AN INTRODUCTION TO MODERN BAYESIAN ECONOMETRICS

Tony Lancaster

AN INTRODUCTION TO MODERN BAYESIAN ECONOMETRICS

Blackwell Publishing

BLACKWELL PUBLISHING

350 Main Street, Malden, MA 02148-5020, USA
9600 Garsington Road, Oxford OX4 2DQ, UK
550 Swanston Street, Carlton, Victoria 3053, Australia

First published 2004 by Blackwell Publishing Ltd

5   2008

Library of Congress Cataloging-in-Publication Data

Lancaster, Tony, 1938–
    An introduction to modern Bayesian econometrics / Tony Lancaster.
        p. cm.
    Includes bibliographical references and index.
        ISBN 978-1-4051-1719-7 (hardcover : alk. paper) – ISBN 978-1-4051-1720-3 (pbk. : alk. paper)
    1. Econometrics. 2. Bayesian statistical decision theory. I. Title: Bayesian econometrics.
    II. Title.
    HB139.L353 2004
    330'.01'519542–dc22

                                                                2003021333

A catalogue record for this title is available from the British Library.

Set in 10/12½ Galliard
by Graphicraft Ltd, Hong Kong
Printed and bound in Singapore
by Markono Print Media Pte Ltd

The publisher's policy is to use permanent paper from mills that operate a sustainable forestry policy, and which has been manufactured from pulp processed using acid-free and elementary chlorine-free practices. Furthermore, the publisher ensures that the text paper and cover board used have met acceptable environmental accreditation standards.

For further information on
Blackwell Publishing, visit our website:
www.blackwellpublishing.com

Contents

3   Linear Regression Models   112

Preface

It was in 1974 that Dennis Lindley visited the Statistics department at the University of Hull. A well-known Bayesian statistician, he gave a talk advocating that point of view, then entirely new to me, and challenged econometricians, specifically me, to reconsider their position. I went away half convinced and resolved to try the Bayesian approach on a problem that then interested me, that of trying to predict the number of events using a poisson regression model. This problem requires high dimensional numerical integration, which I couldn't do, and after several weeks of trying to find reasonable approximations to the predictive distribution that was required, I abandoned the experiment and turned to other problems.

Nearly twenty years later I became aware of intense activity, particularly at Brown University where I then worked, around a new set of techniques, called markov chain monte carlo. This was a method for, in effect, doing high dimensional numerical integration. I tried MCMC and, amazingly, it worked and, moreover, it was not difficult to program. Soon afterwards I began to offer a course in the Brown Economics Graduate Program that described Bayesian methods in econometrics and, more importantly, how to do the calculations that were required using MCMC. But still, in the middle nineties, the method needed programming and some mathematical study and it was not readily accessible to the ordinary applied economist. But by the late nineties the position was quite different as various teams developed software that enabled the ordinary user to describe his model, input his data and rely on the program to use MCMC techniques to good effect in calculating all the probabilities that he required. Now, by 1998, a problem that seemed impossible in 1974 had become trivial.

The only thing lacking was a textbook. One that would explain the Bayesian method and the new computing technology, and how to use it, to applied economists who had a solid sixty year history of innovative thinking about how to confront economic theory with what we would now describe as observational, not experimental, data but who, almost invariably, had done their thinking using an approach to inference radically different from, even opposed to, the Bayesian way. This book is my attempt to fill the gap.

This book explains and advocates a particular formal methodology for our science. Such a formalism is necessary for rigorous work but, in my view, it is only a small part of what is required for excellence in econometrics. Much more important is the skill to match relevant data to careful theory. This is a skill that is very hard to teach. You can only point to superb examples where it is done, of which my own favorite is provided in a book, *A Theory of the Consumption Function* by Milton Friedman, National Bureau of Economic Research (1957), to which I was fortunate to be pointed when I was a graduate student. It still repays study.

I have inevitably accumulated debts to colleagues, students, friends and acquaintances that I am happy to acknowledge. These include, in alphabetical order, Shekhar Aiyar, Manuel Arellano, Chun Chung Au, Sean Campbell, Andrew Chesher, Karsten Hansen, Peter Hansen, Martijn van Hasselt, Joe Hogan, Guido Imbens, Orna Intrator, S. Jun, Frank Kleibergen, Bernard Lindenhovius, Frank Schorfheide, Rusty Tchernis, Wilbert van der Klaauw, Frank Windmeijer, Tiemen Woutersen, A. Zellner. I am sure I have forgotten someone and so apologize. None of these people necessarily agree with the positions I take in this book, nor are they responsible for any errors it contains.

Manuel Arellano, Guido Imbens and Adonis Yatchew helped me by supplying data. The departments of economics at UC Berkeley and University College, London provided hospitality while I worked on the book. As did my wife Jane, historian, who also provided much, much more.

Tony Lancaster,
Department of Economics,
Brown University, May 2003.

Introduction

This book is an introduction to the Bayesian approach to econometrics.[1] It is written for students and researchers in applied economics. The book has developed out of teaching econometrics at Brown University where the typical member of the class is a graduate student, in his second year or higher. If he is an economics student he has taken in his first year a semester course on probability and random variables followed by a semester dealing with the elements of inference about linear models from a classical point of view. It is desirable that the reader is familiar with the laws of probability, the ideas of scalar and vector random variables and the notions of marginal, joint and conditional probability distributions and the simpler limit theorems. It could, therefore, be studied by upper level undergraduates, particularly in Europe and other countries with European style undergraduate programs. The mathematics used in the book rarely extends beyond introductory calculus and the rudiments of matrix algebra and I have tried to limit even this to situations where mathematical analysis clearly seems to give additional insight into a problem.

Some facility with computer software for doing statistical calculations would be an advantage because the book contains many examples and exercises that ask the reader to simulate data and calculate and plot the probability distributions that are at the heart of Bayesian inference. For simple cases these sums can be done in, for example, Matlab or one of the several variants of the S language. I supply code written in S for many of the examples. More complicated calculations rely on purpose-built Bayesian software, specifically a package with the unlikely name of BUGS, and to make full use of this book it is necessary to obtain and learn to use this package.

Whether it is useful to have previous knowledge of econometrics is debatable. On the one hand it is helpful to have some understanding of the method of least squares and of regression, and of fundamental econometric notions such as endogeneity and structure. On the other hand this book deals exclusively with Bayesian econometrics

---

1   The method was first described by Thomas Bayes, an eighteenth century English clergyman, in his paper, An essay towards solving a problem in the doctrine of chances, published in the *Philosophical Transaction of the Royal Society of London*, 53, 370–418, in 1763. This paper was republished in *Biometrika*, 45, 3/4, 293–315, 1958.

and this is a radically different approach to our subject than that used in all[2] existing introductory texts. Because Bayesian inference is different from what is customary, it is, in my experience, extraordinarily difficult for ordinary mortals to change their way of thinking from the traditional way to the Bayesian way or vice versa. At least it is for me, and I notice that most of my students face the same problem. This means that someone whose training has been confined to the conventional approach may find this immersion to be a barrier to understanding the Bayesian method.

This book is about the Bayesian approach to inference; it is not a book about comparative methods and it contains little about traditional approaches which are covered in many textbooks. My aim has been to answer two rather simple questions. The first is "What is Bayesian econometrics?" and the second is "How do I do it?" In the first chapter I explain that Bayesian econometrics is nothing more than the systematic application of a single theorem, Bayes' theorem. I also provide there an answer to the second question, namely that to apply this theorem in an econometric investigation the best method, in general, is to use our new computer power to sample from the probability distributions that the theorem requires us to calculate. In 1989 the computer methods described here were scarcely known; in 1995 they would have been difficult for a beginner to apply; today, application of these computer-intensive methods is little (if any) more difficult than application of the methods traditionally used in applied econometrics. The remainder of the book essentially provides applications of Bayes' theorem and illustrations of the method of calculation using mostly the simplest models; extensions to more complex structures will in many cases be fairly obvious.

These illustrations are not comprehensive; indeed, for an (imaginary) reader who gets the point of the opening chapters, they are unnecessary! Bayesian analysis of important economic models has been going on since the 1960s and significant progress has been made with a number of applications. I do not even deal with all those cases in which the method has been applied, but rather confine my examples to cases that I feel comfortable explaining. My hope is that just a few examples will be sufficient to enable the reader to tackle his own problem using what I shall later call the Bayesian algorithm.

The book could be used as the basis for a one semester course at graduate or advanced undergraduate level. I have used it as such on several occasions with a teaching style that emphasizes calculations and the practicality of Bayesian methods, and demonstrates sampling algorithms including use of markov chain monte carlo procedures in class and requires students to solve problems numerically.

One way to read the book is to get the gist of the Bayesian method from chapters 1 and 2, without necessarily going into the more detailed discussion in these chapters; then to read chapter 4 to get a broad understanding of markov chain monte carlo methods. The reader could then choose among the remaining chapters, which are illustrations of the use of Bayesian methods in particular areas of application, according to his or her interests.

2   947 as of January 2003.

Chapter 1
THE BAYESIAN ALGORITHM

An algorithm is a set of rules for doing a calculation. The Bayesian algorithm is a set of rules for using evidence (data) to change your beliefs. In this chapter we shall try to explain this algorithm. If this explanation is successful the reader may then put down the book and start doing Bayesian econometrics, for the rest of the book is little more than illustrative examples and technical details. Thus, chapter 1 and, to a lesser extent, chapter 2 are the most important parts of the book.

We begin by explaining how we view an econometric analysis and by drawing a distinction between this and statistical analyses.

1.1 ECONOMETRIC ANALYSIS

An econometric analysis is the confrontation of an economic model with evidence. An **economic model** usually asserts a relation between economic variables. For example, a model might assert that consumption, C, is linearly related to income, Y, so that $C = \alpha + \beta Y$ for some pair of numbers α, β. Such a model is typically intended to provide a causal explanation of how some variables, for example C, are determined by the values of others, for example Y. Typically, any model contains both potentially observable quantities, such as consumption and income, called (**potential**) **data**; and it involves quantities, like α and β, that are not directly observable. Variables of this latter type are called **parameters** and will be denoted generically by the symbol θ. They are usually constrained to lie in a set to be denoted by Θ. In our example $\theta = (\alpha, \beta)$ and the set Θ would normally be taken as two-dimensional euclidean space. Any value of θ, for example $\alpha = 10$, $\beta = 0.9$, defines a particular **structure**, in this case $C = 10 + 0.9Y$, and the set of structures under consideration is said to be **indexed** by a parameter, θ.

Evidence is provided by data on the operation of an economy. In the consumption/income example relevant data would be provided by pairs of values for C and Y. There are usually many types of data that are relevant to any particular model. For example, we might have data on the consumption and income of different households, or on the same household observed repeatedly, or on the aggregate income and consumption data of collections of households forming a region or a nation.

The objective of an econometric analysis is to answer two questions. The first question is whether the model is consistent with the evidence: this is called model criticism. This means asking whether any of the structures defined by the model are consistent with the evidence. In our example this would mean asking whether there is any parameter $\theta = (\alpha, \beta)$, lying in Θ, such that, in our data, $C = \alpha + \beta Y$. The second question presumes that the answer to the first is "yes" and it asks what are the probabilities of the different structures defined by the model. Once this question has been answered the model can then be used for purposes of economic decision making, perhaps by a policy maker, perhaps by an individual economic agent. Such use will typically involve predicting the value of the variables for households or regions that are not included in the data. For example, given the structure $\theta = (10, 0.9)$ and told that $Y = 100$ then the economist would predict that $C = 10 + 0.9 \times 100 = 100$.

The practice of econometrics is, in fact, to ask these questions in reverse order. We begin by presuming that our model is consistent with the data and ask for the most likely structure in the light of the evidence. In traditional econometrics this involves forming a good estimate of $\theta_0 \in \Theta$, the particular structure that is presumed to be, in some sense, true. In a Bayesian analysis this step involves using the data to form a probability distribution over the structures in Θ. An estimate, if one is required, might then be provided by reporting, for example, the most probable structure in the light of the evidence provided by the data.

How then do we go about answering these questions in practice? In this chapter we shall focus on the second question in which we presume the consistency of the model with the data and ask how we determine the probabilities of the structures of which the model is composed. The method of doing this is to apply a theorem of probability, Bayes' theorem, and here we shall describe in some detail how Bayes' theorem is used to construct probabilities over alternative structures.

In chapter 2 we shall describe some methods of answering the first question in which the investigator tries to decide whether the model is consistent with the evidence and if it is not, what to do next.

1.2 STATISTICAL ANALYSIS

Statistical analysis deals with the study of numerical data. This is a largely descriptive activity in which the primary aim is to find effective and economical representations or summaries of such data. The point of the activity is to reduce the complexity of a set of numbers to a form which can be more easily comprehended.[1]

---

1   For instance, ". . . the object of statistical methods is the reduction of data. A quantity of data, which usually by its mere bulk is incapable of entering the mind, is to be replaced by relatively few quantities which shall adequately represent the whole, or which, in other words, shall contain as much as possible, ideally the whole, of the relevant information contained in the original data." R. A. Fisher, On the mathematical foundations of theoretical statistics, *Phil. Trans. Royal Soc.*, A222, 1922, p. 309, quoted in T. C. Koopmans, *Linear Regression Analysis of Economic Time Series*, Netherlands Economic Institute, Haarlem, 1937.

The statistician summarizes data by calculating means, standard deviations, trends or regression lines; he represents data graphically by scatter diagrams, histograms, kernel smoothers and many other devices. He typically proposes and applies statistical models as simplified accounts of possible ways in which his data could have occurred. The application of such models involves estimating the parameters of such models and testing hypotheses about them.

Statistical analysis is in many ways very close to econometrics, a subject which, to a statistician, can appear like a branch of applied statistics. Econometric technique is largely drawn from statistics and much of the content of this book will be familiar to a statistician. Indeed, in writing it I have drawn extensively on statistical books and articles. But there are profound differences between econometrics and statistics. The econometrician is primarily concerned with the analysis of the behavior of economic agents and their interactions in markets and the analysis of data is secondary to that concern. But markets can be in, or near, equilibrium; economic agents are presumed to be maximizing or minimizing some objective function; economic agents are often presumed to know relevant things that the econometrician does not. All these considerations tend to be fundamental to an econometric analysis and to dictate the class of models that are worth considering. They make the results of an econometric analysis interpretable to the economist and give parameters solid meaning.

Of course there is not and should not be a sharp line between econometrics and statistics; there is nothing at all wrong with an economist parsimoniously describing data or with a statistician trying to relate the parameters of his model to some underlying theory. But the distinction between the disciplines exists, in my view, and should be kept in mind.

1.3   BAYES' THEOREM

Bayesian econometrics is the systematic use of a result from elementary probability, Bayes' theorem. Indeed, from one angle, that's all it is. There are not multiple methods of using numerical evidence to revise beliefs – there is only one – so this theorem is fundamental.

What is Bayes' theorem?

When A and B are two events defined on a sample space the **conditional probability** that A occurs given that B has occurred is defined as

$$P(A|B) = \frac{P(B \cap A)}{P(B)} \tag{1.1}$$

as long as $P(B) \neq 0$. Here $P(B \cap A)$ is the probability that both A and B occur and $P(A|B)$ is the probability that A occurs given the knowledge that B has occurred. Equation (1.1) is true, of course, with A and B interchanged so that we also have $P(B \cap A) = P(B|A)P(A)$. Substituting this expression into (1.1) then gives

$$P(A|B) = \frac{P(B|A)P(A)}{P(B)}. \tag{1.2}$$

When written in this form the definition is called **Bayes' theorem**. It is a universally accepted mathematical proposition. But there is disagreement about its applicability to econometrics.

Two related questions arise about Bayes' theorem: one is about its interpretation and the other is about its use.

Interpretations of probability

The function $P(.)$ has no interpretation in the mathematical theory of probability; all the theory does is define its properties. When probability theory is applied, as it is in econometrics, we need to decide how to interpret "the probability of an event." In this book we shall take $P(A)$ to measure the strength of belief in the proposition that A is true.[2] Thus the larger $P(A)$ the stronger your belief in the proposition that it represents. This is called a **subjective** view of probability. This interpretation of mathematical probabilities is close to the way we use the idea of probability in everyday language where we say that propositions are "very probable" or "highly unlikely." This closeness to ordinary usage is part of the attraction of Bayesian inference for many people. It allows us to conclude an econometric analysis by saying things such as "in the light of the evidence, theory A is very unlikely whereas theory B is quite probable." Oddly enough, statements like these are impermissible in traditional econometrics where theories are only true or false, not more or less probable.

Similarly, a probability density function for a random variable, $p_X(x)$, will describe degrees of belief in the occurrence of the various possible values of X. Degrees of belief, like utility functions to which they are closely related, are personal to each economic agent, so when you do applied economics using (1.2) you are in fact manipulating your beliefs. On this interpretation Bayes' theorem shows how one belief about A, measured by $P(A)$, is changed into another belief about A, measured by $P(A|B)$.

Range of application of the theorem

The second issue is the range of application of Bayes' theorem. Some people[3] choose to restrict the application of probability theory, including Bayes' theorem, to situations in which there is a series of repetitions in some of which A occurs and in the others it does not. Consequently $P(A)$ is understood as referring to the relative frequency

---

2   **Degrees of belief** may be more precisely defined in terms of willingness to bet on the occurrence of A. We shall not pursue this line of thought but rather take "degree of belief" as a primitive one that most can understand intuitively. Further references on this subjective view of probability are provided in the bibliographical notes.

3   Including virtually all authors of econometric textbooks.

with which *A* occurs during such repetitions. Econometric work that is done solely using this conception of probability as hypothetical relative frequency is often called "frequentist." We shall adopt a much more general range of application in which it will be meaningful to use the expression $P(A)$ to refer to all events, whether they are part of a repeatable sequence or not. Thus we can talk about the probability that the United States was in recession in 1983, that the moon is made of green cheese, or that the economy is in general equilibrium, all of which are events about which you may be sure or quite unsure but about which I assume you have beliefs and those beliefs are capable of being changed by evidence. Unless you have the imagination of a Jules Verne[4] there is no sequence of occasions in some of which the economy was in recession in 1983, or the moon was made of green cheese, and in others of which it was not. Narrower, frequency, interpretations of probability rule out such uses of $P(A)$.

Use of Bayes' theorem to make inferences

How the theorem expressed by (1.2) may be used as the basis for econometric inference from evidence may be shown by considering particular types of events *A* and *B*. Suppose that you have a model containing just two structures θ_1 and θ_2, so Θ contains just two elements, and you also have some data *E*.

EXAMPLE 1.1 *Take the consumption and income relation as an example and let structure 1 assert that C = 10 + 0.9Y and let structure 2 assert that C = Y. Thus*

$$\theta_1 = (10, 0.9); \quad \theta_2 = (0, 1).$$

We now interpret the *A* of Bayes' theorem as referring to particular structures – you can think of these as alternative theories if you like – and we interpret *B* as describing the evidence *E*. So the event *A* is either "θ_1 is true" or it is "θ_2 is true." Suppose you think each structure equally probable so that $P(\theta_1) = P(\theta_2) = 0.5$. (There may be many other structures that you can think of but, for the moment, you are content to consider only these two.) You also, from the content of these two theories, form beliefs about the probabilities of the evidence given that either one is true. This means that you can place a number on both $P(E|\theta_1)$ and $P(E|\theta_2)$. For example, you might think that *E*, the data, is quite unlikely if θ_1 is true but fairly probable if θ_2 is true, say $P(E|\theta_1) = 0.1$ and $P(E|\theta_2) = 0.6$. Now note that these numbers and the rules of probability imply that

$$P(E) = P(E|\theta_1)P(\theta_1) + P(E|\theta_2)P(\theta_2) = 0.1 \times 0.5 + 0.6 \times 0.5 = 0.35,$$

4 Pioneering French science fiction writer.

so E, the event that we have observed, was not particularly probable. We are now in a position to make an inference about the two structures θ_1 and θ_2. It follows from Bayes' theorem (1.2) that

$$P(\theta_1|E) = \frac{P(E|\theta_1)P(\theta_1)}{P(E)} = \frac{0.05}{0.35} = \frac{1}{7},$$

$$P(\theta_2|E) = \frac{P(E|\theta_2)P(\theta_2)}{P(E)} = \frac{0.30}{0.35} = \frac{6}{7},$$

We interpret these numbers as saying that although the theories θ_1 and θ_2 were believed to be equally probable before seeing the evidence represented by E, after the evidence has been seen theory θ_2 is six times more probable than theory θ_1. You have changed your beliefs. This is not an arbitrary change of opinion. It follows as an arithmetical consequence of the beliefs represented by $P(\theta_1) = P(\theta_2) = 1/2$ and $P(E|\theta_1) = 0.1$, $P(E|\theta_2) = 0.6$. Moreover this change of opinion will occur (almost) whatever $P(\theta_1)$ and $P(\theta_2)$ you had. They need not have been equally probable, you might have thought θ_2 very unlikely, yet still the arithmetic of Bayes' theorem will mean that you change your mind on seeing the evidence and, in the present example, you will come to think that θ_2 is more likely than before.

There are two important exceptions to the proposition that evidence will change your beliefs. Suppose that you had assigned probability zero to the theory represented by θ_1, so $P(\theta_1) = 0$ and hence $P(\theta_2) = 1$, then a glance at the arithmetic above shows that $P(\theta_1|E) = 0$ and therefore $P(\theta_2|E) = 1$. This means that if you gave no credence at all to a theory you will never learn that it is right. The other exception is when $P(E|\theta_1) = P(E|\theta_2)$ so that the data are equally probable on both hypotheses. In this case the data carry no information at all about the merits of the two theories. Again, a glance at the arithmetic of Bayes' theorem shows the truth of this remark.

Another way of expressing the change of beliefs uses **odds**. The odds on an event A are the probability of A divided by the probability of its complement. Thus,

$$\text{odds on } A = \frac{P(A)}{1 - P(A)}.$$

So the odds on θ_2 were 1 before you saw E, it was an "even money bet" in gambling jargon, but the odds on θ_2 after you have seen E have become 6, or six to one on. Thus the evidence has swung your beliefs fairly sharply towards theory θ_2 – you have made an inference from the evidence about the plausibility of one of the two theories.

When used in econometrics the A of Bayes' theorem typically is a statement about a parameter of an economic model and the event B is a statement about some data or evidence that bears on the truth of A. We then think of the movement from the right hand side of (1.2) to the left as occurring sequentially. $P(A)$ is the probability assigned to the truth of A *before* the data have been seen and $P(A|B)$ is its probability *after* the evidence is in. When thought of in this way we call $P(A)$ the **prior**

probability of A and $P(A|B)$ the **posterior probability** of A after the Latin phrases "a priori" and "a posteriori." Bayes' theorem can then be interpreted as showing how to revise beliefs in the light of the evidence – how $P(A)$ is changed by the evidence into $P(A|B)$. Notice in particular that the formula does *not* dictate what your beliefs should be, it only tells you how they should change.[5]

Bayes' theorem for random variables

The more usual form of the theorem is in terms of random variables. Suppose that X, Y are a pair of random variables defined on a sample space Ω and assigned, by you, joint probability density $p_{X,Y}(x, y)$ with marginal densities $p_X(x)$, $p_Y(y)$ and conditional densities $p_{X|Y}(x|y)$ and $p_{Y|X}(y|x)$. Then the theorem is

$$p_{X|Y}(x|y) = \frac{p_{Y|X}(y|x)p_X(x)}{p_Y(y)}.$$

In this notation the subscripts indicate the random variables and the arguments indicate particular values[6] of them. Thus, dropping the subscripts, (1.2) becomes

$$p(x|y) = \frac{p(y|x)p(x)}{p(y)}$$

and when used for inference about parameters given data it is conventional to write the parameters with a Greek symbol so we write

$$p(\theta|y) = \frac{p(y|\theta)p(\theta)}{p(y)}. \tag{1.3}$$

Notice that parameter and data are treated symmetrically before the data have been observed and are assigned a joint probability distribution. Notice also that we are now using the symbol y to denote what we previously called E. This is because economic data is almost always in the form of numerical data and y is a conventional symbol in this case.

---

5 Actually there is one constraint on your beliefs: they should satisfy the laws of probability. For example, if A and B are two mutually exclusive and exhaustive events then your beliefs must satisfy $P(A) + P(B) = 1$. Beliefs that satisfy these laws are coherent. If your beliefs are incoherent and you bet according to them then a Dutch book can be made against you. This is a set of bets such that, whatever the outcome, you are sure to lose money. Economists in particular are likely to find such a constraint compelling. See, for example, J. M. Bernardo and A. F. M. Smith, *Bayesian Theory*, Wiley, 1994.

6 We shall in future drop the subscripts unless they are needed for clarity so that random variables will be interpreted by the arguments of their probability function. We also try to follow the convention of using capital letters to denote random variables and lower case letters to denote their realizations but it is not always sensible to do this.

The econometric model

The numerator on the right hand side of (1.3) is the joint probability distribution of the data that are to be observed and the parameter, $p(y, \theta)$. We shall refer to this joint distribution as (your) **econometric model**. It has two components. The first, $p(y|\theta)$, is called the **likelihood** and it describes what you expect to see for every particular value of the parameter $\theta \in \Theta$. It gives your predictions as to what the data should look like if the parameter takes the particular value given by θ. For our little consumption example if $\theta = (\alpha, \beta) = (10, 0.9)$ then you expect to see that C and Y satisfy the relation $C = 10 + 0.9Y$. Formally this is a distribution that assigns probability one to pairs satisfying this relationship and zero to all other possible C, Y pairs. This, incidentally, is an example of a deterministic likelihood in that once the parameter is set there is no uncertainty about what the data should look like. Economic (as opposed to econometric) models often lead to deterministic likelihoods.

The second component $p(\theta)$ is a probability distribution over the parameter space Θ. It is called the **prior distribution** and it gives your beliefs about the possible values of θ. From the point of view taken in this book an econometric model is complete only when it specifies both the likelihood and the prior. Both are required in order to reach probabilistic conclusions either about θ or about the consistency of the model with the evidence.

Digression   Objectivity   *Bayesian inference is not "objective." Some people, believing that science must be objective and its methods objectively justifiable, find this a devastating criticism. Whatever the merit of this position it does not seem to be the way applied econometrics is practiced. The typical seminar in our subject appears to be an exercise in persuasion in which the speaker announces her beliefs in the form of a model containing and accompanied by a set of assumptions, these being additional (tentative) beliefs. She attempts to persuade her audience of the reasonableness of these beliefs by showing that some, at least, embody "rational" behavior by the agents she is discussing and promising that other beliefs will, in fact, be shown by the evidence to be not inconsistent with the data. She then presents her results and shows how some of her beliefs seem to be true and others false and in need of change. The entire process appears to be subjective and personal. All that a Bayesian can contribute to this is to ensure that the way in which she revises her beliefs conforms to the laws of probability and, in particular, uses Bayes' theorem.*

1.3.1 Parameters and data

The material in this section is essential to understanding the point of view taken in this book.

The most useful way to think about the difference between parameters θ and data y is that a parameter is a quantity that is unknown (to you) both before and after the data have been gathered although, of course, your beliefs about it will generally (but not necessarily) have been changed by the evidence; data are unknown before they have been gathered but known afterwards. The word parameter covers several meanings. It may refer to a property of the external world such as the distance from one point on the earth to another or the number of rotten apples in a barrel. Or it may refer to an object appearing in a theory such as "the elasticity of substitution" or "the coefficient of risk aversion." In the latter cases the parameter may well be defined only as a component of a theory and have no existence independent of that theory. And "parameter" does not only mean a constant appearing in a particular economic theory, it may be an index indicating different sub-theories of some larger scheme, as in the introduction to this section where θ_j indicated theory j. And parameters may refer to functions as well as constants as in a setting where it is proposed that $y = g(x)$ where y and x are two economic variables. If $g(.)$ is not given and known (to you), and thus data, this function is a parameter.

Digression   *Randomness*   *In the traditional literature we often find phrases such as "x is random" or "we shall treat x as random" or even "we shall treat x as fixed, i.e. as not random" where "random" means that the object in question will be assigned a probability distribution. In the Bayesian approach all objects appearing in a model are assigned probability distributions and are random in this sense. The only distinction between objects is whether they will become known for sure when the data are in, in which case they are data (!); or whether they will not become known for sure, in which case they are parameters. Generally, the words "random" and "fixed" do not figure in a Bayesian analysis and should be avoided.[7]*

1.3.2 The Bayesian algorithm

We can formulate the Bayesian method as an algorithm.

ALGORITHM 1.1   *BAYES*

1. Formulate your economic model as a collection of probability distributions conditional on different values for a model parameter $\theta \in \Theta$.

2. Organize your beliefs about θ into a (prior) probability distribution over Θ.

3. Collect the data and insert them into the family of distributions given in step 1.

4. Use Bayes' theorem to calculate your new beliefs about θ.

5. Criticize your model.

---

7   Though in chapter 7 we defer to conventional usage and talk, through gritted teeth, about random and fixed effects models.

This book could end at this point, though the publisher might object. All that remains is to offer further explanation and illustration of these steps, not all of which are easy.

1.4   THE COMPONENTS OF BAYES' THEOREM

Let us examine the components of Bayes' theorem as expressed by (1.3), reproduced here for convenience as

$$p(\theta|y) = \frac{p(y|\theta)p(\theta)}{p(y)}, \tag{1.4}$$

using several simple examples. We shall choose examples that are potentially of econometric interest or lie at the heart of models of economic interest. But we shall initially restrict ourselves to cases in which the parameter θ is scalar and not vector valued and we shall consider only situations where each observation is also scalar. This will be rather artificial since in almost all econometric applications the parameter has several, possibly many, dimensions – even in our consumption income example the parameter $\theta = (\alpha, \beta)$ had two dimensions and, as we remarked before, most economic models involve relations between several variables. Moreover the examples use rather simple functional forms and these do not do justice to the full flexibility of modern Bayesian methods. But these restrictions have the great expositional advantage that they avoid computational complexity and enable us to show the workings of Bayes' theorem graphically.

The components of Bayes' theorem are the objects appearing in (1.4). The object on the left, $p(\theta|y)$, is the posterior distribution; the numerator on the right contains the likelihood, $p(y|\theta)$, and the prior $p(\theta)$. The denominator on the right, $p(y)$, is called the marginal distribution of the data or, depending on the context, the predictive distribution of the data. It can be seen that it does not involve θ and so for purposes of inference about θ it can be neglected and Bayes' theorem is often written as

$$p(\theta|y) \propto p(y|\theta)p(\theta) \tag{1.5}$$

where the symbol $\propto$ means "is proportional to." This last relation can be translated into words as "the posterior distribution is proportional to the likelihood times the prior." We shall focus here on the elements of (1.5).

1.4.1   *The likelihood* $p(y|\theta)$

The expression for the distribution of the data to be observed given the parameter, $p(y|\theta)$,[8] has two names. When thought of as the probability density or mass function of Y evaluated at the point y, conditional on the parameter taking the value θ,

---

8   This is $P(B|A)$ in (1.2).

it is called just that, the pdf of Y given θ. But when y is thought of as the actual data that you have gathered, often denoted by the symbol y^{obs} for clarity, it is called the **likelihood function** (of θ). In this case it is often denoted by a different symbol as $\ell(\theta; y)$ and sometimes even more explicitly as $\ell(\theta; y^{obs})$. The likelihood function is not, in general, a probability distribution for θ given data y, nor even proportional to one, though it often is. This is why we separate y and θ by a semicolon and not a conditioning symbol, $|$, when we think of this object as a likelihood function. The likelihood is a function of θ with the data values serving as parameters of that function, hence the semicolon. Many statisticians and some econometricians base their inferences on likelihood functions following the work of the English statistician R. A. Fisher in 1925 and after. People who follow this approach will typically choose as their estimate of θ the value that provides the maximum (strictly the supremum) of the likelihood over Θ. This is called the maximum likelihood (ml) estimator. This tradition is why $p(y|\theta)$ has a special name and symbol when we think of it as a function of θ.

Choice of a likelihood function amounts to choice of a family of probability distributions, one for each $\theta \in \Theta$. The theory of probability offers many such distributions. These range from simple distributions, appropriate to data that can be regarded as conditionally independent realizations from elementary probability distributions with a small number of parameters, to probability models for high dimensional random variables involving many parameters and complex patterns of dependence. Choice among these distributions is an art but this choice must be constrained by a number of considerations. Most importantly, the choice must express the economic model that lies at the center of an econometric investigation. It must allow you to determine from the evidence a probability distribution over the parameter space from which you can calculate which parameter values are probable and which are not. And it must, looking ahead to chapter 2, allow you to conclude that the model itself is wrong or, more precisely, inconsistent with the evidence. But, given this fundamental requirement, many choices remain.

We now give three examples of econometric models and the likelihoods to which they lead. All three involve the dependence of one economic variable upon another. Though simplified here for expository reasons, in more complex and richer forms they lie at the heart of many standard econometric analyses. We preface the examples with a definition.

DEFINITION 1.1 REGRESSION *A regression function is a property of the joint distribution of a pair of random variables. Specifically, it is the expected value in the conditional distribution of one given the other. If the variates are X and Y it is $EX|Y = y$ as a function of y or $EY|X = x$ as a function of x. The term originates with Francis Galton, a nineteenth century English scientist and cousin of Charles Darwin. Galton collected data on heights of parents and their children and calculated the average height of children, $E(Y|X = x)$, of parents of specified height, $X = x$. Plotting these points on a graph he found that the mean height of children increased linearly with their parents' height. He also found that although tall parents tended to have tall children,* *on average they were not as tall as their parents. Children of short parents were also short but tended to be taller than their parents. He called this phenomenon regression (to mediocrity). The term now applies to any conditional mean function, linear or not, and regardless of the numerical character of the relationship. It also applies to any collection of random variables, not just two.*

EXAMPLE 1.2   *LINEAR REGRESSION* Suppose a

*theorist reasons that one variable, for example consumption, c, should be proportional to another, for example income, y, so that $c = \beta y$, where the theory does not specify the numerical value of β. This deterministic model will be inconsistent with any collection of real economic data on c and y. So let us embed this idea in a less rigid econometric model that states that for any collection of c, y data we shall find that each value of c behaves like a realization of a normal[9] random variable with mean – conditional on y and β – equal to βy. This is called a **regression model** because the model specifies the regression function of one random variable given another. It is also a linear regression model because βy is linear in y. If the **precision**[10] of these conditional distributions is denoted by the symbol τ and assumed to be the same regardless of the value taken by y, and if distinct c, y pairs are taken to be independent then the joint probability distribution of, say, n realizations of c given their corresponding y's is*

$$p(c|y, \beta) = \prod_{i=1}^{n}(\tau/2\pi)^{1/2} \exp\{-(\tau/2)(c_i - \beta y_i)^2\}$$
$$\propto \exp\{-(\tau/2)\sum_{i=1}^{n}(c_i - \beta y_i)^2\}. \tag{1.6}$$

*Each component of the product in the first line is a normal density function of a random variable whose realization is c, whose mean is βy, and whose variance is equal to $1/\tau$. The product arises from the assumption that different realizations are independent, and so their probabilities multiply. In the second line we have collected terms together and then dropped all multiplicative terms that do not involve the (scalar) parameter β. To indicate this we have replaced the = sign by the symbol $\propto$ which, as we have noted, means "is proportional to." The expression that remains when we write a probability density without irrelevant multiplicative terms is called the **kernel** of the distribution.*

In all Bayesian work and throughout this book we shall systematically retain only the kernels of the distributions we work with. Once you get used to it this makes for much easier reading, manipulation, and typing.

---

9   The appendix to this chapter gives a brief review of univariate normal distributions.
10   The precision of a normal distribution is the reciprocal of the variance. It is more convenient in Bayesian work to define a normal distribution by its mean and precision rather than the more customary mean and variance.

When we enter into the expression (1.4) the observed values of our c, y pairs and think of it as a function of β this object becomes the likelihood. (Recall that we are working only with scalar parameters so that we are taking τ as a known number.) If we rewrite the expression $\Sigma(c_i - \beta y_i)^2$ and again drop multiplicative terms not involving β we find[11] that the likelihood emerges as

$$\ell(\beta; c, y) \quad \propto \quad \exp\{-(\tau \Sigma y_i^2 / 2)(\beta - b)^2\} \qquad (1.7)$$
$$\text{for} \quad b \;=\; \Sigma_{i=1}^n c_i y_i / \Sigma_{i=1}^n y_i^2.$$

The expression b is the **least squares** estimate of the slope of the regression line, β. Inspection of the likelihood function shows that it has the form of a normal distribution with a mean equal to b and a precision equal to $\tau \Sigma_{i=1}^n y_i^2$.

A valuable thing to do when learning the theory of econometrics is to study the formulae numerically and graphically. Some people prefer to do this using real economic data but in this book we shall often use simulated data in which you, the reader, specify the numerical values of the parameters and then use a computer to generate data. This artificial data can then be inspected numerically and, in particular, you can see what the likelihood looks like. To see this in action with example 1.2 you can proceed as follows (possible S code is provided in brackets).

ALGORITHM 1.2 *SIMULATING DATA FOR A REGRESSION MODEL*

1. Choose values for n, β and τ. (`n <- 50; beta <- 0.9; tau <- 1`)

2. Select n values for $y = (y_1, y_2, ..., y_n)$. (`y <- runif(n, 10, 20)`)

3. On your computer generate n independent realizations of normal variates[12] *with means βy_i and variances equal to $1/\tau$.* (`consump <- rnorm(n, beta*y, 1/sqrt(tau))`)

ALGORITHM 1.3 *PLOTTING THE LIKELIHOOD FUNCTION*

To plot (1.7) you must calculate b; then choose a range of β values over which the plot will be built; then issue the plot command. Possible S code is

1. `b <- sum(consump*y)/sum(y*y)` *# least squares estimate*

2. `betavalues <- seq(0.86, 0.94, length=100)` *# trial and error needed to choose the plot interval*

3. `plot(betavalues, dnorm(betavalues, b, 1/sqrt(tau * sum(y*y))), type="l")` *# dnorm(x, m, s) is the normal density function of mean m, standard deviation s, evaluated at x.*

CALCULATION 1.1
For the following we chose $n = 50$, $\beta = 0.9$, $\tau = 1$ and drew the values of y from a uniform distribution over the interval ten to twenty. Panel 1 of figure 1.1 shows a plot of the data with y on the horizontal axis

---

11 The algebraic manipulation involved here will be explained in more detail in chapter 3.

12 Variate is a shorter version of the phrase "random variable."

and c on the vertical. The straight line is $c = by$ where b is the least squares estimate which turns out to be 0.899. The second panel shows a plot of the likelihood function. As we saw from its mathematical form, it has the shape of a normal curve centered at b and with a standard deviation equal to $1/\sqrt{(\tau\sum y_i^2)} = 0.0096$. Note that the likelihood is centered close to the value of β, 0.9, that was used to generate the data, and that the curve is effectively zero along the entire real line except for the rather short interval shown in panel 2.

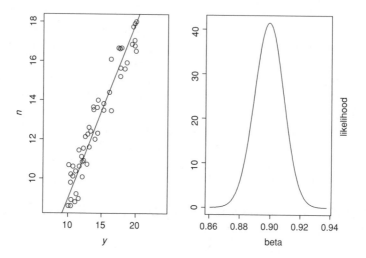

Figure 1.1 Plot of the data and the likelihood for calculation 1.1

For a second example of likelihood we take data that are to be observed in a temporal sequence, i.e. a time series.

EXAMPLE 1.3 AN AUTOREGRESSION *Suppose*

*that your theory describes the way in which a sequence of values of some economic variable depends on earlier values in the sequence. Let the variable be denoted by y and suppose that you are to observe the sequence at successive time points labeled 1 to T. Thus the data are to be the vector $y = (y_1, y_2, ..., y_T)$. A simple theory might be that successive values of y_t follow the law $y_t = y_{t-1}$. As an empirical matter economic data do not follow a (deterministic) law like this just as in the last example data do not follow the deterministic law $c = \beta y$. A simple relaxation of this law to allow for some departure from strict equality would be to write $y_t = y_{t-1} + u_t$, where the sequence $\{u_t\}$, $t = 2, 3, ..., T$ is independently normally distributed random variables with mean zero and precision (reciprocal of the variance) τ. This is called a **random walk**. One way of setting up a likelihood that enables you to test this theory and, if necessary, to reject it is to embed the model* *in the following framework. First note that the theory asserts nothing about the initial observation, y_1, so it seems appropriate to write our likelihood as a probability distribution for y_2, y_3, ..., y_T conditional on the value taken by y_1. Next note that if we enlarge the model, by introducing an additional parameter, to be $y_t = \rho y_{t-1} + u_t$ then the random walk model emerges as the special case in which $\rho = 1$ so we can declare the model inconsistent with the evidence if, after having seen the data, $\rho = 1$ seems to be improbable.*

To complete the argument let us take the parameter of the model as the scalar ρ, taking τ as known for simplicity, and form the likelihood as the joint probability density of $y = (y_2, y_3, ..., y_T)$ conditional on y_1 and, of course, the parameter ρ. This may be derived by first considering the joint density function of $u = (u_2, u_3, ..., u_T)$ given y_1 and ρ. Since the u's form a sequence of independent random variables we may take this distribution as

$$p(u|y_1, \rho) = \prod_{t=2}^{T}(\tau/2\pi)^{1/2}e^{-(\tau/2)u_t^2}$$
$$\propto \exp\{-(\tau/2)\sum_{t=2}^{T}u_t^2\}. \tag{1.8}$$

Now note that $y = (y_2, y_3, ..., y_T)$ is a linear function of $u = (u_2, u_3, ..., u_T)$ because $y_t = \rho y_{t-1} + u_t$ for $t = 2, 3, ..., T$. This function is one to one and its jacobian is readily verified to be unity. Thus the joint density of the data to be observed given the parameter is found by replacing u by y in (1.8) which gives

$$p(y|y_1, \rho) \propto \exp\{-(\tau/2)\sum_{t=2}^{T}(y_t - \rho y_{t-1})^2\}.$$

Rearranging the sum of squares in exactly the same way as in example 1.2 and then regarding the whole expression as a function of ρ gives the likelihood kernel as

$$\ell(\rho; y, y_1, \tau) \propto \exp\{-(\tau\sum_{t=2}^{T}y_{t-1}^2/2)(\rho - r)^2\}$$
$$for \quad r = \sum_{t=2}^{T}y_t y_{t-1}/\sum_{t=2}^{T}y_{t-1}^2. \tag{1.9}$$

This likelihood is again of normal shape centered at r, the least squares estimate of ρ and with precision $\tau\sum_{t=2}^{T}y_{t-1}^2$. The reason for this similarity to example 1.2 is that we are again dealing with a regression model though this time the model is not that of one variable against another but of one variable against its own previous value. To see how this works we can simulate some data using an algorithm like:

ALGORITHM 1.4 *SIMULATING AUTOREGRESSIVE DATA*

1. Choose values for T (which we shall here call n), ρ and τ. (`n <- 51; rho <- 0.9; tau <- 1`)

2. Set up an empty vector to hold the values of y. (`y <- rep(0, n)`)

3. Select the first value for the time series, y_1. (`y[1] <- 0`)

4. Generate, in sequence, the values of y_2, ..., y_T. (`for(i in 2:n){y[i] <- rho*y[i-1]+rnorm(1,0,1/sqrt(tau))})`)

Notice that we have simulated data in which $\rho = 0.9$, not 1, so these data will not provide a realization of a random walk.

CALCULATION 1.2   The panels in figure 1.2 show some simulated data and the likelihood to which they lead. The length of the time series was 51, including the initial observation which was zero, and τ was chosen to be one. The first panel[13] shows a plot of the data against time. The second panel shows the likelihood (1.9) where the least squares estimate is $r = 0.747$ and the quantity $\sqrt{(\tau \sum_{t=1}^{T} y_{t-1}^2)}$ was 9.222. The time series graph showing the actual data seems hard to interpret but the likelihood is much clearer.[14] In particular, the second picture shows that the likelihood is essentially zero over the entire real line except for a very narrow band running from about 0.4 to a little over 1. We shall show later that this likelihood graph can be interpreted as giving the relative probabilities of the different values of ρ in the light of the evidence.

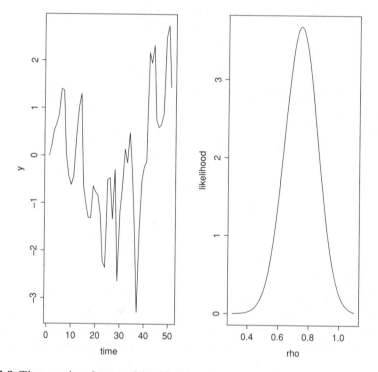

Figure 1.2 Time series data and its likelihood

---

13   Plotting the likelihood follows the same pattern as algorithm 1.3.
14   Some people like to speak of the likelihood graph as providing a window through which some features of the confusing picture on the left can be more clearly seen. But note that many possible windows can be devised.

Both these examples involve a model which began by positing that one random variable was normally distributed given another, and both lead to likelihoods that have the shape of a normal density function – symmetric and bell shaped. But models do not necessarily involve normal distributions nor are likelihood functions invariably shaped like normal distributions. Here is an example of a model whose structure is not normal and whose likelihood function may, or may not, be bell shaped.

EXAMPLE 1.4 *BINARY CHOICE* *Many important economic variables are binary. You either do or do not find work; the economy either grows or declines; the couple do or do not marry. A theorist reasons that such a binary outcome, which we shall denote by y, depends on the value of another variate x. We shall take the sample space for y as zero and one, and maybe the theorist thinks, for example, that y = 1, finding work, growing, marrying, is more likely to occur when x is large than when it is small. A variable like y whose sample space has only two points cannot possibly be normally distributed so this model is quite inappropriate here. Instead a binary variate has a distribution that is specified simply by stating the probability that y = 1. So a way of specifying an econometric model to capture the idea that y is more likely to be one when x is large is to write a probability model as P(Y = 1|x) = p(x) and so the probability distribution of Y given x is*

$$p_{Y|X}(y|x) = p(x)^y(1 - p(x))^{1-y}, \quad y \in \{0, 1\}. \tag{1.10}$$

All that remains is to specify the form of the function $p(x)$. Note that the expected value of Y given x is just the probability, given x, that $Y = 1$, hence this is again, like examples 1.2 and 1.3, a regression model. If $p(x)$ is linear in x we have a linear regression model, but if $p(x)$ is non-linear in x we have a **non-linear regression model**.

A common choice in econometrics is to set $p(x) = \Phi(\beta x)$ where $\Phi(.)$ is the standard normal distribution function so Y has a non-linear regression on x. This choice has the advantage that its value always lies between zero and one as a probability must do; if β is positive it captures the theorists' idea that when x is large then y is more likely to be one; and it enables the discrediting of that idea when the parameter β appears in the light of the evidence to be negative or zero. Since $\Phi(\beta x)$ is a non-linear function of x this is a non-linear regression model.

Given this model – a **probit model** – the likelihood, when n observations on y and x can be presumed to be independent, with probabilities that multiply, is

$$\ell(\beta; y, x) = \prod_{i=1}^{n} \Phi(\beta x_i)^{y_i}(1 - \Phi(\beta x_i))^{1-y_i}. \tag{1.11}$$

No manipulations can simplify this expression further, nonetheless the likelihood can readily be drawn. Here is an example. First we show how to simulate binary data.

ALGORITHM 1.5   *SIMULATING BINARY DATA*

1. *Choose n and β. (*`n <- 50; beta <- 0`*)*
2. *Simulate x values. (*`x <- runif(n, 10, 20)`*)*
3. *Simulate y values. (*`y <- rbinom(n,1,pnorm(beta*x))`*)*[15]

CALCULATION 1.3   We choose $n = 50$ and let the x values lie approximately uniformly between 10 and 20. For the first example we choose $\beta = 0$. The resulting simulated data has 28 ones and 22 zeros. The likelihood is plotted[16] in the first panel of figure 1.3. In the second example we choose $\beta = 0.1$ and the resulting simulated data has 48 ones and 2 zeros. The likeli-hood is plotted in the second panel. The first likelihood points to values around 0 and the second to values around 0.1. In the second graph the value $\beta = 0$ has effectively zero likelihood. For both likelihoods the function is essentially zero everywhere else on the real line!

Notice that both likelihoods are still approximately bell shaped although the second, with strongly unequal numbers of ones and zeros in the data, is slightly

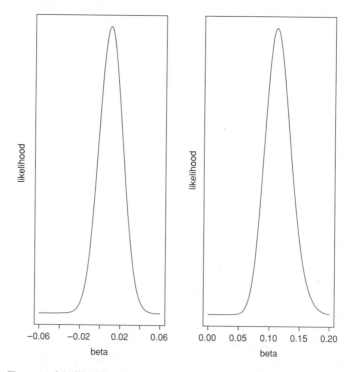

Figure 1.3 Two probit likelihoods

---

15   The function `pnorm(x)` provides the value of the standard normal distribution function, $\Phi(x)$, at x.

16   Plotting is as in algorithm 1.3 except that you would use the S command `pnorm( . . . )`.

asymmetric. This example suggests that even though a model does not involve an assumption of normality likelihoods can nonetheless appear to have the shape of a normal density function. There is a theorem that explains why this is so and we shall describe it later in this chapter.

Before concluding our discussion of likelihood it will be useful to give one final example, one which is mathematically simpler than the first three but which is both fundamental and a convenient vehicle with which to illustrate Bayesian ideas. It does not involve relations between variables and for that reason is of less intrinsic econometric interest, but it is important nonetheless.

EXAMPLE 1.5 *BERNOULLI TRIALS* *There is a very simple model for binary data that is valuable for illustrating some theoretical points in a very simple way and this is to consider a sequence of Bernoulli trials. Suppose the variable of interest is binary and takes the values zero or one. We dealt earlier with such a model in which the probability that y is one depended on the value of a covariate x. Now let us look at a simpler setup in which this probability, say θ, is the same for all agents. A model in which the data are represented as independent with the same probability of a "success" is called (a sequence of) Bernoulli trials. The random variables $Y_1, Y_2, ..., Y_n$ are now taken to be independent and identically distributed (iid) conditional on θ and n.*

The probability mass function of any element in this collection of random variables is $p(y|\theta) = \theta^y(1-\theta)^{1-y}$, for $0 \le \theta \le 1$ and $y \in \{0, 1\}$. Because probabilities multiply when random variables are independent the mass function for n such variates is

$$p(y|\theta, n) = \theta^s(1-\theta)^{n-s}. \tag{1.12}$$

Here, y is now the vector $(y_1, y_2, ..., y_n)$ and $s = \sum_{i=1}^n y_i$ which is the total number of successes (ones) in the n trials. When the number s is replaced by a particular realization the likelihood is

$$\ell(\theta; y) = \theta^s(1-\theta)^{n-s}, \quad 0 \le \theta \le 1. \tag{1.13}$$

This Bernoulli likelihood has the mathematical form of the kernel of the beta family[17] of probability density functions (for θ). This will turn out to be a useful fact when it comes to drawing and simulating such likelihoods and their generalizations.

17 See the appendix to this chapter.

CALCULATION 1.4   *BERNOULLI TRIAL LIKELI-HOODS*

To study (1.13) numerically you can generate some data by choosing n and θ and then using the command y <- rbinom(n,1,θ) which will put a sequence of ones and zeros into y. The value of s can then be found as s <- sum(y). The likelihood can be plotted using the fact that $\theta^s(1 - \theta)^{n-s}$ is the kernel of a beta density with parameters $s + 1$ and $n - s + 1$. Thus, choose a sequence of theta values as, say, thetaval <- seq(0,1,length=100), and plot with plot(thetaval, dbeta(thetaval,s+1,n-s+1,type="1"). Some plots are shown in figure 1.4.

The first row shows the two possible likelihood functions that can arise when only one trial is made. In this case either $s = 1$ or $s = 0$. The likelihood is linear in both cases and not at all bell shaped. The second row examines the case in which $n = 50$ so that s has 51 possible values. We draw the likelihood for two of these. When only one success is recorded the likelihood is concentrated near zero with an (interior) maximum located at $\theta = 0.02$ as can be quickly verified by differentiating $\theta(1 - \theta)^{49}$. On the other hand when there are equal numbers of successes and failures the likelihood looks like a normal curve symmetrical about $\theta = 1/2$.

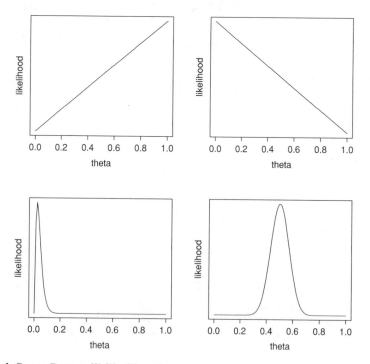

Figure 1.4 Some Bernoulli likelihoods

Parameters of interest

The Bernoulli trials example can be used to make the point that there can be many different parameters of interest, for any of which a likelihood can be constructed. We have taken θ as the parameter of interest but it could have been otherwise. Suppose someone told you that he had carried out n Bernoulli trials with a parameter θ that you and he agree is equal to 0.5 and that he had recorded $s = 7$, say, successes. But he declined to tell you the value of n, so now n is the parameter of interest and θ is data. The probability of s successes in n Bernoulli trials is the binomial expression

$$P(S = s\,|\,n,\,\theta) = \binom{n}{s}\theta^s(1 - \theta)^{n-s} \quad s = 0,\,1,\,2,\,...,\,n,\,0 \le \theta \le 1, \quad (1.14)$$

and on inserting the known data $s = 7,\,\theta = 1/2$ we get the likelihood for the parameter n

$$\ell(n;\,s,\,\theta) \propto \frac{n!}{(n-7)!}\left(\frac{1}{2}\right)^n \quad n \ge 7.$$

This is drawn in figure 1.5 for $n = 7,\,8,\,...,\,30$.

The parameter here, n, is discrete and the evidence constrains the support of the likelihood – the set of points on which it is positive – to be the integers greater than or equal to 7. After all, if you observed 7 successes you could not possibly have had fewer than 7 trials! The picture clearly shows that only a small set of possible

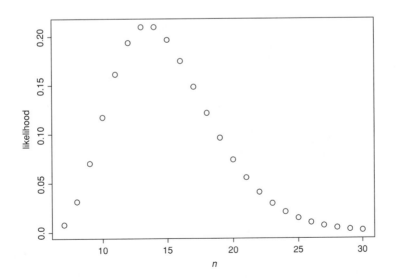

Figure 1.5 Likelihood for n

values of n has much likelihood, and it points to values of n that are close to 14, a number which is equal to $s/\theta = 7/0.5$ which would be most people's guess at the number of trials done to get 7 heads when throwing a fair coin.

The likelihood principle

We remarked earlier that in deducing the posterior we need only consider the kernel of the likelihood (and the same will be true of the prior which we consider in the next section) in order to deduce the posterior distribution of θ. After you have the kernel of the posterior it only takes an integration – $\int p(y|\theta)p(\theta)\,d\theta$ – to find the multiplicative constant that ensures that your posterior density integrates to one.

The fact that you need only the kernel of the posterior to complete your inference has an interesting, and deep, consequence, namely that different likelihoods can lead to the same posterior density and hence to the same inferences. To see this we can again use the Bernoulli trials model with parameter θ to make the point. Consider two investigators with the same prior beliefs about θ but who carry out quite different experiments. The first decides to make $n = 20$ trials and he happens to observe $s = 7$ successes. The second decides to observe Bernoulli trials until seven successes have occurred, and then stop. When he does this he finds that the seventh success occurs on the twentieth trial. The likelihood for the first investigator is the distribution of the number of successes in 20 Bernoulli trials (1.14), as we have seen, and at the observed data this is

$$\ell_1(\theta; n = 20, s = 7) = \binom{20}{7} \theta^7 (1 - \theta)^{13} \tag{1.15}$$

For the second investigator, the probability distribution governing the observations he is about to make is that of the total number of trials, n, necessary to achieve seven successes. This is the negative binomial distribution

$$p(n|s,\theta) = \binom{n-1}{s-1} \theta^s (1 - \theta)^{y-s}, \qquad y = s, s + 1, s + 2, \ldots \tag{1.16}$$

and at the observed data this becomes the likelihood

$$\ell_2(\theta; n = 20, s = 7) = \binom{19}{6} \theta^7 (1 - \theta)^{13}. \tag{1.17}$$

Notice that both (1.15) and (1.17) have the same kernel and so, with the same prior, they lead to exactly the same inferences about θ. The likelihoods (1.17) and (1.15) are, as functions of θ, proportional to each other. This is an illustration of the fact that Bayesian inference satisfies the *likelihood principle*.

DEFINITION 1.2   THE LIKELIHOOD PRINCIPLE   *This states that likelihoods that are proportional should lead to the same inferences (given the same prior). Notice that the data that might have been observed by the two investigators are quite different. What matters for Bayesian inference are the data that were observed; the data that might have been seen but were not are irrelevant.*[18]

The application of the likelihood principle just described is often referred to as "irrelevance of the stopping rule." That is, it doesn't matter whether you chose in advance to do 20 trials or you chose in advance to do trials until you observed 7 successes. It doesn't, in fact, matter whether you had anything in your head at all before you began doing trials. Maybe you just got bored, or felt ill, after 20 trials. Maybe you can't remember what you planned to do. Most people meeting this implication of the likelihood principle feel shocked, even outraged, and some continue to do so. A common complaint is that stopping trials when you have enough successes sounds like cheating, and that if you find this out your inferences about θ would be different than if you were sure that 20 trials had been decided on in advance. The likelihood principle is a radical idea. Think about it carefully. Given that she was conducting Bernoulli trials, would *your* inference about θ depend on what you knew of the trialer's intentions? Would you throw away as worthless the, possibly unique, even priceless, data if you couldn't find out what she planned to do when she started the trials?

The point of this section has been to define the likelihood principle and to point out that Bayesian inference adheres to it. It has not been to argue for or against the likelihood principle as a fundamental principle of statistical inference. Such arguments can be made and there is a rich literature to consult – pointers to this are given at the end of this chapter. Professional opinion is divided on whether inference should adhere to the likelihood principle.

After these examples we now return to the general issue of the art of likelihood construction to embody and test economic theories.

Populations and samples

There is an important branch of statistics called **survey sampling**. In this field there exists a well defined collection of agents – people or households, for example – and

---

18   This is in sharp contrast to standard econometric inference in which the data that might have been observed but were not play a key role through the idea of distributions of estimators in repeated samples. Distributions of statistics over hypothetical repeated samples play no role in Bayesian inference. (See appendix 1.)

Frequentist inferences about θ in this model vary according to whether the data are binomial or negative binomial. That is, they will differ according to the content of the trialer's head when he stopped making his trials. If the frequentist doesn't know this mental state he can make no inferences about θ from the fact that 20 Bernoulli trials produced 7 successes.

each member of this population has a unique vector of characteristics, for example his wage, job, employment status, intention to vote and so on. Call this vector *y*. The object of the calculation is to learn about this collection of vectors, for example the average wage in the population or the fraction of the population without a job. This feature of the population distribution of *y* is *defined* to be the parameter of interest and we learn about it by taking a sample from the population. Often samples are assumed to be random, though there are many other ways of sampling a population. A **random sample** is one in which every time a member of the population is to be selected each member has exactly the same chance as every other of being picked. The data or evidence is provided by the sample and, in frequentist statistics, the parameter is estimated from the sample by choosing a formula, or **estimator**, and applying it to the sample. For example, if the parameter is the average wage in the population an estimator might be "calculate the average wage in the sample." Obeying this instruction with a particular (sample) set of data obtained by selecting individuals from the population then yields an **estimate** of the parameter of interest.

Many applied economists use this story as an aid to thinking about how to embed their economic theory within a probability model, that is, to construct a likelihood. That is, they think of what they are doing as analogous to survey sampling. This point of view holds particular attractions for people whose specialism is microeconomics, since this field typically deals with individual agents and it is often plausible for them to think of their data sets as if they had arisen by some act of randomly sampling a population. Sometimes this story has elements of truth when data really are gathered by sampling a particular collection of individuals, for example the poorly paid or the retired or old. And to think of the object of interest as a characteristic of a real population sounds more practical and concrete than to think of it as a parameter defined within an economic model. In addition it holds particular conviction for those who base their inferences not on Bayes' theorem, as we do in this book, but on imagined sequences of repetitions. The economist can imagine repeatedly drawing a sample from "the population" and then think about the properties of his estimator in such a sequence of repetitions.[19]

In fact economists are rarely, if ever, concerned solely with the properties of some particular, historical population. They wish to generalize and the basis for this generalization is economic theory which points to relationships between variables that are intended to be relatively deep and stable features of the workings of the economy. It is the unspecified constants that appear in this theory that are the ultimate objects of interest.[20]

Nonetheless, thinking about one's data as if they were a sample of some type drawn from a population can be a vivid metaphor and helpful to the applied worker in setting up an econometric model. Moreover, a story about a population and a sample

---

19   We shall not, in the body of this book, undertake a criticism of the frequentist approach, but some comments are given in appendix 1 to the book entitled A Conversion Manual.

20   Economists whose applied work is claimed to rest on "estimating some feature of a population" seem very rarely to define that population precisely.

from it can help the particular model chosen by an investigator seem plausible to his audience and readers, and this is an important consideration in scientific communication which is, in part, an exercise in persuasion. There is no reason why a Bayesian econometrician should not think of his data as a sample from some, possibly hypothetical, population if it assists him in drawing up what appears to be a defensible econometric model. This is as long as he remembers that this is, usually, only a metaphor.

Identification

It is perfectly possible for a likelihood function to point not to one particular value of θ, as in the illustration that we gave earlier, but to be such that all elements of a set of points in Θ give equal values for the likelihood. We saw an example of this at the start of section 1.3 where we remarked that if $P(E|\theta_1) = P(E|\theta_2)$ then no change of opinion about θ would take place. There is nothing problematic about this, though it may be disappointing. You will have to depend on the prior distribution to distinguish among such θ values. And if the prior distribution assigns equal probability to such values they will be equally probable a posteriori.

A deeper phenomenon occurs if such flat spots in the likelihood occur *for any possible data set* that could be observed. Specifically, we can imagine a likelihood derived from the conditional distribution $p(y|\theta)$, $y \in \Omega$, $\theta \in \Theta$ such that for a set of values of $\theta \in \Theta$ we have $p(y|\theta) =$ constant for all $y \in \Omega$. This means that whatever Y realizations occur there is a set of values of θ that all give the same value for the likelihood. In this case we say that θ is not (likelihood) identified. Note that this definition makes no reference to the size of the set of θ values that have equal likelihood. This may be just two points or it may be, for example, the entire real line.

EXAMPLE 1.6 NON-IDENTIFIABILITY *Consider the likelihood for n independent observations of a normal random variable with mean μ and precision = 1. Multiplying n such normal densities together and dropping irrelevant multiplicative constants gives*

$$\ell \propto \exp\{-(1/2)\Sigma_{i=1}^{n}(y_i - \mu)^2\}$$
$$\propto \exp\{-(n/2)(\mu - \bar{y})^2\}$$

after rearranging the sum in the first line and dropping still more terms not involving μ. Now suppose that your theory leads you to assert that μ is the sum of two theoretically quite distinct effects, one represented by a number α and the other represented by a number β. Thus $\mu = \alpha + \beta$ and we can write the likelihood for α, β as

$$\ell(\alpha, \beta; y) \propto \exp\{-(n/2)(\alpha + \beta - \bar{y})^2\}.$$

> *For any particular data set providing a value for* $\bar{y}$, *say* 1.415, *we can see from the above expression that all values of* α *and* β *whose sum is* 1.415 *yield exactly the same value for the likelihood. But, more importantly, this will be true for any and every data set that you obtain. It will always be true that there is a collection of points in the* α, β *parameter space that yield equal values for the likelihood. The parameters* α *and* β *are not identified.*

Technically, we define[21] identification as

DEFINITION 1.3   IDENTIFICATION   *A value* θ_a *of a parameter is identified if there is no other value* θ_b *such that* $p(y|\theta_a) = p(y|\theta_b)$ $\forall$ $y \in \Omega$. *The model is identified if all the parameter values are identified, in which case the parameter* θ *is said to be identified.*

If $p(y|\theta_a) = p(y|\theta_b)$ for all y then θ_a and θ_b are said to be observationally equivalent.

Historically, identification has been a major issue in econometrics and the early discovery of potential non-identifiability in even a simple market demand and supply model was a major event in the evolution of our subject. To find that the economic model you have devised and the likelihood to which it leads does not permit the discovery of a single numerical value for a parameter, whatever the data, can be an important insight. The discovery of non-identifiability has prompted the search for credible prior information that can help to distinguish among non-identified values of θ. Traditionally these have either taken the form of exact restrictions on the parameter space – dogmatic priors – or the discovery of further data.

Flat spots at the top of the likelihood pose a problem for maximum likelihood inference since there will never be unique maxima and second derivative matrices will typically be singular at non-identified points. It is of no special significance from the Bayesian point of view because Bayesians do not maximize likelihoods – they combine them with priors and integrate them. A qualification to this is that if all values of a parameter on, say, the real line are unidentified then an (improper) flat prior distribution on that line would lead to a flat posterior and this is not allowed. We shall illustrate non-identifiability in specific contexts later in the book.

Exchangeability

It is almost impossible to construct an econometric model without, at some stage, invoking a proposition of the form "$(Y_1, Y_2, ..., Y_n)$ are independently and

---

21   Following Bauwens, Lubrano and Richard (1999). This definition refers to parametric identifiability. For a more general definition see Manski (1988).

identically distributed random variables." But this seems to imply that somewhere, out there, is a machine that is similar to the random number generator on your computer and capable of producing a stream of numbers that appear as if they were independent draws from the marginal distributions of any of the $\{Y_i\}$. From the subjective point of view, in which probabilities are private and personal the phrase just cited doesn't look meaningful – it appears to give probability an objective existence.

Because of this some writers prefer, following de Finetti, to derive their likelihoods or probability models via the deeper idea of exchangeability.

DEFINITION 1.4   EXCHANGEABILITY   *A sequence of random variables $Y_1, Y_2, ..., Y_n$ is called exchangeable if its joint probability distribution is unchanged by permutation of the subscripts. For example when $n = 3$, $p(Y_1, Y_2, Y_3) = p(Y_2, Y_3, Y_1)$ etc.*

Exchangeability implies that the random variables $\{Y_i\}$ all have the same means and variances, if they exist, and that the correlations between every pair Y_i, Y_j must be the same as for every other pair. Note that exchangeable sequences are not necessarily sequences of independently and identically distributed (iid) random variables, though sequences of iid random variables are exchangeable. Whether you think a sequence is exchangeable is a matter of judgement. Consider, for example, a sequence of, say, 3 tosses of a coin with Y_i denoting the occurrence of heads on the ith throw. You form a judgement about $p(Y_1, Y_2, Y_3)$ and then you are asked to form a judgement about $p(Y_2, Y_3, Y_1)$: would you give a different answer? If you would not and the same was true for all the six possible permutations of the subscripts then your beliefs about Y_1, Y_2, Y_3 are exchangeable.

The relevance of this idea to the question of the choice of prior is a famous result of de Finetti. We give it for binary random variables though more general versions are available. This states that if a sequence of n binary random variables is exchangeable *for every n* then the joint probability distribution of $Y_1, Y_2, ..., Y_n$ *must* take the form

$$p(y_1, y_2, ..., y_n) = \int \theta^s (1 - \theta)^{n-s} dF(\theta).$$

This has the form of a Bayesian marginal data distribution derived from a likelihood equal to $\theta^s (1 - \theta)^{n-s}$ and a prior distribution function equal to $F(\theta)$. So exchangeability implies the existence of a likelihood and a prior. It is an amazingly powerful idea. It means that you have no need to start your modelling with the assertion that a collection of random variables are independent and identically distributed. You can instead merely state that your beliefs about them are exchangeable and this will automatically imply that the model takes the form of a likelihood and a prior.

Having said this, it is the case in almost all practice by Bayesian econometricians that they begin modeling in the conventional way without any deeper justification. We shall mostly follow that path in this book.

Concluding remarks about likelihood

The likelihood (together with the prior which we shall describe next) is a framework within which to confront an economic model with evidence about the economy. Both are probability distributions and in particular the likelihood is, before the data are seen, the joint probability distribution, conditional on a parameter, of all the random variables that will be observed. To construct a likelihood you choose a family of distributions by drawing on the vast collection of such models available within the theory of probability. The likelihood that you choose must be appropriate to the type of data that are to be observed; it must make it possible for you to represent the economic model within it; and it should make it possible for you to discredit that model when it is clearly inconsistent with the evidence.

Your likelihood is not sacrosanct. After all it carries with it restrictions, for example normality, that are not themselves part of the economic model and such restrictions may be inconsistent with the evidence and, if falsely imposed, distort your conclusions about the economic model. In example 1.2 the theorist who proposed that c is proportional to y did not add "and to the extent that it is not, variations about a line through the origin will have a normal distribution." His theory does not refer to data at all; it exists on a different plane of discourse. This does not imply that you must make no restrictions in constructing your likelihood other than those implied by the theorist. But it does imply that you should explore variations in your inferences over a set of likelihoods each of which embodies the theory. And it also suggests that it is better if your likelihood is relatively unrestricted. Thus, for example, you might want either to assume normality, if this makes sense, and then test whether normality was in fact a restriction consistent with the evidence. Or you might want to begin by assuming not normal variation but some more general distributional family that includes normality as a special case. Both strategies are sensible. The models described in this introductory chapter (of an introductory book) are necessarily very simple and do not represent the full range of probability structures that are available and computionally feasible. In later chapters we shall describe some richer models that are available to the econometrician.

From the subjectivist perspective adopted in this book, a likelihood represents your beliefs about the values of the data conditional on θ. It is *your* likelihood, in the same way that the marginal distribution for θ, the prior $p(\theta)$, will represent *your* beliefs about that parameter. But if your aim is to persuade others of the interest of your results you will be well advised to choose a likelihood that is not clearly inconsistent with the beliefs of your audience and your readers. Assuming that your audience is fellow economists your likelihood should embody both a defensible and coherent economic model and a probability structure that is not obviously inappropriate.

1.4.2 The prior p(θ)

The prior is the other component of Bayes' theorem and together with the likelihood it provides the basis for inference from the evidence. On the subjective view the prior represents *your* beliefs about θ in the form of a probability distribution.[22] You may choose whatever distribution you like in the same way that you can choose whatever likelihood function you like. But a number of points might usefully be made. Some of these points are relatively technical and some are present largely for historical reasons. It may be that a reader willing to accept the simple idea of a prior as a personal probability distribution over the parameter space and anxious to get on with doing Bayesian econometrics would wish to skip over the rest of this section at first and move directly to section 1.4.3 on posterior distributions, or even to chapters 3 and 4 on regression models and markov chain monte carlo methods respectively.

Tentative priors

The first point is that although $p(\theta)$ represents your beliefs you don't need to believe it! You may and indeed should examine the impact of alternative beliefs – alternative priors – on your subsequent, posterior, conclusions. This is done in the spirit of "what if?" You ask "if I had believed this . . . before seeing the data, what would I now believe?" This is called sensitivity analysis and it applies to the likelihood function just as much as to the prior. You may, for example, consider changing the prior from $p(\theta)$ to $q(\theta)$ and you would then recalculate the posterior to study how beliefs about θ have changed. Similarly, you may consider changing the likelihood from $p(y|\theta)$ to $q(y|\theta)$ and seeing how the posterior distribution of θ has changed. The idea here is to explore how sensitive your main conclusions are to alterations in the model, i.e. in the prior and likelihood. We shall illustrate this idea in chapter 2 once we have completed our survey of the main components of Bayesian inference.

In the same spirit, although we usually interpret Bayes' theorem as operating in temporal order, prior beliefs → data → posterior beliefs, this is not a necessary interpretation and it is formally quite legitimate to allow your "prior" beliefs to be influenced by inspection of the data. This is in fact the practice of most applied workers who act in the spirit of Sherlock Holmes' dictum "It is a capital mistake to theorize before one has data."[23] The legitimacy of such data-dependent priors follows from the

---

22   It's also possible to take an objective view of a prior distribution over θ values. On this view there exists a population of agents with different values of θ so there is an objectively existing collection of θ values and you can think of $p(\theta)d\theta$ as referring to the proportion of such agents with θ values in the short interval $d\theta$. This gives a relative frequency interpretation to the prior. Some people feel more comfortable with this interpretation of the prior and there is nothing in what follows to preclude this point of view. It is entirely consistent with the mathematics of Bayesian inference and the reader who prefers such an **objective Bayesian** perspective can use all the techniques described in this book to carry out his econometric analysis.

23   *A Scandal in Bohemia* by Arthur Conan Doyle.

fact that Bayes' theorem does not restrict the choice of prior, it only prescribes how beliefs change.

Encompassing priors

The second point is that it is necessary to take account of the beliefs of your audience and your readers, if any. Prior beliefs[24] that conflict sharply with those of your readers will make your work of little interest to them. You will be saying "If you believed *A* before seeing the data you should now believe *B*." But this will be met with the response "So what, I don't believe *A*." It is therefore a good idea, for public scientific work, to use priors that are not sharply or dogmatically inconsistent with any reasonable belief. In low dimensions this requirement can sometimes be met by using a uniform or flat distribution on some reasonable function of the parameter. In the Bernoulli trials example a uniform distribution for θ on the interval zero to one will not be inconsistent with any belief. It will not *represent* any belief, for example it would not represent the belief of someone who is quite convinced that θ lies between 0.4 and 0.6, but it wouldn't be inconsistent with such a belief. In a sense such a prior encompasses all reasonable beliefs. Such priors are often called **vague**.[25]

As a particular case of this it would be wise to avoid using priors that assign zero probability to parts of the parameter space. Because the posterior density is formed by multiplication of the prior and likelihood – see (1.3) – a prior that assigns probability zero to a set will necessarily assign zero posterior probability to that set. Such a prior is very dogmatic and this is to be avoided wherever possible in scientific enquiry. On the other hand, any model involves some dogmatic assertions since without them the theory would be vacuous. So the recommendation to avoid dogmatic priors can never be strictly fulfilled.

Natural conjugate priors

The posterior density function $p(\theta|y)$ is formed, apart from the multiplicative constant $1/p(y)$, by multiplying the likelihood and the prior. There is some merit in choosing a prior from a family of density functions that, after multiplication by the likelihood, produce a posterior distribution in the same family. Such a prior is called *natural conjugate*. In this case only the parameters of the prior change with the accumulation of data, not its mathematical form. Such priors also have the advantage that they can be interpreted as posterior distributions arising from some earlier, possibly fictional, evidence. Thus we might try to form our prior for θ in the

---

24   And likelihoods, for that matter.
25   There is a history of efforts to find priors that are "uninformative" in some sense, compared to the likelihood. These efforts do not seem to have been very fruitful particularly in the case of models with parameters of several dimensions.

Bernoulli trials example by trying to imagine what our beliefs would currently be had we seen the evidence of some earlier trials prior to which our beliefs were vague.

Before illustrating natural conjugacy it will be helpful to reintroduce the idea of a kernel.

DEFINITION 1.5 A KERNEL *A probability density or mass function of a random variable X typically has the form $kg(x)$ where k is a numerical constant whose role is to ensure that $kg(x)$ integrates to one. The remaining portion, $g(x)$, which does involve x, is called the **kernel** of the function.*

For the beta family of probability density functions the kernel is $x^{a-1}(1 - x)^{b-1}$ while k is the ratio of gamma functions given in the appendix to this chapter. What constitutes the kernel of a density or mass function depends on what you think the argument is. For example if x is of interest the kernel of an $n(\mu, \tau)$ density function is $\exp\{-\tau(x - \mu)^2/2\}$ while the constant is $\tau^{1/2}/\sqrt{(2\pi)}$. On the other hand if one is thinking about the normal density for given x as a function of μ and τ then the kernel would be $\tau^{1/2}\exp\{-\tau(x - \mu)^2/2\}$. In neither case is the numerical factor $1/\sqrt{(2\pi)}$ of any relevance.

The purpose of k is to make the density or mass function integrate to one. Once you know the kernel the constant can be found by integration but it is usually of little interest in itself. Since a family of distributions can be recognized from its kernel it is usually convenient to omit constants when we manipulate probability distributions and we shall follow this convention in this book. It makes for algebra that is much easier to follow.

Indeed, as we remarked earlier, Bayes' theorem itself is often stated up to a missing constant as

$$p(\theta|y) \propto p(y|\theta)p(\theta) \tag{1.18}$$

or, in words, the posterior is proportional to the product of the likelihood and the prior.

EXAMPLE 1.7 *NATURAL CONJUGACY FOR THE BERNOULLI TRIALS PARAMETER* *To illustrate natural conjugacy consider the likelihood of θ in the Bernoulli trials example which has, up to a multiplicative constant, the general form $\theta^s(1 - \theta)^{n-s}$. Since the posterior density of θ is formed by multiplying the prior and the likelihood it is clear, by contemplating the multiplication of such functions, that any prior that is proportional to $\theta^{a-1}(1 - \theta)^{b-1}$ will lead to a posterior density of the same mathematical form. It follows that the natural conjugate family of prior distributions for this problem is the beta family.*

Notice that this argument never needed to mention the constants multiplying these kernels. The property of natural conjugacy was of more importance in the days when posterior distributions were computed analytically and not, as now, numerically.

Improper priors

A "probability distribution" for θ is called improper if its integral over the sample space Θ does not converge. A simple example is the expression

$$p(\theta) \propto 1, \quad -\infty < \theta < \infty \tag{1.19}$$

which is called a uniform distribution on the real line and can be thought of as a rectangle on an infinitely long base. Its integral, the area under the line, does not converge, it is infinite and so (1.19) is not, in fact, a probability distribution. Nevertheless such improper distributions are frequently used in applied Bayesian inference and there are several reasons for this.

One reason is that often it does not matter, at least mathematically, if the prior is improper. Because the object of ultimate interest is the posterior distribution of θ and this is formed by multiplying the likelihood and the prior it is perfectly possible for the posterior distribution to be proper even though the prior is not. To see this consider the following.

EXAMPLE 1.8 *PROPER POSTERIOR FROM IMPROPER PRIOR* *Let the likelihood be formed as the distribution of n independent normal variates with mean θ and precision one. Thus*

$$\ell(\theta; y) \propto \prod_{i=1}^{n} \exp\{-(1/2)(y_i - \theta)^2\}$$
$$= \exp\{-(1/2)\sum_{i=1}^{n}(y_i - \theta)^2\}, \tag{1.20}$$

and using the fact that

$$\sum_{i=1}^{n}(y_i - \theta)^2 = \sum_{i=1}^{n}(y_i - \bar{y} + \bar{y} - \theta)^2$$
$$= \sum_{i=1}^{n}(y_i - \bar{y})^2 + \sum_{i=1}^{n}(\theta - \bar{y})^2,$$

we find that

$$\ell(\theta; y) \propto \exp\{-(n/2)(\theta - \bar{y})^2\}. \tag{1.21}$$

This is (the kernel of) a normal distribution with mean $\bar{y}$ and precision n. It is a perfectly proper probability density function whatever the values of $n > 0$ and $\bar{y}$. So if you multiply the likelihood (1.21) by the improper prior (1.19) the resulting posterior distribution is proper.

Thus, at least mathematically and for at least some models,[26] it is unnecessary for a prior to be proper. Improper priors can lead to proper posteriors.

Another reason is that an improper prior can often be thought of as an approximation to a proper prior that is intended to represent very imprecise or vague beliefs. To see this consider the last example again.

> **EXAMPLE 1.9** *Suppose we multiply the likelihood (1.21) by a prior density for θ that is normal with precision equal to τ and mean zero. This gives a posterior density*
>
> $$p(\theta|y) \propto \exp\{-(n/2)(\theta - \bar{y})^2\}\exp\{-(\tau/2)\theta^2\}$$
> $$\propto \exp\{-(n + \tau)(\theta - \bar{\theta})^2/2\} \tag{1.22}$$
>
> *after a little rearrangement of the exponent and the dropping of irrelevant multiplicative constants. This expression, (1.22), is the kernel of a normal distribution with mean $\bar{\theta} = n\bar{y}/(n + \tau)$ and precision $n + \tau$. Now let the positive number τ approach zero. The prior density $e^{-\tau\theta^2/2}$ approaches a constant, the posterior mean $n\bar{y}/(n + \tau)$ approaches $\bar{y}$ and the posterior precision approaches n and these are the values that correspond to the improper uniform prior underlying (1.21). A proper prior with τ sufficiently small will produce much the same posterior as an improper, uniform, prior.*

It follows from this example that when your prior beliefs are very vague you can (sometimes) act as if your prior was uniform and find a numerically very accurate approximation to what your real posterior beliefs would be. The uniform prior is a labor saving device in that it saves you the trouble of specifying your exact beliefs. It's often used in this way in practice, during preliminary analyses. Many of the standard calculations in econometrics, for example the use of least squares regression and all maximum likelihood methods, can be thought of as flat prior Bayes, as we shall see.

A third reason goes by the name of the **principle of precise measurement**.

Precise measurement

Recall from Bayes' theorem (1.3) that the posterior distribution, which provides our inferences about θ, is formed as the *product* of the likelihood and the prior. This simple fact is of enormous consequence. We have already remarked that because of it you should never assign zero prior probability to a set in Θ since, because zero times any number always gives zero, this action necessarily assigns zero posterior

---

26 In other models improper priors can lead to improper posteriors, as we shall see.

probability to that set so you can never learn that in fact, in the light of the evidence, that set is quite probable. We now use this fact again by remarking that almost always – the first two panels in figure 1.4 are an exception – the likelihood is effectively zero over most of the parameter space. To see this look at examples 1.2, 1.3, and 1.4 where the likelihood is negligible everywhere on the real line except in the region we have plotted. Thus the prior is multiplied by (almost) zero almost everywhere in the parameter space and it does not matter what your prior beliefs were in that region. Whatever they were they will not change the posterior density in regions where the likelihood is negligible. This implies that a prior that is intended to be roughly neutral as between different values of θ need only be so in the region where the likelihood is non-negligible – how the prior behaves outside that region is of no consequence. A conclusion that could be drawn from these remarks is that a prior that is, formally, uniform on the real line is practically equivalent to one which is uniform where the likelihood is non-negligible but behaves in any other (bounded) way outside that region.

We now turn to look at the possibilities of finding objective and default priors.

Objective and default priors

Much ink has been spilt in the search for a rule that would produce a prior distribution for any model and one that would, in some sense, be minimally informative. The search could be said to begin with the Marquis de Laplace in the eighteenth century but in its modern form it could be said to begin with Harold Jeffreys in 1938 and it still continues. In his book Jeffreys proposed a rule that possesses an apparently persuasive property, that of invariance.

JEFFREYS' INVARIANT PRIORS

We can parametrize a model in an infinite number of ways and the parametrization we choose is important in Bayesian inference. For example we can parametrize a zero mean normal distribution in terms of its standard deviation σ, its variance σ^2, its precision $\tau = 1/\sigma^2$ and generally we can use any one-to-one function of σ. Suppose that we choose any particular parametrization, for example σ, and apply a rule for constructing a prior distribution for that parameter and then, using the prior that results from following that rule we construct the posterior distribution of σ. Now suppose that you re-analyze the data but work in terms of a different parametrization, say σ^2, but you apply *the same rule* to form your prior for σ^2. Jeffreys then argued that the beliefs about the first parameter σ that can be deduced from the posterior distribution for σ^2 should be identical to those reached in the first analysis; in Jeffreys' words "equivalent propositions should have the same probability." Posterior beliefs about the same quantity should be *invariant* to the parametrization used. Jeffreys showed that there exists a rule, now named after him, that does satisfy this invariance condition.

His rule is to choose the prior proportional to the square root of the *information*,

$$I_\theta = -E\left(\frac{\partial^2 \log \ell(\theta;y)}{2\theta^2}\right) \tag{1.23}$$

where the expectation is taken with respect to $p(y|\theta)$. This is (the negative) second derivative of the logarithm of the likelihood function averaged over repeated realizations of y. It, and its matrix version, plays a major role in both likelihood and Bayesian inference. Here is the argument that shows that Jeffreys' rule is invariant to reparametrization. Suppose a second parametrization is in terms of $h(\theta)$, for example θ might be σ and $\gamma = h(\theta)$ might be $1/\sigma^2$. Now note that

$$\frac{\partial \log \ell}{\partial \gamma} = \frac{\partial \log \ell}{\partial \theta} \frac{\partial \theta}{\partial \gamma},$$

$$\frac{\partial^2 \log \ell}{\partial \gamma^2} = \frac{\partial^2 \log \ell}{\partial \theta^2}\left(\frac{\partial \theta}{\partial \gamma}\right)^2 + \frac{\partial \log \ell}{\partial \theta}\frac{\partial^2 \theta}{\partial \gamma^2},$$

$$\text{so} \quad I_\gamma = I_\theta\left(\frac{\partial \theta}{\partial \gamma}\right)^2 \tag{1.24}$$

where the last line follows because $E(\partial \log \ell/\partial \theta) = 0$.[27] Here, I_γ is the information about γ and I_θ is the information about θ. Note that (1.24) implies that $I_\gamma^{1/2} = I_\theta^{1/2} |\partial\theta/\partial\gamma|$. Now the posterior distribution of θ for someone who works in terms of θ and follows Jeffreys' rule will be $\ell(\theta)I_\theta^{1/2}$. For someone who works in terms of γ, his posterior distribution for γ will be $\ell(h(\theta))I_\gamma^{1/2}$. From this we can deduce what the second person's beliefs about θ will be by following the standard rule for deducing the distribution of a function of a random variable. This gives the second person's beliefs about θ as $\ell(\theta)I_\gamma^{1/2}|\partial\gamma/\partial\theta| = \ell(\theta)I_\theta^{1/2}|\partial\theta/\partial\gamma||\partial\gamma/\partial\theta| = \ell(\theta)I_\theta^{1/2}$ which are precisely the same as the first person's beliefs about θ. To illustrate this potentially confusing little argument consider the following.

> **EXAMPLE 1.10 JEFFREYS' PRIOR FOR A NORMAL PRECISION** *If $p(y|\sigma)$ is the density of n independent normal variates of mean zero and standard deviation σ then $\log \ell(\sigma) = -n\log\sigma - \sum y_i^2/2\sigma^2$. So the hessian is $\partial^2 \log \ell(\sigma)/\partial\sigma^2 = (n/\sigma^2) - 3\sum y_i^2/\sigma^4$. Since the expected value of y^2 is σ^2 the information about σ, I_σ, is $2n/\sigma^2$ and Jeffreys' prior for σ will be $\propto 1/\sigma$. An alternative parametrization is $\tau = 1/\sigma^2$ and the log likelihood in terms of τ is $\log \ell(\tau) = (n/2)\log\tau - \tau\sum y_i^2/2$. Differentiating twice, taking expectations and changing sign then gives the information*

---

27 Take the identity $\int p(y|\theta)dy = 1$; differentiate with respect to θ; then rearrange using $\partial \log p/\partial\theta = (1/p)\partial p/\partial\theta$.

for τ as $I_\tau = n/2\tau^2$ implying the Jeffreys' prior for τ is $\propto 1/\tau$. The posterior beliefs about σ for the person working in terms of σ will be

$$p(\sigma|y) \propto \sigma^{-(n+1)} \exp\{-\Sigma y_i^2/2\sigma^2\}. \qquad (1.25)$$

The beliefs about τ for the person working in terms of τ will be

$$p(\tau|y) \propto \tau^{n/2-1} \exp\{-\tau\Sigma y_i^2/2\}.$$

Finally, the beliefs about σ held by the latter person are found by the change of variable from τ to σ and are

$$p(\sigma|y) \propto \sigma^{-n+2} \exp\{-\Sigma y_i^2/2\sigma^2\} |-2/\sigma^3| \propto \sigma^{-(n+1)} \exp\{-\Sigma y_i^2/2\sigma^2\}.$$

This is identical to (1.25) which confirms invariance in this case.

Prior beliefs formed using Jeffreys' rule are often improper as the preceding example illustrates – $1/\tau$ is an improper prior over $0 < \tau < \infty$ since $\int_0^\infty \tau^{-1} d\tau$ diverges. The invariance argument generalizes straightforwardly to the case in which θ is a vector parameter. Informations are replaced by information matrices and Jeffreys' takes the form $|I_\theta|^{1/2}$ – the square root of the determinant of the information matrix.

EXAMPLE 1.11   *JEFFREYS' PRIOR FOR BER-NOULLI TRIALS*   *With n Bernoulli trials the likelihood for θ is $\ell(\theta; y) \propto \theta^s(1 - \theta)^{n-s}$. To calculate Jeffreys' prior we need to differentiate the log likelihood twice and take expectations. The calculation, with L denoting $\log \ell$, is as follows.*

$$L(\theta) = s \log \theta + (n - s) \log(1 - \theta)$$

$$\frac{\partial L}{\partial \theta} = \frac{s}{\theta} - \frac{n - s}{1 - \theta},$$

$$\frac{\partial^2 L}{\partial \theta^2} = \frac{-s}{\theta^2} - \frac{n - s}{(1 - \theta)^2},$$

$$since\ E(s|\theta, n) = n\theta,\quad I_\theta = \frac{n}{\theta} + \frac{n}{1 - \theta} = \frac{n}{\theta(1 - \theta)}.$$

It follows that Jeffreys' prior is

$$p(\theta) \propto \frac{1}{\sqrt{\theta(1 - \theta)}}.$$

This is a beta(1/2, 1/2) density which is proper, but U shaped. According to this prior the least likely value of θ is 1/2. Notice that Jeffreys' prior is not uniform, as one might, perhaps, have anticipated.

There remains much debate about the value of Jeffreys' rule. It often doesn't seem to give very appealing results particularly when θ is vector valued but even in a simple model such as an autoregression a Jeffreys' prior on the autoregressive coefficient may seem strange to many. Objective rules in general are not very appealing to those who prefer beliefs to represent subjective opinion based on an informed appreciation of the economic meaning of θ. Jeffreys' prior involves taking expectations with respect to y which is a repeated sampling calculation, and many writers take the view that such calculations are, in general, not well defined and they certainly violate the likelihood principle.

It's also not very clear in what sense Jeffreys' rule produces prior distributions that are minimally informative. There is another strand in the literature, due to Bernardo and Berger,[28] which starts with a precise measure of the amount of information in a probability distribution based on information theory, and asks for the prior distribution whose contribution to the total information in the posterior distribution is minimal. This leads to the class of **reference priors**. Unfortunately these do not always exist, even for econometrically simple models, but where they do exist they typically take Jeffreys' form. So in this sense Jeffreys' priors can be justified as minimally informative.

But even if one doesn't like general rules for forming prior distributions there exists a need for **default priors** to use in standard situations when an investigator, at least initially, doesn't wish to spend much time thinking about the details of his prior beliefs about θ. So just as there are default likelihoods for automatic use in standard models there are default priors in general use. These are typically uniform (and therefore improper) distributions of functions of the parameter concerned. For example linear regression coefficients are usually taken to be uniform on the real line and normal precisions to be such that the log precision is uniform on the real line, so that the precision itself has "density" $1/\tau$ on the positive axis.[29] We shall use such default priors quite often in this book. Application of such default uniform distributions to high dimensional parameters must however be done with great caution[30] and we shall see several illustrations of this caution in the chapters on panel data and on time series.

Hierarchical priors

When dealing with vector valued parameters it is often persuasive to think about your prior distribution hierarchically. Suppose you are dealing with a parameter with, say, n elements and these elements are similar in the sense that they have the same dimension (units of measurement) and play similar roles in the model. An example might be the coefficient of the same variable in a regression model where each agent is allowed to have his own response. Another example might be the set of precisions

---

28 See the bibliographic notes at the end of this chapter.
29 Using a change of variable with jacobian $\partial \log \tau / \partial \tau = 1/\tau$.
30 BUGS, the software package recommended for this book, *requires* the user to employ proper priors.

in a model where each agent is allowed to have his own precision. If the parameter is $\theta = (\theta_1, \theta_2, ..., \theta_n)$ one might construct a prior that expresses the similarity among the elements of θ, by taking these elements to be an independent set of realizations of some appropriate parent distribution, say $h(\theta|\lambda)$, where the parameter of the parent, λ, is of much smaller dimension than θ. This parent or second stage parameter is then assigned a prior distribution, typically one of the default choices. Formally, we want $p(\theta)$ and we get this by stating firstly $p(\theta|\lambda)$ and then forming $p(\lambda)$. This forms $p(\theta)$ implicitly as $p(\theta) = \int p(\theta|\lambda)p(\lambda)d\lambda$. The parameters θ represent the first stage in the hierarchical structure; the parameters λ represent the second stage, and so on. There is no limit to the number of stages in a hierarchical model though in practice two or three is usual. Here is an example.

EXAMPLE 1.12   *A HIERARCHICAL PRIOR* *Let $\tau = (\tau_1, \tau_2, ..., \tau_n)$ be a set of precisions that are thought to be similar, but not identical, and have the same dimension. Since they are non-negative an obvious choice for a hierarchy is to let them be realizations of a gamma variate with parameter $\lambda = (\alpha, \beta)$. Thus (see the appendix to this chapter)*

$$p(\tau|\lambda) \propto \prod_{i=1}^{n} \tau_i^{\alpha-1} e^{-\beta\tau_i}. \tag{1.26}$$

As an application, consider a collection of independent normal variates of mean zero and precisions τ_i. Then the likelihood is

$$\ell(y; \tau, \lambda) \propto \prod_{i=1}^{n} \tau_i^{1/2} \exp\{-y_i^2 \tau_i/2\}, \tag{1.27}$$

and the whole model is

$$\begin{aligned} p(\tau, \lambda|y) &= \ell(y; \tau, \lambda)p(\tau|\lambda)p(\lambda) \\ &= \prod_{i=1}^{n} \tau_i^{1/2} \exp\{-y_i^2\tau_i/2\}\prod_{i=1}^{n}\tau_i^{\alpha-1}e^{-\beta\tau_i}p(\lambda), \\ &= \prod_{i=1}^{n} \tau_i^{\alpha+1/2-1} \exp\{-\tau_i(\beta + y_i^2/2)\}p(\lambda). \end{aligned} \tag{1.28}$$

This prior structure is often used as the basis *for robust Bayesian analysis in the sense that it relaxes the somewhat dogmatic restriction that all y's have the same precision. We shall return to this model in later chapters.*

An interesting feature of hierarchical priors is that they reveal the somewhat arbitrary nature of the distinction between the likelihood and the prior. Take a model written with parameter θ; let θ have a prior that depends upon a hyperparameter ψ; and let ψ have a prior $p(\psi)$ involving no unknown parameters. Then one way of presenting the model is as

$$\ell(\theta; y)p(\theta|\psi)p(\psi)$$

where the prior is $p(\theta|\psi)p(\psi) = p(\theta, \psi)$. Another way is to integrate out θ and write the model as

$$\ell(\psi; y)p(\psi), \quad \text{where } \ell(\psi; y) = \int \ell(\theta; y)p(\theta|\psi) \, d\theta.$$

Which is the likelihood, $\ell(\psi; y)$ or $\ell(\theta; y)$? The answer is that it doesn't really matter; all that does matter is the product of prior and likelihood which can be taken as $p(y, \theta, \psi)$ or as the y, ψ marginal, $p(y, \psi) = \int p(y, \theta, \psi) \, d\theta$.

Priors for multidimensional parameters

While it doesn't matter in principle to the Bayesian method whether θ is scalar or multidimensional it matters quite a lot in practice. Default choice of prior for scalar parameters has been rather thoroughly studied. For example, many reference priors (mentioned above) for scalar parameters have been produced, but the situation for vector parameters is notably less clear or, indeed, simple. Jeffreys' priors for scalars are known to provide acceptable results in most cases but, as Jeffreys himself observed, the position is less satisfactory when I_θ is matrix valued.

One promising line of work has been to try to reduce the situation to one involving many scalar parameters. This can be done if you can separate the likelihood into a product form, each term of which involves only a single element of θ. Then if you can reasonably assume independence of the elements of θ in the prior, the posterior distribution will also factor and you have, at least in a numerical sense, k separate analyses. Separating the likelihood in this way typically will involve finding a different parametrization of the model from the one in which you originally wrote it. That is, working in terms of some one-to-one function $g(\theta)$ instead of θ.

EXAMPLE 1.13 PARAMETER SEPARATION IN REGRESSION *As a fairly simple example of parameter separation consider a version of example 1.2 in which there are two parameters, α and β, so that $\theta = (\alpha, \beta)$. Let the relation between consumption and income be*

$$c_i = \alpha + \beta y_i + \varepsilon_i, \quad \varepsilon_i \sim n(0, 1), \tag{1.29}$$

for $i = 1, 2, ..., n$ with observations independent given the parameters and the y's. By the argument leading to (1.6) the likelihood is

$$\ell(\alpha, \beta) \propto \exp\{-(1/2)\Sigma_{i=1}^n(c_i - \alpha - \beta y_i)^2\}$$

and this, after a little tedious algebra, can be written as a generalization of (1.7)

$$\ell(\alpha, \beta) \propto \exp\{-(1/2)(\theta - \hat{\theta})'X'X(\theta - \hat{\theta})\} \tag{1.30}$$

$$\text{where} \quad X'X = \begin{bmatrix} n & \Sigma y_i \\ \Sigma y_i & \Sigma y_i^2 \end{bmatrix},$$
(1.31)

$$\text{and} \quad \theta = \begin{bmatrix} n & \Sigma y_i \\ \Sigma y_i & \Sigma y_i^2 \end{bmatrix}^{-1} \begin{bmatrix} \Sigma c_i \\ \Sigma c_i y_i \end{bmatrix}.$$

Inspection of (1.30) shows that it will not *break apart into a product of a term involving only α and a term involving only β unless $X'X$ is a diagonal matrix and this requires that $\Sigma_{i=1}^{n} y_i$ is zero, which will not usually be true. But we can make it true.*

To see this let us rewrite the model as

$$c_i = (\alpha + \beta \bar{y}) + \beta(y_i - \bar{y}) + \varepsilon_i$$
$$= \alpha^* + \beta y_i^* + \varepsilon_i$$

with the same distributional assumptions. This is exactly the same model as (1.29) but with a different parametrization: instead of $\theta = (\alpha, \beta)$ it is now parametrized in terms of $g(\theta) = (\alpha^*, \beta)$, a one-to-one function of θ. Now the new $X'X$ matrix has the form

$$\begin{bmatrix} n & 0 \\ 0 & \Sigma(y_i - \bar{y})^2 \end{bmatrix}$$
(1.32)

where the zeros appear because the sum of observations measured from their mean is identically zero. It follows from this diagonality that the likelihood in terms of $g(\theta)$ takes the form

$$\ell(g(\theta); y) \propto e^{-(n/2)(\alpha^* - \hat{\alpha}^*)^2} e^{-(\Sigma y_i^{*2}/2)(\beta - \hat{\beta})^2}$$

where $\widehat{\alpha^*} = \bar{c}$, and $\hat{\beta} = \Sigma(c_i - \bar{c})(y_i - \bar{y})/\Sigma(y_i - \bar{y})^2$.

So the first component of the reparametrized likelihood has the shape of a normal curve centered at mean consumption, and the second component has the shape of a normal curve centered at $\hat{\beta}$, the least squares estimate.

One feature of this example that is particularly important is the effect of the parameter transformation on the information matrix. It's obvious that if a likelihood is multiplicatively separable then the log likelihood is additively separable, and it follows from this that the cross partial second derivatives of the log likelihood will be identically zero. For this model the information matrix for θ is given by (1.31) but the information matrix for $g(\theta)$ is given by (1.32), which is diagonal.

This remark suggests that we can search for separable reparametrization by looking for functions $g(\theta)$ that diagonalize the information matrix. In later chapters we shall show that such new parametrizations, called **information orthogonal**, can often be found and that they tend to simplify the search for default priors in models with multidimensional parameters.

1.4.3 The posterior $p(\theta|y)$

The posterior density represents your beliefs about θ given your prior beliefs and the beliefs embodied in the likelihood. In many applications the posterior is the culmination of an empirical analysis.[31] To report your results you will display the posterior distributions to which your model and data have led. Let us look at examples of posterior distributions before making some general comments.

EXAMPLE 1.14 *BERNOULLI TRIALS* *Suppose that your prior beliefs are described by a member of the (natural conjugate) beta family. Formally, $p(\theta) \propto \theta^{a-1}(1 - \theta)^{b-1}$, $0 \le \theta \le 1$. With a model in which n Bernoulli trials are undertaken, with outcomes which are conditionally independent, with common expectation θ, the likelihood was given by (1.13). Hence, by Bayes' theorem the posterior density of θ has the form*

$$p(\theta|y) \propto \theta^{s+a-1}(1 - \theta)^{n-s+b-1} \tag{1.33}$$

which we recognize as the kernel of a beta density with mean and variance

$$E(\theta|y) = \frac{s + a}{n + a + b}, \quad V(\theta|y) = \frac{(s + a)(n - s + b)}{(n + a + b)^2(n + a + b + 1)}. \tag{1.34}$$

(Note that if both s and n are large and in the ratio r then these moments are approximately

$$E(\theta|y) = r, \quad V(\theta|y) = \frac{r(1 - r)}{n}.$$

When n is large and $r = s/n$ is fixed, the posterior variance becomes small and almost all its probability mass is confined near s/n, the fraction of successes. It is easy to see that this is true whatever member of the beta family was used as the prior and we conclude that for this model, as evidence accumulates, the posterior becomes dominated by the likelihood, virtually independent of the shape of the prior, and ultimately converges to a point.)

---

31 Its counterpart in frequentist econometrics is a table of estimated values of θ with their estimated standard errors.

CALCULATION 1.5   As a numerical example of a posterior distribution
take the case of the likelihood plotted in the first panel of figure 1.4 which arose
when one success was observed in one trial. If our prior was uniform – a beta(1, 1)
density – then the posterior distribution is just the likelihood and is

$$p(\theta|y) \propto \theta$$

which is the 45 degree line plotted in that graph. This is a proper posterior density,
its normalizing constant is 2, and, for example, the posterior expectation of θ after
one success in one trial is

$$E(\theta|s = 1, n = 1) = \int_0^1 2\theta^2 \, d\theta = 2/3.$$

This contrasts rather sharply with the maximum likelihood estimate, which either
doesn't exist or is 1, depending on how you define the parameter space, Θ.

In this example, with a uniform prior, $p(\theta) \propto 1$, the posterior distribution, without its normalizing constant, is identical to the likelihood. This is clearly generally
true. So if you now look back to likelihoods plotted earlier in this chapter, for example in figures 1.1, 1.2, and 1.3, you are, in effect, looking at posterior distributions
under uniform priors. So you can read these figures as if they told you your beliefs
about θ from that model and that data. For example, figure 1.1 tells you that the
most probable value of β is about 0.9; that values in excess of 0.93 or less than
0.86 seem very unlikely; that $\theta = 0.89$ is about five times as probable as, say, $\theta = 0.88$
and so on. Similarly, under a prior for n which is uniform on the positive integers
figure 1.5 shows the posterior distribution which points to values of n of about 14
and indicates that values of n greater than 25 are very improbable.

Reporting the posterior distribution

How might you report your posterior distribution?

DRAW IT

In the case in which θ is scalar the best way of conveying to readers the content of
the posterior distribution is by drawing it. This is also true when θ is vector valued
but the parameter of interest is a one-dimensional function of θ, as it often is in
econometrics. For example economists are often interested in $\partial y/\partial x$, the marginal
effect of x on y. Outside the linear model this may well be a function of many or
all parameters of the model as in the probit model of example 1.4. With x and β
vectors of k elements the general version of that model is

$$P(Y = 1|x, \beta) = \Phi(x\beta)$$

and $\partial P(Y = 1 \mid x, \beta)/\partial x_j$ where x_j is the j'th element of x is given by $\beta_j \Phi(x\beta)$ which involves every element of the k dimensional parameter β. To report this object at some chosen value of x you would compute its posterior distribution from that of β and draw it.

REPORT ITS MOMENTS

Traditional econometric practice is to report an estimate of θ together with an estimate of the standard deviation of its repeated sampling distribution. If you wish to conform to this practice you might want to report the mean (or median) of the posterior distribution together with the standard deviation of that distribution.

REPORT A HIGHEST POSTERIOR DENSITY REGION

Similarly, traditional practice often reports a confidence interval for (scalar) θ. This is a numerical interval with the somewhat arcane interpretation that if you calculated your interval in the same way over many hypothetical repeated samples of the same size and using the same model then, say, 95% of such intervals would contain within them the "true" value of θ. The Bayesian analogue is to find, from the posterior distribution of θ, an interval[32] in Θ such that with probability 0.95 θ lies within it. It's as simple as that. Of course there are many ways of capturing 95% of the probability in a distribution and standard Bayesian practice is to construct the interval in such a way that no point in Θ has smaller probability density than any point outside it. This is called a (95%) *highest posterior density* – hpd – interval. Here is a numerical example. We take the autoregressive model of example 1.3 and artificially generate 51 observations, starting at $y_1 = 0$, with $\rho = 1$ which is called the **random walk** model, and with unit precision. The likelihood was shown to be of the normal form with mean $r = \sum_{t=2}^{51} y_t y_{t-1} / \sum_{t=2}^{51} y_{t-1}^2$ and standard deviation equal to $s = 1/\sqrt{(\sum_{t=2}^{51} y_{t-1}^2)}$. From the data we generated we find that $r = 1.011$ and $s = 0.037$. Now if we take the prior for ρ to be uniform on the real line, $p(\rho) \propto 1$, $-\infty < \rho < \infty$, the posterior density of ρ is equal to the likelihood and so is itself normal (r, s). Then from well known properties of the normal curve we know that 95% of the distribution will lie within 1.96 standard deviations of the mean and 99% will lie within 2.58 standard deviations of the mean. Further, the intervals $r \pm 1.96s$ and $r \pm 2.58s$ are such that all points within them have higher probability density than any point outside them. Thus they are an hpd interval. For our data we find a 95% hpd interval to be $0.939 < \rho < 1.084$ and a 99% interval is $0.916 < \rho < 1.107$. The interpretation of such intervals is very simple: for example, "the probability that ρ lies within the interval 0.939 to 1.084, given the model and data, is 0.95."

32 More generally, a set.

CALCULATE THE MARGINALS

The calculation involved in forming the posterior distribution of the object of interest may well be mathematically challenging, to say the least. To work out the distribution of $\beta_j \phi(x\beta)$ in a probit model is very hard. Similarly, if the object of interest is, say, the third element θ_3 in a model parameter of k elements, to find its marginal density will involve doing the sum

$$p(\theta_3|y) = \int_{\theta_1} \int_{\theta_2} \int_{\theta_4} \dots \int_{\theta_k} p(\theta|y)\, d\theta_1\, d\theta_2\, d\theta_4 \dots d\theta_k, \qquad (1.35)$$

a $k - 1$ dimensional integration. This is, in general, a hard problem.[33] Fortunately there are two solutions, one fairly old and of wide though not universal applicability, the second new, rather easy and of what is apparently universal application. The first is the use of approximations to posterior distributions and the second is the method of (computer) assisted sampling, which we shall treat in chapter 4.

Approximate properties of posterior distributions

If your posterior distribution is mathematically complicated or the dimension of θ is such that the integration (1.35) is hard to do it seems natural to look for a useful approximation. Clues to such an approximation are the likelihood graphs that we have drawn earlier in this chapter. These seem to suggest that likelihoods tend to look roughly normal, at least when the number of observations is not very small. Now if we could prove a theorem that states that when the number of observations in large posterior distributions are approximately normal, then integrals such as (1.35) are easily done. This is because if $p(\theta|y)$ is multivariate normal then all its marginal distributions are themselves normal so we would know immediately that, say, $p(\theta_3|y)$ is just a normal distribution. All that would then remain is to deduce its mean and precision.

The relevant theorem states the following proposition.

THEOREM 1.1   LARGE SAMPLE APPROXIMATE POSTERIOR

Let θ be the parameter, possibly vector valued, and let $p(\theta|y)$ be the posterior distribution, then for sufficiently large n, θ is approximately normally distributed with mean equal to $\hat{\theta}$ and precision (matrix) equal to $-H(\hat{\theta})$ where $\hat{\theta}$ is the posterior mode and H, the hessian, is the matrix of second derivatives of the logarithm of the posterior density function. Under a uniform prior for θ the posterior distribution is equal to the likelihood and so $-H(\hat{\theta})$ is equal to the negative second derivative of the log likelihood evaluated at $\hat{\theta}$. The expected value of the negative hessian of the log likelihood with respect to the

---

33   It's the sort of problem that, as I described in the preface, defeated my efforts many years ago.

*distribution of y given θ is the information (matrix), I_θ, mentioned earlier. In practice, $I_\theta(\hat\theta)$ – called the **observed information** – and $-H(\hat\theta)$ will be close except when the number of observations is relatively small or the prior is far from flat near $\hat\theta$.*

Proof *For further discussion and references to proofs see Bernardo and Smith (1994).*

It should be noted that this multivariate normal approximation to the posterior distribution applies to *any* parametrization of the model. Since for θ the result states that approximately $\theta \sim n(\hat\theta, -H(\hat\theta))$,[34] it also implies that $g(\theta) \sim n(g(\hat\theta), -J(\hat\theta))$, approximately, where

$$J(\hat\theta) = -\left(\frac{\partial^2 p(\theta|y)}{\partial g^2}\right)_\theta = -\frac{\partial^2 p(\theta|y)}{\partial\theta^2}\left(\frac{\partial\theta}{\partial g}\right)_\theta^2 = H(\hat\theta)\left(\frac{\partial\theta}{\partial g}\right)_\theta^2$$

and $g(\theta)$ is any differentiable one-to-one function of θ. A potentially important warning should be made here, that for any given data set and model, the normal approximation for θ can be very accurate, but the corresponding normal approximation for $g(\theta)$ can be very inaccurate, especially if $g(.)$ is a markedly non-linear function. This works in reverse in that $g(\theta)$ can be nearly normal but θ far from normal. Also, since a multivariate normal distribution has a single mode this theorem can't provide a useful approximation when the posterior density has several modes.

Another important warning is that although the theorem is stated as a "large n" result, it is almost always not the sample size that determines when the sample is large but some other function of the data. For example, in a non-linear regression model, which we shall study in chapter 5, it is objects such as $\sum_{i=1}^n (x_i - \bar x)^2$ that determine whether approximate normality of the posterior distribution is, or is not, a good approximation. This sum of squares generally increases with the sample size, n, yet it may be very small, even zero, even though n is very large, and it can be very large even though n is very small. Just looking at the number of observations generally gives a misleading answer to the question of whether approximate normality of the posterior is reasonable.[35]

EXAMPLE 1.15 *PROBIT COEFFICIENT POSTERIOR* *For an example of a normal approximation take the probit model of example 1.4 where, under a uniform prior for β, the posterior density is equal to (1.11) with logarithm equal to*

---

34 The symbol $\sim$ means "is distributed as."
35 We shall see a striking example of this in chapter 8 where we find that 36,000 observations in a model with seven parameters is a very "small" sample indeed.

$$\log p(\beta|y) = \sum_{i=1}^{n} y_i \log \Phi(\beta x_i) + \sum_{i=1}^{n} (1 - y_i) \log(1 - \Phi(\beta x_i)).$$

The derivative of this expression with respect to β is

$$\frac{\partial \log p(\beta|y)}{\partial \beta} = \sum_{i=1}^{n} y_i x_i \frac{\phi(\beta x_i)}{\Phi(\beta x_i)} - \sum_{i=1}^{n}(1 - y_i) x_i \frac{\phi(\beta x_i)}{1 - \Phi(\beta x_i)}$$

$$= \sum_{i=1}^{n} \frac{x_i \phi(\beta x_i)(y_i - \Phi(\beta x_i))}{\Phi(\beta x_i)(1 - \Phi(\beta x_i))},$$

and the posterior mode $\hat{\beta}$ equates this derivative to zero. The solution exists and is unique as long as the y's and x's vary but it must be found numerically. Differentiating this expression to find the hessian results in a rather complicated expression though one which is readily evaluated on the computer. The negative hessian is, however, when the number of observations is not too small, often well approximated by the information. The information matrix is usually a simpler expression than the hessian itself and it is in this case where it is

$$-E\left(\frac{\partial^2 \log p(\beta|y)}{\partial \beta^2}\Big|\beta\right) = \sum_{i=1}^{n} \frac{x_i^2 \phi(\beta x_i)^2}{\Phi(\beta x_i)(1 - \Phi(\beta x_i))} = I(\beta).$$

A normal approximation to the joint posterior density of β would then be

$$p(\beta|y) \approx n(\hat{\beta}, I(\hat{\beta})). \tag{1.36}$$

CALCULATION 1.6 For a numerical comparison we generate some data with $n = 50$ and $\beta = 0$ and plot the posterior density under a uniform prior for β – this is the dotted line in figure 1.6. On this we superimpose as the solid line the normal approximation (1.36). This is the normal density with mean $\hat{\beta}$ and precision $I(\hat{\beta})$ where $\hat{\beta}$ is the maximum likelihood estimate of β – the posterior mode under a uniform prior. The two curves are indistinguishable.

Likelihood dominance

Another important feature of posterior distributions in general is that they typically depend very little on the prior when the number of observations is large relative to the number of parameters and the prior does not assign probability zero to the relevant parts of Θ. To see generally why this is likely, consider the logarithm of

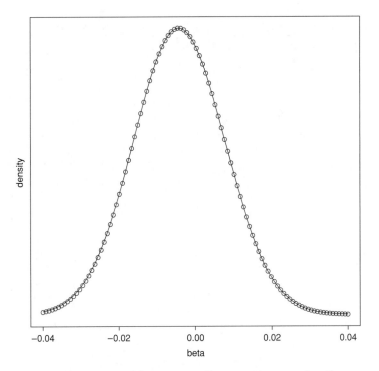

Figure 1.6 Probit posterior and its asymptotic normal approximation

the posterior density of θ using a sample of size n. It has two components,[36] the log likelihood and the log prior,

$$\log p(\theta|y_1, ..., y_n) = \log \ell(\theta; y_1, ..., y_n) + \log p(\theta).$$

Now as data accumulate and n increases the likelihood changes and tends to increase in modulus, but the prior stays the same. To see an example of this increase, consider the likelihood for n independent normal (μ) variates which is $\exp\{-(1/2)\Sigma(y_i - \mu)^2\}$ with logarithm $-(1/2)\Sigma_{i=1}^n(y_i - \mu)^2$. The increment in the likelihood when you add an extra observation is therefore $-(1/2)(y_n - \mu)^2$ which is either negative or zero (which happens with probability zero), for almost all μ, the log likelihood becomes a larger and larger negative number as observations accrue. Hence, in large samples the likelihood will be the numerically dominant term as long, of course, as $p(\theta) > 0$. This is true rather generally and it also works in the case of dependent or non-identically distributed data. This argument will fail if $p(\theta)$ is zero over the region in Θ where $\ell(\theta|y)$ tends to concentrate since $\log p(\theta) = -\infty$ over that region. But if $p(\theta)$ is not dogmatic and assigns some probability to all relevant parts of Θ then it will indeed be eventually dominated. Here is an example of dominance of the posterior by the likelihood.

---

36   Apart from an irrelevant additive constant.

EXAMPLE 1.16   WEAK DEPENDENCE OF THE POSTERIOR ON THE PRIOR

Consider the Bernoulli trials example with likelihood $\propto \theta^s(1-\theta)^{n-s}$ and consider the effect of varying the prior within the natural conjugate beta family, $p(\theta) \propto \theta^{a-1}(1-\theta)^{b-1}$. Suppose that $n = 20$ with $s = 7$. Figure 1.7 shows three quite different beta prior distributions. The horizontal line is a uniform prior with $a = b = 1$; the line composed of circles is beta density with $a = b = 3$; and finally the solid line is the Jeffreys' prior with $a = b = 1/2$. These priors show quite different initial beliefs. Figures 1.8 and 1.9 show posteriors using these priors. In figure 1.8 we had $n = 5$ trials with $s = 2$ successes, while in figure 1.9 we had $n = 20$ trials with $s = 8$ successes. The solid line is the posterior with Jeffreys' prior; the starred line corresponds to the uniform prior; and the remaining line to the beta (3, 3) prior.

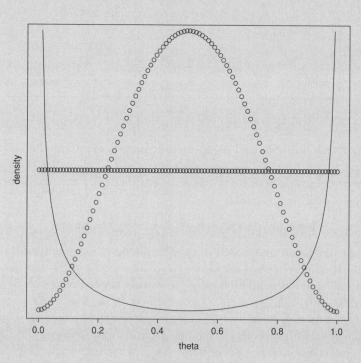

Figure 1.7 Three priors for a Bernoulli parameter

The message of the figures is that divergent prior beliefs can be brought rapidly into rough agreement in the face of quite limited amounts of evidence, and that the agreement is more complete the more data are available.

This argument for the large sample dominance of the likelihood over the prior is sometimes said to mimic a process of rational scientific enquiry in that two individuals with quite different, but non-dogmatic, prior beliefs will be brought into agreement

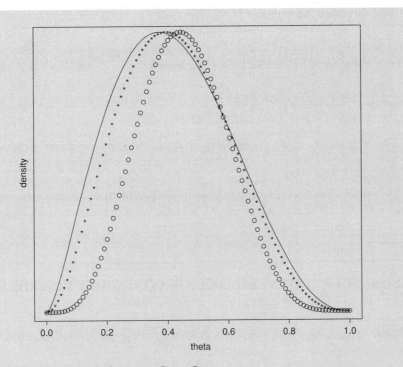

Figure 1.8 Three posteriors: $n = 5$, $s = 2$

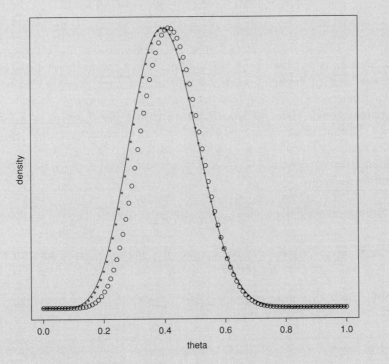

Figure 1.9 Three posteriors: $n = 20$, $s = 8$

by the accumulation of evidence. Note that such individuals must agree on the likelihood even if they disagree in their prior beliefs.

Convergence of the posterior distribution

We have just shown, with an example, that people with quite diverse prior beliefs can be brought into agreement if the sample size is large enough. But a different question also arises. What happens to the posterior distribution when the number of observations becomes large? Do your beliefs tend to concentrate on some element of Θ? And if so, on what? Here's an argument that shows what happens in a special but important case.

THEOREM 1.2   CONVERGENCE OF POSTERIOR DISTRIBUTIONS

Suppose the parameter space Θ is discrete with elements θ_1, θ_2, ... possibly infinite in number. Let the observations be iid conditional on θ with densities $p(x_i|\theta)$ and suppose that there exists in Θ a true parameter labeled θ_t, which is distinguishable from all the other elements of Θ by the condition that

$$\int p(x|\theta_t)\log\left[\frac{p(x|\theta_s)}{p(x|\theta_t)}\right] dx < 0 \quad \text{for all } s \neq t. \tag{1.37}$$

*The integral in this expression is the Kullback–Leibler measure of the divergence between the two probability distributions $p(x|\theta_t)$ and $p(x|\theta_s)$ and what the condition says is that all the possible data distributions (likelihoods) arising from values of θ different from θ_t are different from $p(x|\theta_t)$.[37] Some such identification condition is clearly necessary to prove convergence. After all, suppose that there existed a θ, say θ_s, such that $p(x|\theta_t)$ $= p(x|\theta_s)$ for all x, then there would be no way of deciding whether an observed sample x had been provided by $p(x|\theta_t)$ or by $p(x|\theta_s)$. (1.37) is called an **identification condition**.*

Then the theorem is

$$\lim_{n\to\infty} p(\theta_t|x) = 1$$

This means that all the mass in the posterior distribution comes eventually to concentrate on a single point in the parameter space.

Proof   *Taking the prior as $p_s > 0$ for each $\theta_s \in \Theta$ the posterior density is*

---

37   Cf. definition 1.3 above.

$$p(\theta_s | x) = p_s \frac{p(x | \theta_s)}{p(x)}, \quad \textit{for } p(x | \theta_s) = \prod_{i=1}^{n} p(x_i | \theta_s)$$

$$= \frac{p_s \{ p(x | \theta_s) / p(x | \theta_t) \}}{\sum_j p_j \{ p(x | \theta_j) / p(x | \theta_t) \}}$$

$$= \frac{\exp\{\log p_s + S_s\}}{\sum_j \exp\{\log p_j + S_j\}}$$

where

$$S_j = \log \frac{p(x | \theta_j)}{p(x | \theta_t)} = \sum_{i=1}^{n} \log \frac{p(x_i | \theta_j)}{p(x_i | \theta_t)}.$$

But the right hand expression shows that S_j is the sum of n independent and identically distributed random variables so that, by a strong law of large numbers,

$$\lim_{n \to \infty} \frac{S_j}{n} = E\left(\frac{S_j}{n}\right) = \int p(x | \theta_t) \log \left[\frac{p(x | \theta_j)}{p(x | \theta_t)} \right] dx = \begin{cases} 0 & \textit{if } j = t \\ <0 & \textit{if } j \neq t \end{cases}.$$

If we then apply this result to find the limiting behavior of $p(\theta_s | x)$ as $n \to \infty$ we see that terms like $\exp\{\log p_j + S_j\}$ converge to zero because S_j becomes a larger and larger negative number, except when $j = t$, from which the theorem follows.

This type of theorem can be generalized to continuous parameter spaces and to observations that are neither independent nor identically distributed under suitable further conditions.

This theorem forms a precise statement of how individuals with quite different initial beliefs can be brought into ultimate agreement by the accumulation of evidence.

Sampling the posterior

The material in this section is essential to understanding the point of view taken in this book.

The difficulty with (asymptotic) approximations like the one sketched in the last section is that one can never be sure of their accuracy. Indeed the only way of finding out the accuracy of an approximation to your posterior distribution is to calculate the exact distribution which is what you wanted to avoid doing! This is one reason why approximations, though important, take a second place in modern Bayesian calculations to simulation methods developed during the last ten years or so. These methods depend upon the following remarks.

Suppose that you take a posterior distribution and draw from it a collection of realizations of θ. If you program your machine to produce `nrep` realizations from $p(\theta_1, \theta_2 | y)$ your output will be a matrix with `nrep` rows and as many columns as there are elements of θ. Thus, when θ has two elements, it will look like

$$
\begin{matrix}
\theta_{11} & \theta_{21} \\
\theta_{12} & \theta_{22} \\
\theta_{13} & \theta_{23} \\
\cdot & \cdot \\
\theta_{1,nrep} & \theta_{2,nrep}
\end{matrix}
$$

Each row of this matrix contains a realization of a random variable whose distribution is $p(\theta_1, \theta_2 | y)$. The whole matrix contains nrep realizations from the *joint* distribution of θ_1 and θ_2 while the j'th column contains nrep realizations from the *marginal distribution* of θ_j. To study the distribution of, say, θ_1 given the data, $p(\theta_1 | y)$, just ignore the second column, it's as simple as that. To study the distribution of some function of θ, say $g(\theta)$, just apply this function to every row of your output matrix and the result will be a set of realizations of the random variable $g(\theta)$. (It is desirable, but not essential, that the rows of your output matrix be independent realizations of θ.) Whether they are independent or not, a law of large numbers will generally apply and it can be proved that moments of $g(\theta)$ from a sample of nrep realizations of θ will converge in probability to the moments of the distribution of $g(\theta)$ as nrep $\rightarrow \infty$. Since *you choose nrep* you can make arbitrarily accurate estimates of any aspect of the posterior distribution including, for example, the mean, precision, distribution and density functions. *It follows that if you can sample the distribution in question you can know it with arbitrary accuracy.* Computer assisted sampling to avoid integration is the key feature of *modern* Bayesian econometrics[38] and the approach described in this paragraph is critical to understanding this subject. Increasingly, difficult mathematics is being abandoned in favor of computer power.

Computer assisted sampling requires not only computer power but also effective algorithms that can be proved to sample the distribution in question. We have already in this book made extensive use of computer routines to provide artificial data sets and to sample likelihoods and posterior distributions. These calculations rely on computer languages like S or Matlab that have built in commands, like `rnorm` or `rexp`, to sample most of the standard distributions of elementary probability theory. But where the distribution to be sampled is not standard, researchers either have to have put together their own program or, increasingly, use specialized sampling software. In the rest of this book we shall use one of the most widely used pieces of sampling software, a program called **BUGS**. In chapter 4 we shall give an account of the theory behind this program and in appendix 2 we shall provide some instruction on

---

38   It was only in about 1990 that computer assisted sampling started to become widespread in many areas of applied statistics. This is because it was about that time that powerful computers became readily available to researchers. This development has radically altered applied statistical practice.

its use. We conclude these introductory remarks on the sampling study of posterior distributions with an example of the use of BUGS to solve a complicated problem.

EXAMPLE 1.17 *PROBIT REVISITED* *Consider binary data y whose mean depends on two variables x_1 and x_2 according to*

$$E(Y|x, \beta) = \Phi(x\beta),$$

where $x\beta = \beta_0 + \beta_1 x_1 + \beta_2 x_2$. Thus $\theta = (\beta_0, \beta_1, \beta_2)$ is a three-dimensional parameter. If interest centers on a scalar function of θ then a two-dimensional integration will be needed to find its marginal distribution. For example, you might want to know the posterior distribution of the derivative of the probability that $Y = 1$ with respect to x_1 evaluated at alternative choices of x. This derivative may be of considerable economic interest and so you need to know its most likely value or its expected value or the chance that it is negative. In this case the parameter of interest is

$$\gamma = \frac{\partial \Phi(x\beta)}{\partial x_1} = \beta_1 \phi(x\beta)$$

and it is its posterior distribution that you require. The modern way of finding this distribution is to sample the joint posterior distribution of $(\beta_0, \beta_1, \beta_2)$ then, for each realization of these three numbers, compute γ for some, perhaps typical, x vector of interest.

A first look at BUGS

BUGS calculation To illustrate the method we generated some artificial data and used the BUGS program to generate a sample of 10,000 realizations of $(\beta_0, \beta_1, \beta_2)$. We then substituted these values into the expression for γ at the x vector, say, $x_1 = 1$, $x_2 = 1$ and this gives 10,000 realizations from the marginal posterior distribution of γ. These can then be studied in whatever way you find helpful.

Data were generated with $n = 50$, $\beta_0 = 0$, $\beta_1 = 0.5$, $\beta_2 = -0.5$ The BUGS program follows exactly the Bayesian algorithm and so it requires you to tell it your likelihood and then to tell it your prior. The likelihood is (1.11) and it is written for the program as

```
model
{for(i in 1:n){
y[i]~dbin(p[i],1)
mu[i]<-beta0+beta1*x1[i]+beta2*x2[i]
p[i]<-phi(mu[i])}
```

The third line specifies that the i'th observation is a realization of a binomial (1, p_i) variate, the notation ˜dbin meaning "is distributed binomially." That is, Y_i is 1 with probability p_i and zero with probability $1 - p_i$. The next two lines state the probit model in which $p_i = \Phi(\beta_0 + \beta_1 x_{1i} + \beta_2 x_{2i})$. The statement phi(x) means evaluate the standard normal distribution at x, that is, calculate $\Phi(x)$. Lines two through five together provide the likelihood.

We then give the second component of the model which is the prior for β which in this case is specified as

```
beta0˜dnorm(0,0.001)
beta1˜dnorm(0,0.001)
beta2˜dnorm(0,0.001)}
```

These statements imply that the three elements of β are distributed independently normally with means zero and very low precisions implying standard deviations of $1/\sqrt{(0.001)} = 31$. This means that we are saying that, before seeing the data, we think that each element of β is very likely to lie within −93 and +93 which is plus and minus three standard deviations of zero. This is meant to be a vague prior. If you wish to put in more precise information, including dependence among the elements of β, or even less precise information, you may, of course, do so. Notice that the whole model, the likelihood and the prior, is enclosed by {}.

After supplying the data matrix containing as columns the values of y, x_1 and x_2 and some further details including the number of realizations required which in the present case was chosen to be nrep = 10,000, the program then produces an output matrix containing 10,000 realizations of the three elements of β. Each element of this matrix contains, to a close approximation, realizations from the joint posterior distribution of β corresponding to the likelihood, prior and data that we supplied.

To illustrate the procedure, figure 1.10 gives the smoothed histogram of the realizations of the marginal distribution of β_2. The value of β_2 that generated the data used here was $\beta_2 = -0.5$; the plot, as can be seen, is centered about −0.22. The mean and median of β_2 were both about −0.21. Finally, for comparison, the maximum likelihood estimate of β_2 was also −0.21. The "true" value of β_2 is one of the less probable values, though it would still lie within a 95% highest posterior density region.

To conclude this example we calculate the value of γ for $x_1 = 1$, $x_2 = 1$ for each of our 10,000 realizations and its smoothed histogram is given in figure 1.11. It can be seen that the effect of x_1 on the success probability is certainly positive and most probably about 0.17.

We shall explain in chapter 4 the methods used by BUGS to produce the realizations described here, and we shall make frequent use of this program throughout the book. Appendices 2 and 3 describe the BUGS language and give BUGS programs for many standard econometric models.

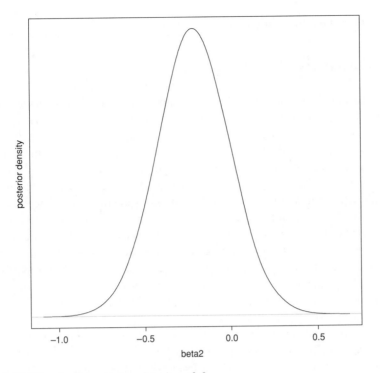

Figure 1.10 Marginal posterior density of β_2

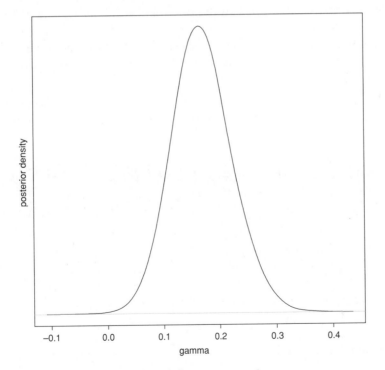

Figure 1.11 Posterior density of $\beta_1 \phi(x\beta)$ at $x_1 = x_2 = 1$

1.4.4 Decisions

Many writers prefer to view the problem of inference from data or evidence as that of making a decision or taking an action. An agent is viewed as setting up a model, including both $p(y|\theta)$ and $p(\theta)$; observing the data, y^{obs}; and then, in the light of the posterior distribution of θ, taking a decision. The decision might be to invest some money, to announce a forecast of Y, to report a single numerical value as an estimate of θ, etc. This is a point of view that is attractive to economists, who want to consider the agents whose behavior and interaction they model to be rationally coping with the uncertainties they face. This book does not take a decision theoretic perspective, though it is not inconsistent with one. This is because the problem faced by most economists or intending economists does not seem well described as one of decision. It seems more like that of sensibly and concisely reporting their findings, and for this the recommended procedure is to draw the marginal(s) of the object of interest. This leaves it up to others, for example policy makers, to use your report as a basis for decision making.

For the sake of completeness we give a very brief review of one version of the decision problem, that of choosing a point estimate of θ. Suppose that you have a model for potential data y involving a parameter θ. After having seen the data you will have a posterior distribution for it, $p(\theta|y)$. You are required to reach a single numerical decision, d, about θ. This decision will depend on the data y so $d = d(y)$. The decision theory approach assumes the existence of a **loss function** $L(d, \theta)$ that gives the loss to the decision maker, you perhaps, of making decision d when the parameter, about which you are uncertain, takes the value θ. A **Bayes decision** minimizes the expected loss

$$\hat{d} = \arg.\min \int_{\Theta} L(d, \theta) p(\theta|y)\, d\theta \quad \text{for } \hat{d} \in \Theta.$$

EXAMPLE 1.18   *SQUARED ERROR LOSS*   *Suppose the loss function takes the symmetric form $L(d, \theta) = (d - \theta)^2$ – squared error loss – then $\hat{d}$ is the posterior mean, $E(\theta|y)$. To prove this note that the expected loss is*

$$\int_{\Theta} L(d, \theta) p(\theta|y)\, d\theta = \int_{\Theta} (d - \theta)^2 p(\theta|y)\, d\theta$$

and a simple differentiation with respect to d provides the result.

A nice application of this is:

EXAMPLE 1.19 *DATA UNIFORM ON 0 TO θ* Let
Y be uniformly distributed between 0 *and* θ *so its density function is*

$$f_Y(y) = \frac{1}{\theta}, \quad 0 \le y \le \theta,$$

and zero elsewhere. Under the default (improper) prior density $p(\theta) \propto 1/\theta$ *the posterior density from n independent realizations is*

$$p(\theta|y) \propto \frac{1}{\theta^{n+1}}, \quad \theta \ge y_{\max} \tag{1.38}$$

where $y_{\max}$ *is the largest of the n sample realizations. (This comes about because* θ *is, by definition, not less than any observation, so it is certainly not less than the largest observation.) The kernel (1.38) is that of a proper density, for* $n \ge 1$, *and after supplying the normalizing constant it can be written as*

$$p(\theta|y) = \frac{n y_{\max}^n}{\theta^{n+1}} \quad \theta \ge y_{\max}. \tag{1.39}$$

Under squared error loss the Bayes decision is the posterior mean. Carrying out the integration we find that the mean exists for $n > 1$ *and is*

$$d(y) = \frac{n}{n-1} y_{\max}.$$

So your Bayes decision under squared error loss is to take the largest observation in your data, multiply it by $n/(n-1)$, *i.e. slightly increase it, and report the resulting number. (The maximum likelihood estimator of* θ *for this problem is* $\hat{\theta} = y_{\max}$ *which will underestimate* θ *for essentially any data set – it will always be too low.)*

Decision making and reporting are not necessarily alternatives. In many situations an economic model will envisage agents taking decisions under uncertainty. An analysis of data using a model that incorporates agents making decisions under uncertainty will lead to you – the uncertain investigator – reporting your analysis of uncertain agents who are presumed to be taking decisions under uncertainty in an optimal (Bayesian) way. So really both the decision making and reporting perspectives on Bayesian inference should receive emphasis in a text on Bayesian econometrics not because econometricians take decisions but because agents do.

1.5   CONCLUSION AND SUMMARY

The Bayesian approach to econometrics is conceptually simple and, following recent developments, computationally straightforward. Following the algorithm given in section 1.3.2 you must formulate your theory as a conditional probability statement for the data that you are about to see and a prior distribution over the parameters of that statement. This is equivalent to making a simple statement about what you think the data should look like on your theory since $\int p(y|\theta)p(\theta)d\theta = p(y)$, a probability distribution for the data. You then study the data and determine whether the model is, at least roughly, consistent with the evidence and, if it is, you proceed to revise your views about the model parameters. Whether the data are consistent with the model or not, you will have learned something. In view of this conceptual and computational simplicity the rest of this book is little more than a series of examples with some account of recently developed computational algorithms.

1.6   EXERCISES AND COMPLEMENTS

In this section we give some further worked examples on priors, likelihoods and posterior distributions and ways to study them and we suggest some exercises.

(1)   Simulation

Study of likelihoods and posterior or prior distributions is, as we have seen, often aided by computer simulation and graphics. In some of the examples in this chapter we simulated some data satisfying the model and plotted both the data and the likelihood they imply. Many computer languages make this easy and you may, of course, use whatever language you like but my own favorite is the language S. An appendix to the book describes the elements of this language and suggests reading. Here are some examples in which data are simulated and graphics used. If you have access to a copy of S – there is a shareware version, called *R*, on the web at *http://www.r-project.org/* – you should try these commands.

To simulate a regression model as in example 1.2 in which y is normal given x with mean βx and precision τ you can use

```
beta <- 0.3 ... specifies the value of β.
tau <- 1 ... specifies the value of τ.
n <- 50 ... chooses the sample size.
x <- runif(n,10,20) ... produces x values uniformly distributed from 10
```
to 20.
```
y <- rnorm(n,beta*x,1/sqrt(tau)) ... produces y values with mean βx
```
and standard deviations $1/\sqrt{\tau}$.
```
plot(x,y) ... plots the data on a scatter diagram.
b <- sum(x*y)/sum(x^2) ... calculates the least squares estimate.
```

`abline(0,b)` ... draws the least squares line $y = bx$ on the scatter diagram, with intercept zero and slope b.

`sdb <- 1/sqrt(tau*sum(x^2))` ... finds the standard deviation of the normal curve that defines the likelihood, (1.7)

`bval <- seq(b-4sdb, b+4*sdb, length=200)` ... chooses 200 points at which to evaluate the likelihood. These points cover the range over which the likelihood will be non-negligible.

`plot(bval,dnorm(bval,b,sdb),type="l")` ... draws the likelihood exploiting the fact that for this model it has the shape of a normal curve with mean `b` and standard deviation `sdb`. The plot command evaluates the function at the 200 points specified in `bval` and then the command `type = "l"` joins the points to form a continuous curve.

EXERCISE Generate your own data using this normal regression model and plot the data and the likelihood.

---

(2) A regression model for counts

Theory suggests that y should depend on x but the data will be counts of how often some events occurred. Econometric applications might be the numbers of strikes occurring in particular industries in a year or the numbers of patent applications filed by different firms over a year. Because the y values will be positive integers or zero such data cannot be normally distributed. The standard model for count data is the poisson with probability mass function

$$p_Y(y) = \frac{\mu^y e^{-\mu}}{y!}, \qquad y = 0, 1, 2, 3, \ldots, \qquad \mu > 0.$$

A (non-linear) regression model then takes Y as poisson with mean $\mu = \exp\{\beta x\}$ given x. The exponential function is chosen because it guarantees that the mean is always positive. This implies that for n independent observations on y and x the likelihood is

$$\ell(\beta; y) \propto \prod_{i=1}^{n} \exp\{\beta x_i y_i\} \exp\{-e^{\beta x_i}\}$$
$$= \exp\{\beta \sum_{i=1}^{n} x_i y_i\} \exp\{-\sum_{i=1}^{n} e^{\beta x_i}\}. \tag{1.40}$$

This does not have the shape of a normal curve but, nonetheless, if you simulate some data and draw the function you will find, for almost all data sets, that the curve is approximately bell shaped.

To simulate some data choose n, β and x as in exercise 1 and then use the command `y <- rpois(n,exp(beta*x))`. To draw the likelihood define a set of

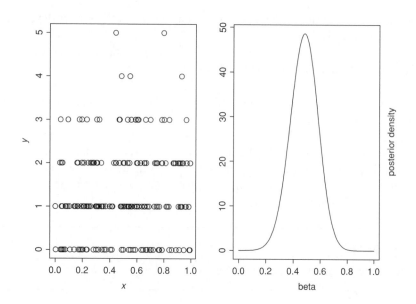

Figure 1.12 Data and likelihood for exercise 2

β values at which to evaluate it and store these in a vector `bval` as before, then define the logarithm of the likelihood function (1.40) by, say,

```
poissonlogl <- function(b){b*sum(x*y)-sum(exp(b*x))}
```

Finally use a "do loop" to evaluate the function at the points in bval, store these values in, say, `val` and plot the elements of exp(val) against bval. This could be done, if bval has `nval` elements, by

```
for(i in 1:nval){val[i] <- poissonlogl(bval[i])}
plot(bval,exp(val),type="l").
```

Figure 1.12 shows the results of such a simulation with $n = 200$, $\beta = 0.5$ and the x's uniform from zero to one. The first panel shows a scatter plot of the data and the second shows the likelihood. The scatter plot, as often with a discrete dependent variable, is quite hard to interpret. The likelihood is much easier and points clearly to a beta value in the neighbourhood of the value, 0.5, that produced the data.

There are two slight difficulties in doing this calculation. One is that, unlike the normal case of exercise 1, it is not evident where the likelihood will take its largest values. One solution is to make a preliminary calculation using a maximum likelihood routine to find the β value that gives maximum likelihood. Another solution is to calculate the likelihood for a wide range of β values to find out where the function is large. Another slight difficulty is that likelihood values can be very large numbers which may be hard to plot. The solution here is to calculate the mean value of the log likelihood and subtract it from `val` before issuing the plot command.

> **EXERCISE** Generate your own count data satisfying a regression model and calculate the likelihood. Try increasing the value of *n* to observe the convergence of the posterior towards a point.

(3)   Exponential likelihoods

The fundamental probability model for the duration of an event – how long it lasts – is the exponential. If a theorist reasons that agents with large values of *x* tend to have longer events than those with smaller *x*'s a natural econometric model within which to embed this idea is to let the duration *y* be exponentially distributed with mean μ depending on *x* as for example $e^{\beta x}$. This would be a non-linear regression model with regression function $E(Y|x) = e^{\beta x}$. The exponential density of mean μ is

$$p_Y(y) = (1/\mu)e^{y/\mu}, \quad \mu, y > 0,$$

so the likelihood for *n* independent realizations corresponding to different *x*'s is

$$\ell(\beta; y, x) = \exp\{-\beta\textstyle\sum_{i=1}^{n}x_i\}\exp\{-\textstyle\sum_{i=1}^{n}y_ie^{-\beta x_i}\}.$$

> **EXERCISE** Generate some durations using the command `rexp(n,exp(b*x))`, if you are using S, and plot the data and posterior density of β assuming a uniform prior.

(4)   A double exponential model

A probability model that is in some ways a useful alternative to the normal distribution is the double exponential or Laplace distribution. In its simplest form this has density function

$$p(y|\theta) = \exp\{-|y - \theta|\}, \quad -\infty < y, \theta < \infty.$$

This function is symmetrical about $y = \theta$ and on each side of θ it declines exponentially, hence the name. The mean, median and mode of *Y* are θ and the standard deviation is $\sqrt{2}$. This distribution is less dogmatic than the normal in that its tails decline like $e^{-|y|}$ which is slower than the normal rate e^{-y^2} so it allows for greater uncertainty about where *y* is located. Figure 1.13 plots the double exponential density function for the case $\theta = 1$.

Then *n* independent realizations of *Y* will have the joint probability density $p(y|\theta)$ $\propto \exp\{-\sum_{i=1}^{n}|y_i - \theta|\}$ and this is also the posterior density under a uniform prior for θ. Figure 1.14 is a Laplace likelihood with $n = 3$.

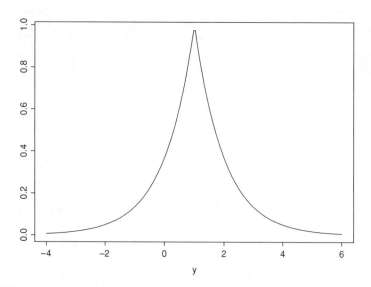

Figure 1.13 A double exponential density

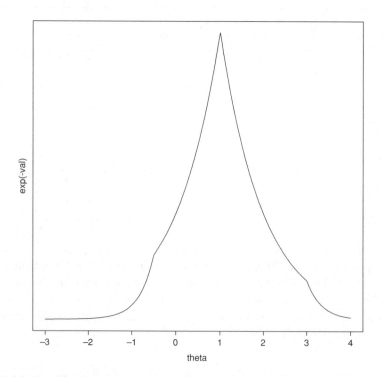

Figure 1.14 The likelihood for 3 observations of a Laplace variate

As can be seen from figure 1.14, the likelihood is kinked at each of the observations, which were $y = (-0.5, 1, 3)$. There are always as many kinks – points of non-differentiability – in the Laplace likelihood as there are distinct observations. (Nonetheless, the likelihood still approaches normality!)

EXERCISE Choose a value for θ and n and generate some data from the double exponential model. This can be done by generating n observations from an exponential distribution with mean = 1, changing the sign of these numbers with probability 0.5, and then adding θ. The first two steps here generate data from a double exponential centered at zero, and the final step centers the distribution at θ. The S command

```
y<-rexp(n)*(-1+2*(runif(n)>0.5))+theta
```

will do this. The statement `runif(n)>0.5` produces n numbers equal to 1 if a uniform variate on 0 to 1 exceeds 0.5, which has probability 0.5, and 0 otherwise; multiplying these numbers by 2 and subtracting 1 turns them into a sequence of plus and minus ones; and these in turn randomly change the sign of the elements of `rexp(n)`.

(1) Choose a small, odd value of n and generate some data.
(2) Sketch the posterior density – by hand – and show that it is continuous but not everywhere differentiable.
(3) Show that the most probable value of θ is the median observation.

EXERCISE Generalize the previous model by setting $\theta = \beta x_i$ for $i = 1, 2, ..., n$, so that each y_i is Laplace distributed about its mean. This is an alternative to the normal regression model. Write down the likelihood for β; generate some data and plot the posterior density of β under a uniform prior for this parameter. Note that the most probable value of β minimizes the expression $\sum_{i=1}^{n}|y_i - \beta x_i|$. This is sometimes called a **median regression** model.

Further exercises

EXERCISE For an example of normal approximation take n independent normal variates with means zero and common precision τ. The likelihood is $\ell(\tau) \propto \tau^{n/2} \exp\{-\tau\Sigma y_i^2/2\}$ and the Jeffreys' prior is $\propto 1/\tau$. Find the log posterior density, calculate the posterior mode of τ and find $-H(\tau)$ and $I_\tau(\hat{\tau})$ at this mode. Hence find the normal approximation to $p(\tau|y)$. Now take $\sigma = \tau^{-1/2}$ as the parameter and find the normal approximation to the posterior density of σ.

EXERCISE The poisson distribution has mass function

$$p(y|\theta) = \frac{\theta^y e^{-\theta}}{y!}, \quad y = 0, 1, 2 ..., \quad \theta > 0.$$

The mean and variance of Y given θ are both equal to θ. Write down the likelihood for n independent realizations of Y and then the posterior density of θ under the conventional vague prior $p(\theta) \propto 1/\theta$. Work out the hessian of the log posterior and the posterior mode and hence construct an asymptotic normal approximation to the posterior. Simulate some data for $n = 5, 10, 20$ and compare the exact (gamma) posterior density of θ to its normal approximation.

1.7 APPENDIX TO CHAPTER 1: SOME PROBABILITY DISTRIBUTIONS

In this appendix we review some of the elementary probability distributions that have been used in the body of this chapter.

THE UNIVARIATE NORMAL FAMILY

The univariate normal family has two parameters, the mean μ and the precision τ. The kernel is $\exp\{-(\tau/2)(y - \mu)^2\}$ and the full density is

$$p(y) = \sqrt{\frac{\tau}{2\pi}} \exp\{-(\tau/2)(y - \mu)^2\}.$$

We refer to such a distribution by writing $Y \sim n(\mu, \tau)$. The standard normal has $\mu = 0$, $\tau = 1$, and kernel $e^{-y^2/2}$ with distribution function $\int_{-\infty}^{y} e^{-u^2/2} du/\sqrt{(2\pi)}$. Its density and distribution functions at the point y are denoted by $\phi(y)$ and $\Phi(y)$. The moment generating of a normal (μ, τ) variate is

$$M(t) = E(e^{tY}) = \int_{-\infty}^{\infty} e^{ty} p(y) \, dy = \exp\{t\mu + t^2/2\tau\}$$

from which the mean and variance are

$$E(Y) = \mu; \quad V(Y) = \frac{1}{\tau}.$$

The variance is denoted by σ^2.

Relevant S commands are as follows.

rnorm(n, m, s) .... *n* independent realizations from a normal distribution of mean *m* and standard deviation (not variance and not precision) *s*.

dnorm(y, m, s) .... the value of the density function at *y* of a normal (*m*, *s*) variate.

pnorm(y, m, s) .... the value of the (cumulative) distribution function at *y* of a normal (*m*, *s*) variate

qnorm(p, m, s) .... the quantile function at *p* of a normal (*m*, *s*) variate. This will produce the number *y* which is exceeded with probability $1 - p$ with such a distribution.

qqnorm(y) .... this will plot the quantiles of the data vector *y* against the quantiles of the standard normal distribution. This provides a graphical test of normality. The plot will be linear if *y* comes from a normal distribution but not otherwise. Non-linearity indicates non-normality.

In S the default values for *m* and *s* are zero and one.

THE GAMMA FAMILY

The gamma family of probability distributions has kernel $p(y) \propto y^{\alpha-1} e^{-\beta y}$; $y > 0$; $\alpha, \beta > 0$. The full density function is

$$p(y) = \frac{y^{\alpha-1} e^{-\beta y}}{\Gamma(\alpha) \beta^{-\alpha}} \tag{1.41}$$

where $\Gamma(\alpha)$ is the complete gamma function defined by

$$\Gamma(\alpha) = \int_0^\infty x^{\alpha-1} e^{-x} dx, \quad \alpha > 0.$$

The family can be thought of as generalizing the exponential family $\beta e^{-\beta y}$ which is a gamma distribution with $\alpha = 1$. The unit exponential has $\beta = 1$ and has mean and variance equal to one.

The mean and variance of a gamma(α, β) variate are

$$E(Y) = \frac{\alpha}{\beta}; \quad V(Y) = \frac{\alpha}{\beta^2}.$$

A one parameter sub-family of the gamma distributions is the χ^2 distributions which have $\alpha = v/2$ and $\beta = 1/2$ where v is positive and usually an integer. Their density functions are

$$p(y) = \frac{y^{v/2-1} e^{-y/2}}{\Gamma(v/2) 2^{v/2}}, \quad y > 0, v > 0.$$

Relevant S commands follow the same format as for the normal, for example `rgamma(n, a, b)` produces n independent realizations from a gamma distribution with $\alpha = a$ and $\beta = b$. Chi-squared (χ^2) results can be got from `rchisq(n, v)` etc.

THE BETA FAMILY

The beta densities are continuous on the unit interval and depend on two parameters. Their form is

$$p(x|\alpha, \beta) = \frac{\Gamma(\alpha + \beta)}{\Gamma(\alpha)\Gamma(\beta)} x^{\alpha-1}(1-x)^{\beta-1}, \quad \alpha, \beta > 0, \ 0 \le x \le 1. \tag{1.42}$$

When α is a positive integer then $\Gamma(\alpha) = (\alpha - 1)!$. In particular, $\Gamma(1) = 0! = 1$. Since probability density functions integrate to one over the sample space it follows from (1.42) that

$$\int_0^1 x^{\alpha-1}(1-x)^{\beta-1}dx = \frac{\Gamma(\alpha)\Gamma(\beta)}{\Gamma(\alpha+\beta)}. \tag{1.43}$$

The means and variances of the densities (1.42) are

$$E(X) = \frac{\alpha}{\alpha + \beta} \qquad V(X) = \frac{\alpha\beta}{(\alpha+\beta)^2(\alpha+\beta+1)}. \tag{1.44}$$

The density is symmetrical about $X = 1/2$ if $\alpha = \beta$. If $\alpha = \beta = 1$ it reduces to the uniform distribution.

S commands are again in standard format in which, for example, `rbeta(n, a, b)` produces n independent realizations from a beta distribution with $\alpha = a$ and $\beta = b$.

THE MULTINOMIAL FAMILY

Suppose a vector discrete random variable $Y = (Y_0, Y_1, ..., Y_L)$ is such that Y_j measures the number of occasions that the j'th of $L + 1$ mutually exclusive and exhaustive events occurs in n trials. Thus each of the $\{Y_j\}$ takes values in the set $Y_j = \{0, 1, 2, ..., n\}$ subject to the condition that $\Sigma_{j=0}^{L}Y_j = n$. Then if $p = \{p_0, p_1, ..., p_L\}$ and p_j is the probability that at any one trial the j'th event occurs,

$$p_Y(y|p) = \frac{n!}{y_0!y_1!\ldots y_L!} p_0^{y_0} p_1^{y_1} \times \ldots \times p_L^{y_L} \tag{1.45}$$

where $\quad \Sigma_{j=0}^{L}y_j = n; \ y_j \in \{0, 1, 2, ..., n\}; \ \Sigma_{j=0}^{L}p_j = 1. \tag{1.46}$

This is best thought of as the distribution of L random variables since the last one is determined by the condition that they sum to n. The means, variances and covariances of the $\{Y_j\}$ are

$$E(Y_j) = np_j; \quad V(Y_j) = np_j(1 - p_j); \quad C(Y_iY_j) = -np_ip_j.$$

A particular case of the multinomial is the binomial which arises when $L = 1$ so there are two categories and the probability mass function takes the form

$$p_Y(y) = \frac{n!}{(n-y)!y!}p^y(1-p)^{n-y}, \quad y = 0, 1, \ldots, n, \quad 0 \le p \le 1. \tag{1.47}$$

And a particular case of the binomial is the Bernoulli family which arises when $n = 1$,

$$p_Y(y) = p^y(1-p)^{1-y}, \quad y \in \{0, 1\}, \quad 0 \le p \le 1. \tag{1.48}$$

THE DIRICHLET FAMILY

This family generalizes the beta family to a vector $p = (p_0, p_1, \ldots, p_L)$ in which $\sum_{i=0}^{L}p_i = 1$ and the $\{p_i\}$ are non-negative. If $\alpha = \sum_{l=0}^{L}\alpha_l$ the density function takes the form

$$f_P(p) = \frac{\Gamma(\alpha)}{\Gamma(\alpha_0)\Gamma(\alpha_1)\ldots\Gamma(\alpha_L)}p_0^{\alpha_0-1} \times \ldots \times p_L^{\alpha_L-1}, \tag{1.49}$$

$$\text{where} \quad \{p_i\} \ge 0; \quad \textstyle\sum_{i=1}^{L}p_i = 1; \quad \{\alpha_i\} \ge 0; \quad \textstyle\sum_{i=0}^{L}\alpha_i = \alpha.$$

The means, variances and covariances are

$$E(P_j) = \frac{\alpha_j}{\alpha}; \quad V(P_j) = \frac{\alpha_j(\alpha - a_j)}{\alpha^2(\alpha + 1)}; \quad C(P_iP_j) = -\frac{\alpha_i\alpha_j}{\alpha^2(\alpha + 1)}.$$

The beta family emerges as the special case in which $L = 1$. Comparison of (1.49) and (1.45) shows that if the prior for p is dirichlet then the posterior is of the same form. This means that the dirichlet is the natural conjugate prior family for the multinomial.

1.8   BIBLIOGRAPHIC NOTES

For a perspective on econometric analysis not dissimilar to that taken in this book the reader might wish to look at Heckman (2001: 673–748).

Almost all books on Bayesian inference are written by statisticians. The main work specifically devoted to Bayesian inference in econometrics is Zellner (1971). This is a useful book and gives a systematic and detailed account of the main analytical results and so it is necessarily confined to the simpler, mathematically tractable, models. Written well before the computer revolution it is naturally dated, but remains a valuable reference. *Bayesian Analysis in Econometrics and Statistics: The Zellner View and Papers*, edited by Zellner (1997), provides convenient access to more recent work by Zellner and others. A stimulating early book by Leamer (1978) is well worth reading but is currently out of print. Bauwens, Lubrano and Richard (1999) is a useful text on econometrics from a Bayesian perspective with a particular emphasis on time series models, but again it shows traces of being written before the computer revolution.

Though statistics and econometrics differ radically in their point of view they have a great deal in common, particularly computational techniques. Useful sources in increasing order of difficulty are Gelman, Carlin, Stern and Rubin (2003) and, particularly, even though it shows the effect of being written before the coming of fast simulation methods, Berger (1993). Bernardo and Smith (1994) is a major study of the principles of Bayesian inference written from a perspective strongly influenced by de Finetti. It contains an account of reference priors, proposed originally by Bernardo. The proof of convergence of posterior mass functions, theorem 1.2 in this chapter, is based on theirs. Another recent statistics text is Press (2003).

The source text for a subjective view of inference is de Finetti's two volumes, *Theory of Probability* (1974 and 1975), though it is not easy reading. See also Cox (1961). Harold Jeffreys' classic *Theory of Probability* (1966) is available in paperback from the Clarendon Press, Oxford. It is not easy reading, partly for notational reasons. Readers curious about foundational issues might like to read Keynes (1920), particularly chapter 24 which gives a subtle discussion of "objective probability". Frank Ramsey replied, arguing for the subjective view, in Ramsey (1931: 156–98). Another valuable source on foundational issues and the subjective versus objective view of probability is Kyburg and Smokler (1964) which contains lengthy excerpts by many of the major contributors to the debate, including de Finetti. An introductory exposition of Bayesian method from a subjective point is by Edwards, Lindman and Savage (1963: 193–242). This article, although published in a psychological journal, is not especially "psychological" and it is not particularly technical. It is recommended to all those interested in Bayesian methods. It is reprinted in *The Writings of Leonard Jimmie Savage – A Memorial Selection*, published by the American Statistical Association and the Institute of Mathematical Statistics (1981).

There is a persistent interest in "objective" Bayesian methods that involve priors or likelihoods that are in some sense minimally informative. A good source, which is strongly recommended even if you aren't interested in objective methods, is the work of E. T. Jaynes, much of it unpublished and which is best accessed through http:\\omega.math.albany.edu/JaynesBook.html.

Zellner (1986) proposes a variant of the natural conjugate prior that has proved popular.

Lindley and Smith's classic article (1972: 1–14) is about hierarchical prior structures as applied to linear regression models.

Lindley and Novick (1981: 45–58) provide an enlightening discussion both of exchangeability and its relation to similar ideas of R. A. Fisher.

Decision theory is dealt with in many books. A recent and clear introductory exposition may be found in Leonard and Hsu (1999). A classic monograph on Bayesian decision theory is DeGroot (1970). Berger (1993), mentioned above, is another recommended source on the decision theoretic approach. A recent paper by Chamberlain (2000: 255–84) is worth study.

Berger and Wolpert (1988) is a very readable study of fundamental principles of inference and is the main source for this book on the likelihood principle.

On the Bayesian view of identifiability see Kadane (1974: 175–91).

On separating models with multidimensional parameters Lancaster (2000: 391–413) and (2002: 647–60) contain a number of examples.

The paper introducing regression is Galton (1886: 246–63).

Full text copies of all but the most recent *Handbook of Econometrics* chapters can be downloaded from www.elsevier.com/hes/books/02/menu02.htm. This source includes the important Leamer (1983).

Chapter 2
PREDICTION AND MODEL CRITICISM

If you don't criticize your results you can be sure that others will. So place yourself in the position of someone who has constructed a model, collected some data, and found the posterior distributions of quantities of economic interest. The results that you announce, whether they are tables of posterior expectations or modes with hpd intervals or frequentist point estimates with estimated standard errors, are open to criticism. How does this work?

In traditional, frequentist, econometrics the criticism is typically that the point estimates (with their standard errors) are not right. And there's a Bayesian counterpart to this, marginal posterior distributions that "look wrong." This means that these estimates are not consistent with the economic theory that is embedded in your econometric model.[1] Often, a theory comes along with quite strong implications about the coefficients that appear in it. The theory sometimes implies that certain coefficients should have particular signs or magnitudes, demand curves should almost certainly slope down; discount rates are non-negative and probably of the order of five to thirty percent; the exponent of labor in a production function should be roughly of the order of labor's proportion of GDP and so on. These remarks imply that an economic theory is not just a set of equations but comes along with a collection of beliefs about the coefficients. These beliefs are derived either from logical considerations such that "the theory would not make sense unless the coefficients have certain signs and not others" or empiricial considerations based on previous studies or general knowledge about the economy.

So what do you do when your coefficients look wrong?

(1) **Check your data and your calculations**   The very first thing is to check your data to see if they have been entered correctly and that they do measure what you thought they were measuring. If you have written your own computer program then check it by using simulated data for which you know what the answers should be.

---

1   This assumes that you used a prior that encompasses a wide range of prior opinion about the coefficients.

(2) **Discard the model**   One reaction is to accept that your economic model is inconsistent with the evidence and discard the results. Sometimes a model is so obviously inconsistent with the data that to abandon the model and think again is clearly the right thing to do. Such a decision can sometimes be reached without elaborate computations. Sometimes just plotting the data is enough. If your economic model suggests that *y* increases with *x* and a scatter diagram shows it clearly decreasing then it's back to the drawing board. Although, since economics usually deals with more than two variables, simple plots are rarely decisive and can be quite misleading.

(3) **Question the model**   Another, more defensive, reaction is to question the econometric model. The econometric model, you will recall, is the economic model together with a likelihood and prior. Such a model inevitably includes dogmatic statements.[2] For example, the Bernoulli model contained the dogmatic assertion that the trials were conditionally independent. The autoregressive model contained several dogmatic assertions, for example the Markov hypothesis that

$$p(y_t|y_{t-1}, y_{t-2}, ..., y_0, \rho) = p(y_t|y_{t-1}, \rho).$$

These dogmatic assertions are often made just for computational convenience and they often concern parameters that are not of primary economic interest. These assertions may turn out, though, to have an important effect on inferences about parameters of interest, or they may not. It's important to know which and the applied economist should always check, if this is possible,[3] to see if such assertions are wrong. Asking whether certain dogmatic features of the model are having an important effect on your inference about the parameter of interest is called **sensitivity analysis**.

In this chapter we shall give an account of some procedures for model checking.

2.1   METHODS OF MODEL CHECKING

There are two ways of checking the dogmatic assertions of your model.

(1) **Take another look at the data**   The first is to examine the data more closely to see if they reveal evidence that the beliefs embedded in the model were wrong. In the Bernoulli trials example this might, for example, include examining the trials to see if they provide any evidence of conditional *dependence*. In the autoregressive example one might examine the posterior distribution of $y_t - \rho y_{t-1} = \varepsilon_t$ to see if these errors show signs of autocorrelation. This process is often called "residual analysis" or carrying out "diagnostic checks." Or you might want to

---

2   These are often called "maintained hypotheses" in the traditional literature.
3   See section 2.3.

look at the posterior distribution of the errors, $(\varepsilon_1, ..., \varepsilon_n)$, to see if they look as they should on the hypothesis that they are, say, conditionally independent homoscedastic normal variates.

Taking another look at the data can be done informally and often graphically or one can turn to a formal calculation. A formal test typically involves calculating the value of some feature of the fitted model, for example the residual autocorrelation or skewness, and then asking how probable such a value was if the model had been as you specified it to be. If you find that the value you have calculated is very improbable under your model then you have reason to doubt that model.

(2) **Enlarge the model**   The second method is by changing the model to one that turns dogmatic assertions into undogmatic ones. This is called *enlarging or expanding the model*. In the autoregressive example one might expand the model to allow for second order dependence by writing $y_t = \rho_1 y_{t-1} + \rho_2 y_{t-2} + \varepsilon_t$ and examine whether ρ_2 is materially different from zero. The original, first order, model can then be construed as containing the dogmatic assertion that $\rho_2 = 0$ while the enlarged model says only that it may be zero, or may not. Or one might expand the model to allow for variances of the $\{\varepsilon_t\}$ to depend upon previous realizations of the series as in an ARCH or autoregressive conditional heteroscedasticity model. In a regression model one might expand the covariate list; relax assumptions of linearity; allow for interactions so that the effect of one covariate depends on the level of another; do separate analysis within sub-groups of the data, and so on.

In the next section we shall begin an account of model checks which are numerical and graphical ways to check the model's dogmatic assertions. These are systematic ways of taking another look at the data. Informal specification checks are usually graphical and we begin by looking at some leading examples.

2.2   INFORMAL MODEL CHECKS

Most econometric models derive from equations like $g(y, x) = 0$ augmented by error terms that allow for agent to agent variation not accounted for by the theory. The augmented model is $g(y, x) = \varepsilon$. Econometric analyses typically use fairly dogmatic assertions about the properties of the error terms and this is especially true of Bayesian methods, since these require a likelihood and this requires distributional assumptions about the $\{\varepsilon_i\}$. There will also usually be hypotheses about the function $g(,)$. An obvious way to check assumptions about the ε is to study their distribution after observing n pairs of the form y_i, x_i. Thus, to check this aspect of the model specification we look at the posterior distribution of the model errors and see if it is broadly consistent with our prior beliefs.

The most common example of this type of check arises in the linear regression model in which $g(y, x)$ takes the linear form $y - \beta_0 - \beta_1 x$ and thus the errors are

$\varepsilon = y - \beta_0 - \beta_1 x$. A Bayesian analysis requires a likelihood and this in turn will require you to formulate prior beliefs about ε. A common example of such a belief is that the n elements of ε can be thought of as independent realizations of a normal variate with mean zero and common precision, say τ. This belief implies a certain, perhaps rather strong, degree of similarity among the $\{\varepsilon_i\}$ but it may be the case that agents we are studying are in fact unexpectedly heterogeneous. If so, this could be an interesting discovery and it might prompt further enquiry into the reasons for this diversity.

So how do we deduce the posterior distributions of the model errors? We shall go into this question in some detail in the chapters on regression and on computational methods but for the moment we just assert that under the belief that the errors are iid $n(0, \tau)$ and that the priors are vague, the errors have posterior means equal to

$$e_i = y_i - b_0 - b_1 x_i, \quad i = 1, 2, ..., n$$

where b_0 and b_1 are the least squares estimates of the coefficients β_0 and β_1. The e_i are the **regression residuals**. They are usually derived by replacing the β coefficients in $y = \beta_0 + \beta_1 x + \varepsilon$ by least squares estimates, which is a correct derivation. Here we emphasize their interpretation as posterior means of the $\{\varepsilon_i\}$. So we may get some idea of how the evidence has changed our beliefs about $\{\varepsilon_i\}$ by looking at the residuals, their posterior expectations.

2.2.1 Residual QQ plots

A simple graphical way of checking to see if the ε_i could reasonably be regarded as iid normal realizations given τ is to look at the frequency distribution of the n model residuals – the $\{e_i\}$. Such a look can be undertaken by doing a QQ plot. This takes the ordered residuals and plots them against what they ought to be if they were a sample from a standard normal distribution – against the **expected order statistics** of a normal distribution. (Note that this is not quite correct. The QQ plot shows the ordered data against a set of numbers that are close numerical approximations to the expected order statistics.)

DEFINITION 2.1   EXPECTED ORDER STATISTICS   *The order statistics of a sample of size n are just the ordered data – the smallest, next smallest and so on up to the biggest. The expected order statistics are the expected values of the smallest (of n), the second smallest of n etc. These expectations depend on the sample size, for example the expected largest of three standard normal variates is 0.846 but the expected largest of six is 1.267 which is, naturally, larger.*

If the data really appear to be standard normal the ordered data should plot linearly against the expected order statistics with a slope of one and an intercept of zero. If the data really appear to be normal but not standard normal the plot should still be linear but the slope will not be one and the intercept not zero. There should be no major departures except for a small proportion of points corresponding to the very largest and the very smallest observations,[4] if the data really are normal. If they are not normal, clear departures can be expected.

The S command to do a QQ plot for a visual test of normality is qqnorm(y) when the data are in the vector *y*; the command qqline(y) adds a straight line showing where the plot should lie under normality.

EXAMPLE 2.1   *QQ PLOTS FOR THICK-TAILED DISTRIBUTIONS* *If the distribution of the data has tails that go to zero less rapidly than the normal then you would expect to see a QQ plot in which the largest observations are larger than would be expected under normality and the smallest are smaller. This is illustrated in figure 2.1 which shows a QQ plot of 1,000 observations from a t distribution with three degrees of freedom.*

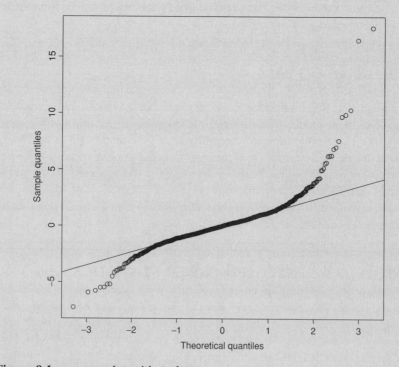

Figure 2.1 qqnorm plot with t_3 data

---

4 This is because the extreme order statistics are much more variable than those in the middle.

EXAMPLE 2.2 *FINITE MIXTURES* *For another example consider a linear regression model in which the $\{\varepsilon_i\}$ are not homogeneous but rather look as if they came from a mixture of normal distributions of the form*

$$p(\varepsilon) = \alpha\; n(\mu_1, \tau_1) + (1 - \alpha)\; n(\mu_2, \tau_2), \quad 0 \le \alpha \le 1. \qquad (2.1)$$

*This is an example of a **finite mixture distribution**. The idea is that the "population" consists of two types of agent, those whose ε values are scattered around a mean of μ_1 and those whose ε values are scattered around μ_2. A density of the form (2.1) can generate a wide variety of shapes including both unimodal and bimodal[5] distributions depending on the values of the five parameters $\theta = (\alpha, \mu_1, \mu_2, \tau_1, \tau_2)$. The raw moments of this mixture distribution are weighted averages of the moments of the two component distributions. In particular, the expected value of ε is $E\varepsilon = \alpha\mu_1 + (1 - \alpha)\mu_2$. If $\mu_1 = \mu_2$ and $\tau_1 = \tau_2$ then (2.1) reduces to a homogeneous normal density so the mixture model generalizes the normal model. The next graph, figure 2.2, shows an example of (2.1) in which $\alpha = 0.15$, $\mu_1 = 2$, $\mu_2 = -1$ and the τ's are both equal to 0.7. It can be seen that this particular mixture is bimodal with a major mode at μ_2 and a minor one at μ_1.*

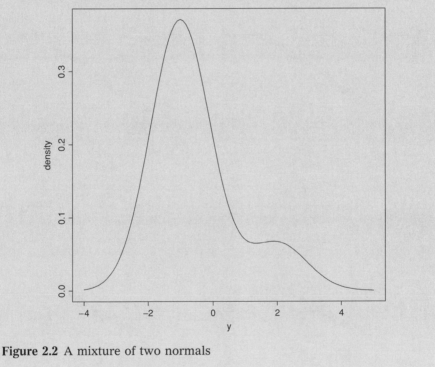

Figure 2.2 A mixture of two normals

5   The classic example of a bimodal mixture arises when you study the heights of a population of adults of whom half are men and half are women. It is asserted that the distribution will show modes at the average male height and at the average female height. Sadly, recent research (Schilling, Mark F., Watkins, Anne E., and Watkins, William, *Is human height bimodal?*, *The American Statistician*, 56, 3, August 2002) has shown that adult heights, though still presumably a mixture of normals, are not bimodal.

Mixing in the errors can be detected by inspecting a residual QQ plot.

Finite mixtures with several, not just two, components can approximate a large variety of distributional shapes and they have been advocated as a good way to make Bayesian econometric modeling more flexible and less dogmatic.

EXAMPLE 2.3 *DETECTING ERROR MIXING FROM THE QQ PLOT*   *We first generate $n = 100$ iid normal errors, say ε_h; generate some x data; and finally generate the y data as $y_h = \alpha + \beta x + \varepsilon_h$. Then we compute the least squares estimates of α and β and calculate the residuals, $e_h = y_h - a - bx$. In the top two panels of figure 2.3 we show QQ plots of the ε_h and then the e_h. Both plots show little evidence of departure from homogeneous normality. Next we generate errors ε_m that come from the mixture population described above; we then redraw some y's as $y_m = \alpha + \beta x + \varepsilon_m$; compute the new least squares estimates and form the new residuals $e_m = y_m - a - bx$. The lower two*

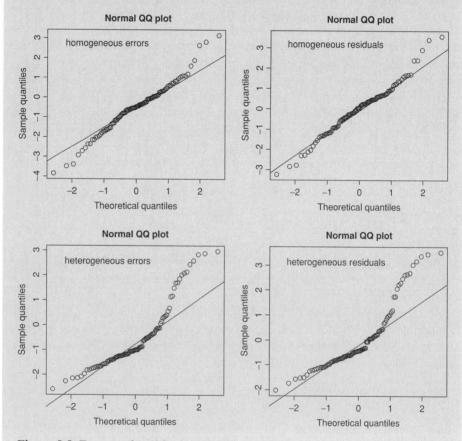

Figure 2.3 Error and residual QQ plots

panels show QQ plots of ε_m and e_m. If we compare the right hand plots to the left we see that the distribution of the residuals strongly resembles that of the errors so there is little loss, at least with this sample size, in having to look at the errors only through the lens provided by the residuals. Turning to the comparison of the upper pairs of plots with the lower we see that the non-normality of the error distribution in the second data set is revealed rather, well, graphically. We conclude that the QQ plot can detect heterogeneity, due to mixing, in the errors in a regression model.

What should the investigator do when faced with regression residuals that look like the lower right figure? A good strategy might be to try to find the identities of the agents whose residuals are systematically different from the rest and then to think about why these agents should satisfy a different structure than the others. Such thought might lead to a valuable revision of the theory underlying this calculation. An alternative is to generalize the error distribution by allowing for it to be a mixture of different normals, and then to see if the posterior distribution of parameters of interest is affected by this change.

There are many other useful graphical ways of examining model errors by inspecting the corresponding model residuals. For example with time series data it is useful to plot the residuals against time, to try to see if they suggest that the errors were dependent when your model assumed that they were independent. We shall illustrate some other graphical methods in later chapters.

One difficulty about graphical methods is that graphs are sometimes hard to read. For instance it may not be obvious that the departures from a straight line in the upper left graph are not, in fact, indicative of a serious departure from normality, (though we know they aren't because the data were generated as normal!). Time series plots are notoriously hard to interpret, and so on. For these reasons most people trying to check a model prefer to rely more on formal, numerical, model checks and to these we shortly turn. Before doing so we need to consider whether some beliefs contained in our model are, in fact, uncheckable by any method, graphical or otherwise.

2.3 UNCHECKABLE BELIEFS?

The collection of beliefs that together represent your model can be thought of as being of two types. The first are the dogmatic beliefs such as that the regression is linear, the errors are independent and so on. The others are the non-dogmatic beliefs as represented by prior distributions that are never exactly zero over the natural parameter space. The non-dogmatic beliefs are revised by the evidence according to Bayes' theorem and you can see how the evidence has altered your views. The dogmatic beliefs can be checked by looking at the data to see if there is evidence that they are false – this is the process that we are describing in this chapter – and then you can do a further calculation to see if such falsity matters for your posterior beliefs about the objects that really interest you. It is, however, true that there are some dogmatic beliefs that, it can be argued, can *never* be checked using data of the type that you are modeling.

This is a very fundamental point. It is related to the phenomenon of **non-identifiability** from the likelihood that we treated in chapter 1. Here is an example that anticipates a little the material of the linear regression chapter but which is central to econometrics. Take the linear equation that we discussed in the last section,

$$y_i = \alpha + \beta x_i + \varepsilon_i$$

where the $\{\varepsilon_i\}$ are terms representing the departure of real data from the strict linear deterministic relation posited by theory. These $\{\varepsilon_i\}$ are, from the Bayesian point of view, additional parameters about which we must form our prior beliefs. A belief that underlies most applications of the linear model is that

$$E\varepsilon_i|x_i = 0, \quad i = 1, 2, ..., n. \tag{2.2}$$

This is called **mean independence** of the error and the covariate. This belief, together with certain additional assumptions, is what justifies the estimation of α and β by least squares. But one might consider, perhaps for solid theoretical reasons, that in fact the errors and covariates are probably linearly related according to

$$E\varepsilon_i|x_i = \gamma x_i, \quad i = 1, 2, ..., n \tag{2.3}$$

given some parameter γ. We see then that mean independence of error and covariate could be interpreted as the adoption of the dogmatic belief that $\gamma = 0$. Can we check this belief? Substituting this last belief into the model for y we see that while under (2.2) the expectation of y in your model is

$$Ey_i|x_i = \alpha + \beta x_i,$$

under (2.3) it is

$$Ey_i|x_i = \alpha + (\beta + \gamma)x_i.$$

Now it can be shown that, for a large variety of extra assumptions that lead to a likelihood for the $\{y_i\}$ given the $\{x_i\}$, the only coefficients that are identifiable from the likelihood alone are firstly α, and secondly $\beta + \gamma$, and that there will *always* be a non-degenerate set of values of α, β, γ that lead to the same value for the likelihood.[6] In particular, we could never learn from the likelihood alone whether or not γ was, in fact, zero.

For a Bayesian this is, in a sense, not an issue since he/she doesn't make inferences from the likelihood alone, but would also use beliefs about β, γ that are described

---

6 Compare the definition of identification, 1.3, in chapter 1, section 1.4.1.

by the prior. But if β, γ are not separately identified from the likelihood this will generally mean that posterior beliefs are sensitive to prior beliefs – and this will be true however many observations we possess. It will also often be difficult to provide a convincing argument for one prior as against another. Inference in this case may well be controversial and unpersuasive and this is an unsatisfactory state of affairs.

We conclude from this example that though all beliefs are checkable in principle, to do so may require priors that would be quite unpersuasive. What should one do about this? What should one do to check if γ is zero, or nearly so? The short answer is that not even Bayesians can make bricks without straw. Part of a longer answer would be that any respectable economic theory should have more implications than the bald statement that $y = \alpha + \beta x$ so you should find other data relevant to the model. Another part is to find additional data to break the deadlock such as instrumental variables – see chapter 8 – or panel data – see chapter 7.

2.4 FORMAL MODEL CHECKS

2.4.1 *Predictive distributions*

Formal model checks depend upon the idea of predictive distributions. This is because *checking a model is a process of comparing its (your) predictions to the evidence.* As its name suggests, a predictive distribution is a probability distribution whose role is to predict. There are two such distributions. The first is the **prior predictive distribution** which indicates what your data *should* look like, given your model, before you have seen them. The prior predictive distribution is sometimes called the **marginal likelihood**. The second is the **posterior predictive distribution** which indicates what another realization from your model should look like given the data that you have seen and, of course, your model. Another realization can be a future (or past) observation or it might be a replication of the type of observation that is in your data file.

2.4.2 *The prior predictive distribution*

This distribution is

$$p(y) = \int p(y|\theta)p(\theta)\, d\theta \tag{2.4}$$

where $p(y|\theta)$ is the likelihood and $p(\theta)$ is the prior. Note that $p(y)$ is the denominator in Bayes' theorem, (1.3). The prior predictive distribution describes all that your model implies for the potential data. You can use it to compare features of the data with what the model predicts. For example you might calculate from $p(y)$ the predictive distribution of the autocorrelations (if y is a time series) and then you might collect the data, calculate the correlations in them and see whether they are probable or not. If you are going to observe pairs of observations, x and y, the prior predictive distribution is an algebraic statement of what the x, y scatter diagram should look like, telling you which diagrams are likely and which are not.

Here is a very simple, yet intriguing, example of a model and a prior predictive distribution.

EXAMPLE 2.4   *A PREDICTIVE DISTRIBUTION FOR BERNOULLI TRIALS*   *As we saw in chapter 1, the likelihood for a model in which n Bernoulli trials are to be done takes the form $p(y|\theta) = \theta^s(1 - \theta)^{n-s}$ on a sample space that consists of all distinct sequences of ones and zeros of length n and where s is the number of ones or successes in the sequence. A simple case of the beta distributions that are natural conjugate for this model is the uniform distribution, $p(\theta) = 1, 0 \le \theta \le 1$. Under this model the prior predictive distribution of the n vector y is*

$$p(y) = \int_0^1 \theta^s(1 - \theta)^{n-s}\, d\theta = \frac{\Gamma(s + 1)\Gamma(n - s + 1)}{\Gamma(n + 2)} = \frac{s!(n - s)!}{(n + 1)!} \qquad (2.5)$$

where the solution of the integration is found by using the beta integral formula of (1.29). This is the probability distribution of the data, Y, that you are about to observe when you plan to conduct a given number, n, of Bernoulli trials. Note that (2.5) is a probability distribution for Y whose sample space is all possible sequences of ones and zeros of length n. It is not the predictive distribution of S, the number of successes in n such trials. But also note that all sequences having the same number of ones have the same probability. Thus, 0, 0, 0, 1, 1, 1 is as probable as 1, 0, 1, 0, 1, 0. This is why the predictive density depends on y only through s.

As a particular case, for $n = 2$ the predictive probabilities over the four distinct sequences of ones and zero are

$$p(0, 1) = 1/6; \quad p(1, 0) = 1/6; \quad p(1, 1) = 1/3; \quad p(0, 0) = 1/3. \qquad (2.6)$$

Note that these are quite different from the predictions you would make if you knew that $\theta = 0.5$, – "the coin is fair." With this dogmatic prior the predictive distribution is just $p(y) = 0.5^s 0.5^{2-s} = (1/2)^2 = 1/4$ leading to

$$p(0, 1) = 1/4; \quad p(1, 0) = 1/4; \quad p(1, 1) = 1/4; \quad p(0, 0) = 1/4. \qquad (2.7)$$

You may find the difference between (2.6) and (2.7) puzzling if, when thinking of Bernoulli trials, you have in your head the image of someone throwing a coin. With two throws of a coin "everyone knows" that the probabilities are given by (2.7). A source of confusion here is that probability statements are being made without a clear statement of the conditions that govern them. The prior belief that θ is exactly $1/2$ appears only via the word "fair" in the phrase "two throws of a fair coin," a word that is easy to miss. And if indeed you believe that the coin is fair, so you believe dogmatically that $\theta = 1/2$, then (2.7) is indubitably right. But if you think that θ is equally likely to lie anywhere between zero and one then (2.6) is certainly right.

If you are still puzzled about the difference between (2.7) and (2.6) the following intuition may be helpful. Under the uniform prior in which θ could be anywhere between zero and one the occurrence of a success at the first trial will lead you to suspect that θ is larger than a half and hence that success is more likely than failure on the second trial. So with this prior the probability of the sequence 1, 1 will be larger than that of 1, 0. But with the dogmatic prior no such learning takes place and success is as probable on the second trial as it was on the first. Hence both 1, 1 and 1, 0 have the same probability.

When your beliefs assert dogmatically that θ takes a particular numerical value, say θ_0, you have a **point prior**. This is the prior that asserts that $p(\theta_0) = 1$ and that the density is zero everywhere else. Then your predictive distribution becomes $p(y|\theta_0)$ and you can use this distribution to compare the mean, variances, covariances and other features of the data with what they are predicted to be. In the Bernoulli trials example one might assert that $\theta = 0.5$ so that the predictive density is $p(y|\theta = 0.5)$ $= 1/2^n$ implying that all sequences of n ones and zeros are equally probable.

Remark *Point prior predictive distributions are sometimes used in the calibration literature[7] where θ_0 is usually a vector of parameter values picked from estimates provided by other studies. In this method predictions of the data to be observed are made on the dogmatic hypothesis that $\theta = \theta_0$. Then the actual characteristics of the data, moments, time series properties and so on, are compared with those provided by their dogmatic predictive distribution. One reason for going about prediction in this way is that the likelihood is often extremely difficult to compute for the type of general equilibrium model that is common in this area of economics. Workers in this area often go a stage further by trying alternative values of θ_0 to see which one provides predictions that correspond most closely with the observed features of the data. This second stage may then turn into a procedure for estimating θ by choosing the θ_0 that best predicts the data. This is not a Bayesian procedure though it may be an approximation to one, and if so it might be justified either by the claim that the integration in (2.4) is impossibly difficult or by the claim that the solution of the general equilibrium model for y, which provides the likelihood, is excessively expensive.*

---

7   See the bibliographic notes at the end of this chapter.

2.4.3   Using the prior predictive distribution to check your model

The prior predictive distribution tells you what the data *should* look like, so if they don't look like they should there is probably something wrong with your model. You calculate $p(y)$ and then look at the data, say, y^{obs}. If the data are reasonably probable then they are consistent with the model; if they are improbable then doubt is cast on the model. While conceptually straightforward this model checking procedure raises a good many further issues. The first one is that data are high dimensional and we normally find it easier to think about one or low dimensional quantities. So usually we calculate not y but a scalar function of y, say $T(y)$, and the checking algorithm is as follows.

ALGORITHM 2.1   *MODEL CHECKING*

1. Use the prior predictive distribution of Y to work out the predictive distribution of $T(Y)$.

2. Use your data to calculate $T(y^{obs})$.

3. If the model is consistent with the data $T(y^{obs})$ is a realization of $T(Y)$, so if $T(y^{obs})$ looks as if it could have come from the distribution of $T(Y)$ then tentatively accept the model; if $T(y^{obs})$ is improbable (i.e. it lies well out in the tails of the distribution of $T(Y)$), reject the model and think again.

To implement this algorithm you need to do step 1 and compute the distribution of $T(Y)$. As usual, this is simple to do numerically although for all but the simplest models and choices of $T(.)$ it is hard to do analytically. To compute the probability distribution of the scalar function of the data, $T(Y)$, one proceeds as follows.

ALGORITHM 2.2   *COMPUTING THE DISTRIBUTION OF A TEST STATISTIC*

1. Sample θ from its prior distribution $p(\theta)$.

2. Use the θ realization to sample a Y value from $p(y|\theta)$.

3. Use this realization, y, to compute $T(y)$.

4. Repeat steps 1 to 3 nrep times.

The result of this calculation will be nrep realizations of $T(Y)$ and the histogram of these values will provide, with an accuracy that you can make as high as you like by raising `nrep`, the prior predictive distribution of the specification test statistic.

The function $T(.)$ defines a Bayesian **specification test** statistic. A choice of test statistic is usually a decision to test some aspect of the model. Typically your model will make some rather specific dogmatic assertions, for example that certain correlations are zero or that certain variances are equal, and then you would naturally choose a test statistic that is well designed to reveal how consistent these assertions are with the evidence. The frequentist literature provides a large number of reasonable statistics that can be adapted and used by the Bayesian econometrician in the manner described above.

There is, however, one additional feature that needs to be taken into account, and this is that many apparently reasonable specification test statistics are a function not only of the potential data Y, but also of the parameter θ. Here is an example.

> ## EXAMPLE 2.5   A TEST STATISTIC FOR THE AUTOREGRESSIVE MODEL   *Consider the autoregressive model in which $y_t | y_{t-1}, ..., y_0 \sim n(\rho y_{t-1}, \tau)$ or, in linear model terms,*
>
> $$y_t = \rho y_{t-1} + \varepsilon_t, \quad t = 1, 2, ..., T$$
>
> *with $\varepsilon = (\varepsilon_1, ..., \varepsilon_T)$ distributed iid $n(0, \tau)$ given y_0. This model asserts that $\{\varepsilon_t\}$ are independent, and therefore uncorrelated, given y_0. A natural way of examining this dogmatic assertion is to choose as your test statistic, $T(Y)$, the **autocorrelation coefficient** of the errors $\{\varepsilon_t\}$. This is the correlation coefficient of the sequence $\varepsilon_2, ..., \varepsilon_T$ with the sequence $\varepsilon_1, ..., \varepsilon_{T-1}$. But since $\varepsilon_t = y_t - \rho y_{t-1}$ the errors are defined in terms both of the data and of the parameter, here ρ. Hence what seems to be a natural test statistic depends on both the data and the parameter and it has the form $T(Y, \rho)$.*

This example indicates that we need to consider specification test statistics of the form $T(Y, \theta)$. How might we proceed with such a form of statistic? Consider (2.4) again. We see that the prior predictive distribution is the marginal of the joint prior distribution of (potential) data and parameter, $p(y|\theta)p(\theta)$. This suggests that we consider the prior predictive distribution of $T(Y, \theta)$ when Y and θ have joint distribution $p(y|\theta)p(\theta)$. This can be easily computed because steps 1 and 2 of algorithm 2.2 already provide us with samples from the joint prior of Y and θ.

The remaining question is, what do we compare to the distribution of $T(Y, \theta)$? The natural answer is $T(y^{obs}, \theta)$ in just the same way as with statistics that did not depend on θ we compared $T(y^{obs})$ with the distribution of $T(Y)$. This argument leads to the following generalization of algorithm 2.1.

ALGORITHM 2.3   *GENERALIZED MODEL CHECKING*

1. Using the joint prior predictive distribution of Y, θ work out the predictive distribution of $T(Y, \theta) - T(y^{obs}, \theta)$.

2. Sample this object by first sampling θ from its prior distribution then using the realized θ values to sample Y from its distribution given θ.

3. Examine the frequency distribution of realizations of $T(Y, \theta) - T(y^{obs}, \theta)$ to see whether zero is a probable value. If it is not, conclude that the data look inconsistent with the particular belief that $T(Y, \theta)$ was designed to check.

We shall illustrate the use of $T(Y, \theta)$ in section 2.5.2 of this chapter.

2.4.4   Improper prior predictive distributions

One (further) difficulty with improper priors is that they tend to lead to improper predictive distributions, since if you integrate the likelihood with respect to an improper prior you typically get an improper predictive distribution. That is, the calculation (2.4) doesn't give a proper distribution for Y. For simple examples consider the following.

EXAMPLE 2.6   NORMAL WITH KNOWN PRECISION   *For a single observation on a normal variate with mean μ and precision $= 1$ and an (improper, Jeffreys) uniform prior on μ, namely $p(\mu) \propto 1$, $-\infty \leq \mu \leq \infty$, the prior predictive density is*

$$p(y) \propto \int_{-\infty}^{\infty} \exp\{-(1/2)(y-\mu)^2\}\, d\mu = \sqrt{(2\pi)},$$

which is constant. So the predictive distribution of Y is also uniform (and improper) on the real line. Roughly speaking, if you've "no idea" about μ then you've equally no idea about Y.

EXAMPLE 2.7   THE AUTOREGRESSIVE MODEL   *Under a flat prior for ρ the predictive distribution is, from (1.9),*

$$p(y|y_0) \propto \int_{-\infty}^{\infty} \exp\{-(1/2)(\rho-r)^2\sum_{t=1}^{n} y_{t-1}^2\}\, d\rho,$$

$$\propto \left(\sum_{t=1}^{n} y_{t-1}^2\right)^{-1/2} \exp\{-(1/2)\sum_{t=1}^{n}(y_t - ry_{t-1})^2\}$$

and this is not a proper probability distribution for the n component vector random variable $Y = (Y_1, Y_2, ..., Y_n)$.

Since improper priors are often a convenient simplification this is a difficulty with their use. If you have no predictions you cannot check your model. It is generally wise to use proper, defensible, prior distributions even though this takes more thought than using default improper priors.

2.4.5   Prediction from training samples

One way of reacting to this difficulty, other than using proper priors, is to set aside part of the data which is then used to form a proper predictive distribution for the rest. If $y = (y_P, y_T)$ then the method is to calculate the posterior distribution of θ using a possibly improper prior and the data y_T, $p(\theta|y_T)$, and then to form the predictive distribution of y_P given y_T,

$$p(y_P|y_T) = \int p(y_P|y_T, \theta)p(\theta|y_T) \, d\theta. \tag{2.8}$$

The subset of the data y_T is called a **training sample**, hence its subscript. This method works because typically it takes only a small number of observations to convert an improper prior into a proper posterior which should then generate a proper predictive distribution.

EXAMPLE 2.8 NORMAL WITH KNOWN PRECISION
For perhaps the simplest example consider n independent observations on a normal variate with mean θ and known precision equal to 1. The likelihood for a single observation is

$$\ell(\theta; y_1) \propto \exp\{-(1/2)(y_1 - \theta)^2\}$$

and on multiplication by $p(\theta) \propto 1$, an improper uniform prior, we see immediately that the posterior density of θ is

$$p(\theta|y_1) \propto \exp\{-(1/2)(\theta - y_1)^2\}.$$

This is a perfectly proper distribution, a normal distribution of mean y_1 and precision 1. So in this case it takes a training sample of just one observation to convert an improper uniform prior into a proper posterior which can then be used to predict other observations.

If it is the case in your model that Y_P are independent of Y_T given θ then (2.8) simplifies further to $p(y_P|y_T) = \int p(y_P|\theta)p(\theta|y_T) \, d\theta$. Either way, this expression immediately suggests an algorithm for simulating from the predictive distribution of Y_P given the training sample.

ALGORITHM 2.4 SIMULATING PREDICTIONS OF THE REST OF THE SAMPLE
  1. *Draw nrep values of θ from $p(\theta|y_T)$.*
  2. *Using these theta values draw nrep vectors y_P from your likelihood given θ (and, if necessary, y_T).*
  3. *For each of the nrep samples compute whatever statistic(s) you wish to predict.*
  4. *Compare the sample value of the statistic to the predictive distribution that you formed in step 3.*
  5. *Draw your conclusions.*

EXAMPLE 2.9 *PREDICTION USING A TRAIN-*
ING SAMPLE *For a numerical example we take the case of the normal with known precision used in example 2.8 and generate n = 5 independent normal variates of mean zero and precision = 1. We use* y[1] *as the training sample leading to a posterior distribution for* θ *as normal with mean* y[1] *and precision 1. We then draw nrep values from this distribution and store them in, say, thetavalues using*

```
thetavalues <- rnorm(nrep,y[1],1).
```

This is step 1 above. Now suppose that you want to predict the mean of the remaining four. Then draw nrep samples of this mean from its predictive distribution by the command

```
for(i in 1:nrep){yb[i]_mean(rnorm(4,thetavalues[i],1))}
```

which draws averages of four normal variates with means drawn from your posterior distribution of θ. *Then draw the histogram or a smooth of the histogram. For the data generated when we use these commands the value of y[1] was −1.154 and the mean of the other four was 0.100. Figure 2.4 shows a histogram smooth of the predictive distribution of the mean of the next four observations given the first and the vertical line shows the actual value of that mean in your data, 0.100. The conclusion to be drawn from the figure is that 0.100 is quite a probable value for the mean of the remaining four observations, and that there is essentially no evidence here that casts doubt on the model. The observed mean of the last four observations is pretty much what we should expect it to be given the first observation and the initial vague prior.*

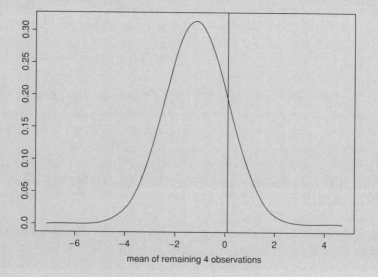

Figure 2.4 The predictive distribution of the mean

Prediction from a regression model

Take a simple regression model with one covariate and no intercept, as in example 1.2 of chapter 1. Suppose that we want to check the model by taking a training sample and predicting the rest of the data given the x values. So the question is, "what do we expect the remaining y's to look like given the x values that are associated with them and given the evidence about β provided by a training sample?" Anticipating later results, the posterior distribution of β from a collection of n_T training observations is normal with mean equal to the least squares estimate, b, of β from the training sample, and precision equal to $\tau\sum_{i=1}^{n_T} x_i^2$ provided the error precision is known and equal to τ. The predictive distribution of the remaining $n_P = n - n_T$ observations, given their x values, is then

$$p(y_P|x_P, y_T, x_T) \propto \int_{-\infty}^{\infty} \exp\{-(\tau/2)\sum_{j=1}^{n_P}(y_j - \beta x_j)^2\}\exp\{-(\tau\sum_{i=1}^{n_T}x_i^2/2)(\beta - b)^2\}\,d\beta.$$

The first term in the integrand is the likelihood for y_P given x_P and β, while the second term is the posterior density of β from the training sample.

EXAMPLE 2.10 *Even though it looks complicated it is simple to sample from the distribution defined by this integral. Here is a numerical example. First generate some x and y data satisfying a regression model $y_t = \beta x_t + \varepsilon_t$ with the $\{\varepsilon_t\}$ iid $n(0, \tau)$. We chose $n = 30$ observations. And then pick n_T $\{y, x\}$ pairs for use as a training sample and call these x_T and y_T. We chose $n_T = 10$. Then compute the least squares estimate of β as $b = \sum_{i=1}^{n_T} y_t x_t / \sum_{i=1}^{n_T} x_i^2$. (If you are working in S the command* summary (lm(yt˜xt-1)) *fits a linear regression model (lm) without an intercept (−1) and reports the results.) Then generate* nrep = *say, 1,000 realizations of the posterior distribution of β, a normal distribution of mean b and precision $\tau\sum_{i=1}^{n_T} x_i^2$, e.g.* bv <- rnorm(1000, b,1/sqrt(tau*sum(xt^2))). *Finally, generate* nrep *realizations of the predictive distribution of y_P given x_P. An S command to do this might be, if $\tau = 0.7$,*

```
for(i in 1:1000){ypred_rnorm(20,bv[i]*xp,1/sqrt(0.7));
am[i]_mean(ypred)}
```

The first command in braces generates 20 predicted y's for each realization of β. The second command finds the average of these predicted y's. The frequency distribution – histogram, for example – provides you with an estimate of the predictive distribution of the mean y and then you can compare this to the mean of the y's in your data set. You may use any other aspect of the predictive distribution *of the y's that you like in place of the mean. For example you can calculate the predicted variance of the y's or their maximum or their autocorrelations, etc.; to do this just replace* mean *in the second command with the function required.*

With data that are not naturally ordered, use of a training sample involves the rather arbitrary division of the data into a training sample and a prediction sample. There have been a number of suggestions to reduce this arbitrariness, including use of all possible training samples – see the papers on model selection in the bibliographic notes to this chapter.

So far as checking your model is concerned, one alternative to comparing features of the data with their prior predictive distribution is to use, instead, the **posterior predictive distribution**. This involves placing yourself after all the data have been seen, not before they have been seen.

2.5   POSTERIOR PREDICTION

Prediction in the usual sense of the word applies exactly the same logic as in the last section. There we predicted what our data would look like before we saw them. In prediction in the usual sense we use both our prior beliefs and the observed data to predict a future, past, or just another realization from the model. The formula is analogous to (2.4). Let y^{obs} represent the data that we have observed and let $\tilde{y}$ represent another set of data generated by the same model, possibly a future observation or sequence of such observations, possibly even a sample of the same size as that which you have observed. Then the posterior predictive distribution of $\tilde{y}$ is

$$p(\tilde{y}|y^{obs}) = \int p(\tilde{y}|y^{obs}, \theta)p(\theta|y^{obs})\, d\theta. \tag{2.9}$$

The integrand is the joint density of $\tilde{y}$ and θ and the only difference from (2.4) is that we have now included y^{obs} in the conditioning set. This is how Bayesians predict and a point prediction or decision might be the mean or mode of $p(\tilde{y}|y^{obs})$ depending on your loss function.

Digression   *Frequentist practice is to replace $p(\tilde{y}|y^{obs}, \theta)$ by $p(\tilde{y}|y^{obs}, \hat{\theta})$ and prediction is based on this object. This is called a "plug-in" method.[8] It has no theoretical justification except as an approximation to (2.9) when θ is concentrated about $\hat{\theta}$.*

---

8   The distribution $p(\tilde{y}|y^{obs}, \hat{\theta})$ is sometimes called an estimative distribution, cf. J. Aitchison and I. R. Dunsmore, *Statistical Prediction Analysis*, Cambridge University Press, 1975.

The integration in (2.9) can sometimes be done analytically but, in general, it is simpler to sample. The sampling method is as follows.

ALGORITHM 2.5   *BAYESIAN PREDICTION*

1. Sample θ from its posterior distribution.

2. Insert such a realization into the conditional distribution, given θ, and y^{obs} if necessary, and sample $\bar{y}$ from this conditional distribution.

3. Repeat steps 1 and 2 nrep times and you will have that many realizations from $p(\bar{y}|y)$.

The following two examples illustrate the method in cases where the calculations are analytically feasible and simulation is unnecessary.

EXAMPLE 2.11 *POSTERIOR PREDICTION OF AN AUTOREGRESSION*

Suppose the model is the first order autoregression, with uniform prior and precision one studied in example 1.3 of chapter 1, where we found the posterior distribution of ρ to be $p(\rho|y) = n(r, \sum_{t=1}^{n} y_{t-1}^2)$. If $\bar{y}$ is the next observation in the sequence, y_{n+1}, then, by the specification of the model,

$$p(\bar{y}|y^{obs}, \rho) \propto \exp\{-(1/2)(y_{n+1} - \rho y_n)^2\}.$$

Thus, putting $s^2 = \sum_{t=1}^{n} y_{t-1}^2$, and using the fact established earlier that the posterior density of ρ is normal with mean r and precision s^2,

$$p(y_{n+1}|y) \propto \int \exp\{-(1/2)(y_{n+1} - \rho y_n)^2 - (s^2/2)(\rho - r)^2\} d\rho$$

$$\propto \exp\left\{-\frac{1}{2}\left(\frac{s^2}{s^2 + y_n^2}\right)(y_{n+1} - r y_n)^2\right\}$$

which is (the kernel of) a normal distribution[9] with mean $r y_n$ and precision equal to $\sum_{t=1}^{n} y_{t-1}^2 / \sum_{t=1}^{n+1} y_{t-1}^2$. Notice that the precision of your prediction is always less than one, even though the precision of the variation about your model, τ, is one. But as the posterior uncertainty about ρ increases – $s^2 \to \infty$ – then the uncertainty of your prediction approaches that which is intrinsic to the model and which would remain even if you knew the value of ρ.

---

9   The derivation here requires rearranging the integrand as proportional to a normal kernel for ρ, carrying out the integration, and then dropping all terms not involving y_{n+1}.

EXAMPLE 2.12 *POSTERIOR PREDICTION OF BERNOULLI TRIALS*
Similarly, in the Bernoulli trials example, let $\bar{y}$ be y_{n+1}, the result of the next trial after the n you have already carried out. Then the posterior predictive distribution of y_{n+1} when your prior was uniform is

$$p(y_{n+1}|y^{obs}) = \int \theta^{y_{n+1}}(1-\theta)^{1-y_{n+1}}\theta^s(1-\theta)^{n-s}d\theta \frac{\Gamma(n+2)}{\Gamma(s+1)\Gamma(n-s+1)}$$

$$= \frac{\Gamma(y_{n+1}+s+1)\Gamma(n+2-y_{n+1}-s)}{\Gamma(n+3)} \frac{\Gamma(n+2)}{\Gamma(s+1)\Gamma(n-s+1)}$$

$$= \frac{(y_{n+1}+s)!(n-s-y_{n+1}+1)!}{(n+2)!} \frac{(n+1)!}{s!(n-s)!}, \qquad (2.10)$$

where we have used the integral of a beta density, given in the appendix to chapter 1, to supply the missing constant of proportionality in the posterior density of θ, and again to evaluate the integral. It follows from this that the general formula for the predictive probability of a success – $y_{n+1} = 1$ – at the $n+1$'th trial in a sequence of Bernoulli trials where the prior probability was uniform can be found by putting $y_{n+1} = 1$ in (2.10) and canceling terms. It is

$$p(y_{n+1} = 1|n, s) = \frac{s+1}{n+2}. \qquad (2.11)$$

So after two successes in two trials the probability of a success is 3/4 but after 98 successes in 98 trials the probability that the next trial will be a success is $99/100 = 0.99$. It is said, rather unfairly, that Laplace used this formula to reassure himself that the sun would rise tomorrow given that it had done so unfailingly for the past 5,000 years.[10]

We now turn to the use of the predictive distribution for model checking.

2.5.1 *Posterior model checking*

Use of a training sample involves using part of a sample to predict the rest. Some writers suggest pushing this idea further by using *all* the data as a "training sample," but then what do you predict?

For this purpose we let $\bar{y}$ now be y^{rep}, an alternative realization, generated by the model, of the data that you have observed – a re-run of history on the assumption

10 To see what Laplace really said read Marquis de Laplace, *A Philosophical Essay on Probabilities*, originally published in Paris in 1814, Dover edition, New York, 1951, page 19. (2.11) is called Laplace's rule of succession.

that the model is what generates histories. Let y^{obs} represent the data that we have observed.[11] The superscript *rep* stands for replication. Then consider the posterior predictive distribution for y^{rep},

$$p(y^{rep}|y^{obs}) = \int p(y^{rep}, \theta|y^{obs}) \, d\theta = \int p(y^{rep}|\theta, y^{obs})p(\theta|y^{obs}) \, d\theta$$

$$= \int p(y^{rep}|\theta)p(\theta|y^{obs}) \, d\theta. \tag{2.12}$$

The left hand term is the probability density function of another realization of the data given y^{obs}, the one that you have observed. It is called the posterior predictive distribution of the data – the prior predictive distribution being $p(y^{rep})$ in the present notation. The posterior predictive distribution tells you the probability to be attached to other realizations given the model and the data that you have observed. If it is plausible, as in some cross-sectional applications, to think of your data as constituting a random sample from a population then the posterior predictive distribution tells you what the next sample should look like, and what it should not look like! The derivation of (2.12) just uses elementary probability rules to get a simple expression for the posterior predictive distribution. In particular it uses, for the final step, the fact that if you knew θ the data observed would be irrelevant to predicting Y. *Given the model*, the only role for the data is to inform you about θ.

2.5.2 *Sampling the predictive distribution*

In the Bernoulli and other simple examples it is relatively easy to do the integration required to find the predictive distribution for another realization of the trials, but for many models, including the simple autoregressive example 1.3 of chapter 1, the integration is not particularly easy and it may be next to impossible. Moreover, once you have found the predictive distribution analytically, it may be that you have to do further algebra to deduce the predictive distribution of some function of the predicted data in which your real interest lies.

This is why in almost every case in which an integration is required it is far simpler to *sample* the required density than to find it by integration. Referring to (2.12) we see that the predictive distribution of y^{rep} given y^{obs} is the marginal of the joint distribution of θ and y^{rep} given y^{obs}. Thus to sample y^{rep} we may sample this joint distribution. This is most easily done by sampling the posterior density of θ and then sampling from the conditional distributions[12] of y^{rep} given θ and y^{obs} where this latter reduces to $p(y^{rep}|\theta)$. *Each realization of y^{rep} comes from its marginal.* So the algorithm is as follows.

---

11   In other contexts we let the data be denoted simply by y. But here it is essential to keep the distinction between observed data and hypothetical alternative realizations clearly in mind.

12   This is just the method described in chapter 1 by which one may sample from $p(x, y)$ by first sampling from $p(x)$ and then from $p(y|x)$ (or the other way round).

ALGORITHM 2.6   *SAMPLING THE POSTERIOR PREDICTIVE DISTRIBUTION*

1. *Sample θ from $p(\theta|y^{obs})$.*
2. *Using this θ realization, sample y^{rep} from $p(y^{rep}|\theta)$.*
3. *Repeat nrep times.*

The nrep realizations of y^{rep} produced by this algorithm are independendent samples from the posterior predictive distribution. Armed with this algorithm we can now tackle the question of how to do posterior model checks or Bayesian residual analysis. Before doing so we give an example of the algorithm.

EXAMPLE 2.13   *SAMPLING THE PREDICTIVE DISTRIBUTION OF A NORMAL VARIATE*   Suppose

that we take n independent realizations of a conditionally normal variate with mean μ and precision $= 1$. The likelihood is thus $\ell(\mu, y^{obs}) \propto \exp\{-(n/2)(\mu - \bar{y})^2\}$ and if the prior on μ is uniform the likelihood is also, apart from a factor of proportionality, the posterior density which will here be normal $(\bar{y}, n)$. The algorithm then proceeds by sampling nrep independent realizations of μ from this distribution and then using each of these nrep values to sample n independent $n(\mu, 1)$ variates. An S implementation might be

```
mu <-rnorm(nrep,ybar,1/sqrt(n))
Yrep <-matrix(0,nrow = nrep,ncol = n)
for(i in 1:nrep){Yrep[i,] <-rnorm(n,mu[i],1)}
```

The first line generates nrep realizations from the posterior distribution of μ; the second line sets up a matrix to hold nrep realizations of n independent normal variates with common unit precision, and the third line fills that matrix row by row. The matrix Yrep then holds nrep realizations of what you think the data should look like, taking account of your current uncertainty about mu.

To check one of the dogmatic assertions in your model you need to compare the predictions of your model (and data), y^{rep}, to the data, y^{obs}. There are many ways of doing this but one formal way that we already looked at in dealing with prior predictive checks is to choose a (Bayesian) test statistic. This will be a function of the potential data, y^{rep}, and the parameter θ, so call it $T(y^{rep}, \theta)$. This statistic will be designed to flag violations of some assumption of the model.

As in section 2.4.3 the simplest case is where the the proposed statistic depends only on the data and not on the parameter so that $T(y^{rep}, \theta) = T(y^{rep})$. In this case the idea is to compare the observed value of the statistic, $T(y^{obs})$, with the posterior predictive distribution of $T(y^{rep})$. If $T(y^{obs})$ lies far out in the tail of the distribution of $T(y^{rep})$ then, remembering that the distribution of $T(y^{rep})$ is computed on the hypothesis that the dogmatic assertions in the likelihood and prior were correct, an extreme value for $Y(y^{obs})$ suggests that at least one of those assertions is false. One might go on to quantify the unlikeliness of $T(y^{obs})$ by reporting the Bayes p value, namely,

$$p = P(T(y^{obs}) - T(y^{rep}) < 0 | y^{obs}). \qquad (2.13)$$

This calculation is easily done using a sample of replications and here is an example.

EXAMPLE 2.14 *AUTOCORRELATION IN A TIME SERIES* *Suppose that your model states that your data are to be a realization of n consecutive independent n(0, 1) variates so the predictive distribution is just that of n independent n(0, 1) variates. This model contains several dogmatic assertions. In particular, it says that the consecutive observations are conditionally independent. One might examine this by calculating the Durbin–Watson statistic,*

$$T(y) = dw = \frac{\sum_{t=2}^{n}(y_t - y_{t-1})^2}{\sum_{t=2}^{n} y_{t-1}^2}.$$

The value of this quantity, when n is not small, should be near 2 for a series that is uncorrelated, and near 2(1 − ρ) for a series that has first order autocorrelation equal to ρ.

Let us first of all generate a sequence of length n = 40 that is independent and distributed as n(0, 1) and compute dw = T(y^{obs}). If we do this we find d = 1.87. Next we sample 10,000 times from the predictive distribution of dw. This means, following algorithm 2.1, generating 10,000 n(0, 1) sequences and for each sequence we compute the Durbin–Watson statistic, dw = T(y^{rep}). The histogram of replications of dw, which approximates its predictive distribution given the model with its assumption of independence, is given in figure 2.5. The mean and median of the 10,000 replications is 1.95. This figure shows the values of dw that are probable given that we have a series of length 40 and the observations are independent standard normal variates. It can be seen that the value of dw = 1.87 in our data is near the center of the distribution, and so pretty much what you would expect from such a model, and gives no grounds for doubting the independence of the successive realizations.

For comparison, if we generate a series that has an autorcorrelation of 0.5 we find a dw statistic of 0.94. Sampling the predictive distribution of dw gives the second histogram (see figure 2.6) from which it can be seen that the value 2 is highly improbable and the sequence is obviously positively autocorrelated.

But, as before, the appropriate statistic may also depend upon θ as, for example, when the mean is some unknown μ and a reasonable statistic for examining skewness might be

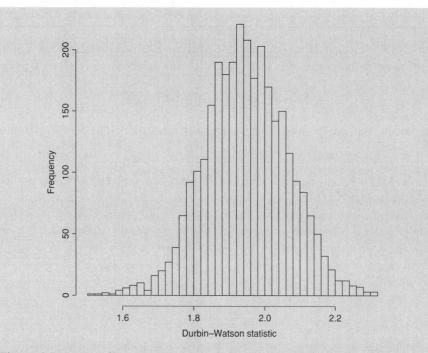

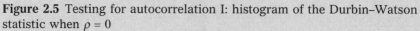

Figure 2.5 Testing for autocorrelation I: histogram of the Durbin–Watson statistic when $\rho = 0$

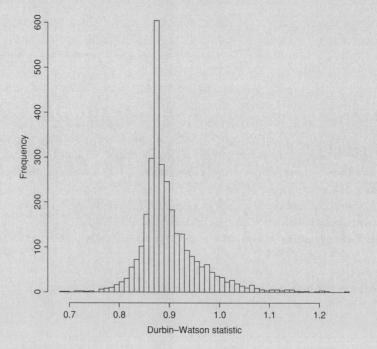

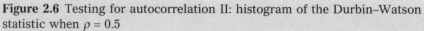

Figure 2.6 Testing for autocorrelation II: histogram of the Durbin–Watson statistic when $\rho = 0.5$

$$T(y^{rep}, \mu) = \frac{\sum_{i=1}^{n}(y_i^{rep} - \mu)^3}{n}.$$

The extension of the Bayes p value to this situation is

$$p = P(T(y^{obs},\theta) \le T(y^{rep},\theta)|y^{obs}). \qquad (2.14)$$

To illustrate the calculation less us return to the first order autoregressive model with a scalar parameter ρ and see how to check for autocorrelation in the errors of the autoregression.

EXAMPLE 2.15   *AUTOCORRELATION IN THE ERRORS OF AN AUTOREGRESSIVE MODEL*

The model is

$$y_t = \rho y_{t-1} + \varepsilon_t$$

where the $\{\varepsilon_t\}$ are believed to be iid $n(0, \tau)$. Suppose that we wish to look for evidence against the hypothesis that the $\{\varepsilon_t\}$ are iid $n(0, \tau)$, then it seems natural to base a model check on the autocorrelation of these errors. Let us do this by studying the Durbin–Watson statistic of the "errors" – the sequence $\{\varepsilon_t\}$. This is

$$dw = \frac{\sum_{t=2}^{n}(\varepsilon_t - \varepsilon_{t-1})^2}{\sum_{t=1}^{n}\varepsilon_{t-1}^2}; \quad \varepsilon_t = y_t - \rho y_{t-1}.$$

But how can we do this since the $\{\varepsilon_t\}$ are not data? The answer is to simulate them from their posterior distribution which, since $\varepsilon_t = y_t - \rho y_{t-1}$, depends only on ρ, given the data. The Bayesian test statistic is $T(y, \rho) = dw$ which now depends both upon the data, y, and upon the parameter, in this case ρ. We need to compute $P(T(y^{obs}, \rho) \ge T(y^{rep}, \rho)|y^{obs})$. The algorithm to do this is just an elaboration of algorithm 2.6, namely:

ALGORITHM 2.7

1. *Generate ρ from its $n(r, \sum_{t=1}^{n}y_{t-1}^2)$ posterior distribution.*
2. *Generate a y^{rep} sequence from the conditional distribution of $Y_1, ..., Y_n$ given ρ, using this ρ value.*
3. *Calculate both $T(y^{rep}, \rho)$ and $T(y^{obs}, \rho)$.*
4. *Repeat steps 1 to 3 nrep times.*
5. *Plot the distribution of $T(\tilde{y}, \rho) - T(y^{obs}, \rho)$ and draw your conclusions.*

For a numerical example we generated a time series of length $n = 100$ starting from an initial value equal to zero. The data follow a first order autoregression with $\rho = 0.7$ and errors that are iid $n(0, 1)$. The realized r was 0.798 and $\sum_{t=1}^{n}y_{t-1}^2 = 241$. We then sampled 5,000 values of ρ from its $n(0.798, 241)$

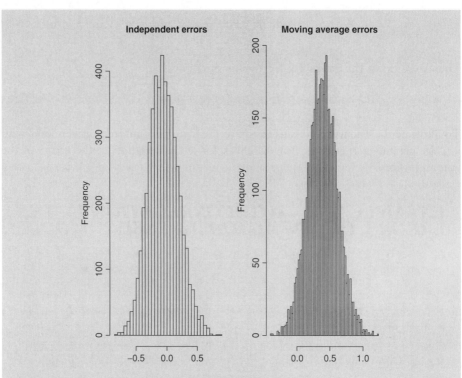

Figure 2.7 Testing for error autocorrelation

posterior density. We next used these ρ values to form 5,000 error sequences of the form $\varepsilon_t = y_t - \rho y_{t-1}$ and for each calculated the dw statistic. This gave 5,000 realizations of $T(y^{obs}, \rho)$. We then repeated this procedure except that, before forming the errors, we used the model to produce a simulated times series of length $n = 100$ with elements $\{y_t^{rep}\}$ and we then formed error sequences of the form $\varepsilon_t = y_t^{rep} - \rho y_{t-1}^{rep}$ where each ρ is one of the 5,000 sampled earlier. Finally we again computed the dw statistics using the newly simulated error sequences. This gives 5,000 realizations of $T(y^{rep}, \rho)$. The left panel in figure 2.7 gives the histogram of the 5,000 values of $T(y^{rep}, \rho) - T(y^{obs}, \rho)$. This distribution should be centered near zero if the model is correct and the errors in the autoregression are independent. As can be seen the distribution is scattered about zero with about 60% of the values negative. This gives little ground for doubting the model is consistent with the evidence. For the right hand panel the data were generated using errors that follow a moving model of the form $\varepsilon_t = u_t + 0.4u_{t-1}$ with u's themselves iid normal. This gives errors with a first order autocorrelation coefficient of 0.34. With these data the hypothesis of independent errors is false. The right panel shows the histogram of 5,000 realizations of $T(y^{rep}, \rho) - T(y^{obs}, \rho)$ using the new data as y^{obs} and it can be seen the realizations are not scattered about zero. In fact only 4 percent of the realizations are negative. This gives rather strong evidence against the hypothesis that errors in the autoregression are uncorrelated.

Digression *The procedure for post-data model checking described here is similar, but not identical, to a class of bootstrap procedures devised by Efron.[13] As we have seen above, (2.12), the posterior predictive distribution takes the form $\int p(y^{rep}|\theta)p(\theta|y^{obs})\,d\theta$ and it is a weighted average of the distributions of y^{rep} given θ, the weights being provided by the posterior distribution of θ. The related frequentist procedure is to replace the averaging in this expression by a single value for θ estimated from the data, and base replications on $p(y^{rep}|\hat{\theta})$. This is sometimes called the **estimative distribution**[14] to contrast it with the predictive distribution of Bayesian inference. Essentially, it neglects the posterior uncertainty about θ. Choosing to replace the unknown θ by a point estimate is often called a **plug-in procedure**. The estimative distribution is an approximation to the predictive distribution and it will be a good approximation if the posterior uncertainty about θ is small. The bootstrap procedure is to choose a quantity $T(y, \theta)$ and estimate its distribution when the model is correct by repeatedly sampling y^{rep} from $p(y^{rep}|\hat{\theta})$ and computing the statistic $T(y^{rep}, \hat{\theta}^{rep})$ for each sub-sample. Here, $\hat{\theta}^{rep}$ is the estimate of θ made from a draw of y^{rep}. When the sample is very informative about θ the conclusions to be drawn from this **parametric bootstrap** procedure will typically be similar to those reached by a Bayesian and described above. There is an analogous procedure called the non-parametric bootstrap and this also is closely similar to the corresponding Bayesian procedure, as we shall see later.*

The use of the posterior predictive distribution for model checking is open to the criticism that it violates the likelihood principle, which it does, and it is therefore strictly inconsistent with the Bayesian approach. Views among Bayesian statisticians are divided and many prefer to compute posterior odds as described in the next section. These calculations involve only the prior predictive distribution.

2.6 POSTERIOR ODDS AND MODEL CHOICE

Early in chapter 1 we considered how a Bayesian might handle the problem of choosing, in the light of the evidence, between two competing theories. The answer was to compute the probabilities of the evidence on both theories, multiply these by the prior probabilities (possibly equal) of the theories, and you have the posterior probabilities of the theories. Then choose the most probable, if you have to choose one or the other. The ratio of the posterior probability of model j to the probability of all other models is the posterior odds on that model. This simple agenda is the essence of Bayesian model choice. Prior predictive distributions play a major role in this Bayesian approach to choosing between models. Specifically, suppose that you have in mind

---

13   See the bibliographic end notes to this chapter.
14   Aitchison and Dunsmore (1975).

J models and that they are denoted by M_j, $j = 1, 2, ..., J$. You tentatively adopt the view that one of these models is right and you assign them prior probabilities P_j which reads,[15] "Assuming that one of these models is right then P_j is my probability that model j is right." Then if you want to see how probable each model is after the data have been seen you can use Bayes' theorem as

$$P(M_j|y) = \frac{p(y|M_j)P_j}{p(y)}, \qquad (2.15)$$

$$\text{where} \quad p(y) = \Sigma_{j=1}^{J} p(y|M_j)P_j.$$

In this equation the $p(y|M_j)$ are the prior predictive probabilities of the data under model j and $p(y)$ is the (weighted) average prior predictive probability of the data. It is the prior predictive distribution of Y under a finite **mixture model** in which model j occurs with probability P_j for $j = 1, 2 ..., M$. Finally the $P(M_j|y)$ are the posterior probabilities of each model. If one model is considerably more probable than the others then this provides strong evidence in favor of that model out of all the models considered. If you are considering just two models then by taking the ratio of the posterior model probabilities you can find the **posterior odds** on model 1 as

$$\frac{P(M_1|y)}{P(M_2|y)} = \frac{P(y|M_1)}{P(y|M_2)} \frac{P(M_1)}{P(M_2)}. \qquad (2.16)$$

The left hand side is called the posterior odds on model 1; the second term on the right hand side is called the prior odds, while the first term on the right hand side is the **Bayes factor**.[16]

DEFINITION 2.2   BAYES FACTOR   *The Bayes factor is the ratio of the prior probabilities of the data under the different models. If the data y was judged highly probable on model 1 but quite improbable on model 2 then the Bayes factor will be larger than one, and the odds on that model will have risen in the light of the data.*

---

15   We are using a capital P to indicate probabilities of events and lower case p to denote probability density or mass functions.

16   The Bayes factor is similar to, but not the same as, the likelihood ratio of frequentist statistics. The likelihood ratio is $P(y|\hat{\theta}_1, M_1)/P(y|\hat{\theta}_2, M_2)$ where the $\hat{\theta}$'s are the maximum likelihood estimates of the parameters of the two models. The Bayes factor does not replace parameters by point estimates; it multiplies probabilities by priors and averages out the parameters, cf. (1.1).

DEFINITION 2.3   COMPARING TWO SIMPLE HYPOTHESES

A simple hypothesis completely specifies the data distribution under that hypothesis. For comparing two simple hypotheses (theories), say that $\theta = \theta_1$ or $\theta = \theta_2$, the predictive probabilities of the observed data take the form $\ell(\theta_1; y^{obs})$ and $\ell(\theta_2; y^{obs})$ and so the posterior odds takes the form

$$\frac{P(\theta = \theta_1 | y^{obs})}{P(\theta = \theta_2 | y^{obs})} = \frac{\ell(\theta_1; y^{obs})}{\ell(\theta_2; y^{obs})} \frac{P(\theta = \theta_1)}{P(\theta = \theta_2)}$$

The posterior odds on θ_1 equals the ratio of the likelihoods on the two theories times the prior odds on θ_1.

EXAMPLE 2.16 *TWO SIMPLE HYPOTHESES*

For an artificial but simple example suppose that $f(y; \theta)$ is the density of a conditionally normal $(\theta, 1)$ variate and the two hypotheses are that $\theta_1 = -1$ and $\theta_0 = 1$ and the sample size is $n = 1$. So you have a single number that comes from one of two possible distributions. The question is – which one? The likelihood ratio is

$$\frac{P(y^{obs} | \theta = -1)}{P(y^{obs} | \theta = 1)} = \frac{e^{-(1/2)(y+1)^2}}{e^{-(1/2)(y-1)^2}}$$

and so, if the hypotheses are equally probable a priori, the posterior odds are

$$\frac{P(\theta = -1 | y^{obs})}{P(\theta = 1 | y^{obs})} = e^{-2y}.$$

Thus, a positive value of y makes $\theta = 1$ more probable than $\theta = -1$; a negative value of y makes $\theta = -1$ more probable than $\theta = 1$; and, finally, a value of y equal to zero leaves the two hypotheses equally probable as, of course, it should.[17] If the mean is either plus or minus one and you observe $y = 0$ then you have learned nothing that would make you incline towards one hypothesis rather than the other.[18] For a numerical value of the posterior odds suppose that you observe $y = 0.5$, then the odds on the theory that $\theta = 1$ are $e = 2.718$ corresponding to a probability of this hypothesis of $P(\theta = 1 | y = 0.5) = e/(1 + e) = 0.73$. When $y = 1$ the probability moves to 0.88.

---

17   What would a Bayesian (or any sane person do) if Y turned out to be, say, -27?

18   You might care to read Berger and Wolpert's (1988, *The Likelihood Principle*, Institute of Mathematical Statistics Lecture Notes – Monograph Series, volume 6) discussion of how a frequentist might approach the question of deciding between $\theta = -1$ and $\theta = 1$.

In general, to compute the posterior odds you need to calculate the prior predictive distributions for each model. Thus if model j involves a parameter vector, say θ_j with prior distribution $p(\theta_j)$, we have to compute $p(y|M_j) = \int p(y|\theta_j, M_j) p(\theta_j) d\theta_j$. In principle this is remarkably simple – pick the model that assigns the greatest probability to what you have seen. But for such a simple idea there has been a surprising amount of discussion and controversy. One issue has been how to compute $p(y)$. Another has been the value of "large sample" approximations to Bayes factors. We shall discuss the computational issue in chapter 4.

2.6.1 Two approximations to Bayes factors

Let the likelihood under model 1 be denoted by $\ell_1(\theta_1; y)$ and that under model 2 by $\ell_2(\theta_2; y)$ so the Bayes factor in favor of model 1 relative to model 2 is

$$B_{12} = \frac{\int \ell_1(\theta_1; y) p(\theta_1) d\theta_1}{\int \ell_2(\theta_2; y) p(\theta_2) d\theta_2}$$

where the distribution $p(\theta_j)$ is the prior distribution of the parameters of model j. When the sample size is large and the likelihoods are sharply peaked about their maxima, we can use Laplace's approximation to each integral in this expression. This amounts to expanding each integrand about the maximum likelihood estimate in such a way that the lower order terms can be integrated analytically and the higher order terms neglected as $n \to \infty$. This is Laplace's approximation,

$$\int \ell_1(\theta_1; y) p(\theta_1) d\theta_1 \approx (2\pi)^{k_1/2} |H_1(\hat{\theta}_1)|^{1/2} \ell_1(\hat{\theta}_1; y) p(\hat{\theta}_1)$$

with a similar expression for the predictive distribution on model 2. In this expression H is the negative hessian of the log likelihood and it is evaluated at the maximum likelihood estimate $\hat{\theta}$. The ratio of this expression to the corresponding approximation for model 2 provides a large sample approximation for the Bayes factors:

$$B_{12} \approx \frac{(2\pi)^{k_1/2} |H_1(\theta_1)|^{1/2} \ell_{\le}(\theta_1; y) p(\theta_1)}{(2\pi)^{k_2/2} |H_2(\theta_2)|^{1/2} \ell_{\ge}(\theta_2; y) p(\theta_2)}.$$

A cruder approximation which works well in regular models with large n is

$$B_{12} \approx \frac{\ell(\hat{\theta}_1; y)}{\ell(\hat{\theta}_2; y)} n^{(k_2 - k_1)/2}.$$

This is known as the Bayesian information criterion (BIC), sometimes known as the Schwarz criterion. Its first factor is the ratio of maximized likelihoods[19] and the

---

19 This is the likelihood ratio of frequentist statistics.

second is a term depending on the difference in the numbers of parameters in each model. This second factor is sometimes said to "penalize" the model with the larger number of parameters. If the BIC is notably larger than one the criterion favors model 1 in the sense that it is judged much more probable than model 2 if both models were judged to be equally likely before observing the evidence. If it is much less than one then model 2 is favored. Note that the BIC approximation completely neglects the priors. This is because it applies in large samples when the prior can be neglected because it is numerically dominated by the likelihood.

Improper priors

As we saw earlier, improper priors cause difficulties for predictive methods and this is even more true when computing Bayes factors. Suppose that both θ_1 and θ_2 are uniform on the real line with "densities" $p(\theta_1) = c_1$ and $p(\theta_2) = c_2$, where c_1 and c_2 are arbitrary, then the arbitrary ratio c_1/c_2 will appear in the Bayes factor which is quite unsatisfactory. To permit improper priors but still compute a meaningful Bayes factor the method of training samples is again invoked. The idea is to select a sub-sample large enough to convert both $p(\theta_1)$ and $p(\theta_2)$ into proper posterior distributions, and then to compute a Bayes factor using the rest of the data with these proper posterior distributions employed in place of $p(\theta_1)$ and $p(\theta_2)$. This clearly depends on what data are used for the training sample, and so the idea is modified by computing Bayes factors for all possible training samples of minimal size and then averaging the results in some way. The arithmetic mean of such factors is called the *intrinsic Bayes factor* and examples and discussion are provided in the survey by Berger and Pericchi mentioned in the bibliographic notes.

2.6.2   Model averaging

Model choice implies that you wish to choose one model out of the J models under consideration but some users, particularly those making forecasts, might wish to keep all models in view but to weight them according to their posterior probabilities. The following logic shows how this works. Let y^{obs} be the observed data and let $\tilde{y}$ denote the object to be predicted. Then your predictions must be made using $p(\tilde{y}|y^{obs})$ which is

$$p(\tilde{y}|y^{obs}) = \Sigma_j p(\tilde{y}, M_j|y^{obs})$$
$$= \Sigma_j p(\tilde{y}|M_j, y^{obs})p(M_j|y^{obs}).$$

The second terms in the sum are the posterior probabilities of each model given the data, while the first terms are predictive probabilities of $\tilde{y}$ from each model. To sample from $p(\tilde{y}|y^{obs})$ the following algorithm can be used.

ALGORITHM 2.8   *MODEL AVERAGING*

1. Calculate the posterior probabilities of each model – these are the $p(M_j|y^{obs})$ for $j = 1, 2, ..., J$.

2. Draw realizations of $\tilde{y}$ from its predictive distribution given each of the models.

3. Construct a weighted average of the draws from step 2 using the $p(M_j|y^{obs})$ as weights.

The result of this calculation will be a draw from $p(\tilde{y}|y^{obs})$. Many such draws will give you the predictive distribution of $\tilde{y}$. To implement this algorithm you need procedures to compute the posterior model probabilities and to sample from the model-specific predictive distributions. Further information on these issues is provided in chapter 4.

2.7   ENLARGING THE MODEL

Formal choice between sets of models in the manner of (2.16) is relatively rare in applied econometrics, though it has attracted theoretical interest. Much more common is the use of a larger model containing additional parameters that nests within it the initial model to which it reduces when the extra parameters take special values. Formally, the enlarged model has the form $p(y|\theta, \phi)$ which reduces to $p(y|\theta)$ when ϕ takes the value ϕ_0, typically zero. What this approach does is to nest the smaller model within the larger one. Comparisons based on Bayes factors do not require that the models to be compared are nested. To make this nesting approach concrete consider the autoregressive model again.

EXAMPLE   2.17   ENLARGING   THE   AUTO-REGRESSIVE MODEL   *The model can be written as*

$$y_t = \rho y_{t-1} + \varepsilon_t, \quad \{\varepsilon_t\}|y_0 \sim iid \; n(0, 1); \quad t = 1, 2, ..., n. \quad (2.17)$$

The model includes the dogmatic assertion that the $\{\varepsilon_t\}$ are independent. In example 2.14 we showed a way of checking this assertion by examining the predictive probability distribution of the Durbin–Watson statistic for the ε_t. Another way of checking the model is to enlarge it, and one way of doing this is to adopt a model for the ε_t that includes their independence as a special case. So consider the extra assertion that

$$\varepsilon_t = \gamma \varepsilon_{t-1} + u_t, \quad \{u_t\}|y_0 \sim iid \; n(0, 1); \quad t = 1, 2, ..., n. \quad (2.18)$$

We can put these models together by noting that (2.17) implies that

$$y_{t-1} = \rho y_{t-2} + \varepsilon_{t-1}. \tag{2.19}$$

If we multiply this equation by γ *and then subtract it from (2.17) we get the enlarged model*

$$y_t = (\rho + \gamma)y_{t-1} - \rho\gamma y_{t-2} + u_t, \quad \{u_t\}|y_0 \sim iid\ n(0,\ 1),$$
$$t = 1,\ 2,\ ...,\ n. \tag{2.20}$$

When $\gamma = 0$ *this collapses back to (2.17). Written in likelihood form the model is that*

$$p(y_t|y_{t-1},\ y_{t-2},\ y_{t-3},\ ...,\ y_0) = n((\rho + \gamma)y_{t-1} - \rho\gamma y_{t-2},\ 1); \quad t = 1,\ 2,\ ...,\ n.$$

*This is a **second order autoregressive model**.*

   To check the original model we just compute the marginal posterior density of γ. If this density is concentrated around zero this indicates the first order model is not inconsistent with the evidence. If zero is an unlikely value, doubt is cast on the simpler model. To compute the marginal posterior density of γ we fit the larger model; sample the joint posterior distribution of all coefficients and from the realizations sample the posterior distribution of γ. To do this we need to specify two initial values for the series, not just y_0, as before and condition the likelihood on these. Call these first two values y_{-1} and y_0. The likelihood for the extended model is:

$$\ell(\rho,\ \gamma;\ y,\ y_{-1},\ y_0) \propto \exp\{-(1/2)\textstyle\sum_{t=1}^{n}(y_t - (\rho + \gamma)y_{t-1} + \rho\gamma y_{t-2})^2\}. \tag{2.21}$$

   We shall describe methods for sampling posterior distributions in this and more general models in chapter 4.

EXAMPLE 2.18   *ENLARGING THE BERNOULLI MODEL*   *For a second example of model enlargement, take the Bernoulli trials example in which your model asserts that trials are conditionally independent with constant probability of a success,* θ. *To examine this question in another way we shall enlarge the model to allow for conditional dependence by letting the probabilities of success and failure at the* t'*th trial depend on the outcome of the trial before. Specifically let us adopt the Markov assumption that* $p(y_t|y_{t-1},\ y_{t-2},\ ...,\ y_1,\ \pi) = p(y_t|y_{t-1},\ \pi)$ *so that the outcome at* t *depends only on that at* $t - 1$. *And write*

$$p(y_t|y_{t-1} = 1,\ \pi) = \pi_1^{y_t}(1 - \pi_1)^{1-y_t},$$
$$p(y_t|y_{t-1} = 0,\ \pi) = (1 - \pi_0)^{y_t}\pi_0^{1-y_t}. \tag{2.22}$$

This two state markov chain model can be represented using a transition probability matrix[20] as

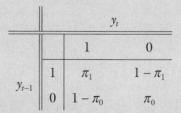

The transition probability matrix here is 2×2 and its rows give probability distributions of the outcome at t for each possible outcome at $t - 1$. Note that the rows must sum to one, because they are probability distributions.

The probability mass function of y_t given all earlier outcomes can be written compactly by raising the first row of the transition probability matrix to the power y_{t-1} and the second to the power $1 - y_{t-1}$ to get

$$p(y_t|y_{t-1}, ..., y_1, \pi) = \pi_1^{y_t y_{t-1}}(1 - \pi_1)^{(1-y_t)y_{t-1}}(1 - \pi_0)^{y_t(1-y_{t-1})}\pi_0^{(1-y_t)(1-y_{t-1})}.$$

Then we form the likelihood recursively by multiplying together such terms for $t = 2$ to n and this then provides the likelihood conditional on the initial observation,

$$\ell(\pi; y_2, ..., y_n|y_1) = \pi_1^{s_{11}}(1 - \pi_1)^{s_{10}}\pi_0^{s_{00}}(1 - \pi_0)^{s_{01}}, \tag{2.23}$$

where s_{ij} gives the number of transitions from $y_{t-1} = i$ to $y_t = j$. Under a prior for π_1, π_0 in which these parameters are independently uniformly distributed, the posterior density of $\pi = (\pi_1, \pi_0)$ is proportional to (2.23).

This simple markov chain reduces to a sequence of Bernoulli trials if, and only if, the distribution of y_t given $y_{t-1} = 1$ is the same as its distribution given $y_{t-1} = 0$. Inspection of the transition probability matrix shows that this requires that $\pi_1 = 1 - \pi_0$ or $\pi_1 + \pi_0 - 1 = 0$. So we can test the Bernoulli model by looking to see if the pi's satisfy this restriction, and to do this we sample the joint posterior density of π_1 and π_0 and study the posterior distribution of $\pi_1 + \pi_0 - 1$. If zero is a plausible value then there is little reason to doubt the Bernoulli model; if it is not then the Bernoulli model appears to be inconsistent with the evidence. One would then tentatively adopt the Markov model and apply model checking to see if this, in turn, was consistent with the evidence.

To implement this we see from (2.23) that the posterior distribution of π is that of independent beta variates; the parameter π_1 is distributed as beta($s_{11} + 1$,

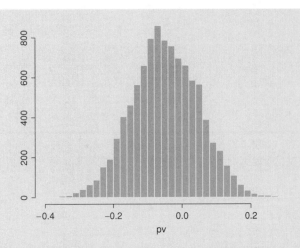

Figure 2.8 Testing for dependence in binary trials I

$s_{10} + 1)$ *and, similarly,* $\pi_0 \sim beta(s_{00} + 1, s_{01} + 1)$. *To implement the test we simulate the pi's from these two densities nrep times and then form* $\pi_1 + \pi_0 - 1$ *and draw its posterior distribution. Here is an example. We first generate the results of 100 Bernoulli trials, calculate the four s's and get* $s_{11} = 24$, $s_{10} = 26$, $s_{01} = 26$, $s_{00} = 23$. *We then draw nrep* $= 10{,}000$ *values from the two beta densities; add the draws together and subtract one and draw the histogram of the results. This gives figure 2.8 where pv stands for pi values. Since zero is near the center of the distribution there is little reason to doubt the independence of successive draws. By contrast, we now draw[21] 100 realizations from a markov chain, starting at* $\pi_1 = \pi_0 = 0.8$. *This is a chain in which successes tend to be followed by successes and failures by failures; it is not Bernoulli. The values recorded were* $s_{11} = 31$,

---

21   An S program to do this is: first set π_1, π_0 and n; then y<<- rep(0, n);

```
y[1] <<- 1
for(i in 2:n) {
  if(y[i - 1] == 1)
    y[i] <<- rbinom(1, 1, pi1)
  elsey[i] <<- rbinom(1, 1, 1 - pi0)
  }
ym<- y[1:n - 1]
yt<- y[2:n]
s11 <<- sum(yt * ym)
s10 <<- sum((1 - yt) * ym)
s01 <<- sum(yt * (1 - ym))
s00 <<- sum((1 - yt) * (1 - ym))
```

The symbol <<- means global allocation and implies that s11 etc. will be available for use after the program has finished. An object allocated by <- is only defined within the program and is lost once the program has finished executing.

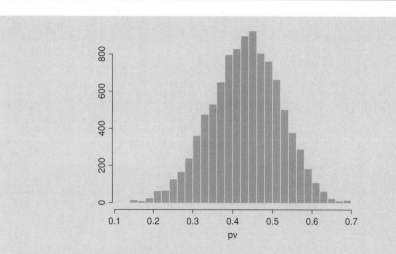

Figure 2.9 Testing for dependence in binary trials II

$s_{10} = 14$, $s_{01} = 13$, $s_{00} = 41$ *and figure 2.9 shows the histogram of 10,000 replications of $\pi_1 + \pi_0 - 1$. Clearly zero is a highly improbable value in this distribution and the hypothesis that the observed draws are from a sequence of Bernoulli trials is in serious doubt.*

2.8   SUMMARY

Informal, usually graphical, methods for taking a critical look at your results can be helpful, and quick, ways to find out what is going wrong, if anything. Formal methods for checking your model, making predictions and choosing among models are all based on the predictive distribution and the basic formula

$$p(y) = \int p(y|\theta)p(\theta)\,d\theta$$

has appeared throughout the chapter in varying disguises. Ideally, model checking involves looking at the data to see if it is as you thought it would be, particularly looking at aspects of the data about which your prior beliefs had been dogmatic. What you thought the data would be like is measured by your prior predictive distribution, and you can construct test statistics to see whether any discrepancies you find are sufficiently significant to warrant changing the model, or abandoning it!

Model comparison involves comparing the predictions of your data provided by alternative models. If you have to choose a single model then, naturally, you would choose that one which has the highest probability given what you have observed. If you don't have to choose a single model but want something to use for making forecasts, for example, then you can average the models under consideration, assigning each model a weight equal to its posterior probability. This is called model averaging. The most general way of comparing and choosing between models is by the construction of Bayes factors. In practice it is more common to use a more restrictive approach that involves nesting your model within some larger one and studying the posterior distributions of the additional parameters.

2.9 EXERCISES

EXERCISE 1 AUTOCORRELATION IN BERNOULLI TRIALS[22]

Recall that the model of chapter 1 for n binary events was to suppose that, conditional on a parameter θ the events occurred independently with constant probability of "success" equal to θ. The model is completed by assigning a uniform prior distribution to θ. So

$$p(y|\theta) \propto \theta^s(1-\theta)^{n-s}; \quad p(\theta) = 1, \quad 0 \le \theta \le 1.$$

The posterior density of θ was $p(\theta|y) = \theta^s(1-\theta)^{n-s}$, a beta distribution with parameters $s+1$, $n-s+1$. Suppose the data are

$$y = (1, 1, 0, 0, 0, 0, 0, 1, 1, 1, 1, 1, 0, 0, 0, 0, 0, 0, 0, 0)$$

with $n = 20$. Since $s = 7$ the posterior density of θ is beta $(8, 14)$ so we draw nrep = 1,000 realizations of theta from this distribution.[23]

One way to examine the hypothesis of conditional independence is to nest the model in a markov chain, as we discussed in example 2.18. Another way, discussed here, is to construct a Bayesian test statistic. The pattern of the data suggests dependence in the y's with a 1 more likely to be followed by a 1 and a 0 by a 0. A statistic to examine this might be the number of switches from 1 to 0 or 0 to 1 in the sequence. This has a maximum of 19 and a minimum of 0, and for these data the value is 3, the observed value of the test statistic, $T(y^{obs})$. The following program in S will calculate the number of switches.

```
switch <- function(y){
ny <- length(y)
n <- ny-1
ind <- rep(0, n)
for(j in 2:ny){i <- j-1; ind[i] <- y[j] != y[j-1]}
return(sum(ind))}
```

---

22 This example is borrowed from the the statistics textbook *Bayesian Data Analysis* by Gelman, Carlin, Stern, and Rubin (2003).

23 `theta<-rbeta(1000,8,14)` in S.

This program sets up an empty vector, ind, *to hold binary indicators of whether there was a switch at observations 2 to n; the* for *loop then scores 1 if there was a switch and zero otherwise. The symbol* != *means not equal to. The test statistic is to be* $T(y^{rep}) - T(y^{obs}) = switch(y^{rep}) - switch(y^{obs})$ *and this does not depend on the parameter. To simulate the predictive distribution we then repeatedly draw* θ *from its posterior beta distribution and for each such realization we generate a binary sequence of length 20. We then apply the switch function to the simulated data. This then gives nrep values for* $T(y^{rep}) - T(y^{obs})$ *and from the histogram of these we can see whether 3 is, or is not, an improbably small number of switches on the hypothesis that successive trials are conditionally independent. Simulate some data and try out this calculation.*

EXERCISE 2   TO SHOW THAT A SINGLE OBSER-VATION CAN TURN AN IMPROPER PREDICTIVE DISTRIBUTION INTO A PROPER ONE

Consider a sample of n independent exponential variates with parameter λ. *The density of a single such variate is* $\lambda e^{-\lambda y}$, λ, $y > 0$. *The log likelihood is* $\log \lambda - \lambda y$ *with first and second derivatives* $(1/\lambda) - y$, *and* $-1/\lambda^2$. *Thus the Jeffreys' prior is* $\pi(\lambda) \propto 1/\lambda$. *We first show that the prior predictive distribution is improper and then show that after a training sample of size 1 the predictive distribution is proper.*

To show the first, consider the predictive distribution of a single observation. This is

$$p(y_1) = \int_0^\infty p(y_1|\lambda)\pi(\lambda)\,d\lambda = \int_0^\infty \lambda e^{-\lambda y_1}\frac{1}{\lambda}d\lambda = \frac{1}{y_1},$$

and this is improper because the integral of $1/y_1$ *is* $\log y_1$ *and this diverges as* $y_1 \to \infty$.

To show the second, consider the posterior density of λ *after we have seen* y_1. *This is*

$$p(\lambda|y_1) \propto p(y_1|\lambda)\pi(\lambda) = e^{-\lambda y_1}$$

and this is a proper density for λ; *it is exponential with parameter* y_1. *We now calculate the predictive density of the observations* $y_2, ..., y_n$ *given* y_1. *This is*

$$p(y_2, ..., y_n | y_1) = \int p(y_2, ..., y_n | y_1, \lambda) p(\lambda | y_1) \, d\lambda$$

$$\propto \int \lambda^{n-1} e^{-s\lambda} e^{-y_1 \lambda} d\lambda$$

$$\propto (s + y_1)^{-n}, \quad for \; s = y_2 + ... + y_n.$$

To see that this is proper consider the case $n = 2$ when the density is proportional to $(y_2 + y_1)^{-2}$. Integrating this expression with respect to y_2 along the positive axis then yields $1/y_1$ so the density is proper as long as $y_1 > 0$.

Simulate some data and plot the predictive distributions of each observation given the preceding ones and an initial Jeffreys' prior.

EXERCISE 3   OVERDISPERSED SUPPOSEDLY POISSON DATA

The usual starting point for analysis of data that are counts of how many times some event occurs is the poisson distribution. This is a discrete distribution with support on zero and the positive integers. Its mathematical form is

$$p(y|\lambda) \propto \lambda^y e^{-\lambda}, \quad \lambda > 0, \; y = 0, 1, 2, \ldots \tag{2.24}$$

The mean of this distribution is λ and this is also the variance. Hence a characteristic feature of the poisson is that mean and variance are equal. But count data often show sample variances that are notably greater than the sample mean and this suggests that a more general model than the poisson is appropriate. In this example we shall describe a Bayesian posterior predictive test of the adequacy of the poisson likelihood, one that exploits this equality of theoretical mean and variance.

Since the log of the probability mass function is $y \log \lambda - \lambda$, with derivatives $y/\lambda - 1$ and $-y/\lambda^2$, the information is, exploiting $E(Y|\lambda) = \lambda$, provided by $I_\lambda(\lambda) = 1/\lambda$, so that Jeffreys' (improper) prior is $p(\lambda) \propto 1/\lambda^{1/2}$. For n independent observations the likelihood is found by multiplying together n terms like (2.24) and is

$$\ell(\lambda; y) \propto \lambda^s e^{-n\lambda}; \quad s = \sum_{i=1}^{n} y_i,$$

leading to the posterior density of λ, using Jeffreys' prior,

$$p(\lambda|y) \propto \lambda^{s-1/2} e^{-n\lambda}.$$

This is a gamma$(s + 1/2, n)$ distribution.

One possible form of the test statistic suggested by the theoretical equality of mean and variance when the poisson hypothesis is true is $T(y) = v(y)/\bar{y}$ where $v(y) =$

$\Sigma(y_i - \bar{y})^2/(n-1)$, *a form of the sample variance. This statistic should be about 1 if the data really are poisson realizations. To compute* $T(y^{rep}) - T(y^{obs})$ *we first note that* $T(y^{obs})$ *is a function of the data alone, and so we just calculate its value for our data and store this information. To calculate values for* $T(y^{rep})$ *we need to generate nrep realizations from the posterior predictive distribution of* $Y = (Y_1, ..., Y_n)$. *To do this we generate a realization of* λ *from its gamma($s + 1/2, n$) posterior distribution and then generate a value for Y, repeating this operation nrep times.*

Simulate some data and, using the test statistic suggested in the last paragraph, compute, by sampling, the distribution of $T(y^{rep}) - T(y^{obs})$ *and calculate the Bayesian p value.*

EXERCISE 4   GENERALIZING THE POISSON MODEL

The standard way of generalizing the poisson model is to allow for variability from observation to observation in the parameter λ. *One way to do this is to write the mean for agent i as* $\lambda \varepsilon_i$ *where* ε *varies from agent to agent according to a gamma law with mean one and variance* $1/\alpha$. *Thus as* $\alpha \to \infty$ *we recover the poisson model as a special case. In particular the mean and variance of Y given only* α *and* λ *are*

$$E(Y|\alpha, \lambda) = E_{\varepsilon|\alpha}E(Y|\lambda, \alpha, \varepsilon) = E_{\varepsilon|\alpha}\lambda\varepsilon = \lambda$$
$$V(Y|\alpha, \lambda) = E_{\varepsilon|\alpha}E(Y^2|\lambda, \alpha, \varepsilon) - \lambda^2$$
$$= E_{\varepsilon|\alpha}(\lambda\varepsilon + \lambda^2\varepsilon^2) - \lambda^2$$
$$= \lambda + (\lambda^2/\alpha) + \lambda^2 - \lambda^2$$
$$= \lambda + (\lambda^2/\alpha).$$

So we see that under this model the variance of Y exceeds the mean but approaches it as $\alpha \to \infty$. *The likelihood for a single observation in this model can be found explicitly by integration of the (poisson) likelihood given* λ, α *and* ε *with respect to the (prior) distribution of* ε *given* α. *The calculation is*

$$p(y|\lambda, \alpha) = \int_0^\infty \frac{\lambda^y\varepsilon^y e^{-\lambda\varepsilon}}{y!} \frac{\varepsilon^{\alpha-1}e^{-\alpha\varepsilon}}{\Gamma(\alpha)\alpha^{-\alpha}}d\varepsilon,$$

$$= \frac{(y+\alpha-1)!}{\Gamma(\alpha)y!}\left(\frac{\lambda}{\lambda+\alpha}\right)^y\left(\frac{\alpha}{\lambda+\alpha}\right)^\alpha, \quad \lambda, \alpha > 0, y = 0, 1, 2, \ldots$$

This two parameter (λ, α) *family of distributions is called the **negative binomial**. The joint posterior density of* λ, α *is found by multiplying n such terms together* *and multiplying by a joint prior density for* α, λ. *The resulting expression is particularly tractable analytically, but the posterior density is easily sampled using monte carlo methods with data augmentation, as we shall see in chapter 4.*

2.10 BIBLIOGRAPHIC NOTES

The review of Bayes factors by Kass and Raftery (1995) is well worth reading. A recent volume in the Institute of Mathematical Statistics Lecture Notes series provides a useful overview of model selection from both Bayesian and frequentist perspectives. This is IMS Lecture Notes Volume 38, *Model Selection*, ed. Lahiri. The paper *Methods and Criteria for Model Selection* by Kadane and Lazar also gives a lucid survey of the use of Bayes factors in the problem of choosing between models. See also papers by Berger and Pericchi (2001) and Efron and Gous (2001). For a recent discussion of model choice and an explanation of a criterion (DIC) that is currently ouput by the program BUGS see Spiegelhalter, Best, Carlin and van der Linde (2002: 583–640). Kass and Wasserman (1995: 928–34) give an account of a connection between BIC and Bayes factors for comparison of models such that one is nested in the other. Fernandez, Ley, and Steel (2001: 381–427) consider model averaging for linear models.

Gelfand and Dey (1994: 501–14) and Gelfand and Smith (1990: 398–409) are valuable early papers. Geweke (1998) is a valuable recent survey on methods of model checking that exploit MCMC simulation output. He provides references to his own software to implement the methods he proposes. This software is called Bayesian Analysis, Computation and Communication (BACC). It is available at http://www.econ.umn.edu/~bacc.

The (frequentist) parametric bootstrap procedure is well described by its inventor, Efron, with Tibshirani as co-author; Efron and Tibshirani (1993: 53–6).

The statistics textbook *Bayesian Data Analysis*, by Gelman, Carlin, Stern and Rubin (2003), advocates the Bayesian p value and is well worth reading more generally. The approach of this book has influenced the view of model checking taken in this chapter.

Two introductory books on the predictive point of view in Bayesian work are Aitchison and Dunsmore (1975), and Geisser (1993).

The method of training samples is closely related to the method of cross-validation, Stone (1974: 111–47).

There are rather few examples of the use of predictive distributions for model checking in econometrics. Canova (1994: S123–44) is a useful survey and advocates predictive methods in the context of rational expectations general equilibrium models. Hirano (1998: 355–69) and (2000: 781–99) uses predictive distributions in the context of modeling the evolution of individual earnings.

Geweke and Keane (2000: 293–356) provide an example of regression modeling using finite mixture distributions for the errors.

Chapter 3
LINEAR REGRESSION MODELS

3.1 INTRODUCTION

In chapter 1 we illustrated the components of Bayesian thinking by using as examples some simple linear and non-linear regression models. In the present chapter we shall try to go more deeply and systematically into the connection between econometric models and regressions. In particular, we shall ask what additional beliefs are required in order that we may use the well-established techniques of regression analysis to estimate econometric models. Having described some beliefs that enable us to make this transition we then explain in some detail the widely used normal linear regression model, regarding it as a valid expression of our economic model. Though such models are usually explained using a great deal of algebra we shall give the mathematics only in simple cases where the various formulae are likely to be reasonably transparent and helpful to intuition. We then describe an alternative Bayesian approach to linear regression inference that is based on a multinomial, not a normal, distribution for the data to be observed. Data on the demand for gasoline are used repeatedly to illustrate ways of using and extending the linear regression model. Mostly we shall focus on practical questions of how an economist can use the linear model easily and effectively.

3.2 ECONOMISTS AND REGRESSION MODELS

An econometric analysis usually deals with relationships between variables. Typically a theory exhibits how one set of variables, say, y, will be determined by another, x. Demand may be determined by price; expenditure by income; labor supply by wage rates and so on. Often these relationships are deterministic in the sense that for any x there will be a unique y chosen by the agent or determined by a competitive market or the current state of technology. A deterministic relationship is represented by a function, say, $g(y, x) = 0$ with a unique solution for y given a value for x. The question faced by the econometrician is to relate this economic model to data on x

and y in such a way that the theory can be tested to see if it is consistent with the evidence, and can be used to make predictions and decisions.

The first difficulty in answering this question is that economic data typically do not exhibit relationships that are deterministic. For agents or markets that show the same values of x the values of y vary in a way that they should not were the theory strictly true. We resolve this by broadening the theory to, say, $g(y, x) = \varepsilon$ where for any particular pair of observations, y, x we expect ε to be zero but allow that it might not be. This source of uncertainty in the comparison between the theory and the data is usually attributed either to *measurement error* or to the fact that the theory was derived under a *ceteris paribus* clause which states that y is determined solely by x in a hypothetical world in which no other relevant factors were allowed to change. From the measurement error point of view there do exist values of y and x for which $g(y, x) = 0$ is true, but the numbers in your data file do not correspond exactly to the variables that the theorist would demand that you measure. In the other point of view, ε arises because the theorist reached his conclusions by mentally holding constant all other possibly relevant factors. For example, demand is determined solely by price when all other prices, consumer income and consumer tastes remain constant.

The next difficulty arises when we consider the possible properties of ε. To carry the argument forward in a reasonably simple way let us linearize the function $g(., .)$ as, say, $y - \beta_0 - \beta_1 x$. This will generally be possible at least locally for some range of possible x values. Note that, if x is scalar, we could have linearized the function the other way round as, say, $x = \gamma_1 + \gamma_2 y$ but since the theory is designed to explain the determination of y by x our intuition, as theorists, will concern objects like β_0 which is the solution for y when $x = 0$, or about $\partial y / \partial x = \beta_1$ which is the effect of a small variation in x upon the solution value. It will not concern $\partial x / \partial y$ and so the linearization that places y on the left expresses our idea of the causal mechanism that, as theorists, we believe to be at work. When we extend the economic model by adding an error term ε we have

$$y = \beta_0 + \beta_1 x + \varepsilon.$$

We now contemplate observing y and x on several occasions, say n of them, corresponding to different points in time or space or different markets or different families or firms. For each of these "agents" the basic relation, $g(y, x) = 0$, is supposed to hold apart from a deviation or disturbance ε that admits the possibility that agents with the same value x will be observed, in spite of the theory, to have different values of y. But since the theory is supposed to hold we also expect that $\varepsilon = 0$ and so $E(\varepsilon) = 0$ is a reasonable way of expressing our belief that the theory is true.

But the restriction that ε has expectation zero is not sufficient to specify a probability model for y, x pairs. Even a complete (mean zero) distribution for ε will not do the trick since the two (or more) dimensional variate (y, x) does not have a distribution determined by that of the one dimensional ε.

3.2.1   *Mean independence*

One possibility is to believe (assume) that the expected value of ε is zero for every possible value of x, that is $E(\varepsilon|x) = 0$ whatever the value of x. This is called **mean independence** of ε and x, and under this belief it follows that

$$E(y|x) = \beta_0 + \beta_1 x + E(\varepsilon|x) = \beta_0 + \beta_1 x \qquad (3.1)$$

and so we have, in the assumption of mean independence, specified the regression function[1] of Y on X. Under mean independence the econometric model has become a **regression model**. Note that this belief is consistent with the basic property of ε that $E(\varepsilon) = 0$ since if $E(\varepsilon|x) = 0$ then it follows from the law of iterated expectations that $E(\varepsilon) = 0$.

If $E(y|x) = \beta_0 + \beta_1 x$ we have a **linear regression model** because this expression is linear in x. This is not as restrictive as it sounds because x can be any function you like of some other, more natural, economic variables. For example x could be the logarithm of income or the square of price and we still, formally, have a linear regression model. A model like $E(y|x) = \beta_0 + \beta_1 x^{\beta_2}$ is conventionally called a non-linear regression model for the slightly confusing idea that although it is linear in x^{β_2} this dependence involves a (presumably unknown) parameter β_2. The variable x in $E(y|x) = \beta_0 + \beta_1 x$ can be, and usually is, vector valued with β_1 a vector valued coefficient.

In this chapter and in chapter 5 we shall describe the Bayesian analysis of regression models. This implies that we shall assume mean independence. Most of the simple one parameter examples in chapter 1 were regression models. We have so far offered no justification for the apparently strong assumption that economic models can be converted into regression models. In chapter 6 we shall offer arguments both for and against this assumption and describe what we might do when this assumption is not credible.

3.3   LINEAR REGRESSION MODELS

Suppose that x has k elements of which one, conventionally the first, is unity and we have n observations each consisting of a value of y, here taken to be scalar, though the theory generalizes to vector y, and a vector $x = (x_1, x_2, ..., x_k)$. In the context of regression models it is customary to call y the *dependent variable* and the elements of x the *regressors, covariates or explanatory variables*. In matrix notation this system can be written as

$$y = X\beta + \varepsilon \qquad (3.2)$$

---

1   Cf. section 1.4.1.

where y is a column vector of the n observations on y; X is an $n \times k$ matrix[2] whose j'th column contains n observations on the j'th covariate and the i'th row of X denoted by x_i contains observations on all k covariates for the i'th agent; β is a column vector of the k partial derivatives $\{\beta_j\}$, and the column vector ε contains the n discrepancies or errors. Thus

$$
y = \begin{bmatrix} y_1 \\ y_2 \\ . \\ . \\ y_n \end{bmatrix}, \quad
X = \begin{bmatrix} x_{11} & x_{12} & .. & x_{1k} \\ x_{21} & x_{22} & .. & x_{2k} \\ .. & .. & .. & .. \\ .. & .. & .. & .. \\ x_{n1} & x_{n2} & .. & x_{nk} \end{bmatrix}, \quad
\beta = \begin{bmatrix} \beta_1 \\ \beta_2 \\ . \\ . \\ \beta_k \end{bmatrix}, \quad
\varepsilon = \begin{bmatrix} \varepsilon_1 \\ \varepsilon_2 \\ . \\ . \\ \varepsilon_n \end{bmatrix}.
$$

If the model contains an intercept, one column of X will consist of a column of n ones, conventionally denoted by the symbol j_n or, when the dimension is obvious, just j. Typical covariates in economic models of household behavior are prices and incomes, while in studies of markets price may be the dependent variable, and in studies of economic growth and inequality it may be income that is explained by the theory and is dependent in the model.

Sometimes other covariates consist only of ones or zeros to denote the presence or absence of some feature of a market, an economy or a household. Covariates other than j_n that consist only of ones and zeros are often called **dummy covariates**.[3]

Parameters and data

The model (3.2) contains (potential) data in the vector y and the matrix X, and numbers in β and ε that will not become fully known when the data have been observed. It therefore contains $n + k$ parameters, β, ε, for which an informative prior must be provided.[4]

Digression *Measuring covariates from their means* *If there is a covariate – column of X – that is identically one, its coefficient plays the geometrical role of an intercept in the linear equation (3.2). If this covariate is omitted the regression line is being forced to go through the origin. Covariates other than a vector of ones are called **real covariates**. When an intercept is allowed for, it is convenient to reparametrize the model by measuring the remaining $k - 1$*

---

2   There is an awkward notational conflict here since it is customary to use X for the random variable whose realization will be x and it is also usual for X to denote a matrix as opposed to a column or row vector which is written in lower case. We shall have to bear with the conflict and hope that the context makes it clear which sense is intended. Similarly, y is sometimes used to indicate a scalar (although then it often has an i subscript) and sometimes to indicate a column vector with n elements.

3   Presumably they should be called "real dummies," but that phrase has other connotations.

4   Cf. section 1.3.1 in which we emphasize that all unknowns have probability distributions.

columns from their means. To see what this means consider simple regression with one real regressor and an intercept so that the i'th row of (3.2) looks like

$$y_i = \beta_0 + \beta_1 x_i + \varepsilon_i.$$

If we let $\bar{x}$ be the average of the n x values in the sample we can rewrite this equation as

$$y_i = (\beta_0 + \beta_1 \bar{x}) + \beta_1 (x_i - \bar{x}) + \varepsilon_i.$$

This redefines the intercept from β_0 to $(\beta_0 + \beta_1 \bar{x})$ while leaving the slope coefficient unaltered. This reparametrization has no substantive effect other than to simplify calculations. If you are really interested in the numerical value of β_0 you can always recover it after you have made an estimate of the slope coefficients. In the general case each real regressor would be measured from its own sample mean and the intercept redefined to be $(\beta_0 + \beta_1 \bar{x}_1 + ... + \beta_k \bar{x}_k)$. The coefficient vector in (3.2) now has its first element given by this redefined intercept. The columns of the real regressors now, because they are measured from their means, have zero sum. In order to avoid a proliferation of notation we shall stick with that in (3.2) with the understanding that the $k - 1$ real covariates in X are measured from their means.

3.3.1 Independent, normal, homoscedastic errors

The assumption that made our economic model into a regression model was that $E(\varepsilon_i | x_i) = 0$ for each possible observation. If we now generalize this to $E(\varepsilon | X) = 0$, which implies that $E(\varepsilon_i | x_j) = 0$, then (3.2) becomes the regression[5] model $E(y | X) = X\beta$. But this, by itself, is not enough to provide the likelihood that we need for Bayesian inference. To see what we do need in order to make inferences about the partial derivatives of the model solution β, and to provide a basis for deciding if the model is consistent with the evidence we need Bayes' theorem. The posterior distribution for β is $p(\beta | y, X)$ after seeing the data in y and X. Use Bayes' theorem to get

$$p(\beta | y, X) \propto p(y, X | \beta) p(\beta). \tag{3.3}$$

So we see that what we need is a joint probability model for X and y (given β), $p(y, X | \beta)$, and a marginal (prior) distribution for β, $p(\beta)$. But we know that $y = X\beta + \varepsilon$ so we can see that if we specify a joint probability model for X and ε (given β)

---

5 If X contains only one real regressor then the model is called *simple regression*, otherwise it is *multiple regression*.

we can then deduce the model for y, X that it implies by changing from the distribution of ε, X to that of y, X (all given β). Now $p(\varepsilon|X)$ is already restricted by the belief that $E(\varepsilon|X) = 0$ but we must now, in the Bayesian approach, go from just a conditional mean assumption to a complete distribution. The obvious way to do this is to assert that ε and X are independent and not just uncorrelated (which is what $E(\varepsilon|X) = 0$ implies). In this case

$$p(\varepsilon, X) = p_\varepsilon(\varepsilon)p(X), \tag{3.4}$$

where ε has mean zero. If we now change the variables from ε, X to y, X using (3.2) we see that

$$p(y, X|\beta) = p_\varepsilon(y - X\beta)p(X|\beta).$$

The mathematical form to be used to express your views about the errors, $p(\varepsilon)$, depends on the nature of the variable y. If it is (approximately) continuous and can take values on the real line a natural initial choice is normality.[6] If y is discrete or binary or strictly non-negative other choices may be more persuasive. It may well be reasonable to transform your dependent variable in order to make normality and linearity of regression more plausible. Many economic variables are non-negative and it is common and sensible to use a normal linear regression model for their logarithms. This practice also has the advantage that regression coefficients can then be interpreted as showing the proportionate effect on y of a change in x. This is because $d \log y/dx = (dy/y)dx$ and the term in brackets is the proportionate change in y. And if x is also measured logarithmically its coefficient would then be an elasticity, and this corresponds to the way economists think and talk about covariate effects. In the main empirical illustration in this chapter we use a linear model relating the logarithm of household gasoline consumption to the logarithm of the price of gas, and the coefficient on log price is the price elasticity of demand for gasoline.

Let us begin with normality and consider the simplest version in which the elements of ε are independent and identically distributed with mean zero, of course, and common precision τ. This is a hierarchical prior with τ as a hyperparameter. Thus

$$p(\varepsilon|\tau) \propto \tau^{n/2} \exp\{-(\tau/2)\varepsilon'\varepsilon\}$$

where we are using matrix notation in which $\varepsilon'\varepsilon = \sum_{i=1}^{n}\varepsilon_i^2$. It then follows that

$$p(y, X|\beta, \tau) \propto \tau^{n/2} \exp\{-(\tau/2)(y - X\beta)'(y - X\beta)\}p(X|\beta). \tag{3.5}$$

---

6 Many other choices for the marginal (prior) distribution of ε could be made. Normality is traditional for variables whose sample space is the real line, partly because the mathematics of the model is easy. Most other error distributions are best handled using MCMC methods as described in chapter 4.

If the marginal distribution of X, $p(X|\beta, \tau)$, does not depend on β, or τ as would normally be a reasonable assumption, then X is called *strictly exogenous*. We shall maintain this assumption. A consequence of it is that $p(X)$ can be absorbed into the factor of proportionality in (3.5) and, finally, we have

$$p(y, X|\beta, \tau) = p(y|X, \beta) \propto \tau^{n/2} \exp\{-(\tau/2)(y - X\beta)'(y - X\beta)\} \qquad (3.6)$$

after dropping the irrelevant term $p(X)$ because it does not involve β, τ.

Let us set out the the assumptions we have made before proceeding with the analysis.

ASSUMPTION[7] 3.1   *INDEPENDENCE* $p(\varepsilon, X|\tau, \beta) = p(\varepsilon|\tau, \beta)p(X)$

This assumption specifies that X and ε are independent conditional on the parameters of the model, and that the marginal distribution of X does not depend on these parameters. This assumption that ε and X are independent can be quite a limiting one. For example it rules out most time series models, in particular those in which a covariate or column of X is a sequence of previous values of y, perhaps as

$$y_t = \alpha + \beta y_{t-1} + x_t\gamma + \varepsilon_t, \quad t = 1, 2, ..., n.$$

For an (autoregressive) model like this we see that y_{t-1} is determined in part by ε_{t-1} so it cannot be true that the column of X that corresponds to the values of y_{t-1} is independent of the column of values of ε. Likelihood construction for time series models requires a separate discussion.

ASSUMPTION 3.2   *IID NORMALITY* $p(\varepsilon|\tau, \beta) = n(0, \tau I_n)$ where I_n is

the identity matrix of order n.

This assumption specifies that the elements of ε are independent of each other and normally distributed with mean zero and common precision τ. They are thus independently and identically distributed – iid – conditional on τ. It is an example of an informative prior that we noted above was required in view of the overparametrization of the regression model. The assumption of conditional independence does not imply that if you happened to know one of the elements of the vector ε your view about the others would not change. It generally would change because you would use that knowledge to take a view about τ. The assumption is independence *conditional on* τ. The assumption of common precision is called **homoscedasticity** and means that you are equally uncertain about each element of ε.

---

7   We use the word assumption because it is customary in the literature and means essentially the same as "tentative belief."

The assumptions of normality, conditional independence and homoscedasticity together with (3.2) constitute the **normal linear model**. The assumptions of normality, common error precision and conditional independence are fairly dogmatic, but they are easy to relax and indeed one can readily check their consistency with the data using the methods described in chapter 2. They are made partly for conventional reasons, partly because this is about the simplest model with which to begin thinking about regression, and partly because they are mathematically tractable, a factor that was significant in pre-computer days.

The more usual way of writing the model specified by (3.6) or by assumptions 3.1 and 3.2 is

$$y = X\beta + \varepsilon, \quad \varepsilon | X, \beta, \tau \sim n(0, \tau I_n). \tag{3.7}$$

One could also write

$$Y | X, \beta, \tau \sim n(X\beta, \tau I_n) \tag{3.8}$$

which says that, given X, β and τ, Y is multivariate normal with mean $X\beta$ and covariance matrix $(1/\tau)I_n$. In this way of writing the model the error vector ε is superfluous – one need never mention it. The assumption that $E(\varepsilon | X) = 0$ is implicit in (3.8). This notation, favored by statisticians, implies the normal linear regression model, and people who write the model in this way wonder why economists bother to waste the ink in writing the model as (3.7). The answer is that most econometricians view the regression version of an economic model as debatable – see chapter 6 – and prefer the regression assumption to be written explicitly as in (3.7).

EXAMPLE 3.1   *NO COVARIATES* *An important special case of the regression model is that in which there are no real covariates in X, only a vector of ones, and conditioning our arguments on X becomes unnecessary. This would be a rather thin sort of economic theory. In this case the model reduces to*

$$y_i = \mu + \varepsilon_i, \quad i = 1, 2, ..., n,$$

or, in matrix form,

$$y = \mu j + \varepsilon, \quad j' = (1, 1, 1, ..., 1),$$

where the single element of β is now denoted by μ. By assumption (3.2) $\varepsilon | \mu$, $\tau \sim n(0, \tau I_n)$. This immediately implies that

$$Y | \mu, \tau \sim n(\mu j, \tau I_n)$$

which can be read as "given numbers μ, τ, the elements of Y are independently and identically distributed with mean μ and precisions τ." Thus μ is the conditional mean of every Y_i and τ is the conditional precision. We have used this model several times in chapters 1 and 2 in the special case in which τ is known.

EXAMPLE 3.2 *SIMPLE REGRESSION* *If the model contains just one real regressor then we have simple regression and the formulation*

$$y_i = \alpha + \beta x_i + \varepsilon_i, \quad i = 1, 2, ..., n$$

or, in matrix form,

$$y = [j_n \quad x]\begin{bmatrix} \alpha \\ \beta \end{bmatrix} + \varepsilon$$

where we have, following convention, denoted the intercept parameter by α. Here j_n is a column vector of n ones and x is a column vector of the values of the real covariate measured from their mean. The partitioned matrix $[j_n \ x]$ corresponds to the X of (3.2).

3.3.2 *Vague prior beliefs about β and τ*

We have already specified a (hierarchical) prior for ε, so to complete the model we need a prior distribution for β and τ. Such prior beliefs will generally be influenced by the economist's understanding of the theory of the model and his (and the profession's) common beliefs about marginal effects of economic variables. But there is a special prior that is of particular interest for two reasons. The first is that it leads to posterior inferences about β and τ that, at least numerically, are identical to those that would be produced by a traditional econometrician. And secondly it is a prior – there are others – that permits exact, analytical, derivation of the marginal posterior distribution of β and τ. This prior is the conventional, vague, improper uniform distribution for β, and $\log \tau$, namely

$$p(\beta, \tau) \propto 1/\tau, \quad -\infty < \beta < \infty, \tau > 0. \tag{3.9}$$

By Bayes' theorem multiplication of the likelihood (3.6) by the prior (3.9) gives the posterior density of the $k + 1$ variates β, τ as

$$p(\beta, \tau | y, X) \propto \tau^{n/2-1} \exp\{-(\tau/2)(y - X\beta)'(y - X\beta)\}. \tag{3.10}$$

EXAMPLE 3.3 *NO COVARIATES* *When $X\beta$ reduces to $j\mu$, a vector with elements all equal to μ, then $(y - X\beta)'(y - X\beta)$ reduces to $\sum_{i=1}^{n}(y_i - \mu)^2$. The whole posterior density then looks like*

$$p(\mu, \tau | y, X) \propto \tau^{n/2-1} \exp\{-(\tau/2)\sum_{i=1}^{n}(y_i - \mu)^2\} \tag{3.11}$$

*where, as in example 3.1, we have written the conventional symbol μ for the sole regression coefficient. The expression (3.11) is (the kernel of) a **bivariate probability density function** and to see it let's produce some data and draw the picture. Generating $n = 10$ independent observations from a standard normal distribution – $\mu = 0$, $\tau = 1$ – we are then able to substitute these realized values of $\{y_i\}$ into (3.11) and explore the shape of the posterior density function for our data. This density of μ and τ, (3.11), is described in figures 3.1 and 3.2 firstly by a contour plot of the (joint) density and secondly by a perspective plot. On the contour plot straight lines are drawn to indicate the location of the joint posterior mode (top of the hill). A little calculus shows these are located at*

$$\mu_{mode} = \bar{y}; \quad \tau_{mode} = \frac{n-2}{\sum_{i=1}^{n}(y_i - \bar{y})^2}$$

which for our data are 0.18 and 1.15.

The contour plot shows clearly where the bulk of the probability lies and that the density is unimodal,[8] the mode being at about $\mu = 0.18$ and $\tau = 1.15$. It also shows that the density is not bivariate normal, for under normality the contours should be elliptical and they are not. The perspective plot enables the reader to judge the relative probability of different regions in the μ, τ space. You can use the contour plot to work out a set of points such that the probability that μ, τ lies within it is, say, 0.95 and is such that no point outside the set has higher density than any point inside it. This would be a 95% highest posterior density region, as explained earlier. The boundary of such a set would follow one of the contour lines in figure 3.1, though to find out which requires a further calculation.

The S commands to produce the contour plot are

```
m<-seq(-1,2,length=40)
p<-seq(0.3,3,length=40)
post<-matrix(0,nrow=40,ncol=40)
post<-outer(m,p,function(m,p){p^(n/2-1)*exp(-(p/2)*sum((y-m)^2))})
contour(m,p,post)
```

The first two commands set the box of points in μ, τ space over which the plots will be built; the third constructs a 40×40 matrix to hold the 1,600 function values; the fourth uses the outer product function on the vectors m and p and evaluates the density function at all 1,600 combinations of a point in m and a point in p. Finally, the fifth command orders up the contour plot.[9] The data y were produced by `n <- 10; y <- rnorm(n)`.

---

8   The contours depict a hill not a hole, as is evident from the perspective plot!
9   To produce the perspective plot the command is `persp(m, p, post)`.

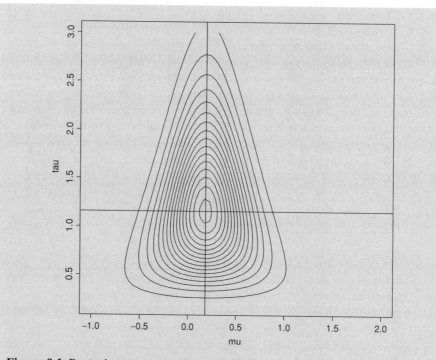

Figure 3.1 Posterior contours of μ and τ

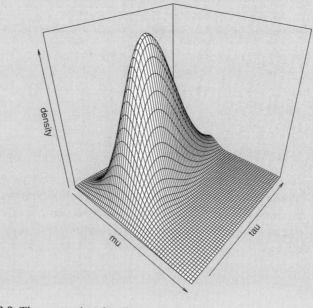

Figure 3.2 The posterior density surface

3.3.3   The two marginals under a vague prior

The marginal distributions of β and τ may be found in several ways. The most general and powerful way, in the spirit of modern Bayesian work, is to sample β, τ pairs from the joint distribution (3.10) and then plot and study either the β columns or the τ column. But in the normal linear model and under a vague prior it is possible to deduce these distributions analytically. In this section we give these analytical results, relegating proofs to the appendix to this chapter.

The first result is an intermediate step showing how the joint posterior density may be written in a way which is different than (3.10) but equivalent to it.

THEOREM 3.1   JOINT POSTERIOR DENSITY   *The joint posterior density (3.10) may be equivalently written as*

$$p(\beta, \tau | y, X) \propto \tau^{n/2-1} \exp\{-(\tau/2)(\beta - b)'X'X(\beta - b)\} \times \exp\{-(\tau/2)e'e\},$$
$$\text{for } b = (X'X)^{-1}X'y \text{ and } e = y - Xb. \tag{3.12}$$

*The vector b is called the **least squares estimate**. It is called this because b is the solution to the problem of minimizing the sum of squares $(y - X\beta)'(y - X\beta)$ with respect to β when $X'X$ is non-singular.[10] The vector e, of length n, gives the deviations of each y value from the plane (line) given by Xb and is the **residual vector** of chapter 2. The scalar e'e is the **residual sum of squares** and $e'e/v$ is called the **residual variance** when v is equal to $n - k$, the **degrees of freedom**.*

We shall discuss the least squares estimate further shortly. The residual vector is crucial in investigating whether the normal linear model is consistent with the evidence.

The next theorem shows that the marginal posterior density of τ, got by integrating β out of (3.12), is a gamma distribution.

THEOREM 3.2   MARGINAL DENSITY OF τ   *In the normal linear model with a vague prior*

$$p(\tau | y, X) \propto \tau^{v/2-1} \exp\{-\tau v s^2/2\}. \tag{3.13}$$

In this expression v is the degrees of freedom, $n - k$, and $s^2 = e'e/v = \sum_{i=1}^{n} e_i^2/v$, the residual variance. This is a gamma distribution.

---

10   To see this, multiply out the sum of squares as $(y - X\beta)'(y - X\beta) = y'y - 2y'X\beta + \beta'X'X\beta$ and then equate to zero the derivative of this expression with respect to beta. See section 3.5.

From the appendix to chapter 1 on the gamma distributions we find that the expected value of τ is equal to $(v/2)/(vs^2/2) = 1/s^2$. Since τ is the reciprocal of the error variance it seems natural to find that its posterior expectation is the reciprocal of the residual variance.

Next, we integrate τ out of the joint posterior density (3.12) to find the marginal posterior (joint) density of β.

THEOREM 3.3   MARGINAL DENSITY OF β   *In the normal linear model with a vague prior*

$$\beta \sim t(b, s^2(X'X)^{-1}, v)$$

which is a multivariate t distribution – see section 3.8.3 in the appendix to this chapter – with location b, scale $s^2(X'X)^{-1}$ and degrees of freedom v. This implies that individual elements of β are univariate t.

$$\beta_j \sim t(b_j, s^2(X'X)^{-1}_{jj}, v),$$

or

$$\frac{\beta_j - b_j}{sd_j} \sim t_v, \quad for \quad sd_j = s\sqrt{(X'X)^{-1}_{jj}}$$

where t denotes the standard t density function with v degrees of freedom and $(X'X)^{-1}_{jj}$ is the j'th diagonal element of $(X'X)^{-1}$.

Since univariate t distributions are unimodal and symmetric about their location we see that β_j is distributed symmetrically about the least squares estimate b_j which is, therefore, the posterior mean, and median of β_j. It is also the posterior mode or most probable value of β_j. If the degrees of freedom v is greater than 2 then sd_j is the posterior standard deviation of β_j.

Posterior moments of the error vector, ε, are also easily derived from these results. In particular:

THEOREM 3.4   POSTERIOR MOMENTS OF ε   *The error vector ε had prior mean equal to zero but has posterior mean equal to e, the least squares residual vector, and posterior covariance matrix equal to $s^2 X(X'X)^{-1}X'$. To see the former, note that*

$$E(\varepsilon|y, X) = E(y - X\beta|y, X) = y - XE(\beta|y, X) = y - Xb = e.$$

To see the latter note that

$$V(\varepsilon|y, X) = V(y - X\beta|y, X) = XV(\beta|y, X)X' = s^2 X(X'X)^{-1}X'.$$

The first of these is the result we used in chapter 2 to justify looking at the residual vector as a way of exploring the posterior distribution of the errors using a QQ plot.

If you look at the least squares residual vector, you are looking at your posterior expectation of the error vector ε. In this way you can form a view about which observations have unusually large deviations from the expected solution of your economic model, and perhaps draw some conclusions about the adequacy of that model.

EXAMPLE 3.4 *NO COVARIATES* *In the case without real covariates in which β_1 is the mean, denoted as μ, then the result of theorem 3.3 reduces to*

$$p(\mu|y) \propto \left[1 + \frac{n(\mu - \bar{y})^2}{vs^2}\right]^{-n/2}$$

which is a univariate t distribution with $v = n - 1$ degrees of freedom, mean $\bar{y}$ and variance (provided $v > 2$) equal to $s^2 v/[(v + 1)(v - 2)]$, where $s^2 = \sum_{i=1}^{n}(y_i - \bar{y})^2/v$.

Figure 3.3 shows the marginal posterior density of μ corresponding to the joint posterior density shown in figures 3.1 and 3.2. Note the symmetry of this t distribution.

Figure 3.4 shows the marginal density of τ corresponding to the joint posterior density shown in figures 3.1 and 3.2. Note the asymmetry of this gamma density.

3.3.4 *Highest posterior density intervals and regions*

We might want to ask whether β_j takes some specific value, typically zero. First we should note that because β_j has a continuous distribution any particular value has probability zero and so, therefore, has the value $\beta_j = 0$. So it doesn't make sense to ask for the posterior probability that β_j is zero. Yet clearly we might still want to ask whether, in the light of the evidence, β_j is zero or thereabouts. There is more than one way to pose and answer this question in the Bayesian literature. One possibility is just to draw the marginal posterior density of β_j and look to see if zero is within the interval where most of the probability lies. Although the most convincing way of doing this is just to look at the graph we might be a bit more formal and construct a highest posterior density (hpd) interval and see whether zero lies within it. We can do this analytically in simple models.

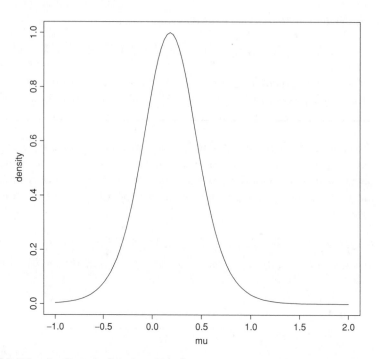

Figure 3.3 Marginal posterior density of μ

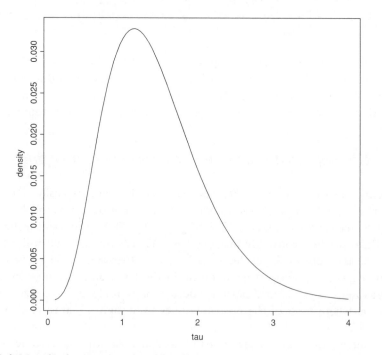

Figure 3.4 Marginal posterior density of τ

In the case of the normal linear model with improper uniform priors we can deduce the form of the, say, 95% hpd interval by the following argument. From the observation that the t distribution is symmetrical about zero and unimodal we can immediately find highest posterior density intervals for β. To do this note that since β_j is distributed as univariate Student's t with mean b_j and scale equal to $s^2(X'X)_{jj}^{-1}$, where $(X'X)_{jj}^{-1}$ is the j'th diagonal element of $(X'X)^{-1}$, then $(\beta_j - b_j)/sd_j$ is distributed as standard t with v degrees of freedom, where $sd_j = s\sqrt{((X'X)_{jj}^{-1})}$. So the S commands qt(0.975,v) and qt(0.025,v) will produce upper and lower quantiles that contain between them a 95% highest posterior density interval for $(\beta_j - b_j)/sd_j$ from which the hpd interval for β_j may be deduced. Specifically,

$$P\left(\text{qt(0.025, }v) < \frac{\beta_j - b_j}{sd_j} < \text{qt(0.975, }v)\right) = 0.95$$

which implies that

$$P(b_j + sd_j\text{qt (0.025, }v) < \beta_j < b_j + sd_j\text{qt (0.975, }v)) = 0.95. \quad (3.14)$$

EXAMPLE 3.5 *NO COVARIATES* *Using the data underlying figures 3.1, 3.2, 3.3 and 3.4 with $n = 10$ we find that $\bar{y} = 0.182$; the sum of squared residuals comes to $\Sigma(y_i - \bar{y})^2 = 6.915$; since $k = 1$ then $v = 10 - 1 = 9$; so that $s^2 = 6.915/9 = 0.768$. Further, since in this case $X'X = n$, and so $(X'X)^{-1} = 1/n = 1/10$ then $sd = \sqrt{(0.768/10)} = 0.277$. Using* qt(0.975,9) *gives the answer 2.262 which is also equal to* -qt(.025,9) *by symmetry about zero. Thus the 95% percent hpd interval for μ is from $0.182 - 0.277(2.262) = -0.445$ to $0.182 + 0.277(2.262) = 0.809$. So,*

$$P(-0.445 < \mu < 0.809|y, X) = 0.95. \quad (3.15)$$

This statement means that μ lies in the interval from -0.445 to 0.809 with probability 0.95 given the data we have seen and the (normal linear) model and vague prior we have used. It is also true that no point outside this interval is more probable than any inside it – because this is a highest posterior density interval. *This hpd interval is numerically identical to the 95% confidence interval for μ recommended in traditional econometrics. This is one of the main examples of Bayesian and frequentist arguments leading to numerically identical conclusions, though the reasonings behind the conclusion are quite different, as is the interpretation of the interval. An hpd interval for τ could similarly be constructed from figure 3.4.*

This formal argument only works when the prior is improper uniform (or natural conjugate) and in most Bayesian applications one would want to place acceptable, but more reasonable priors on unknown parameters. In these cases analytical derivation of hpd intervals is both infeasible and unnecessary, in general. All that is required is to draw the marginal posterior density; construct, by eye or trial and error, an hpd interval; and decide whether, for practical purposes, the coefficient can be treated as if it was zero. Such pictures of marginal posterior densities can be readily constructed by the device of sampling from the joint posterior density of model parameters, as we shall explain shortly.

The situation is a bit more complicated if you are interested simultaneously in *several* functions of the vector β. For instance you might be interested in whether β_3, β_4, and β_5 are all zero. More generally the question might be whether β satisfies a specified restriction of the form $R\beta = r$ where R is an $m \times k$ matrix and r is a vector of length m. R and r are given by you, R being of rank m. This is called a set of m linearly independent restrictions on β. Here is an example of this formalism.

EXAMPLE 3.6   *LINEAR RESTRICTIONS*   *When*

$$R = \begin{bmatrix} 0 & 0 & 1 & 0 & 0 \\ 0 & 0 & 0 & 1 & 0 \\ 0 & 0 & 0 & 0 & 1 \end{bmatrix} \quad and \quad r = \begin{bmatrix} 0 \\ 0 \\ 0 \end{bmatrix}$$

then the assertion that $R\beta = r$ is equivalent to the assertion that $\beta_3 = 0$ and $\beta_4 = 0$ and $\beta_5 = 0$. This amounts to three independent linear restrictions on β.

What is the question you want to ask? It is whether, in the light of the evidence (and the model), the view that $R\beta = r$ has any reasonable probability, or is very unlikely. To answer this, first call $\delta = R\beta - r$ and think of the posterior distribution of δ which, in the case of the example, is a point in three-dimensional space. Some regions in this space will be very probable and others quite improbable, and we can think of a region in δ space that contains within it all the points that have the highest posterior probability density. If we can find a region that contains within it 95%, say, of the posterior probability and such that no point outside it has higher probability density than any point inside it then we have a 95% highest posterior density region. Then one way to answer the question, is $R\beta = r$? i.e. is $\delta = 0$?, is to look to see if the point $\delta = 0$ lies in the highest posterior density region. If it does not then you might reasonably conclude that the restriction $R\beta = r$ is improbable. And if you want to be even more cautious in your judgement you might want to construct a 99% (or larger) region.

Just as in the case of a single linear restriction like $\beta_j = 0$ we can construct a procedure to see whether the set of β values such that $R\beta = r$ lies within an hpd region in the normal linear model with vague or natural conjugate priors. The argument in the vague prior case is as follows.

The vector β has a multivariate t distribution with parameters b, the least squares estimate, and $s^2(X'X)^{-1}$ where s^2 is the residual variance, and $v = n - k$ degrees of freedom. It follows rather easily from this[11] that $\delta = R\beta - r$ has an m-variate t distribution with kernel

$$p(\delta|\text{data}) \propto \left[1 + \frac{(\delta - d)'[R(X'X)^{-1}R']^{-1}(\delta - d)}{vs^2}\right]^{-(v+m)/2} \tag{3.16}$$

and that

$$q(\delta) = \frac{(\delta - d)'[R(X'X)^{-1}R']^{-1}(\delta - d)}{ms^2}$$

has an F distribution with m and v degrees of freedom[12] and where $d = Rb - r$. Call the hpd region H and let the posterior density function of δ be denoted here by $p(\delta)$ for notational simplicity. Then we have the following equivalences:

$$\delta \in H \Leftrightarrow p(\delta) > c \Leftrightarrow q(\delta) < c'$$

for some c', where the relation $A \Leftrightarrow B$ means that the events A and B are equivalent, either one implies the other. The first equivalence is because H is a *highest posterior density* region and the second because $p(\delta)$ is monotone decreasing in $q(\delta)$. Suppose that H is to contain $100(1 - \alpha)\%$ of the posterior probability. Then

$$1 - \alpha = P(\delta \in H) = P(q(\delta) < c')$$

(because equivalent events must have the same probability), so the number c' must be the $1 - \alpha$ quantile of the $F(m, v)$ distribution of $q(\delta)$. Quantiles of the F distribution can be obtained in S by qf(1-α, m, v).

We conclude that to see whether $\delta = 0$ or, equivalently, $R\beta = r$, you should compute the value of

$$q(0) = \frac{d'[R(X'X)^{-1}R']^{-1}d}{ms^2}; \quad d = Rb - r,$$

and find out whether it is less than the $1 - \alpha$ quantile of the $F(m, v)$ distribution. If it is, then the points β such that $R\beta = r$ are in the $100(1 - \alpha)$'th posterior hpd region and thus rather probable; if it is not you would conclude that $R\beta = r$ is an improbable restriction.

This is a somewhat controversial area of Bayesian inference. Many authors prefer to assimilate questions like "Is $R\beta = r$ probable?" to the problem of model choice by setting up two models in one of which we dogmatically set $R\beta = r$ and in the other of which β is not so restricted. This amounts to assigning a positive probability

---

11 See section 3.8.3 in the appendix to this chapter.
12 See section 3.8.3 in the appendix to this chapter for proofs.

to the event that $R\beta = r$, thus avoiding the zero probability issue that we raised at the start of this section. This approach enables you to consider the posterior probability of more general hypotheses than $R\beta = r$, for example the probability that, say, $\beta_3 > 0$ and $\beta_4 < 0$. We shall say more about this method in section 3.6.3.

3.3.5   The least squares line

The least squares (LS) line is $y = xb$ which reduces to $y = b_0 + xb_1$ when we are dealing with observations on two variables and the model contains an intercept. This line has been used for over two hundred years as a way of calculating a line of best fit to a set of data and thus effecting an economical description of a scatter of points in two-dimensional space. It is by far the most widely used of all descriptive statistical methods for multivariate data. Since the least squares estimate arises as the posterior expectation of β in what is probably the simplest version of the linear model, and because the properties of b are important components of the general knowledge of applied economists we devote here a section to this line.

   The line $y = xb$ is called the least squares line because it minimizes with respect to variation in β the sum of squares

$$S(\beta) = e'e = (y - X\beta)'(y - X\beta) = y'y - 2y'X\beta + \beta'X'X\beta.$$

Differentiating with respect to β we get the first order condition

$$\frac{\partial S}{\partial b} = X'Xb - X'y = 0 \tag{3.17}$$

with second derivative matrix

$$\frac{\partial^2 S}{\partial b \partial b'} = X'X.$$

If the symmetric matrix $X'X$ is positive definite and thus has a unique inverse $(X'X)^{-1}$ the solution of (3.17) – the normal equations – is $b = (X'X)^{-1}X'y$. Since the second derivative or hessian matrix is, in this case, positive definite, b provides the unique minimizer of S.[13] So we can conclude that the vector b uniquely minimizes the sum of squares $S(b)$ which is why it is called the *least* squares vector. The minimized sum of squares $e'e$ is a measure of the deviations of the y data from a straight line.

   The line has a number of interesting properties. For example, the least squares residual vector $e = y - Xb$, which provides the posterior expectation of the error

---

13   If $X'X$ is singular there will be many values of b providing the same minimal sum of squares.

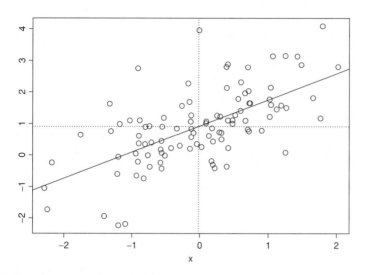

Figure 3.5 Least squares fit and data means

vector, is orthogonal to X in the sense that the inner products of the columns of X with e are identically zero. To see this note that

$$X'e = X'(y - Xb) = X'y - X'Xb = 0$$

from the first order condition (3.17). In particular, if the $n \times k$ matrix X contains a column of ones so that the line $y = Xb$ contains an intercept then

$$[1 \quad 1 \quad . \quad . \quad 1] \begin{bmatrix} e_1 \\ e_2 \\ . \\ . \\ e_n \end{bmatrix} = \Sigma_{i=1}^n e_i = 0.$$

The (LS) residuals sum to zero, identically.[14] When a sum of terms equals zero their average also equals zero so this result implies that

$$\bar{e} = \bar{y} - b_0 - b_1 \bar{x}_1 - ..., b_{k-1} \bar{x}_{k-1} = 0$$

and the line $y = xb$ goes through the means of the data. This is illustrated in figure 3.5.

---

14   This is useful as a computational check on b. If your residuals don't sum to zero then (provided your coefficients include an intercept) you have made an arithmetical mistake in your calculation of b.

The dashed lines show the means of the $n = 100$ simulated pairs of y and x values, their intersection being the point $\bar{y}$, $\bar{x}$. The solid line shows the least squares line which for these data is

$$y = 0.921 + 0.828x$$

and, since an intercept is included in the model, this line goes through the point $\bar{y}$, $\bar{x}$. The residuals e_i correspond on the graph to the vertical distances from the points on the scatter diagram to the least squares line, where by vertical we mean measured parallel to the y axis.

It is often of interest to measure how closely the points are represented by the least squares line. Clearly if all the points lie on the line all the residuals are zero, and to the extent that the points are widely scattered about the line the residuals will be larger, so a natural measure of **goodness of fit** might be based on the size of the residuals. One such measure is their sum of squares, $e'e$. Since the residuals have the same dimensions as y they are not scale invariant and so to make comparisons between one fit and another it is usual to divide $e'e$ by ($n - k$ times) the variance of y. This gives $e'e/\sum_{i=1}^{n}(y_i - \bar{y})^2$ as a dimensionless measure of goodness of fit of the straight line to the data. Customarily the measure is such that the number one measures a perfect fit – all the points lie on the least squares line – and so we actually use

$$R^2 = 1 - \frac{\sum_{i=1}^{n}e_i^2}{\sum_{i=1}^{n}(y_i - \bar{y})^2}$$

sometimes called the **coefficient of determination**. This is equal to its maximum value of one only when all residuals are zero. Its minimum value is zero. In simple regression R^2 is identical to the squared correlation of y and x.

For the sample data shown in figure 3.5 we see that $\sum_{i=1}^{n}(y_i - \bar{y})^2 = 140.590$ and when we calculate the residuals using `e <- y - 0.921 - 0.828x` we find that $\sum_{i=1}^{n}e_i^2 = 85.265$ leading to an R^2 of $1 - 85.265/140.590 = 0.394$. R^2 is often described as the proportion of the variance of y explained by its linear regression on x so this particular result could be described by saying that "x explains about 40% of the variance of y."

It should be noted that there is no economic theory that implies that R^2 should be either high or low and its value cannot be used as a way of determining whether a theory is true or false.

S commands

S commands to fit a linear model to data include `lsfit(X, y, intercept=T)` with X an $n \times k$ covariate matrix and y an $n \times 1$ vector. This will automatically add an intercept column to X and so the calculation will fail if X already contains such a column. In this case set `intercept=F`. The output is a list with the coefficients, b, found as `lsfit(X, y, intercept=T)$coef` and the residuals, e, found as `lsfit(X, y, intercept=T)$res`.

More useful and flexible is `lm(y~X)` where again X should not include a column of ones. If you want to exclude an intercept the command is `y <- lm(y~X - 1)`. The command `lm` stands for linear model. The command `summary(lm(y~X))` produces b, the residual sum of squares $e'e$, the posterior standard deviations, R^2, etc.

3.3.6 Informative prior beliefs

Our discussion of the normal linear regression model has focused on the case in which the prior beliefs were vague, $p(\beta, \tau) \propto 1/\tau$. This gave an analytically tractable model and allowed us to see clearly the role of least squares in Bayesian inference. But in practice you may well want to build into your analysis informative beliefs about these parameters, possibly even rather rigid ones such as constant returns to scale in a production function model. There is no difficulty in doing this in practice, as we shall shortly see, but the *analytical* derivation of results with informative priors is generally tedious and not specially enlightening.

One exception to this rule is when your beliefs can be represented by a natural conjugate prior for β, τ. Since the likelihood takes the form

$$p(y, X|\beta, \tau) \propto \tau^{n/2} \exp\{-\tau(\beta - b)'X'X(\beta - b)/2\} \exp\{-\tau e'e/2\} \quad (3.18)$$

where b is the least squares estimate and e contains the ls residuals, the natural conjugate prior has the form

$$p(\beta, \tau) \propto \tau^{\alpha/2-1} \exp\{-\tau(\beta - \beta_0)'A(\beta - \beta_0)/2\} \exp\{-\tau c/2\}. \quad (3.19)$$

This prior, as always with natural conjugate forms, has the appearance of the posterior of a hypothetical (possibly real) previous analysis in which the least squares estimate was β_0, the precision was τA, the residual sum of squares was c, and the number of observations was α. Its structure is that of a normal distribution given τ with mean β_0 and precision τA and a marginal gamma prior with parameters α, c. The parameter β_0 is the prior mean of β, and its precision is τA. To specify this prior numerically you must provide $k(k + 1)/2$ elements for A – making sure the result is non-negative definite; k elements for β_0; and the scalars c and α. This is demanding of time and patience and in practice A is usually taken to be diagonal with perhaps only a few positive elements on the diagonal. After some algebra the multiplication of prior (3.19) and likelihood (3.18) yields a posterior density for β, τ in which β is distributed with mean

$$E(\beta|y, X) = (X'X + A)^{-1}(X'Xb + A\beta_0).$$

This has the form of a (matrix) weighted average of the ls estimate, b, and the prior mean β_0. The weights attached to these two points are their precision matrices, $X'X$ and A. This is interesting in that it shows the posterior mean emerging as a compromise[15] between prior and "data" means of β. (In the scalar case the posterior mean lies between β_0 and b, nearer the latter if β is estimated very precisely from the data and vague prior alone.)

Unfortunately the prior (3.19) is often not very appealing because it asserts that your prior beliefs about β and τ are dependent – your beliefs about β imply that you know something about τ. Often, it seems, prior beliefs about β and τ derive from completely separate considerations and in this (3.19) would not be appropriate. We therefore turn immediately to practical methods that allow you to specify whatever prior beliefs seem appropriate, natural conjugate or not.

3.3.7 Sampling the posterior density of β

It often happens that economic interest centers not on the elements of β themselves but on some possibly non-linear function of them. Although in simple cases the distribution of such functions can be deduced mathematically, the simplest and most generally applicable way to study them is to sample from the posterior distribution.[16] If interest centers on $g(\beta)$ then sample `nrep` times from the posterior distribution of β and apply the function $g(.)$ to each realization. The result will be a sample from the posterior distribution of $g(\beta)$. This is also a good way of studying the joint distribution of pairs of elements of β, say β_j and β_k. Just pick out the realizations of β_j and β_k and plot their scatter diagram.

Under the vague or natural conjugate priors used so far we have deduced the exact posterior – t – distribution of β, but to sample from it we needn't have gone through this mathematics. There are easier ways to proceed.

In the vague prior case a simple way to sample exactly from $p(\beta, \tau|y, X)$ is to do it in stages. In the first step we sample from the marginal (posterior) distribution of τ, and in the second we substitute these τ values into the posterior distribution of β given τ and then sample from these conditional distributions. The reason this works is that the joint posterior density can be broken up as $p(\beta, \tau|y, X) = p(\beta|\tau, y, X)p(\tau|y, X)$. These two steps are easy since a glance at (3.12) shows that, for given τ, β is multivariate normal with mean b and precision $\tau X'X$,

$$p(\beta|\tau, y, X) = n(b, \tau X'X), \tag{3.20}$$

and, from (3.13), we know that τ is gamma($v/2$, $vs^2/2$). After these two steps the end product is a sample from the joint posterior density of β and τ and from this sample the distribution of any function of β and τ can be estimated with arbitrary accuracy.

---

15 Though matrix weighted averages are not as simple to interpret as scalar weighted averages. See the bibliographic notes for further references.

16 The material of this section anticipates part of chapter 4. Some readers might want to look at that chapter before tackling this section.

ALGORITHM 3.1 *DO-IT-YOURSELF SAMPLING OF THE POSTERIOR DISTRIBUTIONS OF β AND τ* *If you wish to write your own code to compute posterior distributions in the normal linear regression model with vague prior here is an algorithm – in S – to do so.*

1. If your data is an n vector y and an n × k matrix X (which would include a column of ones if you want to include an intercept in the model) first calculate the ls estimate b, then the ls residual vector e, then the residual variance s^2. You could use

```
XXI  <-  solve(t(X)%*%X) # this forms X'X and then inverts it.
v <- n-k; # degrees of freedom
b <-  XXI %*% t(X)  %*%  y # least squares coefficients
e <- y - X%*%b # residual vector
s2 <- sum(e^2)/v # residual variance
```

Alternatively you could get these from `lm(y~X)`, *for example* `b <- lm(y~X - 1) $coef`.

2. Sample τ from its marginal gamma posterior.

```
nrep <- 5000
tauval <- rgamma(nrep, v/2, vs^2/2)
```

3. Sample β from its conditional multivariate normal distribution given τ.

```
bval <- matrix(0, nrow=nrep, ncol=k) # bval will hold the simula-
```
tion output
```
for(i in 1:nrep){V <- (1/tauval[i])*XXI
bval[i,] <- rmvnorm(1,b,V)} # realization of multivariate normal with
```
mean b and covariance V

X is the n × k matrix holding the covariate values; b is the least squares estimate; v is n − k. The command `t(X)` *transposes X and* `solve` *finds* $(X'X)^{-1}$. *The command* `rmvnorm(1,b,V)` *draws one realization of a multivariate normal variate with mean b and covariance matrix* V. *The loop defines the covariance matrix of β as* $\tau(X'X)^{-1}$ *and draws a multivariate normal vector with mean b and this covariance matrix for each of the* `nrep` *realizations of τ.*

4. You may then study the distribution of any function of the elements of β. For example if you are interested in the ratio of $β_3$ to $β_4$ you might use

```
r  <-  bval[,3]/bval[,4]; summary(r); hist(r); plot(den-
sity(r)) etc.
```

3.3.8 *An approximate joint posterior distribution*

We stated in chapter 1 that when the sample size is "large" a joint posterior distribution can often be well approximated by a multivariate normal distribution with mean equal to the maximum likelihood (ml) estimate and precision equal to the negative hessian matrix at that estimate, $\theta \sim n(\hat{\theta}, -H(\hat{\theta}))$. To see what this amounts to here, take the likelihood in the form (3.18) and form its logarithm giving

$$\log \ell(\beta, \tau) = \frac{1}{2}\{n \log \tau - \tau(\beta - b)X'X(\beta - b) - \tau e'e\}$$

where b is the least squares estimates and e contains the least squares residuals. The log likelihood derivatives are

$$\frac{\partial \log \ell}{\partial \beta} = -\tau X'X(\beta - b)$$

$$\frac{\partial \log \ell}{\partial \tau} = \frac{n}{2\tau} - \frac{1}{2}\{(\beta - b)X'X(\beta - b) + e'e\}.$$

Equating these to zero and assuming that $X'X$ is non-singular we get a unique solution for the maximizing values, namely

$$\hat{\beta} = b \quad \text{and} \quad \hat{\tau} = n/e'e.$$

Note that the maximized value of the log likelihood is

$$\log \ell(\hat{\beta}, \hat{\tau}) = \frac{1}{2}\{n \log n - n - n \log e'e\}. \tag{3.21}$$

Differentiating again and changing signs gives the negative hessian matrix

$$-H(\theta) = \begin{bmatrix} \tau X'X & X'X(\beta - b) \\ (\beta - b)'X'X & n/2\tau^2 \end{bmatrix}.$$

When evaluated at the solution of the first order conditions this matrix is positive definite confirming that b and $n/e'e$ are maximum likelihood estimates. Evaluating the negative hessian at these values we have an approximate posterior distribution for β, τ as

$$\begin{pmatrix} \beta \\ \tau \end{pmatrix} \sim n\left(\begin{bmatrix} b \\ n/e'e \end{bmatrix}, \begin{bmatrix} nX'X/e'e & 0 \\ 0 & \dfrac{(e'e)^2}{2n} \end{bmatrix}\right). \tag{3.22}$$

This states that β and τ are approximately normally distributed with means equal to the least squares estimate, b, and the reciprocal of the residual mean squares (but divided by n and not by the degrees of freedom $v = n - k$), respectively. Moreover, these parameters are independent and with precisions that depend only on n, $X'X$ and the residual sum of squares.

One useful implication of this result is that a Bayesian can make use of some of the output of frequentist least squares regression programs. The programs, such as lm() in S, produce b and e, and calculate estimates of repeated sampling standard deviations for least squares estimators as the square roots of the diagonal elements of $(e'e/v)(X'X)^{-1}$. When n is large relative to k this will differ little from the posterior standard deviations of the $\{\beta_k\}$ constructed from (3.22).

In summary, in large sample situations frequentist least squares estimates and their standard deviations will be essentially the same as Bayesian posterior means and standard deviations.

EXAMPLE 3.7 *DEMAND FOR GASOLINE* *To*

illustrate the linear model with real data we consider household survey information about the demand for gasoline.[17] A total of $n = 6{,}491$ households supplied information on their purchases of gasoline, the price they paid for it, their income and many other possibly relevant characteristics. The theory of consumer demand leads to a model in which demand is a function of the price of gas, consumer income and the prices of competing and complementary goods. A log linear version[18] of this theory, leaving aside the other prices, with an error term attached would be

$$gas = \beta_1 + \beta_2\,price + \beta_3\,income + \varepsilon \qquad (3.23)$$

where we would expect the coefficient β_2, the own price elasticity of demand, to be negative, and the income elasticity β_3 to be positive. Under the hypothesis that the elements of $\{\varepsilon_i\}$ are iid normal with precision τ with vague priors the posterior means and standard deviations of the coefficients are found to be

$$gas = 2.68(0.16) - 0.47(0.07)price + 0.20(0.02)income, \qquad (3.24)$$
$$E(\tau) = 2.58(0.05)$$

The first figures attached to each variable are the posterior means and the figures in brackets are posterior standard deviations. The calculations were done in BUGS[19] using the program given below. Since n is equal to $6{,}491$ here it is probably reasonable to use the large sample approximation to the joint posterior density, given above, in which $\beta \sim n(b, nX'X/e'e)$,[20] so these results could also have been found from a frequentist regression program. Specifically, the S command

```
summary(lm(log(gascon)~log(price) +log(income)))
```

produces the output

```
lm(formula = log(gascon)~log(price) + log(income))
Coefficients:
            Estimate Std. Error t value Pr(>|t|)
```

---

17 Supplied by A. Yatchew in Yatchew and No (2001).
18 The term "gas" is log gasoline consumption; "price" is log price paid per litre; and "income" is log household income.
19 See chapter 4 and appendix 3.
20 Or you could replace n by $v = n - k$ to the same order of approximation.

```
(Intercept)  2.68254  0.16440  16.317  < 2e-16  ***
log(price)  -0.46854  0.06818  -6.872  6.9e-12  ***
log(income)  0.19576  0.01517  12.903  < 2e-16  ***
---

Residual standard error: 0.6229 on 6488 degrees of freedom
Multiple R-Squared: 0.03349, Adjusted R-squared: 0.03319
F-statistic: 112.4 on 2 and 6488 DF, p-value: < 2.2e-16
```

The figures under the heading "Coefficients" show the least squares coefficients and next to them are estimates of the standard deviations of their repeated sampling distributions. Comparing these to the Bayes estimates above we see that they are the same. The "Residual standard error" is an estimate of $1/\sqrt{\tau}$ so taking $1/0.6229^2$ we find 2.58 which is the Bayes posterior mean of τ.

Figure 3.6 shows the histogram of 3,000 draws from the marginal posterior density of the price elasticity, and the accompanying QQ plot, Figure 3.7, confirms marginal normality. The joint posterior density of the price and income elasticities is shown in the form of a scatter diagram in figure 3.8. It is clear that these parameters are almost uncorrelated – $r = 0.03$ – and approximately bivariate normal.

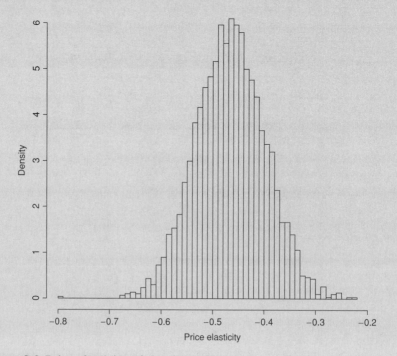

Figure 3.6 Price elasticity of the demand for gas

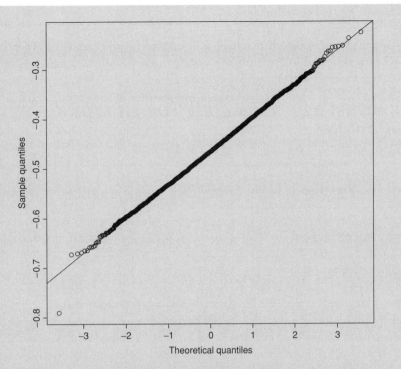

Figure 3.7 QQ plot of the gas price elasticity

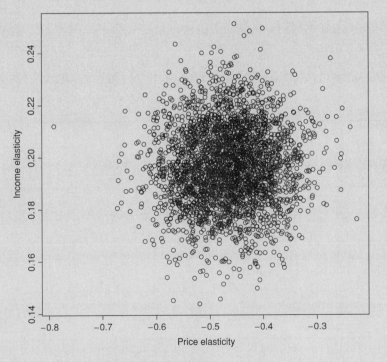

Figure 3.8 Gas price and income elasticities

To anticipate material from chapter 4 and to provide indication of how an MCMC program works here is BUGS code to sample from the joint posterior of a normal linear model with two real regressors.

ALGORITHM 3.2   *BUGS CODE FOR MULTIPLE REGRESSION*

```
model{
for(i in 1:n){
y[i] ~ dnorm(mu[i],tau)
mu[i] <- b0 + b1*x[i,1] + b2*x[i,2]}
b0 ~ dnorm(0, 0.0001)
b1 ~ dnorm(0, 0.0001)
b2 ~ dnorm(0, 0.0001)
tau ~ dgamma(1.0E-3, 1.0E-3)}
```

Lines 2 through 4 give the likelihood (3.8) while lines 5 through 8 give independent vague priors for the four model parameters, in particular, the priors for the β_j centered at zero with a precision equal to 0.0001 implying a standard deviation of $\sqrt{10,000} = 100$. These priors are proper but will be essentially equivalent to (3.9) unless the information in the data is very weak. You may replace the four lines specifying the prior by any other proper prior distribution for β, τ including ones like b1 ~ dnorm(1.0, 100) that specify that β_1 is distributed normally with a mean of one and a standard deviation of 0.10.

Use of such an algorithm enables you to compute rapidly the marginal and joint posterior distribution of all parameters and *any functions of them*. For example, if you intended to study the posterior density of β_2/β_1 you would simply add the line ratio <- b2/b1 before the final brace and ask the package to produce for you realizations of the new parameter ratio.[21]

Summary of results on the normal linear model

The normal linear model with a diffuse prior on β, $\log \tau$ is the fundamental linear regression model.

- It provides a rationale for least squares estimation of the coefficients of the regression. The ls estimates are posterior means and thus optimal Bayes decisions under quadratic loss – see chapter 1.
- We can deduce exactly the form of the marginal and joint posterior distributions of all coefficients and thereby make exact inferences.

---

21 For more on BUGS see appendix 2. Appendix 3 collects together all BUGS code used in this book.

- It is also easily simulated, and the output of such simulations from the joint posterior distribution enables you to make exact inferences about any functions of the model parameters.
- The extension of the model to informative priors on β and τ is computationally straightforward and requires only the changing of a few lines of your simulation program.
- The model is extremely flexible in the sense that the simple expression for the regression function, $x\beta$, can encompass a huge variety of forms. These would include polynomials; piecewise polynomials; indicator or dummy variables; interactions between variables (so that the marginal effect of x_3 depends on the level of x_2); interaction between dummy and real variables which allow for heterogeneous regression slopes etc. We have illustrated only a few possibilities but give several more examples in section 3.6.
- The model is, however, based on a rather restrictive hierarchical prior for the regression errors, namely that they are independent of the covariates and iid $n(0, \tau)$. This belief incorporates a dogmatic belief in homoscedasticity and lack of error correlations. In section 3.5 we shall discuss ways of checking these dogmatic beliefs and in section 3.6 relaxing them. Before doing so we give a brief account and illustration of a Bayesian method that uses an alternative, and possibly weaker, set of beliefs about the distribution of the data.

3.4 A MULTINOMIAL APPROACH TO LINEAR REGRESSION

The material in this section is novel and readers might wish to return to it after reading the rest of the chapter.

In section 3.2.1 we introduced the idea of mean independence of error and covariate, namely that $E(\varepsilon|X) = 0$, while in section 3.3.1 we went on to add to the structure of the model by introducing the beliefs that the errors were uncorrelated, homoscedastic, $E(\varepsilon\varepsilon'|X) = \sigma^2 I_n$ and multivariate normal. Let us now back away from these latter beliefs and focus solely on mean independence and ask whether Bayesian inference is possible under mean independence alone. Clearly, for such inference we require a likelihood, so can we find one that embodies mean independence but avoids further, arguably dogmatic, beliefs? There have been several attempts along these lines[22] and here we shall describe one that is based on the multinomial distribution.

The multinomial distribution – see the probability appendix to chapter 1 – is a probability model for the occurrence of one out of, say, $L + 1$ mutually exclusive and exhaustive categories. Binary data with two categories, employed or unemployed for example, is an instance of multinomial data. Another example might be selection of a number out of the first M integers which would be multinomial with M categories.

---

22 Mainly by Zellner and his co-workers. See the bibliographic notes.

If $\{p_l\}$, $l = 0, 1, ..., L$ represent the probabilities that the outcome Y falls in category l, the probability distribution for a single realization of a multinomial variate is given by the table $P(Y = y_l | p) = p_l$, where the $\{y_l\}$ indicate the $L + 1$ categories. If we consider N independent realizations of the same multinomial variate the joint distribution can be written as

$$p(n|p) = \frac{N!}{n_0! \, n_1! \, ... \, n_L!} p_0^{n_0} p_1^{n_1} \times ... \times p_L^{n_L};$$

$$\sum_{l=0}^{L} n_l = N; \; n_l \in \{0, 1, 2, ..., N\}; \; \sum_{l=0}^{L} p_l = 1.$$

In this notation the $\{n_l\}$ count the number of times event l occurs or, in another language, category l is chosen, during the N realizations. For example, in a multinomial model with three categories, the probability that the first category occurs twice, the second never, and the third five times in $N = 7$ realizations is

$$p(y|p) = \frac{7!}{2! \, 5!} p_0^2 (1 - p_1 - p_0)^5.$$

When $L = 1$ the multinomial distribution reduces to the binomial.

How does the multinomial model help us to formulate a likelihood for a linear regression model that relies only upon the hypothesis of mean independence? To answer this question let us first consider the simpler case in which there are no covariates, just an overall mean μ. Thus

$$Y = \mu + \varepsilon$$

and "mean independence" simply amounts to $E(\varepsilon) = 0$ which is equivalent to saying that $E(Y) = \mu$.

(1) Now suppose that Y is a multinomial variate whose categories correspond to the L distinct numbers $y_0, y_1, ..., y_L$ called the **points of support** of the distribution and let $p = (p_0, p_1, ..., p_L)$ be the probabilities that $Y = y_l$. Then for N independent realizations of Y the likelihood is

$$\ell(p; n) \propto p_0^{n_0} p_1^{n_1} \times .... \times p_L^{n_L}$$

where the $\{n_l\}$ count the number of times that $Y = y_l$. The $\{p_l\}$ are the parameters of the model[23] and for these we require a prior. The natural conjugate prior for the multinomial is the dirichlet.

---

23   You could also think of the support points $\{y_l\}$ as parameters of the model, but we shall think of these as given and known.

(2) Take the prior for p as dirichlet with parameters $v = (v_0, v_1, ..., v_L)$.

$$p(p|v) \propto p_0^{v_0-1} p_1^{v_1-1} \times .... \times p_L^{v_L-1},$$

where the elements of p are non-negative and sum to one and the v_l are positive. It follows from these two hypotheses that

(3) The posterior density function of p is

$$p(p|n, v) \propto p_0^{n_0+v_0-1} p_1^{n_1+v_1-1} \times .... \times p_L^{n_L+v_L-1}.$$

These three steps have produced a (conditional) model for the data that we are to observe and a posterior distribution for its $L + 1$ parameters but, amazingly, we have nowhere mentioned the parameter μ that was the original object of our interest here. This is where mean independence comes in. The condition that $E(\varepsilon) = E(Y - \mu) = 0$ amounts to asserting that

$$\sum_{l=0}^{L} p_l y_l = \mu \tag{3.25}$$

since the expression on the left is precisely the expected value of Y (given p). The equation (3.25) *defines* μ as a function of the fundamental model parameters; technically, it is a function of the data distribution which in the present case is discrete with $L + 1$ points of support.

Having now defined μ in terms of the model parameters it remains to deduce its posterior distribution from that of p. As usual the simplest approach is to simulate its distribution.[24] It is shown in an appendix to this chapter (section 3.8.2) that dirichlet variates may be simulated by generating $L + 1$ independent gamma variates with parameters which, in the present case, would be $\{n_l + v_l\}$. Call these $\{g_l\}$, and form

$$p_l = \frac{g_l}{\sum_{j=0}^{L} g_j}, \quad \text{for } j = 1, 2, ..., L. \tag{3.26}$$

Then p is dirichlet distributed (with $p_0 = 1 - \sum_{l=1}^{L} p_l$). So to simulate the $\{p_l\}$ we need only to simulate the relevant number of gamma variates. We can write this fact conveniently by substituting the algorithm (3.26) into the definition (3.25) giving

$$\mu = \sum_{l=0}^{L} p_l y_l \cong \frac{\sum_{l=0}^{L} y_l g_l}{\sum_{l=0}^{L} g_l} \tag{3.27}$$

where the symbol $\cong$ means that the left and right hand sides have the same distribution.

The remaining problem concerns the points of support $\{y_l\}$ of the multinomial model for the realizations of Y. The trick (and it is little more than this) here is to allow the $\{v_l\}$ to approach zero (from above). The shape parameters of the gamma

---

24 The alternative is to deduce mathematically the distribution of a linear function of a dirichlet variate. This is left as an exercise!

densities of the $\{g_i\}$ are equal to $\{n_l + v_l\}$. For v_l very small these shapes approach n_l which is the number of times that support point y_l appears in your data file. If y_l does not appear as one of your data points, and so $n_l = 0$, the corresponding gamma shape will approach zero. But a gamma variate with shape v (and scale one) has mean v and variance v, so its realizations will with high probability be close to zero when v is itself close to zero. This in turn implies that support points y_l that do not appear in the data receive negligible weight in forming the weighted average on the right hand side of (3.27). So if we take all the $\{v_l\}$ close to zero we can interpret $L + 1$ as the number of distinct data points and the observed $\{y_l\}$ as being those distinct points. In particular if all N data values are distinct, as would often be the case with data suitable for linear regression, we can write

$$\mu \cong \frac{\sum_{i=1}^{N} y_i g_i}{\sum_{i=1}^{N} g_i} \tag{3.28}$$

where the $\{g_i\}$ are now gamma(1) variates, that is, unit exponentials with density $\propto e^{-g}$. Moreover this formula would still be correct even if some data points occur multiple times, since while the correct weight for such a point is a gamma(n_l) such a variate has the same distribution as the sum of n_l independent unit exponential variates, and this is precisely the weight such a point would get in the formula (3.28).

Implementation of this simulation procedure is easy in this and indeed all linear models with mean independence. An S command to simulate nrep times from the posterior distribution of μ for the model without covariates would be

```
for(i in 1:nrep){g<-rexp(n);mu[i]<-sum(y*g)/sum(g)}
```

The method generalizes to the linear model $y = X\beta + \varepsilon$ with the mean independence condition

$$E(X'\varepsilon) = E(X'(y - X\beta)) = 0$$

by noting that this condition implies that β is *defined* as

$$\beta = [E(X'X)]^{-1} E(X'y).$$

We take the support of the joint distribution of y, X to be a collection of $L + 1$ vectors $z_l = (y_l, x_l)$ where x_l is a vector of values of the covariate. Taking the data distribution to be multinomial over these support points with probabilities denoted by $\{p_l\}$ then a typical element of $E(X'y)$ would be $\sum_{l=0}^{L} x_{kl} y_l p_l$ and a typical element of $E(X'X)$ would be $\sum_{l=0}^{L} x_{jl} x_{kl} p_l$. We now observe that matrices with such elements can be written in the form $E(X'X) = X'PX$ and $E(X'y) = X'PX$ where P is an $L + 1$ dimensional diagonal matrix with typical diagonal element equal to p_l. Thus the definition of β is

$$\beta = (X'PX)^{-1} X'Py. \tag{3.29}$$

If we now use the algorithm (3.26) we can see that

$$\beta \cong (X'GX)^{-1} X'Gy \tag{3.30}$$

where G is a diagonal matrix with l'th diagonal element equal to g_l, a unit exponential variate, and with X and y the familiar data matrices of the linear regression model. Since the right hand side of (3.30) is a generalized – in this case weighted – least squares estimate (see section 3.6.2) we can see that simulation of the posterior distribution amounts to repeatedly doing weighted least squares.

In the case of simple regression the simulation formulae are

$$\alpha \cong \bar{y} - \beta\bar{x}$$

$$\beta \cong \frac{\sum g_i \sum y_i x_i g_i - \overline{yx}}{\sum g_i \sum x_i^2 g_i - \bar{x}^2},$$

where $\bar{x} = \sum x_i g_i$ and $\bar{y} = \sum y_i g_i$

and the summations are over $i = 1, 2, ..., N$.

EXAMPLE 3.8 *MULTINOMIAL ANALYSIS OF THE GASOLINE DATA*

Let us take the gasoline demand model (3.23) and drop any hypotheses about ε other than its mean independence from the covariates. Adopting instead the multinomial model with improper dirichlet prior we can sample the posterior distribution using (3.30). When we do this 3,000 times we can compare the posterior distributions of β under the full assumptions of the normal linear model and under the presumably weaker assumptions of the multinomial model. This is a variety of sensitivity analysis. We can compare two distributions using a QQ plot with the instruction qqplot(x,y). *This plots the ordered values of x against the ordered values of y. It differs from* qqnorm *which compares the ordered data against what they would be expected to be under normality.*

When we construct such plots we find that the coefficient posterior distributions are essentially the same with the exception of the distributions of the price elasticity. Figure 3.9 shows the price elasticity QQ plot comparing the posterior distributions of this coefficient under the two models. The solid line has intercept zero and slope one so that if the distributions were the same all points should lie on that line. In fact, they do not and the larger multinomial realizations are larger than their normal linear model counterparts and the smaller are smaller. The posterior distribution under the multinomial model, while basically similar to that under the normal linear model, is somewhat more dispersed. This is confirmed by computing the posterior standard deviations of the two sets of realizations. Under the homoscedastic normal linear model the posterior standard deviation of β_2 is 0.067 while under the multinomial model it is 0.075. The hypothesis of homoscedastic normality for the errors has, perhaps, caused a slight understatement of posterior uncertainty about the price effect.

One striking feature of this result is that the hypothesis of normality of the errors, present in the conventional model but absent in the multinomial model, has apparently no effect whatever on our posterior inferences.

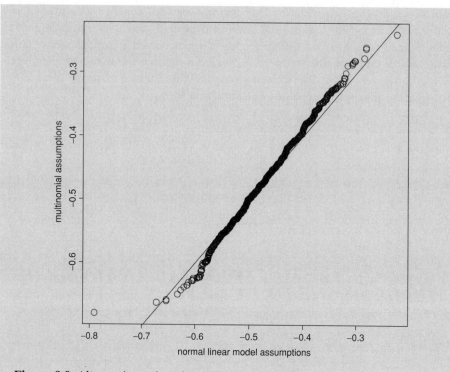

Figure 3.9 Alternative price elasticity posterior distributions

3.4.1   *Comments on the multinomial approach*

This approach, which is an example of the **Bayesian bootstrap** in the terminology of Rubin (1981), who devised it, has a number of attractive features.

- It requires only that the user specify a collection of mean independence restrictions and does not require either homoscedasticity or any tightly parametrized model for the error distribution.
- It is similar to the frequentist bootstrap procedure which will be familiar to some readers. The bootstrap procedure of Efron is a device for approximating the **sampling distribution** of an estimator. The method is to draw repeatedly a random sample (with replacement) of size N from your data set, and for each sample compute the corresponding estimate, for example least squares in the present case. Many such (re)samples provide an approximation to the required sampling distribution. In the frequentist bootstrap an observation, (y_i, x_i), either does or does not appear in any particular resample, whereas in the Bayesian bootstrap all observations are used in every repetition but they receive weights that are not binary but vary from zero to one.
- The method has a resemblance to frequentist generalized method of moments (GMM) procedures.

- It extends easily to any situation where we can uniquely define a parameter by a set of expectations. This includes both methods that use instrumental variables[25] and methods in which the parameter is defined as the (unique) solution to an optimization problem.

To set against these it has a number of unattractive features.

- It appears to be incapable of permitting the user to specify a proper prior for β. Indeed the improper dirichlet prior for p does not imply any unique prior for β, let alone one which the Bayesian user might find reasonable.[26]
- By defining the parameter as the unique solution of a set of mean independence or, more generally, moment conditions we are apparently not permitted to add restrictions to the model. For example, in the model without covariates we might think it possible to enforce homoscedasticity on the model by appending an extra moment of the form $E(\varepsilon^2) = \sigma^2$, so that the moments are

$$E(Y - \mu) = 0$$
$$E(Y - \mu)^2 - \sigma^2 = 0.$$

  But all the second condition does is to define a new parameter σ^2 to add to the definition of μ provided by the first equation. The (simulation) solutions for μ will be identical to those from using the first condition alone.
- Since the mean independence (moment) conditions define the parameter, any change to those conditions redefines the parameter. This is disconcerting if, as often in economics, we think of parameters as being defined independently of the statistical model that is used to make inferences about them.
- The method assumes that the data are independent realizations from the same multinomial distribution, so the method as given above does not immediately apply to dependent data, for example, time series.
- The requirement of an improper dirichlet prior for the multinomial probabilities means that it is not possible to construct a proper (prior) predictive distribution, or to construct Bayes factors for choosing between alternative models.

The multinomial method has so far proved unappealing to most Bayesians, who prefer to adopt more restrictive parametric models and to check them as illustrated in chapter 2 and in the next section, and then, if necessary, to extend the model to relax some of its more dogmatic features.

3.5 CHECKING THE NORMAL LINEAR MODEL

Once you have calculated your posterior distributions for the coefficient vector β you may well find that the results don't look consistent with your theory (or with common sense) or you may worry that your results are sensitive to some of the dogmatic beliefs

---

25 We shall show this in chapter 8.
26 Chamberlain and Imbens (2004).

that you have (tentatively) adopted. How do you react to this? You might want to re-examine the economics of your model, but most people prefer, at least initially, to act defensively. Specifically you might want to ask whether some of the particular, dogmatic, beliefs that you embedded in your econometric model were clearly inconsistent with the data. The reason that this question is interesting is that those beliefs may have distorted your inferences about β. If this is so it would be preferable to relax some of the more dogmatic elements to see if this relaxation markedly changes your posterior beliefs about β. If this is so you would probably want to use a less dogmatic model.

Let us work with the gasoline demand example to illustrate some ways of checking your model against the evidence and extending it if necessary.

EXAMPLE 3.9   *GASOLINE CONSUMPTION* One

useful way of checking the consistency of dogmatic prior beliefs with the evidence is to study the posterior distribution of the model errors, ε, and in particular, their expectation, the least squares residuals e. A good way of doing this is to QQ plot the residuals, as in figure 3.10. This plot suggests that the model errors are rather more dispersed than they would be if the hypothesis of homoscedastic normality was totally consistent with the evidence. In fact, a little experimentation shows that this plot is similar to the plot you would get in sampling from a t distribution with about seven degrees of freedom. There is a good reason for this as we shall explain shortly.

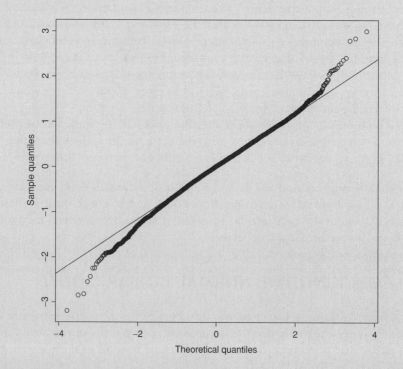

Figure 3.10 Gasoline demand residuals

Numerical checks

From a Bayesian perspective these graphs, while helpful in the task of model check-ing, do not do a complete job. Recall that ε is a random vector with a particular, posterior, probability distribution. When we plot the residuals, e, all we are doing is plotting the mean of ε and we are taking no account of its variability. Thus, for example, we cannot say how statistically significant is the departure from linearity shown by the QQ plot in figure 3.10. To get an impression of variability in the plot one could sample from the posterior distribution of ε and overlay the QQ plots of each sample. This is straightforward since $\varepsilon = y - X\beta$ and so to sample e you just sample β and then construct ε. But overlaid graphs can be cluttered and hard to read. It would therefore be useful to have scalar numerical measures of the depar-ture of the errors from prior assumptions. Here are some illustrations.

Heteroscedasticity

EXAMPLE 3.10 *HETEROSCEDASTICITY IN THE GASOLINE DATA* *If we want to see whether the errors have equal variances it seems sensible to look at the variation in their squared values, which means looking at $\sum_{i=1}^{n}(\varepsilon_i^2 - \sigma^2)^2/n$ where σ^2 is the reciprocal of τ, the model error precision. This is the mean squared deviation of the squared residuals from a common value. For a test statistic we would want to compare this statistic to what we would expect it to be if the data are homoscedastic. This value is*

$$E(\varepsilon^2 - \sigma^2)^2 = E(\varepsilon^4 - 2\sigma^2\varepsilon^2 + \sigma^4)$$
$$= 3\sigma^4 - 2\sigma^4 + \sigma^4 = 2\sigma^4$$

where we have made use of the fact that a normal variate with mean zero and variance σ^2 has a fourth moment equal to $3\sigma^4$. This then suggests that we look at the statistic

$$T(\beta, \sigma^2) = \sum_{i=1}^{n}((y_i - x_i\beta)^2 - \sigma^2)^2/n - 2\sigma^4. \tag{3.31}$$

In words, this is the mean squared deviation of the squared errors from a common value, less its expectation. Simulation of this distribution can be carried out by:

ALGORITHM 3.3 *CHECKING HETEROSCEDASTICITY*

1. Simulate β, σ^2 from the joint posterior distribution.
2. Evaluate T using the observed y and x and the simulated β, σ^2.
3. Repeat nrep times.

EXAMPLE 3.11 *HETEROSCEDASTICITY* *(contin-ued)* *Since we have already computed* 3,000 *draws from the joint posterior distribution of β and* $\tau = 1/\sigma^2$ *this program is easily carried out. Figure 3.11 shows the histogram of the test statistic using the gasoline model and data.*

The statistic can be seen to be strictly positive which indicates strongly the presence of heteroscedasticity in the errors of the model. The earlier QQ *plot of the model residuals had suggested this to be the case.*

The statistic (3.31) is being used here just as a test in that we are looking to see whether its posterior distribution overlaps zero or not. The numerical values of the statistic do not in themselves provide a measure of how severe this heteroscedasticity is. There may be alternative versions of the statistic that are more helpful in this respect, but all versions should show clearly, with over 6,000 *observations, that heteroscedasticity is present.*

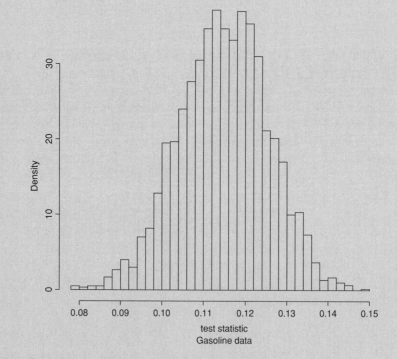

Figure 3.11 A test for error heteroscedasticity

Autocorrelation

The gasoline data are cross-sectional so the ordering of the observations in the data file is arbitrary and a test of error autocorrelation, which depends on a natural ordering, is meaningless with such data. With time series data, which have a natural ordering, the natural test statistic would be the autocorrelation of the errors as measured by, for example, the first order autocorrelation coefficient

$$\rho = \frac{\sum_{t=2}^{T}(\varepsilon_t - \bar{\varepsilon})(\varepsilon_{t-1} - \bar{\varepsilon}_-)}{\sqrt{\sum_{t=2}^{T}(\varepsilon_t - \bar{\varepsilon})^2 \sum_{t=2}^{T}(\varepsilon_{t-1} - \bar{\varepsilon}_-)^2}}$$

where $\bar{\varepsilon}_-$ is the mean of $\varepsilon_1, \ldots, \varepsilon_{T-1}$, or by the Durbin–Watson statistic

$$dw = \frac{\sum_{t=2}^{T}(\varepsilon_t - \varepsilon_{t-1})^2}{\sum_{t=1}^{T}\varepsilon_t^2}.$$

We have already illustrated such tests in chapter 2 in the context of the first order autoregressive model, and the approach taken there is equally applicable here so we shall omit further discussion of autocorrelation tests.

Digression and warning   *It is easy to misinterpret the calculations that we have just described since they have a formal similarity to ones recommended in the standard econometrics texts. So let us re-emphasize their interpretation. Recall that in the normal linear model the errors $\{\varepsilon_i\}$ are viewed as an additional collection of parameters about which you have opinions expressed by independence of X and ε and that marginally the $\{\varepsilon_i\}$ are iid $n(0, \tau)$. In the hypothetical and extreme case in which you knew β you could, when the data are observed, calculate ε as $y - X\beta$ and study this vector's properties to see whether they do indeed look like a realization of iid $n(0, \tau)$ variates as you had supposed. There is no need for simulation in this case. But in the practical case in which you don't know β you can't calculate ε but you can compute its posterior probability distribution, and under a standard diffuse prior this distribution has mean $e = y - Xb$, the least squares residual vector. So to see whether ε is autocorrelated or heteroscedastic you can compute various statistics applied to the ls residuals. The point of sampling from the posterior distribution of, say, dw, is to add to the single number calculated from e a measure of the (posterior) uncertainty surrounding that number that arises from the fact that we do not know β. The value of these statistics, such as dw, is that they reveal, often quite accurately, the properties of the vector $\varepsilon_1, \ldots, \varepsilon_n$.*

Mean independence

The belief that $E(X'\varepsilon) = 0$ is generally viewed as an uncheckable belief. In what sense is this so? If we again take an extreme position and suppose that we knew β, then, as we argued in the last paragraph, we could compute ε and measure the value of the vector $X'\varepsilon$ and ask whether that value is or is not consistent with our prior belief that it could be expected to be zero. So in this case the hypothesis of mean independence *is* checkable. On the other hand, under a diffuse prior for β we cannot deduce ε, we can only make inferences about it. We can compute the expected value of ε, namely the residual vector e, and then we can compute the posterior expectation of $X'\varepsilon$, namely $E(X'\varepsilon|y, X) = X'E(\varepsilon|y, X) = X'e$ but this is zero identically as we showed – the covariates are orthogonal to the least squares residual. This implies that any test statistic using the posterior distribution will always be centered at zero regardless of the actual value of $X'\varepsilon$. So under a uniform prior for β (and the hypotheses of the normal linear model) mean independence is *un*checkable – your test statistic will always be centered on zero. For intermediate cases, with, for example, informative but not dogmatic priors for β the hypothesis of mean independence *is* checkable, but how persuasive others will will find the results of such a check depends upon how persuaded they are about your β prior.

The last few sections have dealt with a Bayesian version of what is traditionally called residual analysis in which the econometrican is encouraged to pore over the evidence to look for signs of serious failure in the dogmatic features of his prior beliefs. But given existing computer power many modern workers prefer to formulate models in a way that minimizes the number of dogmatic beliefs that have to be held. The multinomial model discussed earlier was an example of trying to rely only on a dogmatic belief in mean independence and very little more.

3.6   EXTENDING THE NORMAL LINEAR MODEL

In critically assessing a regression calculation you will have to assess all the dogmatic assumptions made in your model. These include not only hypotheses about the error distribution but also, and arguably more importantly, decisions that you have made about the covariates. In this section we shall first discuss covariate choice in the context of the gasoline demand model. Then we shall consider the more statistical topic of generalizing the model for the error distribution.

3.6.1   *Criticizing the gasoline model*

Our standing "real" illustration in this chapter has been the model relating household gas consumption to prices and income using the log linear form

$$gas = \beta_0 + \beta_1 price + \beta_2 income + \varepsilon. \tag{3.32}$$

Regardless of your beliefs about the distribution of ε, this is a very naive model. It ultimately derives from a consideration of the consumption choices of a rational individual, with given preferences, facing given prices and constrained by a given income. In this theory one can imagine varying price and income and tracing out the consequential variations in gasoline consumption. The coefficients β_1 and β_2 are supposed to tell us about these comparative static effects. Some of the more obvious criticisms of our econometric calculation are:

(1) The theory refers to individuals but the data refer to households.
(2) Gasoline consumption is a derived demand. The ultimate service that provides utility is transportation.
(3) Demand for transportation must vary over households, times of year, location and the prices and availability of alternative modes of transport.

Much of this line of criticism accuses the model of neglecting additional sources of variability across households, or rather sweeping these sources into the error term, ε. (These sources of variation do not exist in the economic model in which consumer tastes were taken as given and constant over comparative static calculations.) One could counter this criticism by remarking that "whatever factors affecting gasoline demand are hidden in the error term, I have assumed they are such that $E(X'\varepsilon)$ = 0 which here means that the total effect of these factors is uncorrelated with both log *price* and log *income*." So the criticism amounts to asserting that there is little a priori reason to believe that omitted covariates *are* uncorrelated with price and income. The best way of reacting to this criticism is to take whatever additional covariates are present in your data file and to see whether indeed they *are* correlated with price and income. An obvious way to do this is to fit the model (3.32) to your data; compute the ls residual vector e; then see if e is correlated with the omitted covariate. This is similar to using residuals to check for heteroscedasticity or autocorrelation. An alternative procedure is to add those omitted covariates to the model. In effect, this is to pull them out of the error term. This is the recommended procedure and here is how it might work with the gasoline model.

When you include additional covariates representing factors that have been assumed constant in the theory these covariates are called **controls**. A reason for this terminology can be seen by imagining a hypothetical experiment in which a scientist is able to confront individuals with alternative gas prices and income and then watch how their demand for gasoline changes. In order to interpret their reactions as being due to the price and income variations he must make certain that nothing else changes – control the laboratory environment – for only in this case can he be certain that changes in demand are solely attributable to price and income changes. This is a hypothetical *controlled experiment*. Addition of covariates is meant to have an effect analogous to the control exercised by our hypothetical experimenter.[27] The way this works is as follows. Suppose your model is $y = \beta x + \varepsilon$ and you add a new variable z as a control, giving the new model $y = \beta x + \gamma z + \varepsilon'$; then one could, if sufficient agents have the same value of z, imagine regressing y on x within each stratum defined by z. But within such strata z *is* constant so it is, in effect, controlled, even if there was no human experimenter doing that controlling.

----

27 For more on experimentation and control see chapter 6.

EXAMPLE 3.12 *EXTENDING THE GASOLINE MODEL: ADDITIVE DUMMY COVARIATES*

There are many additional covariates in the gasoline data file and many of these refer to factors that seem likely to be associated with variations in the demand for transportation. We shall illustrate model extension by considering a few cases. Gasoline demand is likely to be affected by whether the household is located in an urban or a rural district. One way of accounting for this is by defining an additional, dummy, covariate, u (for urban), that takes the value one if the household is in an urban area and zero otherwise.[28] The model then becomes

$$gas = \beta_0 + \beta_1 price + \beta_2 income + \beta_3 u + \varepsilon.$$

If we treat this as a normal linear model with diffuse prior we find the least squares result to be

$$gas = 2.27(0.16) - 0.49(0.07)price + 0.23(0.02)income - 0.22(0.02)u,$$
$$gas = 2.68(0.16) - 0.47(0.07)price + 0.20(0.02)income$$

where we have placed the results from our previous model in the second row for comparison. We see that the coefficient β_3 is located many (posterior) standard deviations from zero, so we conclude that location does affect gasoline consumption with urban households consuming less gas, other things being equal, than rural ones. But more importantly we see that although there is little sensitivity of the price elasticity to the prior that dogmatically excluded u from the model, the inference about the income elasticity was somewhat sensitive to this exclusion. Allowing for u has changed our posterior opinion about the income elasticity and so the earlier inference was somewhat sensitive to the prior.

We could perform a formal comparison of the two models by the methods described in chapter 2 but these would, in the present case, all be equivalent to seeing whether β_3 was well removed from zero, which it is. Zero is not a credible value for β_3, at least under normal linear model assumptions with a diffuse prior.

S commands

Additive dummy covariates can be conveniently included in a model in the following way. If your data file contains a variable coded, say 1 if the household is urban and 2 if the household is rural, and this variable is denoted by UR then the S command

```
lm(lgascon ~price + income + factor(UR))
```

28 An alternative way would have been to define two new dummy covariates of which the first is u and the second is, say, r taking the value one if the household is in a rural area and zero otherwise. If you take this course you must suppress the dummy intercept covariate since otherwise the columns of X would be linearly dependent and the matrix $X'X$ singular.

will create and add to the model a single scalar dummy covariate with the value one if UR = 1 and zero if UR = 2, that is, it will create u. The same is true if UR is a variable with any finite number of levels – if UR has 16 levels then 15 new dummy covariates will be added to the model.

EXAMPLE 3.13 *EXTENDING THE GASOLINE MODEL: MULTIPLICATIVE DUMMY COVARIATES*

Instead of adding the new dummy covariate to the model we could enter it multiplicatively as, say,

$$gas = \beta_0 + \beta_1 price + \beta_2 income + \beta_3(u*income) + \varepsilon \qquad (3.33)$$

or both additively and multiplicatively as

$$gas = \beta_0 + \beta_1 price + \beta_2 income + \beta_3(u*income) + \beta_4 u + \varepsilon. \qquad (3.34)$$

What is the interpretation of such extended models? In (3.33) the model for urban areas has mean equal to

$$E(gas|urban) = \beta_0 + \beta_1 price + (\beta_2 + \beta_3)income$$

while for rural areas it is

$$E(gas|rural) = \beta_0 + \beta_1 price + \beta_2 income$$

so the effect of introducing an urban dummy covariate multiplicatively is to permit the income elasticity of demand to vary between urban and rural areas. But the level of the regression, as measured by the intercept, and the price elasticity are constrained to be the same in both urban and rural areas. In the more general specification (3.34), both the income elasticity and the level of the regression are allowed to change between town and country but, again, the price elasticity is constrained to be the same. To see what happens with our data let us fit the model (3.34) and compare it to the original model that contained only an additive urban/rural effect.

$$gas = 2.34(0.19) - 0.48(0.07)price + 0.22(0.02)income$$
$$- 0.00(0.35)u - 0.02(0.03)(u*income) \qquad (3.35)$$

$$gas = 2.27(0.16) - 0.49(0.07)price + 0.23(0.02)income$$
$$- 0.22(0.02)u \qquad (3.36)$$

It can be seen from the coefficient of u*income that allowing for an income elasticity that changes between urban and rural areas is probably unnecessary. This can be seen immediately from the fact that this coefficient is within a posterior *standard deviation of zero so that β_3 is centered close to zero. Note also that the coefficients of income and price scarcely change with this addition. On the other hand, the coefficient of u falls to zero and looking at the coefficients of u and (u*income) separately even suggests that u has no role to play in this model! This seems puzzling. So clearly we need to be a bit more clear-headed about comparing these two models. A good way to do this is to use Bayes' theorem. The way to do this is to assign prior probabilities to the two models whose estimates are given in (3.35) and (3.36) and then to compute their posterior probabilities, or rather the ratio of posterior probabilities. In other words we should calculate a Bayes factor in favor of or against one of the two models. We shall describe and illustrate Bayes factors in this model in section 3.6.3.*

There is another dogmatic belief contained within the original gasoline model and this is that the income elasticity of demand is independent of the level of income. This implies that both rich and poor households respond in the same proportionate way to an increase in income. There are many ways to relax this belief.

EXAMPLE 3.14   *EXTENDING THE GASOLINE MODEL: FLEXIBLE FUNCTIONAL FORMS*   *One method of being more flexible about the way income affects gasoline demand is to add squared (and possibly higher order) powers of income to the model. For example if we write*

$$gas = \beta_0 + \beta_1 price + \beta_2 income + \beta_3 income^2 + \varepsilon$$

then the income elasticity of demand found by differentiating this relation is $\beta_2 + 2\beta_3 income$, which varies with income. This is called fitting a polynomial. Here is an example in which we fit a quadratic in income together with price and the urban/rural dummy.

$$gas = -17.11(3.53) - 0.48(0.07)price + 3.90(0.66)income$$
$$- 0.17(0.03)income^2 - 0.22(0.02)u$$
$$gas = 2.49(0.16) - 0.49(0.07)price + 0.23(0.02)income - 0.22(0.02)u$$

The additional term in income squared has a coefficient that is about five standard deviations from zero and so almost certainly negative, the income effect is clearly non-linear and the income elasticity of demand is not constant. In fact, from these estimates, it behaves like $3.90 - 0.34*income$ which is decreasing – people with higher income have gas demands that are less responsive to income variations.

Fitting a polynomial in income is still fairly inflexible – maybe the income effect is not at all like a polynomial in shape. A totally flexible method is to treat income as a factor, just as we did with the urban–rural covariate. This allows the regression *to shift up or down at each particular level of income but imposes no restriction at all on the way the line shifts. In this sense it is "non-parametric."[29] The whole model, containing both a non-parametric and a parametric component, is called, of course, semiparametric. If we inspect the income data we find that it takes only nine distinct values, ranging from $20,000 to $100,000 per year, so it has been very coarsely observed and is presumably subject to considerable measurement error (an issue we shall not consider here). So we can enter income non-parametrically by, say,*

$$gas = \beta_0 + \beta_1 price + \beta_2 factor(income) + \beta_3 u + \varepsilon.$$

This produces price and urban coefficients which are essentially unchanged from previous calculations and a set of eight $(9 - 1)$ income coefficients. It is most convenient to display these graphically, as in figure 3.12. If the income elasticity of demand is constant these points should lie on a straight line; if the effect of income on demand is quadratic these points should lie on such a curve. But they don't, the income elasticity of demand seems to fall with income at high income levels but not quadratically as the parametric model supposed.

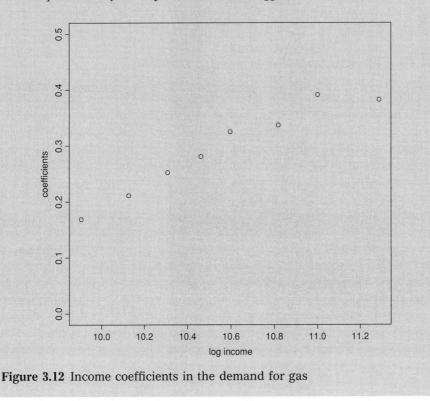

Figure 3.12 Income coefficients in the demand for gas

29   In practice almost all non-parametric methods used in econometrics are distinguished from regular methods only in that they contain more parameters.

Treatment of covariate effects as factors will typically be possible with many, perhaps most, cross-sectional data sets where large sample sizes permit the use of models that are not tied to simple functional forms, and in practice all covariates take only a finite number of distinct values. A serious "non-parametric" form for a covariate effect would require thought about the prior on the coefficients. The analysis above assumed that the eight coefficients describing the effects on demand of different levels of income were independent and uniform on the real line. Typically, however, it would be reasonable to think of these coefficients as similar and thus use an exchangeable, hierarchical prior. One might want to go further and assume that the income coefficients lie on some smooth curve, for example a curve made up of connected low order polynomials, which is called a spline. We shall say more about this in section 3.6.3.

> **Warning**   *These analyses of the gasoline data do not in any sense represent serious pieces of econometrics. We are merely using these data to illustrate some of the many ways the model might be extended.*

3.6.2   *Generalizing the error distribution*

We can generalize the model by relaxing the assumption that the covariance matrix of ε, conditional on a scalar τ, is τI_n. This belief meant that, for you, the errors are equally uncertain and that your belief about one error is independent of your belief about any other. So let us replace the previous belief represented by τI_n with the general statement that ε is multivariate normal with covariance matrix $\tau \Lambda$, where Λ is an $n \times n$ symmetric positive definite matrix. Thus the model is

$$y = X\beta + \varepsilon, \quad \varepsilon | X, \Lambda, \tau, \beta \sim n(0, \tau \Lambda). \tag{3.37}$$

This generalized model will be heteroscedastic if the elements of the principal diagonal of Λ vary, and it will show conditional dependence if its off-diagonal elements are not zero. To make inferences about β we shall, of course, have to construct prior beliefs about all the parameters, which are now β, τ and Λ. We shall shortly specify particular alternative beliefs about Λ, but first we note a simple fact about this generalized normal linear model. This fact is that if we knew the matrix Λ a simple transformation reduces the inferential problem to the normal linear model whose solution we have already described.

If we premultiply (3.37) by the square root of Λ, denoted by $\Lambda^{1/2}$, we get

$$\Lambda^{1/2}y = \Lambda^{1/2}X\beta + \Lambda^{1/2}\varepsilon$$
$$\text{or} \quad y^* = X^*\beta + \varepsilon^*.$$

But the conditional covariance matrix of ε^* is

$$\begin{aligned}
E(\varepsilon^*\varepsilon^{*\prime}) &= \Lambda^{1/2}E(\varepsilon\varepsilon')\Lambda^{1/2} = (1/\tau)\Lambda^{1/2}\Lambda^{-1}\Lambda^{1/2} \\
&= (1/\tau)\Lambda^{1/2}\Lambda^{-1/2}\Lambda^{-1/2}\Lambda^{1/2} \\
&= (1/\tau)I_n.
\end{aligned}$$

Since ε^*, being a linear function of a normal variate, is itself normal, we see that y^*, X^* satisfy a standard linear model.

THEOREM 3.5   *For given Λ the transformed data $y^* = \Lambda^{1/2}y$ and $X^* = \Lambda^{1/2}X$ satisfy a standard normal linear model, $y^* = X^*\beta + \varepsilon^*$, $\varepsilon^*|X, \Lambda, \beta, \tau \sim n(0, \tau I_n)$.*

It follows immediately from (3.20) and the results of section 3.3 that, under a uniform prior for β and $\log \tau$ the conditional posterior density $p(\beta|\tau, \Lambda, data)$ is normal with mean equal to X^*b^* where b^* is the least squares regression coefficient of y^* on X^*, namely

$$\begin{aligned}
b^* &= (X^{*\prime}X^*)^{-1}X^{*\prime}y^* = (X'\Lambda^{1/2}\Lambda^{1/2}X)^{-1}X'\Lambda^{1/2}\Lambda^{1/2}y \\
&= (X'\Lambda X)^{-1}X'\Lambda y,
\end{aligned}$$

and precision matrix

$$P = \tau(X'\Lambda^{1/2}\Lambda^{1/2}X) = \tau(X'\Lambda X).$$

The vector b^* is known as the **generalized least squares** estimate. It reduces to ordinary least squares when Λ is the identity matrix. Similarly it follows from standard normal linear model results that the marginal posterior density of τ, given Λ, is

$$\begin{aligned}
&\tau|\Lambda, data = gamma(v/2, e^{*\prime}e^*/2), \\
&\text{where}\quad e^* = y^* - X^*b^*.
\end{aligned}$$

This fact is of theoretical and possibly computational interest but we wouldn't want in general to do inference conditional on Λ. We would instead want to do inference marginal with respect to Λ and this requires us to adopt some parametrization of this matrix. Here are some possibilities.

Heteroscedasticity

To allow for varying precisions associated with different elements of ε consider the generalization described above in which $p(\varepsilon|X, \tau, \lambda) = n(0, \tau\Lambda)$ where Λ is now a *diagonal* matrix with elements $\lambda = (\lambda_1, \lambda_2, ..., \lambda_n)$ so that each ε is allowed to have its own precision. Note that τ is a scalar. The transformation from y to $y^* = \Lambda^{1/2}y$ in scalar form is

$$y^* = \begin{bmatrix} \lambda_1^{1/2} y_1 \\ \lambda_2^{1/2} y_2 \\ . \\ . \\ . \\ \lambda_n^{1/2} y_n \end{bmatrix}$$

since $\Lambda^{1/2}$ is a diagonal matrix with typical element $\lambda^{1/2}$. This transformation is referred to as doing **weighted least squares** since the transformation of multiplying the dependent variable and the covariate matrix by $\Lambda^{1/2}$ amounts to weighting each observation according to the square root of its precision. This means that observations which are relatively precise receive high weight and those with imprecise errors get low weight in forming the posterior distribution of β and τ. The generalized least squares based on this model is then a weighted least squares estimator.

The most usual situation in which it is reasonable to assign a dogmatic prior to Λ, that is to take Λ as known, is where the y_i are averages of differing numbers of observations. For example, y_1 might be the average wage in a small village and y_2 the average wage in a larger village. Since averages have precisions proportional to the number of observations on which they are based, it would be reasonable to take the $\{\lambda_i\}$ equal to the numbers of workers in each village.

The more common case is where the $\{\lambda_i\}$ are not known but exchangeable and so are assigned a proper prior distribution conditional on a **hyperparameter**. The standard version of such a **hierarchical model** would be to have the $\{\lambda_i\}$ be independently gamma distributed with mean one.[30] Thus $p(\lambda_i) \propto \lambda_i^{v/2-1} e^{-v\lambda_i/2}$, where v, the scalar hyperparameter, controls the precision of the prior. Reference to the appendix to chapter 1 shows that the coefficient of variation of this distribution is $\sqrt{(2/v)}$, so large values of v correspond to precise priors and the view that λ_i is probably quite close to one and imply nearly homoscedastic errors, while small values convey the view that errors may well be quite variable or heteroscedastic. For this exposition we shall take v as a number assigned by the econometrician, though it is possible to assign it a prior distribution and make posterior inferences about it.

To understand how this structure compares with the normal linear model let us look at the marginal distribution of ε_i. Since $\varepsilon_i | X, \beta, \tau, \lambda_i = n(0, \tau\lambda_i)$, multiplying by $p(\lambda_i)$ and integrating out λ_i gives the density of ε_i given only the covariates and τ. This is

$$p(\varepsilon_i | X, \beta, \tau) \propto \int_0^\infty \tau^{1/2} \lambda^{1/2} \exp\{-\tau\lambda\varepsilon_i^2/2\} \lambda^{v/2-1} e^{-v\lambda/2} \, d\lambda,$$

$$\propto \int_0^\infty \lambda^{(v+1)/2-1} \exp\{-(\lambda/2)(v + \tau\varepsilon_i^2)\} \, d\lambda,$$

$$\propto \left(1 + \frac{\tau\varepsilon_i^2}{v}\right)^{-(v+1)/2},$$

---

30   Any non-unit mean would be absorbed into τ.

and comparison with (3.55) shows this is a t distribution with mean zero, scale τ and degrees of freedom equal to v. Thus we have produced a linear model with errors that are distributed not normally but as Student's t. When the degrees of freedom, that is v, become large the t distribution converges to normality so this is a genuine generalization of the normal linear model. It is sometimes called the **robust linear model**, though a better name is the **Student linear model**. The appearance of t errors when you allow for heteroscedasticity is consistent with our earlier finding, using the gasoline data, that the residuals from that model looked rather like independent draws from a t distribution with low degrees of freedom.

With this model you might explore how posterior inferences about β or interesting functions of this vector change by repeating the calculation for different values of v. Choosing v small, say 3 or 4, so the prior density of the errors approaches the Cauchy form, would be a way of producing very conservative – heteroscedasticity robust – estimates of β and its precision. By choosing v large, say 15 or more, you essentially revert to the standard normal linear model – least squares – estimates and their standard errors. BUGS code to sample the joint posterior distribution of β and τ is given in appendix 3.

EXAMPLE 3.15   *ROBUST LINEAR REGRESSION*

We use simulated heteroscedastic data with $n = 100$, two real regressors and an intercept, so $k = 3$ and errors are generated as normal with mean zero and precisions varying according to a gamma distribution with parameters 3 and 1. This means the error precisions have coefficient of variation $1/\sqrt{3} = 0.577$ so they are moderately heteroscedastic. We first ran the model with $v = 4$ which is a very thick-tailed distribution and then we re-ran the analysis with $v = 20$ and we shall compare the results for β_2, the coefficient of the second real regressor whose "true" value, used in generating the data, was -1. The calculations are based on 3,000 simulations of the posterior distribution and a summary of the results is given in the table.

	Mean	*Standard deviation*	*Inter-quartile range*
$v = 4$	-0.966	0.071	0.491
$v = 20$	-0.988	0.070	0.482

The least squares estimate of β_2 is -0.997 with a posterior standard error under homoscedastity of 0.072. There is very little difference between the two distributions, indicating that for these data inference about β_2 is rather insensitive to heteroscedasticity.

Heteroscedasticity in time series data

While a prior in which the precisions of different observations vary independently of each other, as in the notion that they look like independent realizations of a gamma variate, has some plausibility for cross-section data, independence is less attractive for time series. A simple model to capture the idea of correlated error precisions is to suppose that

$$\log \tau_t = \alpha_0 + \alpha_1 \log \tau_{t-1} + u_t, \quad \{u_t\} \sim n(0, \pi), \quad \text{for } t = 2, 3, ..., T. \quad (3.38)$$

This is a first order autoregression for the log precisions. If α_1 is positive then successive precisions tend to be similar to each other which evidence suggests is likely to characterize particularly financial time series. (Note that a normal linear autoregressive model for τ as opposed to $\log \tau$ would not be a good idea because, of course, τ is strictly positive.) This version of heteroscedasticity, (3.38), is called a stochastic volatility model and such models are further explored in chapter 9.

Autocorrelation

When the linear model with strictly exogenous covariates is applied to time series data it is reasonable to believe the equation errors, now ε_t, say, tend to be more similar the closer they are in time, so in such applications it is important both to test for error autocorrelation and to allow for it in making inferences about β. So consider again the linear model

$$y_t = x_t \beta + \varepsilon_t, \quad t = 1, 2, ..., T. \quad (3.39)$$

Here x_t is the t'th row of the $T \times k$ matrix X and the observation subscript is written as t, not i, to remind ourselves that we are dealing with time series data. We continue to suppose that $\{x_t, \varepsilon_t\}$ are independent so we have strict exogeneity, but now we allow the successive parameters to be autocorrelated. This, of course, is your prior belief and to choose a specific form for this belief suppose that

$$\varepsilon_t = \rho \varepsilon_{t-1} + u_t, \quad \{u_t\} \sim \text{iid } n(0, \tau) \quad -1 < \rho < 1. \quad (3.40)$$

This is a first order autoregression with the condition added that ρ lies between minus one and one which ensures that the process is stationary. The error covariance matrix implied by this formulation takes the form

$$\Lambda = \begin{bmatrix} 1 & \rho & \cdots & \rho^{T-1} \\ \rho & 1 & \cdots & \rho^{T-2} \\ \vdots & \vdots & \ddots & \vdots \\ \rho^{T-1} & \rho^{T-2} & \cdots & 1 \end{bmatrix}$$

assuming the process $\{\varepsilon_t\}$ is remote from its starting point.

In order to sample the posterior density of β, ρ and τ we need the likelihood and prior, of course. To derive the likelihood note first that if we take (3.39) and subtract from it ρ times the corresponding equation for period $t - 1$ we get

$$y_t - \rho y_{t-1} = x_t \beta - x_{t-1} \rho \beta + u_t, \quad \text{for } t = 2, 3, \ldots, T.$$

This shows that, given y_{t-1}, ρ, β, τ, y_t is distributed normally with mean $\rho y_{t-1} + x_t \beta - x_{t-1} \rho \beta$ and precision τ,

$$y_t | y_{t-1} \sim n(\rho y_{t-1} + x_t \beta - x_{t-1} \rho \beta, \tau), \quad \text{for } t = 2, 3, \ldots, T. \tag{3.41}$$

The distribution of the initial observation follows from the observation that for a stationary process like (3.40) the variance of ε_t is $\sigma^2/(1 - \rho^2)$ and so the precision is $\tau(1 - \rho^2)$.[31] Thus

$$y_1 \sim n(x_1 \beta, \tau(1 - \rho^2)). \tag{3.42}$$

Possible reasonably vague priors might be low precision normal densities for β; low precision gamma for τ; and a uniform density for ρ on the interval, say, -0.999 to 0.999 – to avoid division by zero when we compute $1/(1 - \rho^2)$.

EXAMPLE 3.16 *BUGS code to implement this likelihood and prior when* $x_t \beta = \beta_0 + \beta_1 x_t$, *might be*

```
model{
for(i in 2:n){
y[i]~dnorm(mu[i],tau)
mu[i]  <-  rho*y[i-1]+b0*(1-rho)+b1*x[i]-rho*b1*x[i-1]
}
y[1]~dnorm(mu1,tau1)
mu1<-b0+b1*x[1]
tau1<-tau*(1-rho*rho)
b0~dnorm(0,0.0001)
b1~dnorm(0,0.0001)
tau~dgamma(1.0E-3,1.0E-3)
rho~dunif(-.999,.999)
}
```

Notice that the code is a very direct translation of the specification given in (3.41) and (3.42). Lines 3 and 4 specify that Y is normally distributed with mean depending on lagged Y and current and lagged X. Lines 6 and 7 give the stationary distribution for the initial observation. And the remaining code specifies

---

31 See chapter 4.

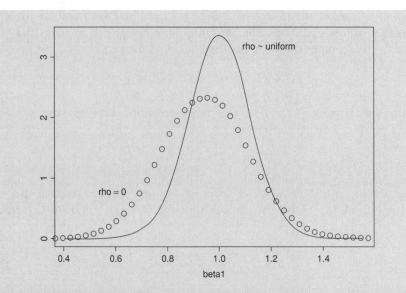

Figure 3.13 Regression with error autocorrelation

priors which can, of course, be changed as you wish. We ran this program for a model in which $\beta_0 = 0$, $\beta_1 = 1$, $\tau = 1$ and $\rho = 0.5$. For comparison we ran a regression, using the same data, with the errors believed to be uncorrelated so the prior on ρ was set dogmatically as $\rho = 0$. The results for β_1 are shown in the table and figure 3.13.

	Slope (ρ uniform)	*Slope ($\rho = 0$)*
Mean	1.001	0.947
Standard deviation	0.112	0.161

We see that for these fifty observations the results for the slope coefficient, β_1, are sensitive to the prior on ρ. When the prior fails to recognize possible correlation in the errors the posterior density of β_1 is both more dispersed and less accurately centered than with a prior that allows for error autocorrelation. These results suggest that with time series data it would be wise to allow for potential error auto-correlation and to use a prior that doesn't dogmatically set $\rho = 0$.

This approach also provides a test for error autocorrelation by looking at the posterior density for ρ which is shown in figure 3.14 with the value used in generating the data indicated by a vertical line.

It is clear from this graph that the errors are positively autocorrelated.

This approach may be generalized by using a higher order autoregressive model for the errors, for example

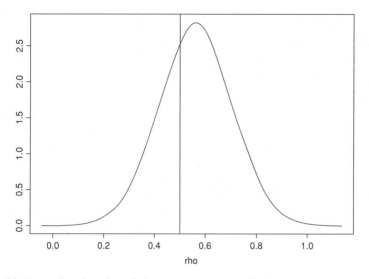

Figure 3.14 Posterior density of the error autocorrelation

$$\varepsilon_t = \phi_1 \varepsilon_{t-1} + \dots + \phi_p \varepsilon_{t-p} + u_t \quad \text{for } t = p + 1, p + 2, \dots, T, \qquad (3.43)$$

where the $\{u_t\}$ are independent $n(0, \tau)$ variates conditional on $\varepsilon_{t-1}, \varepsilon_{t-2}, \dots, \varepsilon_{t-p}$. This is a p'th order autoregressive model. It is also possible to avoid the hypothesis of stationarity by writing the likelihood only for the distribution of y for $t = 2, 3, \dots,$ T conditional on the initial value y_1. To implement this you would simply delete the code referring to `y[1]`, `tau1` and `mu1`. In this approach it is straightforward to allow for p'th order error autocorrelation by conditioning on the first p values of the y series.

Semiparametric regression

In section 3.6.1 we introduced factors into the gasoline model which allowed the coefficient on income to vary with the level of income, so there were as many regression coefficients estimated as the number of distinct income values in the data. This generalization amounts to semiparametric regression in that it imposes no restrictions on the income part of the regression function. The prior on the coefficients of the income factor made them independently uniform. We noted that we could have imposed further structure on them but that this was scarcely necessary given the large number of observations at almost all distinct values of income. Sometimes, however, the situation arises in which one has very few, perhaps only one observation at the relevant x values, and in this case a structured prior is essential. Consider a regression model of the form

$$y_i = x_i \beta + s(z_i) + \varepsilon_i, \quad i = 1, 2, \dots, n. \qquad (3.44)$$

This is the standard normal regression model, assuming the $\{\varepsilon_i\}$ are iid normal, except that the effect of the variable z is not of the conventional form, say γz_i, but written in a slightly mysterious way as $s(z)$. This formulation is intended to express the idea that variations in z have an effect on the mean of y but that the way in which this effect operates is unknown and must be determined in the light of the evidence. A model of this type is sometimes called semiparametric although perhaps a more explicit name is **partially linear**. The word semiparametric is intended to capture the idea that part of the model involves not a finite collection of unknown parameters but rather an unknown function. It includes as a special case the fully linear model if $s(z_i)$ takes the form $\alpha + \gamma z_i$ but here we do not presume this to be so. An example might be time series data in which the covariate z is time and $s(z)$ represents potential, possibly seasonal, variations in the mean value of y.

If we write down the likelihood for this model under the belief that the $\{\varepsilon_i\}$, for the sake of argument, are iid $n(0, \tau)$ then it will look like

$$\ell(\beta, \tau, s) \propto \tau^{n/2} \exp\{-(\tau/2)\textstyle\sum_{i=1}^{n}(y_i - x_i\beta - s_i)^2\}$$

where

$$s_i = s(z_i), \quad i = 1, 2, ..., n.$$

So we see that we have written down a model that, far from being non-parametric, involves $n + k + 1$ parameters composed of the n values $\{s_i\}$, (assuming the $\{z_i\}$ are all distinct), the k elements of β and τ. Since there are more parameters than observations these parameters are not identifiable from the likelihood and to proceed we must supply an informative prior.

The usual way of supplying an informative prior is to suppose that the function $s(.)$ is, in some sense, smooth. You could implement this idea of smoothness in many ways. For example you could suppose that $s(.)$ is a polynomial, but that would just return us to the linear model setup with covariates z, z^2, z^3, etc. Or you could suppose that $s(.)$ is piecewise polynomial in that it looks like a collection of, say, quadratic or cubic curves connected at each end in such a way that the first and maybe second derivatives at each junction of the curve exist. Such methods are called **fitting polynomial splines** and they can be an effective way of learning about an unknown component of a regression function. When you take the points $\{s_i\}$ to lie on a smooth curve then you can extrapolate from the values of the function at the points $\{z_i\}$ to its values at all other points on the z axis.

Bayesian ways of implementing these regression smooths exist but given the present state of software it is currently simpler to implement frequentist software that has been available in R and S for some years. This is represented by the function gam() which stands for **generalized additive model** and which fits a regression model of the form

$$y = s_1(x_1) + s_2(x_2) + ... + s_k(x_k) + \varepsilon. \tag{3.45}$$

Here each $s(.)$ is a smooth, possibly piecewise cubic, function of its argument. Any of the regression terms on the right hand side can be specified parametrically as, say, $\beta_k x_k$ and a model fitted that includes some parametric and some non-parametric terms like (3.44). Here is an example.

EXAMPLE 3.17 *A SMOOTH PRICE EFFECT*

Take the gasoline demand model and data and specify the demand function as

$$gas = s(price) + \beta_2 income + \varepsilon.$$

This relaxes the assumption that the marginal effect of price is constant as $\beta_1 price$ and replaces it with the view that it is some smooth function. The R commands to implement this model are[32]

```
smooth <- gam(gas ~ s(price) + income) #s stands for "smooth"
summary(smooth)
plot(smooth)
```

Figure 3.15 shows an aspect of the output of these commands. It shows the estimated function $s(price)$ together with a 95% (frequentist) confidence band around it. The shaded band at the foot of the graph shows the density of data points associated with the various levels of price, darker shading indicating more data and hence narrower confidence bands. The parametric linear model gave the price effect as $-0.47(0.07)price$ which is, of course, downward sloping, but with a constant slope; the gam effect is also decreasing but with a mildly non-constant slope which suggests relatively inelastic demand over most prices but some more elasticity at relatively high and low prices. If the parametric model had been superimposed on this graph it would have shown a downward sloping straight line with a slope not far from that of the middle part of graph where most of the data lie. Many variants on this approach to modeling are explained in the gam help file. For instance it is possible to fit a model permitting interaction between price and income of the form

$$gas = s(price, income) + \varepsilon,$$

which allows the price elasticity to depend on income and conversely.

Semi- and non-parametric regression modeling tends to move us away from the strict structural approach to econometric modeling in the direction of data exploration and description. We shall leave the subject to the exercises at the end of the chapter and turn to issues of model choice.

---

32 From within an *R* session, to make the gam function available you will need to issue the command `library(mgcv)`.

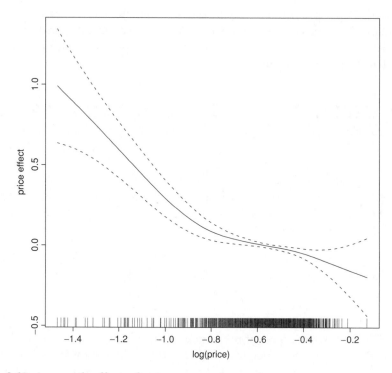

Figure 3.15 A smooth effect of price on gas demand

3.6.3   *Model choice*

As soon as you extend or vary the model from which you began you face the problem of model choice. The Bayesian approach, described in section 2.6, is conceptually straightforward. To compare a set of models we must compare the probabilities they assign to the data. If one model assigns the data much higher probability than all the others, and if we had to choose one model, we would choose that one, at least if all models seemed equally probable a priori. If you don't have to choose a single model then you can select a mixture of all models considered, each weighted by their posterior probabilities. In particular, if m indexes models, y are the data, and θ_m is the parameter of model m, then the probability of the data given model m is $p(y|m) = \int p(y|, \theta_m, m)p(\theta_m, m)\,d\theta_m$. When comparing two models labeled 1 and 2 the Bayes factor in favor of model 1 is

$$B_{12} = \frac{p(y|1)}{p(y|2)}$$

and the posterior odds on model 1 is equal to the Bayes factor times the prior odds. Under certain "large sample" circumstances the posterior odds in favor of model 1 compared to model 2 can be approximated by the Bayesian information criterion, BIC, which as we showed in chapter 2 is

$$BIC = \frac{\ell(\hat{\theta}_1; y)}{\ell(\hat{\theta}_2; y)} n^{(k_2 - k_1)/2}$$

where k_1 and k_2 are the numbers of parameters in the two models. If we now refer back to (3.21), which gave the value of the maximized log likelihood for the normal linear model, we see that the BIC becomes

$$BIC = \left(\frac{e_2' e_2}{e_1' e_1} \right)^{n/2} n^{(k_2 - k_1)/2}.$$

This depends on the two residual sums of squares, the number of parameters in each model, and the sample size, n.

It is enlightening to look at some hypothetical cases.

- Suppose that two models gave identical residual sums of squares, then if the second had more parameters than the first, $k_2 > k_1$, the BIC would exceed one and favor the first, more parsimonious model. The strength of this effect would be larger the larger the sample size.
- If two models involve the same number of parameters, the one with the smaller residual sum of squares – the better fitting model – would be favored. This effect is stronger (because of the power $n/2$) the larger is the sample size. Note that because the squared multiple correlation coefficient is the ratio of the residual mean square to the variance of y the BIC can be written as

$$BIC = \left(\frac{1 - R_2^2}{1 - R_1^2} \right)^{n/2} n^{(k_2 - k_1)/2}.$$

So if model 1 had the larger R^2 it would be favored provided it did not have too many more parameters.

Here is an example of model choice using BIC.

EXAMPLE 3.18 *GASOLINE MODEL CHOICE*
Consider two models,

$$\text{model 1} \quad gas = \beta_0 + \beta_1 price + \beta_2 income + \beta_3 income^2 + \beta_4 u + \varepsilon_1$$
$$\text{model 2} \quad gas = \beta_0 + \beta_1 price + \beta_2 factor(income) + \beta_3 u + \varepsilon_2.$$

So we are comparing a model in which the income effect is constrained to be quadratic with one in which it can take any shape it likes. It seems appropriate to call this a comparison of a parameteric and a semiparametric model.

In model 1 the number of parameters is five betas and tau so $k_1 = 6$. In model 2 the number is three betas plus eight factor coefficients (corresponding to the nine income values) plus tau so $k_2 = 12$, twice as many parameters as model 1. The log of the BIC is

$$\log BIC = \frac{n}{2}(\log e_2' e_2 - \log e_1' e_1) + \frac{k_2 - k_1}{2} \log n.$$

Since $n = 6491$ the second term is $3 \times 8.77817 = 26.33$. The residual sums of squares are

$$e_1' e_1 = 2436.138$$
$$e_2' e_2 = 2433.823$$

so the introduction of the semiparametric model has reduced the residual sum of squares, but not by very much. The first term in $\log BIC$ is then $3245.5 \times (7.79817 - 7.7972) = -3.085$ which is negative but the whole of $\log BIC$ is

$$\log(BIC) = 23.25$$

and this implies a very large BIC, strongly favoring model 1, the model with a quadratic income effect as opposed to the semiparametric one.

EXAMPLE 3.19 *GASOLINE MODEL CHOICE AGAIN*   *In example 3.13 we looked at the whether the income elasticity of demand varied between urban and rural households. We did this by adding a covariate to the model that represented an interaction between the urban/rural dummy variable u and income. The estimated models were*

$$gas = 2.34(0.19) - 0.48(0.07)price + 0.22(0.02)income - 0.00(0.35)u$$
$$- 0.02(0.03)(u * income)$$
$$gas = 2.27(0.16) - 0.49(0.07)price + 0.23(0.02)income - 0.22(0.02)u.$$

The larger model has 6 coefficients and the smaller has 5 so the second term in the Bayes factor is

$$\frac{6 - 5}{2} \log(6491) = 4.389.$$

The model without interaction has a residual sum of squares of 2447.718 and when the interaction term is added the residual sum of squares falls only a little, to 2447.562. So the first term in log *BIC is*

$$\frac{n}{2} \log \left(\frac{2447.562}{2447.718} \right) = -0.207.$$

So the whole log *BIC in favour of the model without interactions – the simpler model – is*

$$\log BIC = -0.207 + 4.389 = 4.182$$

giving large sample posterior odds in favor of the simpler model of about 65, which is very strong evidence against adding the interaction term.

It will be noticed that in example 3.19 the model without the interaction term is nested in the model with it, in the sense that the former can be obtained from the latter by constraining one parameter – that of the interaction – to equal zero. Thus the smaller model is said to be **nested** in the larger. But in example 3.18 this is not so. This illustrates that nesting of models being compared is not necessary for construction of Bayes factors to discriminate between models.

Exact, as opposed to large sample, construction of Bayes factors requires that the user formulate proper prior distributions for the parameters of each model being compared. Default improper priors won't do, for reasons explained in chapter 2.

3.7 CONCLUSION AND SUMMARY OF THE ARGUMENT

This chapter has dealt with linear regression models in which the error terms are mean independent or distributed independently of the covariates. We began with a hierarchical model for the errors in which they were independently normally distributed with common precision, which is the assumption of homoscedasticity and absence of error autocorrelation, and showed some properties of the posterior distributions under alternative likelihoods and priors and how to sample these. We then digressed a little to consider a less structured, multinomial, approach to linear regression models. We then outlined and illustrated some simple tests for heteroscedasticity and error autocorrelation. We continued by extending the model to allow for more general functional forms both for the regression function and for the error distribution. For each model and test we illustrated the calculations and provided code with which they could be carried out.

Linear regression models can be generalized to the case in which an observation on y is a vector not a scalar. This leads to the consideration of **systems of linear regression equations**. The error terms in each of these equations may be believed to be correlated. But for most practitioners, most of the time, it is the single equation (with y_i scalar) that is required, so we shall omit this extension, though it is not difficult. Implementation in BUGS is straightforward.

An important generalization is to the case of **non-linear regression models** and this is the subject of chapter 5. In the next chapter we turn to a description of some of the main methods of computer simulation from probability distributions.

3.8   APPENDIX TO CHAPTER 3

3.8.1 Analytical results in the normal linear model

In this appendix we give derivations of the main analytical results for the normal linear model under a vague prior. The joint posterior density of β, τ was given in (3.10) which we reproduce here as

$$p(\beta,\ \tau | y,\ X) \propto \tau^{n/2-1} \exp\{-(\tau/2)(y - X\beta)'(y - X\beta)\}.$$

To find the marginals we need to integrate this expression with respect either to β or τ.

The first thing to do is to note that the sum of squares in the exponent, $(y - X\beta)'(y - X\beta)$, can be written in another way using the following useful general result, which we have already used several times, called **completing the square**.

DEFINITION 3.1   COMPLETING THE SQUARE

$$(y - X\beta)'A(y - X\beta) = (\beta - b)'X'AX(\beta - b) + (y - Xb)'A(y - Xb)$$
$$where\ b = (X'AX)^{-1}X'Ay$$

which is true as long as $X'AX$ is non-singular. The proof is by multiplying out the right hand side and checking that it equals the left hand side.

Applying this result to (3.10) with $A = I_n$ we get, as long as $X'X$ is positive definite, the following *alternative form* of the joint posterior distribution of β, τ:

$$p(\beta,\ \tau | y,\ X) \propto \tau^{n/2-1} \exp\{-(\tau/2)(\beta - b)'X'X(\beta - b)\} \times \exp\{-(\tau/2)e'e\},$$
$$\text{for } b = (X'X)^{-1}X'y \text{ and } e = y - Xb. \tag{3.46}$$

The k vector b is called the **ordinary least squares** estimate and it is by far the most common way of estimating the slopes and intercept of an assumed linear model.

Similarly, the n vector of deviations from the estimated line, $y - Xb$, is called the **residual vector** and denoted by e. It is quite a different object than ε the error vector in the linear model, although they are related and e does, in fact, provide the posterior expected value of ε in this model. Its sum of squares divided by the number of observations less the number of covariates is the **residual mean square** or **residual variance** and denoted by s^2.

$$s^2 = (y - Xb)'(y - Xb)/n = e'e/(n - k). \tag{3.47}$$

It is convenient to denote $n - k$ as v, known as the **degrees of freedom** of the model. Thus $s^2 = e'e/v$.

EXAMPLE 3.20 *NO COVARIATES* *In this case (3.46) reduces to*

$$p(\mu, \tau | y) \propto \tau^{(n/2)-1} \exp\{-(\tau/2)(\mu - \bar{y})^2\} \times \exp\{-(\tau/2)\Sigma_{i=1}^n (y_i - \bar{y})^2\},$$

with

$$b = (X'X)^{-1}X'y = \frac{1}{n}\Sigma_{i=1}^n y_i = \bar{y}; \quad e_i = y_i - \bar{y} \text{ and } e'e = \Sigma_{i=1}^n (y_i - \bar{y})^2 = vs^2.$$

So b is the sample mean and $e'e$ is $v (= n - 1)$ times the sample residual variance.

The marginal density of the precision

The τ marginal is most easily found from (3.46) noting that β enters this expression only in the second term, which looks like, and is, the kernel of a (multivariate) normal distribution with mean b and precision matrix $\tau X'X$. So carrying out the integration we find from the fact that

$$\int \exp\{-(\tau/2)(\beta - b)'X'X)(\beta - b)\} \, d\beta \propto \tau^{-k/2},$$

that

$$p(\tau | y, X) \propto \tau^{v/2-1}\exp\{-\tau vs^2/2\} \tag{3.48}$$

which we immediately(!) recognize as the kernel of a gamma density with parameters $v/2$ and $vs^2/2$. Thus, from the gamma mean and variance formulae (see appendix to chapter 1) we see that

$$E(\tau|y, X) = \frac{1}{s^2}; \quad V(\tau|y, X) = \frac{2}{vs^4}.$$

Notice that the posterior mean of the precision $\tau = 1/\sigma^2$ is equal to the reciprocal of the variance of the residuals. Note also that the posterior variance of τ is of the order $1/n$ as $n \to \infty$ for fixed k and s^2 so that it will be small – you will be rather certain about τ – when the sample size is large enough.

The marginal density of β

To find the marginal posterior distribution of β we must integrate τ out of the joint density (3.46). This is most easily done by using the first form (3.10) of the joint density of β and τ together with definition 3.1 and integrating with respect to τ using the formulae for the gamma density given in the appendix to chapter 1. This gives

$$p(\beta|y, X) \propto [(\beta - b)'X'X(\beta - b) + vs^2]^{-(v+k)/2}$$

$$\propto \left[1 + \frac{(\beta - b)'X'X(\beta - b)}{vs^2}\right]^{-(v+k)/2} \tag{3.49}$$

for $v = n - k$. Reference to appendix section 3.8.3, definition 3.4 shows that this is a multivariate t distribution with $v = n - k$ degrees of freedom and that if $v > 1$ the expected value of β exists and is b, the least squares estimate; and if $v > 2$ the covariance matrix of β exists and is $[v/(v - 2)]s^2(X'X)^{-1}$. Thus we have:

THEOREM 3.6 *In the normal linear model*

$$\beta|y, X \sim t_v(b, s^2(X'X)^{-1});$$
$$E(\beta|y, X) = b;$$
$$V(\beta|y, X) = [v/(v - 2)]s^2(X'X)^{-1}.$$

This implies, in particular, that any particular component of β, say β_j, is univariate Student's t distributed as stated in the probability appendix, 3.8.3, to this chapter.

Linear and quadratic functions of t variates

In section 3.3.4 we needed to consider expressions of the form

$$q = \frac{(\delta - d)'[R(X'X)^{-1}R']^{-1}(\delta - d)}{ms^2}$$

where $\delta = R\beta - r$ and $d = Rb - r$. We claimed that q was distributed as an F variate with m and v $(= n - k)$ degrees of freedom. To see this note that, given τ, δ is normal (being a linear function of normal variates) with mean d and covariance matrix $(1/\tau)(X'X)^{-1}$. So

$$p(\delta|\tau, y, X) \propto \tau^{m/2} \exp\{-(\tau/2)(\delta - d)'[R(X'X)^{-1}R']^{-1}(\delta - d)\}$$

Now it is easily proved – via its moment generating function – that $\tau(\delta - d)'[R(X'X)^{-1}R']^{-1}(\delta - d) = \tau qms^2$ is a chi-squared variate[33] with m degrees of freedom. And it follows by a change of variable that q itself has density function

$$p(q|\tau, y, X) \propto q^{(m/2)-1}\tau^{m/2}\exp\{-\tau qms^2/2\}.$$

If we multiply this by the marginal posterior density of τ, given by (3.48), and integrate out τ we have the marginal posterior density of q as

$$p(q|y, X) \propto q^{(m/2)-1}(1 + qm/v)^{-(m+v)/2}$$

which is the kernel of the density of an F_v^m variate.

3.8.2 *Simulating dirichlet variates*

The dirichlet[34] has density

$$p(w|v) \propto \prod_{l=0}^{L} w_l^{v_l-1}, \tag{3.50}$$
$$\text{where } w_0 = 1 - \sum_{l=1}^{L} w_l, \text{ and } v_l > 0, \, l = 0, 1, \dots, L.$$

This is best thought of as distribution for the L (not $L + 1$) variates $w_1, w_2, \dots, w_L$ since w_0 is determined from these latter by the condition that the w's sum to one. The best way to simulate from this distribution is:

ALGORITHM 3.4 *SIMULATING DIRICHLETS*
1. Draw $L + 1$ independent gamma variates of which the l'th has density $\propto z^{v_l-1}e^{-z}$, $l = 0, 1, \dots, L$. (See the probability appendix to chapter 1.)
2. Form

$$w_l = \frac{z_l}{\sum_{j=0}^{L} z_j} \quad \text{for } l = 1, 2, \dots, L.$$

Then the $\{w_l\}$ have the dirichlet distribution (3.50).

---

33 See appendix to chapter 1 on gamma distributions.
34 Pronounced dir-ish-lay.

The proof of this proposition is as follows.

PROOF Consider the joint distribution of

$$w_0 = \sum_{l=0}^{L} z_l \quad \text{and} \quad w_l = \frac{z_l}{\sum_{j=0}^{L} z_j}, \qquad \text{for } l = 1, 2, ..., L \qquad (3.51)$$

We need to prove that $w_1, w_2, ..., w_L$ are dirichlet distributed. We do this by forming the joint distribution of $z_0, z_1, ..., z_L$; transforming to $w_0, w_1, ..., w_L$; then integrating out w_0.

The joint density of the $\{z_l\}$ is

$$p(z|v) \propto \prod_{l=0}^{L} z_l^{v_l-1} e^{-z_l}. \qquad (3.52)$$

From (3.51) we can express the $\{z_l\}$ as

$$z_0 = w_0(1 - S); \; z_l = w_l w_0, \quad l = 1, 2, ..., L \qquad (3.53)$$
$$\text{with } S = \sum_{l=1}^{L} w_l.$$

The matrix of the transformation from $\{w_l\}$ to $\{z_l\}$ is

$$\begin{bmatrix} 1 - S & -w_0 & -w_0 & . & . & -w_0 \\ w_1 & w_0 & 0 & . & . & 0 \\ w_2 & 0 & w_0 & 0 & . & 0 \\ . & . & . & . & 0 & 0 \\ . & . & . & . & w_0 & 0 \\ w_L & 0 & 0 & . & . & w_0 \end{bmatrix}$$

and its determinant is $J = w_0^L$. Thus, substituting (3.53) into (3.52) and multiplying by J gives for the joint density of the w's

$$p(w_0, w_1, ..., w_L|v) \propto (1 - S)^{v_0-1} w_0^{\sum_{l=0}^{L} v_l - 1} e^{-w_0} \prod_{l=1}^{L} w_l^{v_l-1}.$$

Finally, integrating out w_0 using the gamma integral formula, and ignoring multiplicative constants, gives

$$p(w|v) \propto \prod_{l=0}^{L} w_l^{v_l-1}, \text{ where } w_0 = 1 - \sum_{l=1}^{L} w_l.$$

This is the dirchlet density, as required.

3.8.3   Some probability distributions

DEFINITION 3.2   *The* **multivariate normal family** *of probability density functions, denoted as* $mvn(\mu, P)$ *or, in terms of the mean and* **covariance matrix**, $\Sigma = P^{-1}$, $mvn(\mu, \Sigma)$, *is*

$$p(x|\mu, P) \propto \exp\{-(1/2)(x - \mu)'P(x - \mu)\},$$
$$x, \mu \in R^k, \quad P \text{ positive definite.}$$

Its contours of constant probability density are ellipsoids – ellipses in the bivariate case $k = 2$ – centered on μ. For $k = 1$ the density reduces to the univariate normal density function. The missing constant of proportionality is

$$\frac{|P|^{k/2}}{(2\pi)^{k/2}}$$

so that

$$\int_{-\infty}^{\infty} .. \int_{-\infty}^{\infty} \exp\{-(1/2)(x - \mu)'P(x - \mu)\} \, dx_1 \ldots dx_k = |P|^{-k/2}(2\pi)^{k/2}.$$

The mean vector and the covariance matrix are

$$E(X|\mu, \Sigma) = \mu, \quad V(X|\mu, \Sigma) = \Sigma = P^{-1}.$$

P is called the **precision matrix**. *The diagonal elements of $\Sigma = P^{-1}$, denoted by $\{\sigma_{ii}\}$, are the* **variances** *of each element of X; the off diagonal elements, denoted by $\{\sigma_{ij}\}$, are the* **covariances** *of pairs of elements of X. The numbers $\rho_{ij} = \sigma_{ij}/\sqrt{(\sigma_{ii}\sigma_{jj})}$ are the* **correlations** *of pairs of elements of X. If $\Sigma = diag\{\sigma_{ii}\}$ then the elements of X are both uncorrelated and independent and the joint density function reduces to the product of n univariate normal densities with means μ_i and variances equal to σ_{ii}. Note the important point that for a multivariate normal vector X if its elements are uncorrelated then they are independent. This is not generally true for other multivariate distributions. The moment generating function (mgf) of the $mvn(\mu, P)$ distribution is*

$$M(t) = \exp\{t'\mu + (1/2)t'P^{-1}t\}. \tag{3.54}$$

The marginal densities of any subset of multivariate normal variates are also multivariate normal with mean equal to the corresponding subvector of μ and covariance matrix equal to the corresponding submatrix[35] of Σ. This is immediate from the mgf (3.54) by putting appropriate elements of the vector t equal to zero. As a particular

---

35   Note that the precision matrix of such a subset is found by taking the inverse of the corresponding submatrix of the inverse of P, i.e. of Σ^{-1}. This is a slight disadvantage of working in terms of the precision rather than the covariance matrix.

case, single elements of X, say the i'th, are univariate normal with mean μ_i and variance σ_{ii}, usually written as σ_i^2, the i'th diagonal element of Σ.

If we partition x as x_1, x_2 the conditional density of X_1 given $X_2 = x_2$ is also multivariate or univariate normal. In the bivariate normal case when x_1 and x_2 are scalar:

$$p_{X_1|X_2}(x_1|x_2) = n(\mu_1 + (\sigma_{12}/\sigma_{22})(x_2 - \mu_2), \sigma_{11}(1 - \rho_{12}^2)).$$

Note that X_1 has linear regression on X_2.

S commands take the form dmvnorm(x,m,S); rmvnorm(n,m,S); pmvnorm(x,m,S) *where x is a k vector, e.g.* x <- c(0,0,0) *for k = 3, n is the required number of realizations, m is a k vector providing the means, and S is a nonsingular symmetric k × k covariance matrix, e.g.* S <- diag(1,nrow=3). *There is no function* qmvnorm.

DEFINITION 3.3   *The **univariate t family**, called **Student's distribution**, and denoted as $t_v(v, \mu, \pi)$, is*

$$p(x|v, \mu, \tau) \propto \left(1 + \frac{\tau}{v}(x - \mu)^2\right)^{-(v+1)/2}, \quad \tau > 0, \; -\infty < x, \mu < \infty, \; v > 0. \quad (3.55)$$

The missing constant of proportionality is

$$\frac{\Gamma\left(\dfrac{v+1}{2}\right)\tau^{1/2}}{\Gamma\left(\dfrac{v}{2}\right)\Gamma\left(\dfrac{1}{2}\right)v^{1/2}}.$$

*The parameter v, often integer valued, is called the **degrees of freedom**. If $v > 1$ the mean exists and is equal to μ; if $v > 2$, the precision exists and is equal to $\tau(v - 2)/v$. The distribution is symmetric about μ and unimodal. The standard form, denoted $t(v)$ or t_v, has $\mu = 0$ and $\tau = 1$. The random variable $\tau^{1/2}(x - \mu)$ has the standard t distribution. When $v = 1$ the distribution has kernel*

$$p(x|\mu, \tau) \propto \frac{1}{1 + \tau(x - \mu)^2}$$

*and is called the **Cauchy distribution**. It has no finite positive integer moments. The t distribution has thicker tails than the normal in the sense that for large x the density function falls like $x^{-(v+1)}$ while the tails of the normal fall like $e^{-x^2/2}$ which is faster. For degrees of freedom greater than about 12 the distribution is well approximated by a normal distribution of the same mean and precision except in the extreme tails. S commands for the standard t are* dt(x,v) *(density at x);* rt(n,v), *(n realizations);* pt(x,v) *(distribution function at x);* qt(p,v) *(quantile function at p).*

DEFINITION 3.4 *The* **multivariate t family** *for a vector x of length d, written* $t_\nu(\nu, P)$*, is*

$$p(x|\nu, \mu, P) \propto \left(1 + \frac{1}{\nu}(x - \mu)'P(x - \mu)\right)^{-(\nu+d)/2}$$

for $x, \mu \in R^d$*,* $\nu > 0$ *and P positive definite. For* $\nu > 1$ *the mean exists and is equal to* μ*; for* $\nu > 2$ *the covariance matrix exists and is equal to*

$$\frac{\nu}{(\nu - 2)}\Sigma \ \text{for} \ \Sigma = P^{-1}.$$

The marginal distributions of scalar elements of x are univariate t variates with means equal to the corresponding element of μ *and variances equal to the corresponding diagonal element of the covariance matrix of x assuming these moments exist.*

DEFINITION 3.5 *The* **Wishart family** *is a collection of distributions of the* $m(m + 1)/2$ *distinct elements of the inverse of an m-dimensional covariance matrix, i.e. a precision matrix. In this respect it generalizes to the multivariate case the gamma distribution which was used as a prior, and posterior for a precision in the univariate linear model. If W is that precision matrix the kernel of the density is*

$$p(W|\nu, S) \propto |W|^{(\nu-m-1)/2} \exp\{-(1/2)tr(SW)\} \quad W \ \text{positive definite,} \ \nu \geq m.$$

The parameter ν *is called the degrees of freedom and S is typically proportional to a matrix of sums of squares and products. The mean of the distribution is* νS^{-1}*. Note that when* $m = 1$ *and S and W are scalar, the density kernel becomes* $p(w|\nu, s) \propto w^{(\nu/2)-1} \exp\{-(1/2)sw\}$ *which is a gamma density of mean* ν/s*.*

   A command to simulate from the Wishart density is typically not available in general statistical software, though it is available in the BUGS package. But simulations can be easily done by yourself using a multivariate normal simulator. Specifically, assuming that ν *is integer, draw* $x_1, x_2, ..., x_\nu$ *independently from an m variate normal distribution with mean zero and covariance matrix* S^{-1}*. In S the command would be* x<-rmvnorm(ν, 0, V)*. Then* $W = \sum_{i=1}^{\nu} x_i x_i'$ *is a realization from a Wishart (* ν*, S) distribution. This representation indicates that* ν *should be thought of as the number of independent normals and W as the matrix of sums of squares and products of such normal vectors.*

3.9   EXERCISES AND COMPLEMENTS

(1) Generate some data from a normal distribution and use `qqnorm(x)` and `qqline(x)` to see if it plots normally. Generate some other data, possibly from a different family of distributions, and compare the distributions by using `qqplot(x,y)`.

(2) Generate or otherwise obtain some y, x data and apply a normal linear regression to it, sampling the posterior density using algorithm 3.1. Then use the BUGS algorithm 3.2 and compare your results.

(3) Use your sampler output from exercise 2 to study the posterior distribution of some non-linear function of β, for example the ratio β_2/β_1.

(4) For your calculations in exercise 2 compute the residuals and study their QQ plot to determine whether homoscedastic normality was a reasonable model for your data.

(5) Generate some data by, for example, `y <- rnorm(20,2,1)` or `y <- rt(20, 5)` and then use the S command

```
for(i in 1:nrep){v_rexp(n);mu[i]_sum(y*v)/sum(v)}
```

to study the Bayesian bootstrap distribution of the expected value of Y.

(6) Repeat exercise 5 but define σ^2 by a second moment condition – $E(Y - \mu)^2 - \sigma^2 = 0$ – then use the Bayesian bootstrap to study the posterior distribution of $var(Y)$.

(7) Generate or acquire some data satisfying a regression model and explore the possibilities of the `factor` and `gam` commands in R. For example, `x_rnorm(n);` `y <- rnorm(n, sin(x), 1); lm(y ~ factor(x)); gam(y ~ s(x))`.

(8) **Sets of linear models**   Suppose that you have not one normal linear model but $m > 1$ of them. Write the j'th as

$$y_j = X_j\beta_j + \varepsilon_j, \quad V(\varepsilon_j) = \sigma_{jj}I_n, \quad j = 1, 2, ..., m$$

where X_j is $n \times k_j$ and set $\Sigma_j k_j = k$. Such a collection of linear models is called a seemingly unrelated system or SURE – seemingly unrelated regression equations – for short. Then we can write all m models together as

$$y = X\beta + \varepsilon$$

where

$$X = \begin{bmatrix} X_1 & 0 & 0 & \cdots & 0 \\ 0 & X_2 & 0 & \cdots & 0 \\ . & . & . & \cdots & 0 \\ 0 & 0 & 0 & 0 & X_m \end{bmatrix}; \quad \beta = \begin{bmatrix} \beta_1 \\ \beta_2 \\ . \\ \beta_m \end{bmatrix}; \quad \varepsilon = \begin{bmatrix} \varepsilon_1 \\ \varepsilon_2 \\ . \\ \varepsilon_m \end{bmatrix},$$

and the covariance matrix of ε is

$$V(\varepsilon) = \Sigma \otimes I_n$$

where $\otimes$ is the kronecker product and $\Sigma = \{\sigma_{jk}\}$. The element σ_{jk} of Σ is the covariance of the i'th element of ε_j with the i'th element of ε_k. Let P denote the precision matrix corresponding to Σ, namely Σ^{-1}. Assuming each ε_j is normal the likelihood is

$$\ell(\beta, P) \propto |P|^{n/2} \exp\{-(1/2)(y - X\beta)'(P \otimes I_n)(y - X\beta)\}.$$

(a) Show that the likelihood may be written as

$$\ell(\beta, P) \propto |P|^{-n/2} \exp\{-(1/2)\operatorname{tr} SP\} \tag{3.56}$$

$$\text{where} \quad S = \begin{bmatrix} \varepsilon_1'\varepsilon_1 & \varepsilon_1'\varepsilon_2 & \cdots & \varepsilon_1'\varepsilon_m \\ \cdots & \varepsilon_2'\varepsilon_2 & \cdots & \cdots \\ \cdots & \cdots & \cdots & \cdots \\ \cdots & \cdots & \varepsilon_m'\varepsilon_{m-1} & \varepsilon_m'\varepsilon_m \end{bmatrix}$$

(b) Show, using definition 3.1 above – completing the square – that, analogously to theorem 3.1, the likelihood may be written as

$$\ell(\beta, P) \propto |P|^{n/2} \exp\{-(1/2)\{(\beta - \hat{\beta})'X'(P \otimes I_n)X(\beta - \hat{\beta})\} \\ \times \exp{-(1/2)e'(P \otimes I_n)e\} \tag{3.57}$$

$$\text{where} \quad \hat{\beta} = (X'(P \otimes I_n)X)^{-1}X'(P \otimes I_n)y \quad \text{and} \quad e = y - X\hat{\beta}. \tag{3.58}$$

Note that $\hat{\beta}$ is a generalized least squares estimate.

(c) A conventional "diffuse" prior for β, P is $\propto |P|^{-(m+1)/2}$. Show that β is multivariate normal given P and that, given β, P is Wishart distributed. Hence devise a Gibbs Sampler algorithm – chapter 4, section 4.4.1 – for sampling the joint posterior density of β, P.

(d) Suppose that, as a special case, $X_1 = X_2 = \ldots = X_m = Z$ so that each linear model has the same covariate data. Show that $X = I_m \otimes Z$ and hence, by simplifying $\hat{\beta}$, show that it is equivalent to applying least squares to each equation separately.

3.10 BIBLIOGRAPHIC NOTES

There are few specifically econometric textbook discussions of Bayesian inference in the linear model since Zellner's classic work of 1971. This book considers, among many other topics, SURE systems, analysis of which originated with that author. Bauwens, Lubrano and Richard (1999) is an exception. Poirier (1995) compares Bayesian and frequentist inference and includes material on the linear model. The

Bayesian statistics literature on this subject is, of course, huge and the subject is included as an early chapter in essentially all the texts referenced at the end of chapter 1. Much of the Bayesian statistics literature on linear models derives from the classic article Lindley and Smith (1972: 1–41). A valuable early statistics text is Box and Tiao (1973).

For a view of errors in a linear model similar to that taken in this chapter see Zellner (1975: 138–44).

Useful journal articles include Chib (1994: 183–206) and (1993: 275–94). These papers focus on MCMC algorithms[36] for computation of posterior distributions, for example the second paper gives a Gibbs Sampler algorithm for fitting the model (3.41), but so rapid is progress in this area that programs such as BUGS mean that the user can now largely avoid going into the question of which algorithm to choose. It is, at least for these simpler models, a solved problem in that essentially exact Bayesian inferences for all parametric variants of the linear model can be routinely done in BUGS. Fernandez and Steel (2000: 80–101) go into more detail about Student linear models and their relatives. The bibliography to Bauwens, Lubrano and Richard (1999) gives many more references to theoretical and applied econometric studies of the linear model and its variants.

The multinomial method of section 3.4 is explained by Rubin (1981). An early econometric application is in Lancaster (1997: 291–303). A more recent contribution is Chamberlain and Imbens (2003). This paper suggested section 3.4.

The text by Hastie and Tibshirani (1990) explains about gam techniques and is well worth reading.

Yatchew and No collected and analyzed the gasoline consumption data used in this chapter in Household gasoline demand in Canada, *Econometrica*, 69, 6, 1697–709 (2001). Dr. Yatchew supplied the gasoline data, with the permission of Cambridge University Press.

---

36   See chapter 4.

Chapter 4
BAYESIAN CALCULATIONS

The objects that tell you about your model and about your results are the posterior distribution $p(\theta|y)$, the prior predictive distribution $p(y)$, and the posterior predictive distribution $p(\tilde{y}|y)$. The first of these describes your beliefs given the data and your model; the second describes your beliefs about the data before you have seen it; and the third describes your beliefs about new data given the model and your old data. In the case of the posterior distribution $p(\theta|y)$, on which we shall focus, the object of interest is often a scalar function of the parameter vector θ, for example a single element of it, or you might wish to study each component in turn. This means that you want a marginal distribution(s) associated with θ and to get these involves integration of $p(\theta|y)$ over all elements other than the one of interest. While these distributions can be deduced analytically in simple cases,[1] as we have seen above, or you can use large sample approximations, it is in general far more straightforward to let the computer do the work by providing for you *simulated samples* from the required distribution. With a sample from the posterior you can find any feature of the joint distribution that you require with an accuracy that you can make arbitrarily high simply by increasing the sample size. Thus, for example, if you want to determine the mean of some element θ_j or the probability that $\theta_j > 0$ then you just form the corresponding sample averages

$$\frac{1}{nrep}\sum_{i=1}^{nrep}\theta_{ji} \quad \text{or} \quad \frac{1}{nrep}\sum_{i=1}^{nrep}I(\theta_{ji} > 0)$$

where $I(\theta_{ji} > 0)$ is an indicator of the event that the i'th realization of θ_j exceeds zero. Typically, a law of large numbers will apply and these averages will converge in probability as $nrep \to \infty$ to $E(\theta_j)$ and to $P(\theta_j > 0)$ respectively. Since you choose $nrep$ these estimates can be made as accurate as you like.

So the main remaining problem in implementing the Bayesian algorithm is how to program the computer to *sample* from the required distribution. In this chapter we shall describe the more important ways in which an econometrician can sample a probability distribution. The starting point is a mathematical expression for $p(\theta|y)$.

---

1 Or you can do what used to be done and apply traditional methods of numerical integration such as Simpson's rule.

There are four main cases.

(1) **Available distributions** The distribution from which you want to sample – usually called the **target distribution** – may be of standard form with properties that are well understood and such that computer routines to sample from it are widely available. It is customary to use the word "available" to refer to distributions that can be sampled by a single call to a function provided in standard packages. This is a common situation with the simpler models that fill textbooks. Typically the distributions that are available for sampling in statistics programs are univariate, for example all but one of the distributions available in S are univariate, the exception being the multivariate normal. When this is the case the study of the target distribution is essentially straightforward – it amounts to doing descriptive statistics with a sample that can be made indefinitely large. You enter a statement such as x <- rgamma(10000, alpha, beta) in S or its counterpart in other packages and then proceed to examine the 10,000 numbers in x using the standard techniques of descriptive statistics. We have already seen, in chapters 1 and 2, several examples of this approach. The algorithms underlying functions such as rgamma(...) are well explained in the literature. To describe these methods here would be of as little relevance as describing how a computer calculates a logarithm.

(2) **Effectively available distributions** It may be that the target distribution is not of standard form but it can be sampled exactly by a sequence of calls to available distributions. One common case is where the target density is, say, $f(x, y) = f(x)f(y|x)$ in which although $f(x, y)$ is not available, both $f(x)$ and $f(y|x)$ are. Then $f(x, y)$ can be sampled by first drawing x from $f(x)$ and then substituting this x into the conditional density and drawing y from $f(y|x)$. This produces a realization from the joint distribution of y and x.

A good example of this is the normal linear regression model in which x is the common precision of the error terms and y is the vector of regression coefficients. Then, as we saw in chapter 3, $f(x)$ is a gamma density and $f(y|x)$ is multivariate normal. Thus if a, b are the parameters of the marginal density of the precision, τ, and $\hat{b}$ is the conditional mean of β given τ, then

```
tau <- rgamma(n,a,b); beta <- rnorm(n,bhat,tau)
```

will produce realizations from the joint distribution of β and τ in the model without covariates and

```
beta <- rmvnorm(1, bhat,(1/tau[i])*XXI)
```

where tau[i] is an element of tau and XXI is $(X'X)^{-1}$, and will produce a realization of β in the regression model.

(3) **Distorting or transforming samples from available distributions** It may be that the required distribution is not of standard form yet it is possible to sample from it by combining samples from an available distribution with an

ingenious computational trick. An example of this is **rejection sampling** in which samples from a standard distribution are used to obtain a sample from the required distribution. Rejection sampling algorithms are already starting to fall into category (1) as they become built into packages for doing Bayesian inference, but we shall briefly describe rejection sampling in section 4.2.1.

Another example is **importance sampling**. Suppose that you wish to calculate an expression such as $\int h(\theta)f(\theta)\,d\theta$ where $f(.)$ is an unavailable probability density function, but there exists another density function $g(\theta)$ which is in some sense close to $f(\theta)$ and which is available. Then you can write the integral as

$$\int h(\theta)f(\theta)\,d\theta = \int h(\theta)[\,f(\theta)/g(\theta)]\,g(\theta)\,d\theta$$

and then draw a sample from $g(\theta)$ and calculate the integral as

$$\int h(\theta)f(\theta)\,d\theta = \frac{1}{nrep}\sum h(\theta_i)w_i \quad \text{for} \quad w_i = \frac{f(\theta_i)}{g(\theta_i)}.$$

This method needs good judgement in choosing a "good" importance sampling density $g(\theta)$. Another example is **inverting the distribution function** which we shall describe in section 4.2.2.

(4) **Markov chain monte carlo** The fourth case is that in which the required distribution is not of standard form nor can the methods of rejection or importance sampling be easily used. One solution here is to construct a stochastic process which is such that (a) it has a stationary distribution, (b) it converges to that stationary distribution, and (c) that stationary distribution is the target distribution. One then simulates the stochastic process until realizations derive from the stationary distribution and then uses such samples for inference in the same way as in case (1) above. This method is called **markov chain monte carlo (MCMC)**. It is not an exact way of sampling the target distribution but rather one for which the realizations can be made as close as one likes to exact samples by observing the stochastic process for sufficiently long. The samples it yields are typically not independent draws from the target distribution but each draw considered individually comes from the target. That is, the draws are identically but not independently distributed provided the process is observed for long enough. We shall describe MCMC methods in section 4.3, but again they are increasingly supplied in packages for Bayesian inference, for example BUGS. MCMC methods are typically applied to sample multivariate distributions. These methods are sufficiently powerful that there are few, if any, distributions arising in econometric practice that cannot be sampled using MCMC.

These general solution methods provide samples that are realizations from the target distribution. Since they can occasionally be complicated to implement they are usefully complemented by approximate methods. In these methods we approximate the target distribution by a standard distribution – almost always the multivariate normal – and study that approximation.

4.1   NORMAL APPROXIMATIONS

We saw in chapter 1 that in many circumstances, when the sample size is large, the joint posterior distribution is approximately normal with mean equal to the joint posterior mode and precision matrix equal to the negative hessian evaluated at the mode. That is,

$$p(\theta|y) \simeq |P|^{1/2} \exp\{-(1/2)(\theta - m)'P(\theta - m)\}(2\pi)^{-k/2} \qquad (4.1)$$

where k is the dimension of θ. This result, (4.1), provided an explanation of why, when we drew the posterior density of θ in the examples given earlier in this book, they often seemed to look roughly normal.

   The approximation (4.1) is a multivariate normal distribution with mean equal to the posterior mode and precision equal to the negative hessian at that mode. To locate m you can either use a standard function minimization routine or make use of a routine in a frequentist package to calculate maximum likelihood estimates. Such ml estimates provide m if the prior component in $p(\theta|y)$ is ignored. Neglecting the prior is mathematically legitimate since the large n approximation (4.1) remains valid because the prior does not change with the sample size whereas the log likelihood typically grows at the rate n. Whether neglecting the prior worsens the quality of the normal approximation in practice depends on how much information the prior contains relative to the likelihood.

   A multivariate normal approximation to the posterior distribution, if it applies, is very convenient because of its simplicity. Specifically,

(1) We are typically interested not in the joint distribution of the elements of θ but in the marginal distribution of a single element, say θ_j. But it is a property of the multivariate normal that its marginal distributions are univariate normal and can be read from (4.1). For example θ_j is (approximately) univariate normal with mean m_j and variance equal to the j'th diagonal element of P^{-1}.

(2) Another convenient feature is that we will often be interested in the most likely value for θ_j. But in general this mode of the marginal distribution of θ_j is not equal to the j'th element of the joint mode of the posterior distribution. That is, if $p(\theta|y)$ is the joint posterior distribution the mode of the marginal distribution of θ_j is not generally provided by the j'th element of the maximizer of $p(\theta|y)$. But for the normal distribution the joint mode *is* equal to the vector of modes of the marginal densities and for this distribution m is both the joint mode and the vector of marginal modes.

(3) Finally, a normal approximation is convenient from the computational point of view because a Bayesian can borrow frequentist software. This is because a

maximum likelihood program locates $\hat{\theta}$, the mode of the likelihood function, and it provides an estimate of the repeated sampling covariance matrix of $\hat{\theta}$. This sampling covariance matrix is, in regular cases, the inverse information matrix $I(\theta)^{-1}$, and the estimate of the information matrix is typically $I(\hat{\theta})$, or an approximation to this. But in a large sample or under a diffuse prior for θ we will have $\hat{\theta} \simeq m$ and $P(m) \simeq I(\hat{\theta})$ since, ignoring the prior, $I(\theta) = E(P(\theta))$ for the value of θ that generated the data, and m is a consistent estimate of this value – typically $I(m) = P(m) + O(n^{-1})$. This means that the standard errors that the maximum likelihood analyst reports will be approximately the Bayesian standard deviations of the marginal posterior densities of the elements of θ. Bayesians and maximum likelihood analysts will tend to draw the same conclusions when the data is very informative about θ. It is usually in so-called "small sample" situations that Bayesian results may disagree strongly with those of frequentists. But in economics small sample or weakly identified situations occur rather frequently.

What can we say about the conditions under which a normal distribution will give an accurate approximation to the posterior distribution?

(1) The distance between $p(\theta|y)$ and a normal distribution, for any given n, depends strongly on the configuration of the data. An example that the reader can easily try for himself is the binomial model with a uniform prior for θ. When there are roughly equal numbers of successes and failures in the data the normal approximation to the posterior distribution of θ is very good even for n in high single figures. But when there are radically unequal numbers of successes and failures the normal approximation can be terrible even for quite large n.
(2) For any given sample size n, the normal approximation is usually worse the larger the number of elements of θ.
(3) The normal approximation cannot be useful when the posterior distribution has multiple modes because the normal has only one.[2]

The observations that the posterior distribution can fail to be approximately normal, and that it is hard to tell whether it is approximately normal without computing the exact posterior density, which we wished to avoid, suggests that attention should be focused on methods for computing the exact density and this is the thrust of most current Bayesian work.

Nonetheless, the majority of models and data sets with which applied economists work are such that approximate normality is at least not a terrible belief and most workers are advised to calculate the mode, m, and the negative hessian, $P(m)$. The elements of m then provide rough point estimates of the means of the marginal distributions of each element of θ and the diagonal elements of P^{-1} provide rough estimates of the variances of these marginal posterior distributions. These values may

---

2 A multimodal posterior can sometimes be approximated by a mixture of multivariate normal distributions with modes at the local modes.

be enough for you to decide either to continue working to get the exact posterior density, or to change/abandon the model if, for example, the values of the elements of *m*, together with their posterior standard deviations, are inconsistent with reasonable economic beliefs.

We shall now turn to some exact sampling methods, dealing first with those not involving MCMC.

4.2   EXACT SAMPLING IN ONE STEP

In MCMC methods, as we shall see, samples from the target distribution are obtained only asymptotically. In this section we describe some methods that yield such a sample in one step. We focus on univariate distributions, and in particular on the method of rejection sampling because it is used extensively in the BUGS MCMC program.

Suppose that the target density is $f = f(\theta)$ and there is a computer routine available to sample from $g = g(\theta)$. Then we could use rejection sampling.

4.2.1 Rejection sampling

Suppose that f and g are such that for all θ, $f(\theta)/g(\theta) \leq M$ so there is a finite upper bound on the ratio of the two density functions. Let $h(\theta) = f(\theta)/g(\theta)M$ and let U be uniformly distributed on zero to one. Let $g()$ be available. Then the following algorithm produces a realization from f.

ALGORITHM 4.1   *REJECTION SAMPLING*
1. *Generate y from g.*
2. *Compute $h(y) = f(y)/g(y)M$.*
3. *Draw u, a realization of U.*
4. *If $u < h(y)$ accept y; otherwise return to step 1.*

The accepted realizations, *y*, have density function *f* and are independent. The proof of this is as follows.

Proof   The probability that $Y \leq x$ and Y is accepted is the integral of the joint density of Y and U over the region $y \leq x$ and $u < h(y)$. Because U and Y are independent and U is uniform this is

$$P(Y \leq x \text{ and } Y \text{ accepted}) = \int_{-\infty}^{x} \int_{0}^{h(y)} g(y)\, du\, dy = \int_{-\infty}^{x} h(y)g(y)\, dy.$$

But $h(y) = f(y)/g(y)M$ so

$$P(Y \leq x \text{ and } Y \text{ accepted}) = \int_{-\infty}^{x} f(y)\, dy/M = F(x)/M.$$

It follows from this, by letting $x \to \infty$, that

$$P(Y \text{ accepted}) = 1/M.$$

Hence,

$$P(Y \leq x|Y \text{ accepted}) = \frac{P(Y \leq x \text{ and } Y \text{ accepted})}{P(Y \text{ accepted})}$$

$$= \frac{F(x)/M}{1/M} = F(x).$$

It follows that *accepted* Y's have density f as required.

Some comments on this method:

Firstly $M \geq 1$ because from $f(y) \leq g(y)M$ integrating both sides over the sample space gives $1 \leq M$. Secondly, the number of draws from g until one is accepted is a geometric random variable with success probability equal to $1/M$. It follows that the expected number of draws until an acceptance is M. It is therefore desirable to choose g, if possible, so that M is small. The function $g()$ is called an **envelope**.

Thirdly, there is a rather large class of density functions f for which a bounding density function g can always be found. This is the class of **log-concave densities**.

DEFINITION 4.1 LOG-CONCAVITY *A density $f(y)$ is log-concave if its logarithm is twice differentiable, with second derivative everywhere non-positive definite.*

For example, normal-based posterior densities for regression parameters β and error precision τ are log-concave in β and in τ considered separately as long as $X'X$ is non-singular. More generally, virtually all of the off-the-shelf models used by applied economists are log-concave.

The reason why a log-concave density can be bounded is because we can bound the log of f by a continuous piece-wise linear curve formed from its tangents as in figure 4.1. This shows the log of a standard normal density bounded above by its tangents at plus and minus 2. To the left of zero the tangent line is of the form $a + bx$ and to the right it is $a - bx$. So the density itself is bounded above by e^{a+bx} or e^{a-bx} depending on whether $x \gtrless 0$.

More generally it is clear that we can bound any log-concave density function by a continuous curve consisting of pieces of the form $e^{a_j+b_j x}$ for $x_{j-1} < x < x_j$, that is,

$$f(x) \leq e^{a_j+b_j x} \quad \text{for } x_{j-1} < x < x_j, \quad j = 1, 2, ..., J. \tag{4.2}$$

Finally, let M be the number that makes the **piecewise exponential curve** (4.2) a probability density function that integrates to one over the real line, then

$$f(x) \leq \frac{e^{a_j+b_j x}}{M} M = g(x)M \quad \text{for } x_{j-1} < x < x_j, \quad j = 1, 2, ..., J.$$

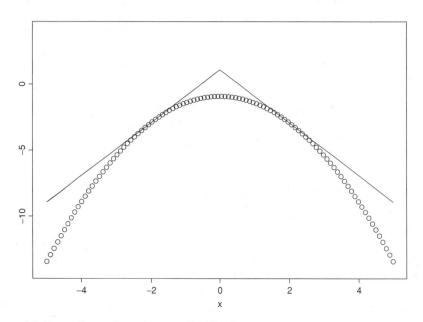

Figure 4.1 Bounding a log-concave distribution

In other words, we can always find a piecewise exponential density function $g(\theta)$ such that $f(\theta)/g(\theta) \leq M$ whenever $f(.)$ is log-concave. Since we can easily sample from a piecewise exponential distribution by a slight elaboration of sampling from a standard exponential distribution (rexp in S), we can always sample, exactly, from a log-concave density function. A sophisticated version of univariate rejection sampling plays a key role in markov chain monte carlo sampling, to which we turn in section 4.3.

4.2.2 *Inverting the distribution function*

We can always sample from the uniform distribution on the interval zero to one. For example runif(n) in S produces n pseudo-random realizations. But the distribution function of any scalar random variable is uniformly distributed. Thus $F(Y) \sim U$ or $Y \sim F^{-1}(U)$ where $F^{-1}(.)$ is the inverse distribution or quantile function. Hence if we generate a realization u from the uniform distribution on zero to one then $F^{-1}(u)$ will be a realization from F. Specifically:

THEOREM 4.1 SAMPLING BY INVERSION   *Define F^- by $F^-(u) = \min\{x \mid F(x) \geq u\}$. Then if $U \sim U(0, 1)$, $Y = F^-(U)$ is a realization from F.*

Proof   *See Ripley (1987).*

The theorem is somewhat abstract because it refers both to continuous *and* discrete random variables. The more usual and simpler version refers solely to random variables with a continuous strictly increasing distribution function. In this case the theorem is that $F(Y) \sim U(0, 1)$ and the proof is:

PROOF: CONTINUOUS CASE A uniform $(0, 1)$ variate is characterized by its distribution function $F(u) = u$, $0 \leq u \leq 1$. To prove that $F(Y) \sim U(0, 1)$ note that

$$P(F(Y) \leq u) = P(Y \leq F^{-1}(u)) = F(F^{-1}(u)) = u$$

for every $0 \leq u \leq 1$. Hence $F(Y) \sim U(0, 1)$.

A useful example is as follows.

EXAMPLE 4.1 *SAMPLING TRUNCATED NOR-MAL VARIATES* *To sample from a normal distribution with mean μ and standard deviation σ truncated to the interval from a to b, note that the distribution function of such a Y is*

$$G(y) = \frac{F(y) - F(a)}{F(b) - F(a)} \quad a \leq y \leq b$$

and zero elsewhere, where $F(.)$ is the distribution function of an $n(\mu, \sigma)$ variate. Equating $G(.)$ to a uniform variate U yields

$$F(y) = F(a) + u(F(b) - F(a))$$
$$or \quad y = F^{-1}(F(a) + u(F(b) - F(a))).$$

In S this would be, say,

```
y <- qnorm(pnorm(a, m, s)+runif(10000)*(pnorm(b, m, s)
-pnorm(a, m, s)), m, s)
```

where $m = \mu$ and $s = \sigma$. If you pick m, s, a and b and issue this command you will obtain in y 10,000 realizations of a normal(m,s) variate truncated below at a and above at b.

It will have been noticed that several of these techniques, such as inversion, basically apply only to scalar random variables. But we have argued the econometric problem is almost always to sample vector parameters. The relevance of scalar sampling techniques is that perhaps the main MCMC technique, Gibbs Sampling, requires repeated sampling from low dimensional, often scalar, conditional distributions. This is where scalar sampling techniques, such as rejection sampling for log-concave densities, come into their own.

4.3 MARKOV CHAIN MONTE CARLO

Markov chain monte carlo[3] (MCMC) is a method of sampling a (target) probability distribution by constructing a markov chain such that the target distribution is the stationary distribution of the chain, and such that the chain converges in distribution to that stationary distribution. When convergence occurs, realizations of the chain are realizations of the stationary distribution. The task of the econometrician is to construct a chain having a given target as its stationary distribution.[4] In the next sections we give a brief guide to markov chains, stationarity and convergence. The aim of these sections is to answer some elementary[5] questions about markov chains and to provide at least an intuitive understanding of how markov chains provide us with a way of sampling posterior distributions. By the end of this section the reader should be able to find the stationary distribution of a finite markov chain; to construct an MCMC program to sample from simple multivariate distributions; and to run the corresponding chains on his own computer. At the end of this chapter we provide a guide to the literature in which more detailed and rigorous accounts are given.

4.3.1 Markov chains and transition kernels

A markov chain is a sequence of random variables $X_0, X_1, X_2, \ldots$ such that the probability distribution of any one, given all preceding realizations, depends at most on the immediately preceding realization. Specifically, if χ is the sample space for the $\{X_t\}$ and A is a subset of a collection of sets on χ then

$$P(X_{t+1} \in A | x_0, x_1, \ldots, x_t) = P(X_{t+1} \in A | x_t) \tag{4.3}$$

for all $t = 1, 2, 3, \ldots$ and any such A. The value taken by X_t is called the **state of the chain** at t. An expression like (4.3) is called a **transition probability**. The chain is **homogeneous** if the transition probabilities do not depend on the date, t, and

---

3 The phrase monte carlo refers to the use of random number generators to solve mathematical problems. The phrase itself is a reference to the Principality of Monte Carlo in southern France, which is famous for its casino. When you type `rnorm` in S you are using a monte carlo method. The phrase markov chain refers to a sequence of random variables whose probability law satisfies a certain restriction. So when we use markov chain monte carlo methods we use random number generators to sample from this sequence of random variables.

4 Most probability texts focus on the converse problem: given a chain find out its stationary distribution.

5 All current published expositions of MCMC presume a knowledge of elementary markov chain theory.

we shall assume homogeneity throughout this chapter. In most applications of MCMC methods in Bayesian inference the state X is a vector random variable, often a parameter vector, and its value is a value for each component of X.

In view of the limited type of dependence expressed by (4.3) it is almost obvious that a homogeneous markov chain can be fully described by its initial state and the rule describing how the chain moves from its state at t to its state at $t + 1$. This latter rule is described by the **transition kernel**.[6] This is a function $K(x, y)$ that for each x provides a probability distribution for y. Thus it is a collection of conditional probability distributions, one for each x. When the sample space, χ, is discrete:

$$K(x, y) = P(X_{t+1} = y \mid X_t = x) \quad x, y \in \chi.$$

And when χ is also finite we can write this collection of distributions as a table.

EXAMPLE 4.2   *A TWO STATE MARKOV CHAIN*
Consider the family of laws described by

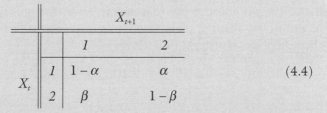

(4.4)

which is intended to show that when $X_t = 1$ then $X_{t+1} = 1$ with probability $1 - \alpha$ and $X_{t+1} = 2$ with probability α; and when $X_t = 2$ then $X_{t+1} = 1$ with probability β and $X_{t+1} = 2$ with probability $1 - \beta$. The two by two matrix

$$K(x, y) = \begin{bmatrix} 1 - \alpha & \alpha \\ \beta & 1 - \beta \end{bmatrix} \qquad (4.5)$$

*is, for a chain like this with a discrete state space, called a **transition probability matrix** and a process which moves between two states according to the probability law (4.4) is a **two state markov chain**.*

Notice that the elements of a transition probability matrix are non-negative and that the rows, being probability distributions, sum to one. A matrix such as this is also called a **stochastic matrix**. The space χ in this example is $\chi = \{1, 2\}$. Much of the intuition about MCMC can be gained by thinking about finite discrete chains.

When the sample space is continuous the transition kernel is usually described by a formula.

---

6   A transition kernel is not the same as the kernel of a probability density or mass function.

EXAMPLE 4.3 *AUTOREGRESSIVE MODEL*
The expression

$$K(x, y) = \frac{1}{\sqrt{2\pi}} \exp\{-(1/2)(y - \rho x)^2\} \qquad (4.6)$$

represents a process such that when $X_t = x$, then X_{t+1} is normally distributed with precision one and mean equal to ρx. Both x and y lie in a parameter space which is the whole real line.

4.3.2 The state distribution, $p_t(x)$

The probability distribution of X_{t+1}, say p_{t+1}, can be described in terms of the transition kernel and the analogous distribution of X_t. This is because the probability that $X_{t+1} = y$ is equal to the sum or integral of the probabilities that $X_t = x$ times the probability that the chain moves to y given that it had been in x. Algebraically, when there are M states, this is

$$P(X_{t+1} = j) = \sum_{i=1}^{M} P(X_t = i) P(X_{t+1} = j | X_t = i), \; j = 1, 2, \ldots, M, \qquad (4.7)$$

that is,

$$p_{t+1}(j) = \sum_{i=1}^{M} p_t(i) K(i, j). \qquad (4.8)$$

EXAMPLE 4.4 *For the two state chain, for example,*

$$\begin{aligned} P(X_{t+1} = 2) &= P(X_{t+1} = 2 | X_t = 1) P(X_t = 1) + P(X_{t+1} = 2 | X_t = 2) P(X_t = 2) \\ &= \alpha P(X_t = 1) + (1 - \beta) P(X_t = 2). \end{aligned}$$

The matrix version of (4.8) is

$$p'_{t+1} = p'_t K \qquad (4.9)$$

for a chain with finite discrete sample space and where K is a transition probability matrix of order $M \times M$. Here p'_t and p'_{t+1} are *row* vectors describing the probability distributions of X_t and X_{t+1} respectively. For a chain with continuous sample space the sum is replaced by an integral and the analogous expression is

$$p_{t+1}(y) = \int_\chi K(x, y) p_t(x) \, dx. \qquad (4.10)$$

EXAMPLE 4.5 *For the autoregressive model the analogue of (4.7) is*

$$p_{t+1}(y) = \int_{-\infty}^{\infty} \frac{1}{\sqrt{2\pi}} \exp\{-(1/2)(y - \rho x)^2\} \, p_t(x) dx \tag{4.11}$$

which shows the density of the state at the point y in terms of its density at all points a period ago and the transition kernel.

In this case $p(.)$ is a density function not a vector.

4.3.3 Stationary distributions

For relations like (4.9) and (4.10) it is natural to ask whether there exists a distribution such that if $p_t = p$ then also $p_{t+1} = p$ so that once the state distribution becomes p it remains p thereafter. Such a distribution is called a **stationary or invariant distribution** of the chain. Mathematically, this is the question of whether there exists a solution, p, to the vector or functional equations

$$p = pK \tag{4.12}$$

$$\text{or} \quad p(y) = \int_{\chi} K(x, y) p(x) \, dx \tag{4.13}$$

where p is a row vector. The answer to this question is yes, subject to some verifiable conditions on the kernel K.

4.3.4 Finding the stationary distribution given a kernel

The discrete case

To find a solution, if it exists, for the finite discrete case is rather straightforward since $p = pK$ implies that $p(I - K) = 0$ or $(I - K')p' = 0$. Thus p' is a right eigenvector associated with a *unit* eigenvalue of the matrix K. Since a square matrix with non-negative entries and rows summing to one always has a real unit eigenvalue a stationary distribution always exists.[7] (But there may be multiple unit eigenvalues

---

7   For K to have a root of 1 the matrix $I - K$ must be singular. But $I - K$ has zero row sums so it is singular. Note that eigenvalues of stochastic matrices are not necessarily real, though the root of largest modulus is.

and multiple stationary distributions.) Let us look at some examples of finite discrete chains and their stationary distributions.

EXAMPLE 4.6 *THE GENERAL TWO STATE CHAIN*   *For the general two state chain with transition kernel given by (4.5) the equation (4.12), with $p = (q, 1 - q)$, becomes*

$$[q \ \ 1 - q] = [q \ \ 1 - q] \begin{bmatrix} 1 - \alpha & \alpha \\ \beta & 1 - \beta \end{bmatrix}$$

whose unique solution is readily found to be

$$p' = \begin{bmatrix} q \\ 1 - q \end{bmatrix} = \begin{bmatrix} \dfrac{\beta}{\alpha + \beta} \\ \dfrac{\alpha}{\alpha + \beta} \end{bmatrix}. \tag{4.14}$$

Thus a stationary distribution of the chain with kernel given in (4.5) exists and it is

$$P(Y = 1) = \beta/(\alpha + \beta); \quad P(Y = 2) = \alpha/(\alpha + \beta)$$

as long as $\alpha + \beta \neq 0$. This solution is clearly unique. Alternatively, note that the eigenvectors of K' are 1 and $1 - \alpha - \beta$ and that the eigenvector corresponding to the unit eigenvalue, when normalized to sum to one, is $\beta/(\alpha + \beta)$, $\alpha/(\alpha + \beta)$.

EXAMPLE 4.7 *A PARTICULAR TWO STATE CHAIN*   *On the other hand, if $\alpha + \beta = 0$ so that both α and β are zero, the transition probability matrix becomes*

$$K = \begin{bmatrix} 1 & 0 \\ 0 & 1 \end{bmatrix},$$

the identity matrix. In this case the equations $p = pK$ are satisfied by any two point probability distribution p, so there are infinitely many stationary distributions!

EXAMPLE 4.8 *For a numerical example consider the three state chain with transition probability matrix*

$$K = \begin{bmatrix} 0.410 & 0.390 & 0.200 \\ 0.313 & 0.577 & 0.110 \\ 0.158 & 0.376 & 0.466 \end{bmatrix} \tag{4.15}$$

so that, for example, $P(X_{t+1} = 1 \mid X_t = 1) = 0.410$. The eigenvalues of K' are

$$eigenvalues(K') = \begin{bmatrix} 1.000 \\ 0.280 \\ 0.172 \end{bmatrix}$$

and the eigenvector corresponding to the unit eigenvalue of K', when normalized to sum to one, is

$$unit\ eigenvector(K') = \begin{bmatrix} 0.310 \\ 0.476 \\ 0.214 \end{bmatrix}$$

which gives the unique stationary distribution of the chain over its three states.[8]

EXAMPLE 4.9 *Consider the transition probability matrix*

$$K = \begin{bmatrix} 0 & 1 \\ 1 & 0 \end{bmatrix}.$$

This is a process that alternates between the two states; if it is in state one it must then go to two and conversely. The eigenvalues of $K' = K$ are 1 and -1 and the eigenvector corresponding to the unit root, when normalized, is $(0.5, 0.5)$. Thus even this deterministic chain does have a unique stationary distribution. It is one in which each state is equally probable!

On the other hand, as in example 4.7, a chain might have more than one stationary distribution.

---

8 These calculations can be done in S using `eigen(t(K))` which produces a vector of eigenvalues and a matrix of eigenvectors. The command `v <- eigen(t(K))$vectors[,1]` stores the eigenvector corresponding to the unit eigenvalue in `v` and the command `v <- v/sum(v)` normalizes it.

EXAMPLE 4.10   *NON-UNIQUENESS*   *Consider the transition probability matrix*

$$K = \begin{bmatrix} 1/2 & 1/2 & 0 \\ 1/2 & 1/2 & 0 \\ 0 & 0 & 1 \end{bmatrix}.$$

This is symmetric with eigenvalues of 1, 1, and 0 so there are two *unit eigenvalues. The eigenvectors are*

$$p_1 = \begin{bmatrix} 0 \\ 0 \\ 1 \end{bmatrix}; \quad p_2 = \begin{bmatrix} 0.707 \\ 0.707 \\ 0 \end{bmatrix}; \quad p_3 = \begin{bmatrix} 0.707 \\ -0.707 \\ 0 \end{bmatrix}$$

so there are at least two *stationary distributions. The first is p_1 and the second is (0.5, 0.5, 0) derived from p_2 after normalizing it to sum to unity. Both vectors satisfy (4.11). The first says that if the process starts in state 3 it will remain there; the second says that if the process is, at any stage, equally likely to be in states 1 or 2 then it will always be equally likely to be in 1 or 2 and never in 3.*

There are, in fact, an infinity of stationary distributions of this chain, all of which have the first two probabilities equal.

The continuous case

In the continuous case, finding the stationary distribution (and the conditions under which it exists) is usually trickier. Here is the solution for the autoregressive model.

EXAMPLE 4.11   *When the transition kernel is (4.6) we can represent the kernel by the linear model expression*

$$x_{t+1} = \rho x_t + \varepsilon_t$$

where ε_t is independent of x_t and the $\{\varepsilon_t\}$ are themselves iid $n(0, 1)$. It follows, because X_t and ε_t are independent, that

$$E(X_{t+1}) = \rho E(X_t) \quad and \quad V(X_{t+1}) = \rho^2 V(X_t) + 1.$$

Stationarity of the distribution requires that the mean and variance are unchanging over time so that, in the stationary distribution,

$$E(X) = \rho E(X) \quad and \quad V(X) = \rho^2 V(X) + 1.$$

The first of these conditions implies that in the stationary distribution, if it exists and unless $\rho = 1$, the mean must be zero, and the second implies that the variance in that distribution must be equal to $1/(1 - \rho^2)$, assuming that $\rho^2 < 1$. This is because if $\rho^2 \geq 1$ there is no positive $V(X)$ satisfying the equation $V(x) = \rho^2 V(X) + 1$. Hence we see that it is necessary for the existence of a stationary distribution with finite mean and positive variance that $|\rho| < 1$. This suggests that a stationary distribution will exist under this condition and that it is normal with mean zero and precision $1 - \rho^2$. To check this conjecture we can carry out the integration in (4.13) with

$$p(y) = n(0, 1 - \rho^2) \quad and \quad K(x, y) = \frac{1}{\sqrt{2\pi}} e^{-(y-\rho x)^2/2}.$$

This gives

$$\int_{-\infty}^{\infty} \frac{1}{\sqrt{2\pi}} e^{-(y-\rho x)^2/2} \frac{\sqrt{1-\rho^2}}{\sqrt{2\pi}} e^{-(1-\rho^2)x^2/2} \, dx$$

$$= \int_{-\infty}^{\infty} \frac{1}{\sqrt{2\pi}} e^{-(x-\rho y)^2/2} \frac{\sqrt{1-\rho^2}}{\sqrt{2\pi}} e^{-(1-\rho^2)y^2/2} \, dx$$

$$= \frac{\sqrt{1-\rho^2}}{\sqrt{2\pi}} e^{-(1-\rho^2)y^2/2} = p(y).$$

This shows that $p(y) = n(0, 1 - \rho^2)$ does satisfy the integral equation (4.13) and so provides a stationary solution to the process. Note that $|\rho| < 1$ is both necessary and sufficient for the existence of a stationary distribution of this chain.

4.3.5 *Finite discrete chains*

Before giving general results let us look a little closer at the algebra of the finite discrete chain. For a finite discrete chain repeated application of (4.8) shows that, generalizing (4.7),

$$p_{n+m} = p_n K^m. \tag{4.16}$$

Now the j'th element of p_{n+m} is the probability of the chain being in state j at time $n + m$. But by the law of conditional probability this must be equal to the sum over *i* of the probabilities of being in state *i* at time *n* times the conditional probability of moving from state *i* to state *j* in *m* steps,

$$P(X_{n+m} = j) = \Sigma_i P(X_n = i) P(X_{n+m} = j \mid X_n = i). \tag{4.17}$$

Comparison of (4.16) to (4.17) shows that K^m must have elements of the form $P(X_{n+m} = i \mid X_n = j)$. These are called the *m* step transition probabilities and K^m is the **m step transition probability matrix**. The elements of K^m provide the probabilities of being in state *j*, *m* steps after being in state *i*, conditional on being initially in state *i*. These elements are denoted by $p_{ij}(m)$; of course $p_{ij}(1)$ is just p_{ij}, the *i*, *j*'th element of *K*. For example, if the states correspond to employed and unemployed then $p_{ij}(m)$ supplies the probability that a man unemployed at any date is found to be employed *m* weeks (days, ...) later.

Now consider the existence of a unique stationary distribution of the chain. The theorem on the existence of a unique stationary distribution of such a chain depends on the notion of irreducibility. State *j* is said to be accessible from state *i* iff there exists an $m > 0$ such that $p_{ij}(m) > 0$. In words, there must be a positive probability of going from state *i* to state *j*, if not immediately then after some number *m* of steps have elapsed. This is not vacuous since it is perfectly possible to write down a transition probability matrix such that, if the chain is in state *i*, state *j* can never be reached, as in example 4.7. If state *i* is accessible from state *j* and state *j* is accessible from state *i* the two states are said to communicate. A set of states that communicate is called a communication class. This enables the following definition.

DEFINITION 4.2 IRREDUCIBILITY *A chain is irreducible if and only if there is only one communication class.*

What does this tell us about the structure of *K*? One thing is immediate and this is that if every element of the transition probability matrix is positive, denoted by $K > 0$, then the chain is irreducible. This is because in such a chain all states are accessible from every other in $m = 1$ steps so all states communicate and the complete set of states forms a communication class. But $K > 0$ is by no means necessary for the chain to be irreducible; that would be very restrictive. In fact one can show that a non-negative square matrix is irreducible if there is no permutation of the rows and columns, that is, a relabeling of the states, such that it can be put in the partitioned matrix form

$$K = \begin{bmatrix} K_{11} & K_{12} \\ 0 & K_{22} \end{bmatrix}.$$

So what is the connection between irreducibility and the existence of a unique stationary distribution? For a finite chain the theorem is:

THEOREM 4.2 EXISTENCE FOR A FINITE CHAIN *An irreducible finite chain has a unique stationary distribution. Every element of the stationary distribution is positive.*

Proof *The proof is essentially that of the famous Perron–Frobenius theorem[9] which states that*

if K is m × m, non-negative and irreducible, then

(1) *one of its eigenvalues is positive and greater than or equal to (in absolute value) all other eigenvalues;*
(2) *there is a positive eigenvector corresponding to that eigenvalue;*
(3) *that eigenvalue is a simple root of the characteristic equation of K.*

See, for example, Bremaud (1998b).

Here are some comments on this theorm. Firstly, it helps to explain the examples. In example 4.6 K is positive when α, $\beta \neq 0$ therefore the chain is irreducible, a unique stationary distribution exists and its probabilities are all positive. In example 4.7 all powers of K are equal to the identity matrix so, for example, $p_{12}(m)$ is never positive; states 1 and 2 do not communicate and there are, in fact, two communication classes, therefore the chain is reducible. In example 4.8 $K > 0$. In example 4.9 K^m is the two by two identity matrix when m is even and K when m is odd, therefore both states communicate and the chain is irreducible. This is an example of a non-positive K that is nevertheless irreducible. In example 4.10 there are two communicating classes, states $\{1, 2\}$ and state 3, so the chain is reducible. This manifests itself in the non-uniqueness of stationary distributions.

The second comment on the theorem is that it has a nice intuitive connection with MCMC. In markov chain monte carlo where the target is the stationary distribution one evidently needs the chain to "visit" every state – every possible value of θ – regardless of its starting point and, moreover, to do this infinitely often. A chain that is irreducible will certainly return to any initial state because $p_{ij}(m) > 0$ for some m. But extra conditions are needed to ensure that it does so infinitely often.

4.3.6 More general chains

There are two further types of homogeneous markov chain, chains with a countably infinite state space and chains with continuous state spaces. Theorems analogous to theorem 4.2 are available but they are a little bit more fussy in that they demand

---

9 The Perron–Frobenius theorem has been well known in economics for over fifty years. See for example Debreu and Hernstein (1953).

conditions additional to irreducibility. We can give the gist of the extra requirement by considering the chain with a countably infinite state space.

The countably infinite case

The relevant theorem in this case involves an additional idea, that of **recurrence**.

DEFINITION 4.3   RETURN TIMES   *The return time to state i is*

$$T_i = \inf\{n \geq 1; \, X_n = i\}.$$

In words, the return time is the first time a chain starting from state i will again be in state i. Clearly, $T_i \geq 1$.

DEFINITION 4.4   RECURRENCE   *A state is recurrent if $P_i(T_i < \infty) = 1$.*
   *A state is recurrent if its return time is finite with probability one. A state that is not recurrent is **transient**.*

DEFINITION 4.5   POSITIVE RECURRENCE   *A state is positive recurrent if $E(T_i) < \infty$.*
   A state is positive recurrent if the mean time to return to it is finite. If all states are positive recurrent the chain is positive recurrent.

Positive recurrence is the extra condition mentioned above that is needed to make sure the chain returns to any particular state often enough for it to do an effective tour of the parameter space. These definitions enable us to state the relevant theorem for countably infinite chains. It is:

THEOREM 4.3   EXISTENCE FOR A COUNTABLE CHAIN   *An irreducible positive recurrent markov chain on a countable state space has a unique stationary distribution.*

   Proof   *See Norris (1997), theorem 1.7.7.*

So we need to add positive recurrence when the state space is countable. This was unnecessary when the state space is finite because then irreducibility implies positive recurrence. For the continuous state space case positive recurrence needs strengthening to Harris recurrence: see Robert and Casella (1999), for example.

4.3.7 Convergence

We turn next to convergence which means asking about whether the state distribution p_t will, in some sense, get arbitrarily close to the unique stationary distribution p when that exists. We clearly need such convergence in MCMC sampling since we want to use realizations from the chain as if they were realizations of the stationary (target) distribution. It is not enough to design a chain that has the target distribution as its stationary distribution; we need also to show that the state distribution will converge to the target, wherever we start the chain. Roughly speaking, we can establish convergence when we add yet another condition on the chain, a condition that will rule out chains like that in example 4.9.

First, what do we mean by convergence? Consider a finite chain. Then we know that

$$p_t = p_0 K^t$$

and that K^t contains the t step transition probabilities $p_{ij}(t)$. Now if p_t is to approach a constant vector then K^t must approach a matrix with identical rows, each of which is equal to the stationary distribution. So we can define convergence in terms of the limiting behavior of the t step transition probabilities $p_{ij}(t)$. In particular, for a countable chain with stationary distribution p we define convergence as

$$\lim_{n \to \infty} p_{ij}(t) = p_j, \quad \text{for all } i, j. \tag{4.18}$$

EXAMPLE 4.12 *EXAMPLE 4.9 REVISITED* *The transition probability matrix*

$$K = \begin{bmatrix} 0 & 1 \\ 1 & 0 \end{bmatrix}$$

gives a chain with a unique stationary distribution equal to $p = (0.5, 0.5)$. But $K^2 = I_2$ and $K^3 = K$ and successive powers alternate between I_2 and K so the elements of K^n cannot converge.

The sort of alternating behavior shown by example 4.9 must be ruled out before we can have convergence. This is done by the condition that the chain is aperiodic.

DEFINITION 4.6   APERIODIC   *A state i is aperiodic if $p_{ii}(n) > 0$ for all sufficiently large n.*

A chain is aperiodic if all its states are. This condition rules out example 4.9 in which, for example, $p_{11}(n)$ is zero for $n = 1, 3, 5, \ldots$

Then the theorem stating convergence for countable chains is:

THEOREM 4.4   CONVERGENCE   *If the chain with kernel K is irreducible and aperiodic with stationary distribution p then*

$$P(X_n = j) \to p_j, \text{ as } n \to \infty \text{ for all } j$$

independently of the initial state distribution p_0. This result implies (4.18).

   Proof   *See Norris (1999), for example.*

   Again there is a version of this theorem for chains on a continuous state space.

4.3.8 Ergodicity

Even though a chain has a unique stationary distribution and converges to it there remains one further set of results before we can be fully content. These relate to the behavior of sample averages and are known as ergodic theorems. If we have a chain we would want to estimate features of the stationary distribution by forming averages of the successive realizations, in the way described in the first paragraph of this chapter, when the chain is run. We would want to be assured that such averages converge in some useful sense to the corresponding expectations with respect to the stationary distribution. This means we want an ergodic theorem to be applicable to our chain.

   The main theorem, at least for a distribution on a countable state space, is:

THEOREM 4.5   ERGODIC   *An irreducible positive recurrent chain, starting from any initial distribution, and with stationary distribution p, is such that*

$$P\left(\frac{1}{n} \sum_{k=0}^{n-1} f(X_k) \to E(f) \text{ as } n \to \infty \right) = 1$$

where $E(f) = \sum p_i f_i$ where $\{f_i\}$ are the values of the function at each possible state of the chain, and $f(.)$ is bounded. In words, the average of functions of realized states converges (almost surely) to the expectation of the function with respect to the stationary distribution. There are analogous theorems for continuous state spaces.

The effect of this result is as follows. Suppose you have a target distribution p of a random variable X (or in another notation θ) and you construct a markov chain that has p as its unique stationary distribution. Then if you run the chain through many steps, from any starting point deterministically or randomly chosen, you will find that the average of (functions of) the successive realizations will approach the expectation of that function of X with respect to p. In particular, the average number of times that $X \in A$ will converge to $P(X \in A)$ for any set A. Thus you can learn about p and any (finite) expectations with respect to it. But this is exactly what you want to do when using sampling in order to study a posterior distribution: you want to generate realizations from the distribution and study their properties. The ergodic theorem tells you the conditions that enable you to do so via markov chain sampling.[10]

4.3.9 *Speed*

A remaining question which we mention briefly for completeness is that of the speed of convergence. The ergodic theorem tells us that state probabilities and sample averages converge, but how fast? With a finite chain this is the question of how rapidly p_t approaches p. Now in this case, from the fundamental equation (4.9), $p'_{t+1} = p'_t K$, we must have $p'_t = p'_0 K^t$ so if $p_t \to p$ then it must be that $p'_0 K^t \to p'$ so the speed of convergence depends on the properties of the transition kernel (probability matrix) K, in particular its eigenvalues. Let us examine this point by the simple example of the general two state chain. Recall that the kernel was

$$K = \begin{bmatrix} 1 - \alpha & \alpha \\ \beta & 1 - \beta \end{bmatrix}.$$

A fairly straightforward calculation then shows that the crucial matrix K^t takes the form

$$K^t = \frac{1}{\alpha + \beta} \begin{bmatrix} \beta & \alpha \\ \beta & \alpha \end{bmatrix} + \frac{(1 - \alpha - \beta)^t}{\alpha + \beta} \begin{bmatrix} \alpha & -\alpha \\ -\beta & \beta \end{bmatrix}.$$

The first matrix on the right has identical rows and each row is the stationary distribution of the chain. The second matrix measures the departure of p_t from p. If its elements are zero you're home; if not you want them to go to zero rapidly, and it can be seen that the speed at which they do so is (a) geometric and (b) depends on the magnitude of $(1 - \alpha - \beta)$. But, from example 4.6, we know that the eigenvalues of K are 1 and $1 - \alpha - \beta$. This example then suggests two propositions. The first is that convergence to the stationary distribution is geometrically fast – this is true for finite chains but not necessarily so in general. The second is that the speed

---

10 Ergodic theorems are a standard and necessary part of econometric time series analysis. Indeed, without them time series econometrics would not be possible.

of convergence depends on the modulus of the second largest eigenvalue. This is generally true and we leave the issue at this point.

We have now completed a brief tour of markov chain theory which aimed to show that (homogeneous) markov chains will have unique stationary distributions to which they converge, and we have given and tried to explain some sufficient conditions for such existence and stationarity to be true. The only remaining problem then is that of constructing a chain (a kernel) that has the target distribution as its stationary distribution.

4.3.10   Finding kernels with a given stationary distribution

For MCMC the relevant question is not whether a given kernel (and chain) has a stationary distribution but whether we can find a kernel corresponding to a given stationary distribution. This is because we want to sample from a given distribution by constructing a chain, i.e. a kernel, and running that chain until realizations come from the given target. So, we ask, given a target distribution, can we find a kernel that has that target as its stationary distribution? The answer is yes, and we can usually find infinitely many chains that have a given target as their stationary distribution.

To demonstrate this point we can first look at our two main examples and then give general methods of chain construction.

> **EXAMPLE 4.13 *THE TWO STATE CHAIN REVISITED*** *The chain with two states, 1 and 2, and transition probability matrix (kernel) given by*
>
> $$K = \begin{bmatrix} 1 - \alpha & \alpha \\ \beta & 1 - \beta \end{bmatrix}$$
>
> *has stationary distribution in which the probability of state 1 is $\beta/(\alpha + \beta)$. Now suppose that you are given a target distribution over the two states in which the probability of state 1 is required to be some specific number $p^\star$. Then you can construct a kernel with $p^\star$, $(1 - p^\star)$ as its stationary distribution by choosing any number α, β such that*
>
> $$\frac{\beta}{\alpha + \beta} = p^\star, \tag{4.19}$$
>
> *or $\beta - \alpha[p^\star/(1 - p^\star)] = 0$. This is a line through the origin in α, β space and any point on that line that satisfies (4.19) with $0 \le \alpha, \beta \le 1$, $\alpha + \beta \ne 0$ will do. Thus there is an infinity of two state chains that have any given stationary distribution.*

EXAMPLE 4.14 *THE AUTOREGRESSIVE PROCESS* *The chain with kernel*

$$K(x, y) = \frac{1}{\sqrt{2\pi}} e^{-(1/2)(y-\rho x)^2}$$

has the unique stationary distribution $p(y) = n(0, 1 - \rho^2)$ *when* $|\rho| < 1$*. Now if we wish to create a chain with stationary distribution* $p(y) = n(0, \theta)$ *we can do so by setting* $\theta = 1 - \rho^2$*, that is, by choosing* $\rho = \pm\sqrt{(1 - \theta)}$*. Thus we can find a chain whose stationary distribution is* $n(0, \theta)$ *only if* $\theta < 1$*. And even in this case there is not an infinity of kernels that will do the job but only two, corresponding to the two solutions in the equation for* ρ*. However, if we look at a larger class of kernels such as*

$$K(x, y) = \frac{\tau^{1/2}}{\sqrt{2\pi}} e^{-(\tau/2)(y-\rho x)^2}$$

there is an infinity of kernels in this class that will do the job. From the equation $x_t = \rho x_{t-1} + \varepsilon_t$ *we see that, in the stationary distribution,*

$$V(X) = \rho^2 V(X) + 1/\tau.$$

So to create a chain with $n(0, \theta)$ *as its stationary distribution we need to choose* ρ *and* τ *such that*

$$\theta = \tau(1 - \rho^2)$$

and this can clearly be done in an infinity of ways for every $\theta > 0$*.*

4.4 TWO GENERAL METHODS OF CONSTRUCTING KERNELS

The two examples of the last section suggest that for any given univariate target distribution we can find a kernel that will have that target as its stationary distribution. But since target distributions in econometrics are almost always multivariate and come in diverse forms it is time to give a general method for finding an appropriate kernel. In this section we shall describe two such methods. The first and most intuitive is called the **Gibbs Sampler**.

4.4.1 *The Gibbs Sampler*

Let the target random variably – the state variable – be vector valued, so that to specify a state of the process we must give a list of numbers as long as the dimension of y. Partition its elements into, say, two blocks, so $y = (y_1, y_2)$ where the y_j may themselves be vectors. Let the target distribution be $p(y) = p(y_1, y_2)$. The kernel is, as before, a specification of the distribution of Y given $X = x$ and is of the form $K(x, y)$ which now is

$$K(x, y) = K(x_1, x_2, y_1, y_2)$$

in which, when the state of the process is x_1, x_2, $K(,)$ gives the probability of going to y_1, y_2. Our problem is to choose the form of K, so that the stationary distribution of the process is a given target (posterior) distribution $p(y_1, y_2)$. One way of doing this is to note that associated with the density p are two **component conditionals**, $p_{Y_1|Y_2}(y_1|y_2)$ and $p_{Y_2|Y_1}(y_2|y_1)$ and this[11] may suggest a kernel which proceeds in the following way from any given origin $x = (x_1, x_2)$.

ALGORITHM 4.2   *GIBBS SAMPLER*

   1. Sample y_1 from the conditional distribution of Y_1 given $Y_2 = x_2$, $p_{Y_1|Y_2}(y_1|x_2)$.
   2. Using the realization y_1, sample y_2 from the conditional distribution of Y_2 given $Y_1 = y_1$, $p_{Y_2|Y_1}(y_2|y_1)$.
   3. Repeat steps 1 and 2.

This algorithm is known as the Gibbs Sampler[12] and it was the first MCMC algorithm to be used in statistics and econometrics and it remains popular. One of several reasons for this is that it is often easy, just from the structure of the problem, to recognize a set of component conditional distributions to be used in the algorithm.[13]

The Gibbs Sampler kernel thus takes the form

$$K(x, y) = p_{Y_1|Y_2}(y_1|x_2)p_{Y_2|Y_1}(y_2|y_1) \qquad (4.20)$$

The idea, once grasped, is quite intuitive and thus is another reason for its popularity as an MCMC method. It says, "to make a move in the chain sample in turn from each of the component conditionals." Moreover, for many models the component conditionals are available so that programming the Gibbs Sampler is easy – at each step you just make two[14] calls to standard random number generators.

To verify that (4.20) does have $p(y_1, y_2)$ as its stationary distribution we just substitute this kernel into the stationarity condition (4.13), getting

---

   11   We are here reverting to the more careful notation in which we distinguish between random variables, which are capitalized, and realizations, which are in lower case.
   12   Willard Gibbs was an early twentieth century American statistical physicist. The initial letters of the phrase Gibbs Sampler provide the last two letters of BUGS.
   13   When y is more than two-dimensional there is more than one way of choosing a partition of y into blocks but the computationally effective choice is usually pretty clear.
   14   Or however many blocks y has been divided into.

$$\int K(x, y)p(x)\, dx = \int p_{Y_1|Y_2}(y_1|x_2)p_{Y_2|Y_1}(y_2|y_1)p_{Y_1,Y_2}(x_1, x_2)\, dx_1\, dx_2$$

$$= \int p_{Y_1|Y_2}(y_1|x_2)p_{Y_2|Y_1}(y_2|y_1)p_{Y_2}(x_2)\, dx_2$$

$$= p_{Y_2|Y_1}(y_2|y_1)\int p_{Y_1,Y_2}(y_1, x_2)\, dx_2$$

$$= p_{Y_2|Y_1}(y_2|y_1)p_{Y_1}(y_1) = p_{Y_1,Y_2}(y_1, y_2) = p(y),$$

as required. Thus we conclude that sampling in sequence from component conditionals provides the kernel of a chain with stationary distribution given by the corresponding joint distribution.

From the technical point of view it is not immediate that a Gibbs Sampler chain satisfies irreducibility, aperiodicity or positive (Harris) recurrence, so the convergence theorems given earlier do not automatically apply. Conditions on (Gibbs) kernels to show convergence have been provided, though they are sometimes difficult to apply – sources are mentioned at the end of this chapter. Thus there is always a slight theoretical doubt about convergence in any Gibbs Sampler application unless the relevant conditions on the kernel have been checked mathematically. Practice, which is doubtless imperfect, is often to neglect this mathematical checking and rely on practical, ex post, convergence checks as discussed later in this chapter even though such checks can never confirm convergence.

EXAMPLE 4.15 *BIVARIATE NORMAL* *As a first example, consider sampling from a bivariate normal distribution with mean zero, unit variances and correlation* ρ. *Then we know that, conditional on* y_2, Y_1 *is normal with mean* ρy_2 *and variance* $1 - \rho^2$. *Similarly,* $Y_2|Y_1 = y_1$ *is normal with mean* ρy_1 *and variance* $1 - \rho^2$. *So a Gibbs Sampler algorithm would be:*

ALGORITHM 4.3 *GIBBS SAMPLING FOR THE BIVARIATE NORMAL*

1. Choose an initial value y_1 *– it would be sensible to choose this value within a couple of standard deviations of its marginal mean, i.e. within* ± 2 *of the origin.*

2. Generate $y_2 \sim n(\rho y_1, 1/(1 - \rho^2))$;

3. Generate $y_1 \sim n(\rho y_2, 1/(1 - \rho^2))$;

4. Go to 2.

After a number of steps in this algorithm the pairs y_1, y_2 *will look like realizations from the stationary, bivariate normal, distribution.*

To see how this works consider the following S program in which we create a function called gibbs whose arguments are the length of the chain, *n*; the correlation in the bivariate distribution, *r*; and the initial value of y_1.

EXAMPLE 4.16   *A GIBBS SAMPLER PROGRAM*[15]

```
gibbs <- function(n, r, y0){
y1 <<- rep(0, n); y2 <<- rep(0, n)
y1[1] <<- y0
for(i in 2:n){
y2[i] <<- rnorm(1, r*y1[i-1], sqrt(1-r^2))
y1[i] <<- rnorm(1, r*y2[i], sqrt(1-r^2))
}}
```

This function is intended to simulate from the bivariate normal with means zero, unit variances and correlation r. The first statements set up empty vectors to hold the output in two vectors y1 and y2; they set the first value of y1 to an arbitrary start or initial condition and then generate the first value of y2 from its conditional distribution given y1; finally, the do loop implements the algorithm by sampling in turn from the component conditionals. To show how this Gibbs Sampler works we choose y0 = 0, its marginal mean, and produce the first 30 steps of the sampler with ρ = 0.9. These are plotted in figure 4.2 and each step is joined by a

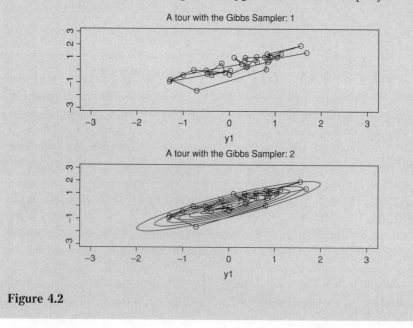

Figure 4.2

15   The S operator <<- is global assignment as opposed to <- which is local assignment. Use of <<- ensures that when the function is called, values, for y2 for example, created within it are stored and available for inspection when the program is done. Under local assignment they would be erased when the program has finished executing.

line to its preceding one. The first graph shows the realizations connected by straight lines, and the second graph shows the same information with contours of the target normal distribution superimposed. The outermost contour contains within it about 95% of the mass of the bivariate distribution. These graphs show rather vividly that the sampler is, in effect, exploring the y_1, y_2 space and, after the sampler has run through a burn-in period, it will visit each region of the space in proportion to its probability. In particular, it will rarely stray far outside the outermost contour in the second graph.

EXAMPLE 4.17   PROBIT REGRESSION   *The probit model is a model for binary choices, labeled $y = 0$, 1, as a function of covariates x. Specifically we suppose that choice is based on the value of a variable y^* that satisfies a normal linear regression model. Thus*

$$y_i^* = x_i\beta + \varepsilon_i, \quad i = 1, 2, ..., n,$$

with the $\{\varepsilon_i\}$ distributed independently as $n(0, 1)$. The agent's decision rule is that $y_i = 1$ if $y_i^* > 0$ and $y_i = 0$ otherwise. The data are $\{y_i, x_i\}$ and the parameter is $\theta = (\beta, y^*)$ where $y^* = (y_1^*, ..., y_n^*)$. We can construct the joint posterior density of θ, $p(\theta|y)$, by Gibbs Sampling using the two blocks β and y^*.

The component conditionals are $p(\beta|y^*, y)$ and $p(y^*|\beta, y)$. The first is the posterior for β in a normal linear model with known, unit, precision and this, assuming a vague prior for β, is known from chapter 3 to be $n(b, X'X)$ where b is the least squares regression coefficient of y^* on the covariates and $X'X$ is the matrix of sums of squares and product of the covariates.

The second component conditional is the distribution of the y_i^* when they have known means $x_i\beta$, known unit precision, and when they are known to be either positive – if $y_i = 1$ – or negative – if $y_i = 0$. Moreover the y_i^* are independent across agents given β. Thus the distribution of y^* is that of n independent left (or right) truncated normal variates.

The Gibbs algorithm for this model is then:

ALGORITHM 4.4   GIBBS SAMPLING FOR THE PROBIT MODEL

1. Choose an initial value for β – perhaps the maximum likelihood estimate.

2. Generate y_i^* for $i = 1, 2, ..., n$ by sampling from $n(x_i\beta, 1)$ truncated on the left at zero if $y_i = 1$ or truncated on the right at zero if $y_i = 0$, using the method of example 4.1.

3. Generate β as $n((X'X)^{-1}X'y^*, X'X)$.

4. Return to 2.

Since both component conditionals, the truncated normals for the $\{y_i^*\}$ and the multivariate normal for β are available or can be sampled exactly in one step – see example 4.1 – the sampler is straightforward to implement.

The probit application demonstrates what statisticians call **data augmentation**. This means taking the original set of parameters, in this case β, and augmenting them with the parameters[16] $\{y_i^*\}$. On the face of it this leads to a more difficult problem since $\{\beta, y^*\}$ is much higher dimensional than β alone. But in fact, in the light of the Gibbs algorithm, it is *much* easier to sample from $p(\beta, y^*|y)$ than from $p(\beta|y)$. This idea has immediate appeal to economists whose models often involve latent (unobserved) variables which are such that, had they been observed, inference would have been straightforward. So the Gibbs algorithm is of immediate application to a large number of models of economic interest.

> **EXAMPLE 4.18   *JOB SEARCH***   *In the standard job search model an agent receives job offers from time to time and eventually accepts one. We typically observe the time until he accepts a job and possibly the accepted wage. Inference would be much simpler if we could also observe the offers, if any, that he/she didn't accept. Gibbs algorithms using the rejected offers as additional parameters have a very simple structure – see Lancaster (1997a).*

As a final note on Gibbs, there is one mistake into which users should definitely not fall! It is possible to write down a Gibbs algorithm such that each component conditional is a proper distribution but such that there is *no* proper joint distribution having those conditionals. So it is unclear what the Gibbs Sampler could possibly be sampling. Casella and George (1992) give an entertaining example.

4.4.2 The Metropolis method

Let the target distribution be $p(y)$ where y may be vector valued. For the **Metropolis method** we first choose a sequence of **jumping** or **proposal distributions** $q(y|x)$ which are, for each $x \in \Theta$, probability distributions over Θ. The function $q(y|x)$ must be symmetric in y and x. The families $q(y|x)$ are not transition kernels because in this method draws from $q(y|x)$ can be rejected. When this happens the state of the chain remains unchanged. We can then construct a chain (kernel) having $p(y)$ as its stationary distribution using the following algorithm.

---

16   So a better name would be parameter augmentation.

ALGORITHM 4.5 *METROPOLIS*

1. *Choose an initial value, y_0, and set $t = 0$.*
2. *Draw y^* from $q(.|y_t)$.*

3. *Calculate the ratio* $r = \dfrac{p(y^*)}{p(y_t)}$.

4. *If $r \geq 1$ set $y_{t+1} = y^*$; otherwise set*

$$
\begin{aligned}
y_{t+1} &= y^* &&\text{with probability } r, \\
y_{t+1} &= y_t &&\text{with probability } 1 - r.
\end{aligned}
$$

5. *Increase t by one and then proceed to step 2.*

The probability that a y^* is accepted is, from step 3 of the algorithm, equal to

$$
\rho(y_t, y^*) = \min\left(\frac{p(y^*)}{p(y_t)}, 1 \right). \tag{4.21}
$$

The rationale of this expression is that the chain is most likely to accept y's that, according to the stationary distribution, are probable relative to the current value of the chain – the chain tends to move to higher probability regions of the sample space, but does not always do so – it sometimes goes downhill. A useful feature of (4.21) is that the constant multiplying $p(y)$ does not have to be calculated since it cancels from the ratio $p(y^*)/p(y_t)$. You only need the kernel of the target distribution.

A Metropolis chain will sometimes show sequences of identical values when realizations are repeatedly rejected and y_{t+1} is set equal to y_t. Nonetheless, for sufficiently large t the random variables $y_t, y_{t+1}, \ldots$ will be identically distributed as $p(.)$.

We now give a proof that the Metropolis chain has $p(.)$ as its stationary distribution.

The Metropolis chain has stationary distribution $p(.)$

To show this we have to show that the kernel defined by the Metropolis procedure satisfies the integral equation (4.13) which we reproduce here for reference:

$$
p(y) = \int_\chi K(x, y)p(x)\, dx.
$$

THEOREM 4.6   METROPOLIS HAS STATIONARY DISTRIBU-TION $p(.)$

Proof   *First, suppose that a kernel satisfies the condition, called **detailed balance**, that*

$$
K(x, y)p(x) = K(y, x)p(y) \tag{4.22}
$$

for all x, y. Then p(.) is the stationary distribution of the chain. Consider any set B and note that

$$\int_Y K(y, B)p(y)\, dy = \int_Y \int_B K(y, x)p(y)\, dx\, dy,$$

$$= \int_Y \int_B K(x, y)p(x)\, dx\, dy \quad \text{by detailed balance}$$

$$= \int_B p(x)\, dx,$$

because $\int_Y K(x, y)\, dy = 1$. Thus p(.) is a stationary distribution of the chain – cf. (4.13).

It only remains to show that the Metropolis kernel satisfies detailed balance. To see this, note that the Metropolis kernel can be written

$$K(x, y) = \rho(x, y)q(y|x) + (1 - r(x))\delta_x(y) \tag{4.23}$$

where $\delta_x(y)$ is the Dirac delta function equal to one if $y = x$ and zero otherwise. Here,

$$\rho(x, y) = \min\left(\frac{p(y)}{p(x)}, 1\right)$$

and

$$r(x) = \int \rho(x, y)q(y|x)\, dy.$$

The explanation for (4.23) is, roughly, that $q(y|x)$ is the probability that y is produced and $\rho(y|x)$ is the chance that it will be accepted so the first term is the probability that $Y = y$ is produced and accepted. $r(x)$ is the sum of these probabilities over y and so is the chance that a y produced is accepted. It follows that the final term is the probability of y being produced and not accepted so the chain stays still with $y = x$. Finally, multiply (4.23) by $p(y)$ and it is straightforward to verify that the Metropolis kernel satisfies detailed balance and thus has p(.) as its stationary distribution.

4.4.3 *Metropolis–Hastings*

More often used than Metropolis is the generalization introduced by Hastings. In this the algorithm is essentially the same as that given above except that r is no longer $p(y^*)/p(y_t)$ but is rather

$$r(y_t, y^*) = \frac{p(y^*)}{p(y_t)} \frac{q(y_t|y^*)}{q(y^*|y_t)}$$

and the probability that y^* is accepted is not (4.21) but rather

$$\rho(y_t, y^*) = \min\left(\frac{p(y^*)}{p(y_t)} \frac{q(y_t|y^*)}{q(y^*|y_t)}, 1 \right). \tag{4.24}$$

Notice that if $q(x, y)$ is symmetric then (4.24) reduces to the Metropolis algorithm. The proof that the Metropolis–Hastings (M–H) algorithm has $p(y)$ as its stationary distribution is a simple generalization of the proof for the Metropolis algorithm. A very large number of Metropolis–Hastings algorithms have been proposed in the literature and pointers to this literature are given at the end of this chapter. One common choice is the Independence M–H Sampler in which $q(y|x)$ does not depend on x and the acceptance criterion reduces to

$$\rho(y_t, y^*) = \min\left(\frac{p(y^*)}{p(y_t)} \frac{q(y_t)}{q(y^*)}, 1 \right).$$

Another is the Random Walk M–H Sampler in which $y_t^* = y_t + \varepsilon_t$ where ε_t is a random perturbation of the current state of the chain. In this case $q(y|x)$ takes the form $g(y - x)$. Convergence and ergodic theorems are available for many special cases of the Metropolis–Hastings algorithm – see Robert and Casella (1999).

As compared to Gibbs the Metropolis–Hastings algorithm[17] is more flexible through the choice of $q(.|.)$ but perhaps less intuitive than Gibbs. The latter is often the first choice in a simulation problem and M–H is used if some component conditional is difficult to sample. This practice, which creates a hybrid chain, can introduce complications in convergence proofs.

4.4.4 Practical convergence

We have briefly discussed the question of convergence and the speed at which this happens earlier in this chapter, but this is not really the operational question for the user, which is "I have run the chain through 1,000 steps; has it converged?" So how do you tell by looking at your realizations whether the chain is producing realizations from the target distribution? Many answers to this question have been proposed but first note that in a strict sense the question is unanswerable. The output from your chain may look stationary; you may have run the sampler from many diverse starting points; and yet still it is possible that the realizations do not originate from the target distribution. To see this, suppose the target distribution has many isolated

---

17 Actually, Gibbs is a special case of M–H for a particular choice of the proposal density.

modes, then it is possible to have sampler output that never visits one of the modes even if it is theoretically guaranteed to do so eventually. Of course one should not overstate this point and it is usually ignored in practice, and the same problem besets any numerical integration procedure.

Perhaps the most widely used of practical convergence checks derives from running a number of chains simultaneously and comparing the variation in the output between and within chains. It works like this. Suppose that you run n realizations from m parallel chains each of which starts at a different point in θ space. Pick a scalar function of θ, perhaps a single element of this vector, and call it ω and consider using the realizations of ω in each chain to do your convergence check. Let the i'th realization of ω in the j'th chain be denoted by ω_{ij}. Then the "variance" *between* chains is defined to be

$$B = \frac{n}{m-1} \Sigma_{j=1}^{m} (\bar{\omega}_j - \bar{\omega})^2$$

where $\bar{\omega}$ is the overall mean of all mn realizations and $\bar{\omega}_j$ is the mean of the n realizations in chain j.[18] The variance *within* chains is defined to be

$$W = \frac{1}{m(n-1)} \Sigma_{i=1}^{n} \Sigma_{j=1}^{m} (\omega_{ij} - \bar{\omega}_j)^2.$$

This is the average of the variances within each chain. Now assuming that the chain is ergodic, both B and W will be consistent estimates of σ^2, the variance of ω, as $n \to \infty$ and so will their weighted average,

$$\hat{\sigma}_\omega^2 = (1 - 1/n)W + (1/n)B.$$

The idea of the convergence check is to compare W and $\hat{\sigma}_\omega^2$ using the statistic

$$R = \sqrt{\hat{\sigma}_\omega^2/W}.$$

This is called the Gelman–Rubin statistic (as modified by Brooks).

The intuition behind the test is as follows. If the starting points of the chains are overdispersed relative to the variation that you expect in ω then the between variation, B, will initially overstate the variability of ω. By contrast, the within variance will tend to understate the variability in ω because the early draws will not yet have thoroughly explored its state space. This indicates that R will initially be larger than one but fall towards it as the length of the chains increases. The BUGS software prints out the evolution of R as the chains evolve. A common practice is to compute

18   So B is really n times the variance in the sample means of the m chains, using the conventional divisor $m - 1$.

R for all or a selection of the components of θ. Remember that R values that have reached one are indicative of convergence but do not prove it.

Many alternative checks for convergence have been proposed: Gammerman (1997) provides a useful review.

4.4.5 Using samples from the posterior

Suppose that the random variables of interest are, say, $\theta = (\theta_1, \theta_2)$, and that you have obtained a sample from their joint posterior distribution giving you a data file with two columns and nrep rows of which the first column contains θ_1 realizations and the second contains θ_2 realizations. This sample may have been drawn by an exact sampling method or it may consist of the output of an MCMC calculation; for the purpose of this section it doesn't matter which. Suppose that your aim is to calculate some feature(s) of the marginal posterior distribution of, say, θ_2. How should you do this?

The natural answer is to look at the θ_2 realizations. For example, if you want to know the mean of θ_2 then average the nrep θ_2 realizations; if you want to know the most likely value of θ_2 then form a histogram of the θ_2 realizations, draw a smooth curve through it and find the point at which the curve is highest; if you want to know the precise shape of the marginal posterior density of θ_2 then also use a smoothed histogram.[19] But, oddly enough, none of these natural choices are the best ways to use the sampler output.

The reason for this is that they neglect the information about the distribution of θ_2 that is contained in the θ_1 realizations. Such information will exist if θ_2 and θ_1 are dependent. To see this, consider two estimators of, say, μ_2, the mean of θ_2. Let $\phi(\theta_1)$ denote the conditional expectation of θ_2 given θ_1 and *assume that this is a known function*. Denote the n realizations of θ_1 and θ_2 by $\theta_{11}, \theta_{12}, ..., \theta_{1,n}$ and $\theta_{21}, \theta_{22}, ..., \theta_{2,n}$ and take the first estimator to be the sample mean of the θ_2 values and let the second estimator be the sample mean of $\phi(\theta_1)$. Thus,

$$\acute{\mu}_2 = (1/n)\sum_{i=1}^{n}\theta_{2i}; \quad \tilde{\mu}_2 = (1/n)\sum_{i=1}^{n}\phi(\theta_{1i}).$$

The first thing to note is that these two estimators have the same expectation and this is the mean of θ_2. Clearly this is true for $\acute{\mu}_2$ since each θ_{2i} has mean μ_2. And that it is true for $\tilde{\mu}_2$ follows from:

THEOREM 4.7 THE LAW OF ITERATED EXPECTATIONS *This states that, provided the expectations exist,*

$$E(Y) = E(E(Y|X)).$$

In words, the average is the same as the average of the (conditional) averages.

19 Perhaps using a standard kernel smoother such as is provided in S by `density(x)`.

Proof *The proof is*

$$E(Y) = \iint yp(x, y)\,dy\,dx$$

$$= \int p(x) \int yp(y|x)\,dy\,dx$$

$$= \int p(x)\,E(Y|x)\,dx = E(E(Y|X)).$$

It follows from this law that

$$E\phi(\theta_1) = E(E(\theta_2|\theta_1)) = E(\theta_2) = \mu_2$$

and both estimators of the mean of θ_2 are unbiased.

The second property of these two estimators is that $\tilde{\mu}_2$ has, in general, a smaller sampling variance than $\hat{\mu}_2$.

THEOREM 4.8 RAO–BLACKWELL *This theorem states that, provided the expectations exist,*

$$E(Y - \mu)^2 \geq E(E(Y|X) - E(Y))^2, \tag{4.25}$$

where μ is $E(Y)$. The left hand side is the variance of Y. The right hand side of (4.25) is the expected value of the squared deviation of $E(Y|X)$ from its mean which is $E(Y)$ by the law of iterated expectations. Thus the r.h.s. is the variance of the conditional mean of Y given X and (4.25) becomes

$$V(Y) \geq V(E(Y|X)),$$

or, in words, the variance exceeds or equals the variance of the conditional mean.

Proof *The proof is as follows. Note that*

$$E(Y - \mu)^2 = E(Y - E(Y|X) + E(Y|X) - \mu)^2.$$

Let $a = Y - E(Y|X)$ and $b = E(Y|X) - \mu$ so that

$$E(Y - \mu)^2 = E(a^2) + E(b^2) + 2E(ab). \tag{4.26}$$

Now note that $E(b^2) = E((E(Y|X) - \mu)^2)$ and this is $V(E(Y|X))$, the variance of the conditional mean. Furthermore, $E(a^2) \geq 0$ so the proof is done if we can show that $E(ab) = 0$. But $E(ab) = E(E(ab|X))$ by the law of iterated expectation, and b is a function of X alone, and $E(a|X) = 0$. It follows that $E(ab) = E(E(ab|X)) = E(bE(a|X)) = 0$.

To see how this applies to a comparison of $\hat{\mu}_2$ and $\tilde{\mu}_2$ note that the variance of $\hat{\mu}_2$ is the variance of θ_2 divided by n but the variance of $\tilde{\mu}_2$ is the variance of the conditional mean of θ_2 given θ_1 also divided by n. So the theorem implies that, in general, $\tilde{\mu}_2$ is the more precise estimator. It is in this sense that it is "wrong" to use $\hat{\mu}_2$.

The preceding discussion did not restrict the form of $E(Y|X)$ but the theorem will appear more familiar to those familiar with regression analysis if we look briefly at the linear regression case. Specifically, suppose that

$$Y = X\beta + \varepsilon$$

where $E(\varepsilon|X) = 0$ and so $X\beta$ is the conditional expectation $E(Y|X = x)$. Then the theorem says that $V(Y) \geq V(X\beta)$ which is true because $V(Y) = V(X\beta) + V(\varepsilon)$.

Rao–Blackwell density estimates

Perhaps the most common use of the Rao–Blackwell theorem is to construct, from sampler output, a good estimate of the marginal probability density function of some scalar component of the parameter vector θ. Again let $\theta = (\theta_1, \theta_2)$ with joint density $p(\theta_1, \theta_2)$, conditional density $p_{2|1}(\theta_2|\theta_1)$, and marginal densities $p_1(\theta_1)$ and $p_2(\theta_2)$. The problem is to use nrep realizations from $p(\theta_1, \theta_2)$ to estimate $p_2(\theta_2)$. Now

$$p_2(y) = \int p(\theta_1, y) \, d\theta_1$$

$$= \int p(y|\theta_1) p_1(\theta_1) \, d\theta_1$$

$$= E(p_{2|1}(y|\theta_1)).$$

Thus the marginal density of θ_2 at the point y is the expected value of the conditional density of θ_2 given θ_1 at the point y. The Rao–Blackwell theorem implies that it is generally better to estimate $p_2(y)$ by averaging the conditional densities at y than by using the θ_2 realizations alone. With the realizations denoted by $\theta_i = (\theta_{1i}, \theta_{2i})$ the Rao–Blackwell estimate of $p_2(\theta_2)$ at the point $\theta_2 = y$ would take the form

$$\hat{p}_2(y) = (1/n)\sum_{i=1}^{n} p_{2|1}(y|\theta_{2i})$$

Constructing an estimate using conditional distributions in this way is known, rather clumsily, as Rao–Blackwellizing. To apply the method you need to know the conditional mean or distribution of θ_2 given θ_1. In MCMC work this is often the case, particularly when using the Gibbs Sampler. Often a glance at the joint posterior distribution reveals to you $p(\theta_2|\theta_1)$ even though $p(\theta_2)$, which requires an integration, remains unclear. Here is a simple numerical example, one in which the answer happens to be known analytically.

EXAMPLE 4.19 *Let X, Y be standard bivariate normal with means zero, unit variances and correlation ρ. Then the joint density is*

$$p(x, y) \propto \exp\left\{-\frac{1}{2(1-\rho^2)}(x^2 + y^2 - 2\rho xy)\right\}.$$

It should (!) be obvious from this expression that the conditional distribution of y given x is normal with mean ρx and variance $(1 - \rho^2)$. Of course, the marginal density of y is $n(0, 1)$, but pretend we don't know this but that we do know $p(y|x)$. If we have, say, 40 realizations of X, Y then we could use the Y observations to construct a kernel smooth estimate of the density of Y – this is the "natural" way to estimate the density of Y; or we could construct a Rao–Blackwell estimate. The latter is the average of the conditional densities at the 40 X points, namely

$$\tilde{p}_Y(y) = \frac{1}{40}\sum_{i=1}^{40}\frac{1}{\sqrt{1-\rho^2}\sqrt{2\pi}}\exp\left\{-\frac{1}{2(1-\rho^2)}(y - \rho x_i)^2\right\}.$$

In the calculations plotted in figure 4.3 we generated 40 bivariate normal realizations with $\rho = 0.5$ and then plotted (a) a kernel estimate of the ($n(0, 1)$) marginal density of Y using the S command `density` *with the default Gaussian kernel and default bandwidth – this is plotted with crosses; (b) the Rao–Blackwell estimate at 100 distinct y's from –3 to 3 – this is plotted with circles; and (c) the true $n(0, 1)$ density – plotted as a solid line. It can be seen that the R–B estimate does rather well, and better than the kernel estimate using only y data, but then it's using much more information than the kernel estimate.*

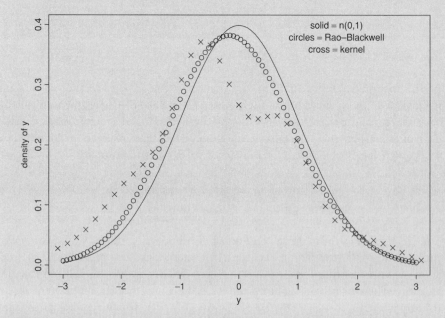

Figure 4.3 Three estimates of the standard normal density function

4.4.6 Calculating the prior predictive density

In comparing the probabilities of alternative models the prior predictive density plays a central role, as we showed in chapter 2. This distribution is just the probability of the data that you have on the model you are using, and to compare two models you look to see which of them accords your data higher probability. The formula for this distribution is

$$p(y) = \int p(\theta, y)\, d\theta = \int p(y|\theta)p(\theta)\, d\theta. \qquad (4.27)$$

This quantity is also sometimes called the **marginal likelihood**. Looked at from another angle $p(y)$ is (one over) the constant that makes the posterior density of θ integrate to one. This is directly from Bayes' theorem:

$$p(\theta|y) = \frac{p(y|\theta)p(\theta)}{p(y)}.$$

In models of simple structure this normalizing constant can be calculated analytically. For example with Bernoulli trials and a uniform prior the posterior was $p(\theta|y) \propto \theta^s(1 - \theta)^{n-s}$ and the normalizing constant is found from the beta density formula to be

$$p(y) = \frac{\Gamma(s + 1)\Gamma(n - s + 1)}{\Gamma(n + 2)}.$$

Or it can be calculated numerically by taking a large sample from the prior and estimating (4.27) as

$$\hat{p}(y) = \frac{1}{nrep} \sum_{i=1}^{nrep} p(y|\theta_i) \qquad (4.28)$$

since $p(y)$ is just the expectation of $p(y|\theta)$ with respect to $p(\theta)$ and this formula estimates this expectation by a sample average. This can be made as accurate as you like by taking nrep big enough.

But for more complex models analytical calculation may be impossible and (4.28) may demand a very large sample indeed. So there is need for another method and the following technique makes effective use of Rao–Blackwellizing.

By rearranging Bayes' theorem we have

$$p(y) = \frac{p(y|\theta)p(\theta)}{p(\theta|y)} \qquad (4.29)$$

and since the left hand side does not involve θ this formula must be true for *any* θ. Pick a point, call it θ^*, and assume we can calculate the likelihood at θ^*, and the prior at θ^*. Then all that remains is to calculate the posterior density at θ^*. There are several ways to calculate this posterior density ordinate but the following can be effective. Suppose that you have been doing Gibbs Sampling with data augmentation so that you worked with an enlarged parameter vector θ, y^* and you know the component conditional $p(\theta|y^*, y)$. Then we can make a Rao–Blackwell estimate of $p(\theta^*|y)$ by

$$\hat{p}(\theta^*|y) = \frac{1}{nrep} \Sigma_{i=1}^{nrep} p(\theta^*|y_i^*, y) \tag{4.30}$$

where the $\{y_i^*\}$ are the sample from the marginal posterior density of y^* that is available in your Gibbs Sampler output file. This follows because

$$p(\theta^*|y) = \int p(\theta^*, y^*|y)\,dy^* = \int p(\theta^*|y^*, y)p(y^*|y)\,dy^*.$$

Finally, insert (4.30) in (4.29) to get

$$\hat{p}(y) = \frac{p(y|\theta^*)p(\theta^*)}{(1/nrep)\Sigma_{i=1}^{nrep} p(\theta^*|y_i^*, y)}. \tag{4.31}$$

All that remains is to choose θ^* and a sensible choice will be a point of high posterior density such as the posterior mode. The denominator in (4.31) is a Rao–Blackwell estimate of $p(\theta|y)$.

The paper by Chib (1995) gives extensions and applications.

4.4.7 *Implementing markov chain monte carlo*

Until recently if you wanted to sample using MCMC you had to write your own sampler algorithm. But for most models economists might want to use, this is no longer the case.[20] There are several packages now available that enable you to write down your model and the package will choose an appropriate MCMC algorithm and produce for you sampler MCMC output and summary and diagnostic statistics. The package used in this book is BUGS (Bayesian analysis Using the Gibbs Sampler).[21] In appendix 2 we provide a fairly detailed guide to the use of this package. Here we shall briefly explain the principles of the use of this program. *These principles are a direct implementation of the principles of Bayesian inference.*

Presuming that you have downloaded a copy of BUGS – in writing this book I have used an MS Windows version called WinBUGS – the package requires you to supply the following:

---

20 Much of the recent literature in Bayesian econometrics has consisted in presenting MCMC algorithms for particular classes of model.

21 The acronym is a peculiarly English joke, not necessarily appreciated in other parts of the globe.

(1) Your data.
(2) Your likelihood.
(3) Your prior.

After all, what else does a Bayesian econometrician require!

Providing these items to the program and retrieving the sample output has historically involved a somewhat sharp learning curve but now there exists an interface to WinBUGS from the R implementation of S.[22] In this, described in more detail in appendix 2, your data exist as an R data file (data in other formats, e.g. SAS, can be easily imported into R) and you must write down a data statement as a list whose components are, well, the data. These would include the sample size, the actual y's and x's, and any other specified numerical parameters, for example parameters that appear in hierarchical prior structures. A simple example of a data statement might be

```
data <- list(n = 100, y = y)
```

where the left hand y refers to a variable that appears in your likelihood and the right hand y refers to a vector of numbers stored in R.

The next requirement for input to BUGS is the likelihood. This is a direct translation of what, in mathematical notation, is $\ell(\theta; y)$. For example if your model states that the T values of Y follow a first order autoregressive process, $y_t = \alpha + \rho y_{t-1} + \varepsilon_t$ with the $\{\varepsilon_t\} \sim n(0, \tau)$ independently, then you would write in your model file, say, "mymodel.txt,"

```
model{
for(i in 2:T){y[i] ~dnorm(mu[i], tau)
mu[i] <- alpha + rho * y[i-1]
}
```

The final element of your model statement is the prior of which a simple example might be

```
alpha ~ dnorm(0, 0.001)
rho ~ dnorm(0, 0.001)
tau ~ dgamma(0.001,0.001)
```

This provides independent low precision normal distributions for α, ρ and a low precision gamma distribution for the precision τ. All priors used in BUGS must be proper.

The likelihood and the prior will be written in a file with extension .txt in R.

In addition to the model file and the data list, the interface requires a statement of which of the model parameters you wish to monitor and save for subsequent study. This might be

```
parameters <- c("alpha", "rho", "tau")
```

---

22   Interfaces to WinBUGS from SAS and Matlab are also available. Go to the WinBUGS home page, www.mrc-bsu.cam.ac.uk/bugs/winbugs/contents.html for current details.

Finally, since you are asking the package to produce markov chain(s) you must tell the chain what state to start from (although you can sometimes get BUGS to sample starting points from the prior). This means providing initial values for all the components of the chain, for example

```
inits <- list(alpha = 0, rho = 0.8, tau = 1)
```

In practice it is wise to run several markov chains from diverse starting values so you would provide several inits statements, inits1, inits2, etc. and combine them in an overall general statement such as

```
inits <- list(inits1, inits2, ...)
```

Finally, you must tell the program how many steps to run the sampler for. If it appears not to have converged for your initial choice of number of steps, raise the number and try again. You must also tell the program how many steps to discard and therefore how many steps to use in calculating the posterior distributions that you want.

The sampler is then run by a call of the form

```
mysim <- bugs(data, inits, parameters, "mymodel.txt",
n.chains=3, n.iter = 5000, debug=T)
```

which will start WinBUGS and store realizations of the "parameters" under the names used in "parameters."

4.5 CONCLUSION

Bayesian inference requires you to compute probability distributions and this can be done by sampling from them. There are many ways to sample probability distributions using a computer. This is the currently effective way – don't deduce probability distributions, sample them. They may be sampled by single calls to available subroutines; they may be sampled as a sequence of independent realizations; they may be sampled as a sequence of dependent realizations, as in MCMC. All these methods are now well within the capacity of an applied economics researcher. In this chapter we have tried to provide the basis for a good, if intuitive, understanding of the main sampling methods. For many purposes the most significant one of these is markov chain monte carlo.

4.6 EXERCISES AND COMPLEMENTS

(1) Use the S functions `runif`, `rbinom`, `rexp`, and `rnorm` to produce pseudo-random realizations from such distributions. Then use descriptive statistics methods such as `hist`, `table`, `plot(density)`, and `summary` to examine the realizations and explore the shapes of these distributions.

(2) Take the posterior density of θ corresponding to n independent poisson variates with mean θ and an improper prior $p(\theta) \propto 1/\theta$. Show that the likelihood depends only on n and the sum of the observations, $s = \sum_{i=1}^{n} y_i$. Deduce the asymptotic normal approximation to $p(\theta|y)$ and find, by calculation or by drawing, how large n and s must be to ensure accuracy of the normal approximation.

(3) The error precision, τ, in a linear regression model with a vague prior has a posterior density that is gamma $(v/2, e'e/2)$ where n is the sample size, $v = n - k$ is the degrees of freedom, e is the vector of least squares residuals and so $e'e$ is the residual sum of squares. Conditional on τ the vector of regression coefficients β is multivariate normal with mean equal to the least squares estimate b and precision matrix $\tau X'X$ where $X(n \times k)$ is the matrix of regressor values. Generate some data and show how to sample from the marginal density of β by first sampling τ with a call to the function `rgamma` and then using the realized τ in a call to `rmvnorm`.

(4) Consider the three state markov chain with transition matrix

$$K = \begin{bmatrix} 0.384 & 0.238 & 0.378 \\ 0.434 & 0.221 & 0.345 \\ 0.338 & 0.379 & 0.283 \end{bmatrix}.$$

Using the S commands `eigen(t(K))` and `K <- K%*%K` (matrix multiplication) find the stationary distribution of the chain and study how rapidly the chain converges.

(5) About the simplest method of simulating a scalar random variable is by *inverting the distribution function*. Try simulating truncated normal variates using the method of example 4.1. Plot the realizations and check that they make sense. Extend example 4.1 to truncated versions of other distributions, for example the exponential or gamma.

(6) A simple application of the result of theorem 4.1 is in sampling from an exponential (θ) distribution. Show that $Y = -(1/\theta) \log U$ is indeed distributed as exponential (θ) and use that fact to draw a sample from it given a uniform sample.

(7) Try sampling from a bivariate normal distribution using the Gibbs algorithm 4.3. Plot your output and observe the elliptical shape of the contours. Try sampling from a joint distribution with ρ close to ± 1 to see if the sampler takes longer to converge than when ρ is close to zero.

(8) You can do the same operation using BUGS with the program

```
model{
y1 ~ dnorm(mu1, tau)
y2 ~ dnorm(mu2, tau)
mu1 <- rho*y2
mu2 <- rho*y1
tau <- 1/(1-rho*rho)
}
```

Try this using the value of rho as data, for various values of rho.

4.7 BIBLIOGRAPHIC NOTES

Ripley (1987) gives a concise but readable account of methods for exact simulation of random variables, while Devroye (1986) is a nearly exhaustive monograph on the subject.

There is a large and rapidly growing journal literature on MCMC methods and there is now a large selection of books that provide an account of the subject. Robert and Casella (1999) is a clear, though mathematically advanced, account of the subject. It contains discussion and further references on the question of convergence of Gibbs Sampler algorithms. An easier and clear introductory stochastic process book is Bremaud (1998a). Norris (1997) is a clear account of countable chains and I have drawn upon it in writing this chapter. Gammerman (1997) is a good introduction to MCMC written at a slightly higher level than this book and it contains a useful survey of methods for monitoring convergence of MCMC output. Meyn and Tweedie (1993) and Nummelin (1984) are two relevant advanced references. Possibly the best recent book on markov chains with applications to MCMC is by Bremaud, *Markov Chains* (1998b). *The Handbook of Econometrics* (2001) contains a survey article by Chib. This is a useful survey and gives a number of algorithms for popular classes of econometric model as well as a valuable bibliography. A fine introduction to the Gibbs Sampler at an elementary level is by Casella and George (1992). This is strongly recommended. Chib and Greenberg (1995: 327–35) is useful. Important early papers in the statistics literature are by Smith and Gelfand (1992: 84–8), Gelfand and Smith (1990: 398–409), and by Smith and Roberts (1993: 3–23).

Chib (1995: 1313–21) proposed the method for constructing the prior predictive distribution discussed in section 4.4.6. See also Newton and Raftery (1994: 3–48).

There have already been several examples of Gibbs with data augmentation in the econometrics literature – see the bibliography to Chib's *Handbook of Econometrics* chapter. Lancaster (1997b: 165–79) applies the technique to an optimal job search model.

Congdon has two, soon to be three, books providing many examples of WinBUGS code both in the text and at the book's web site. Those already published are Congdon, *Bayesian Statistical Modelling* (2001) and Congdon, *Applied Bayesian Modelling* (2003).

For a precise statement of theorems proving asymptotic posterior normality and the regularity conditions required for them to hold see Heyde and Johnstone (1979: 184–9). The proofs depend on central limit theorems. Typical regularity conditions require that the dimension of θ remain constant as $n \rightarrow \infty$, and that the sample space for Y not depend on θ.

Some other useful articles are Cowles and Carlin (1995: 883–904); Brooks and Roberts (1998: 319–35); Brooks and Gelman (1998: 434–55), following on from (generalizing and correcting) Gelman and Rubin (1992: 457–511).

Chapter 5
NON-LINEAR REGRESSION MODELS

In this chapter we shall resume the thread of chapter 3 and present some examples of *non-linear* regression models that are of economic interest. These will still be regression models so that mean independence of errors and regressors will still be assumed. It is not until the following chapters that we shall look at econometric models that are not naturally posed as regressions. In traditional econometrics non-linear regression models are felt to be more difficult than linear because exact sampling distributions are hard or impossible to calculate and reliance has to be placed on approximate, asymptotic results. But from the modern Bayesian point of view such models are no more difficult than linear ones except, on occasion, numerically. Essentially exact posterior inference can be carried out for a large class of non-linear econometric models.

5.1 ESTIMATION OF PRODUCTION FUNCTIONS

Production functions are technical relations between inputs and outputs. For the first application we examine inference about the parameters of the **constant elasticity of substitution** (CES) production function

$$Y = A[\delta L^{-\beta} + (1 - \delta)K^{-\beta}]^{-1/\beta}, \qquad (5.1)$$

where Y is output, K is capital and L is labor. The parameters are

$$A, \text{ a scale parameter, } A > 0;$$
$$\delta, \text{ a distribution parameter, } 0 < \delta < 1;$$
$$\beta, \text{ a substitution parameter, } \beta \geq -1.$$

The parameters of main economic interest are δ and

$$\sigma = \frac{1}{1 + \beta},$$

the elasticity of substitution. Since $\sigma \geq 0$ this implies that $\beta \geq -1$. An important limiting case is $\sigma = 1 \Rightarrow \beta = 0$. Taking the limit of (5.1) as $\beta \to 0$, using l'Hôpital's rule, gives

$$Y = AL^{\delta}K^{1-\delta}, \tag{5.2}$$

the **Cobb–Douglas production function**. Past estimates of the elasticity of substitution often seem to suggest values not very far from 1, the Cobb–Douglas case.

To turn this deterministic model into an econometric one let us introduce an error term of mean zero and assume that K, L are exogenous. Thus they are believed to be independent of the errors in the model and to have a marginal distribution that does not involve the model parameters. It follows that we have a regression model, though a non-linear one. Thus, if the error is introduced multiplicatively,

$$Y = A[\delta L^{-\beta} + (1 - \delta)K^{-\beta}]^{-1/\beta}e^{\varepsilon},$$

and, after taking logarithms, we get

$$y = a - (1/\beta)\log[\delta L^{-\beta} + (1 - \delta)K^{-\beta}] + \varepsilon, \quad a = \log A, \ y = \log Y. \tag{5.3}$$

By pulling $L^{-\beta} = e^{-\beta l}$ out of the term in square brackets this may be put in a more convenient form as

$$y - l = a - (1/\beta)\log[\delta + (1 - \delta)e^{-\beta(k-l)}] + \varepsilon, \quad k = \log K, \ l = \log L. \tag{5.4}$$

This is a non-linear regression model in which the mean value of the logarithm of output per man, Y/L, depends on the logarithm of capital per man, K/L. The model is non-linear in two senses. The mean is a non-linear function of K/L; and it is a non-linear function of the parameters (δ, β).

To complete the model assume, for purposes of exposition only, that the $\{\varepsilon_i | \tau\} \sim$ iid $n(0, \tau)$, which then provides the likelihood, and then provide a prior for $\theta = (a, \delta, \beta, \tau)$. The likelihood is

$$\ell(\theta|y) \propto \tau^{n/2} \exp\{-(\tau/2)\Sigma_{i=1}^{n}(y_i - l_i - \mu_i)^2\} \tag{5.5}$$

$$\text{for} \quad \mu_i = a - (1/\beta)\log[\delta + (1 - \delta)e^{-\beta(k_i - l_i)}].$$

For the sake of illustration we choose conventional diffuse normal and gamma priors for a and τ respectively. The prior for δ, which lies between zero and one, was chosen to be uniform over this interval. The prior for β, which lies between minus one and infinity, is a little more difficult. We choose to place a uniform prior over what seems to be an economically plausible region giving elasticities of substitution ranging from 0.02 to 50. Notice that a uniform prior for β implies a non-uniform prior for σ. Alternatively one might want to put in a prior for β that recognizes that σ is probably not far from 1.

EXAMPLE 5.1 *POSTERIOR INFERENCE FOR THE CES MODEL*

To illustrate Bayesian inference using this model we generated $n = 100$ independent draws from a CES production function, for which $\sigma = 1$ and so $\beta = 0$, with capital/labor shares varying about $2/3$. The labor share parameter δ was set to be $\delta = 0.4$; τ was set to 1; and a was set to zero. Thus the model generating the data was

$$y - l = 0.6(k - l) + u, \quad u \sim n(0, 1),$$

which is the Cobb–Douglas special case. The model we fit, however, is the general CES function, (5.4). The MCMC sampler in BUGS was run through 3,000 steps and the last 1,500 retained. Three chains were run to check convergence using the GR statistic. We report only posterior densities of β and $\sigma = 1/(1 + \beta)$ since the posterior densities of a and δ are nearly normal and centered near the values used in generating the data. Figure 5.1 shows smoothed histograms of the $3 \times 1,500 = 4,500$ realizations, first of β and then of σ. The fact that there is some density near $\beta = -1$ translates into a long right tail for the density of σ. However, both distributions have modes that point to the right values, namely zero for β and one for σ. Notice that to derive the posterior density of σ from that of β all that is necessary is to apply the function `sig <- 1/(1 + b)` *to the vector b containing the 4,500 realizations of this parameter. No mathematical derivation involving a jacobian is required, nor are asymptotic approximations needed.*

The BUGS model statement was

```
model{
for(i in 1:n){
yl[i]~dnorm(mu[i],tau)
mu[i]<- a-(1/b)*log(d+(1-d)*exp(-b*kl[i]))
}
b ~dunif(-0.8,50)
a ~dnorm(0,0.001)
d ~dunif(0.05,0.98)
tau ~dgamma(.01,.01)
}
```

in which `yl` *stands for $y - l$ and* `kl` *for $k - l$. All the priors used here are readily modified to see the effect of alternative forms on the posterior density of, say, σ or δ. We could have put in an additional line telling the program to calculate $\sigma = 1/(1 + \beta)$. This would have the form* `sig <- 1/(1+b)` *and its effect would be to include realizations of σ in the output file. Instead we chose to do this transformation ourselves in R. Extensions of the model to allow for non-normality, heteroscedasticity or autocorrelation are also straightforward and follow the same pattern as in the linear model.*

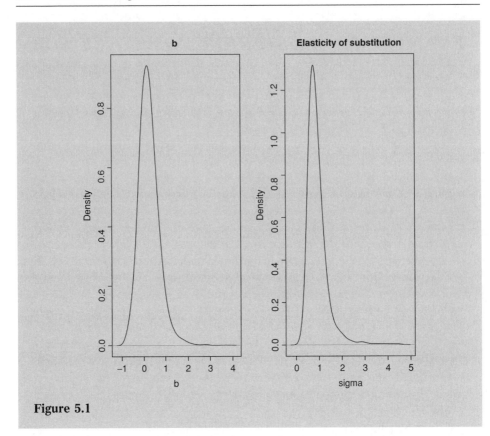

Figure 5.1

5.1.1 Criticisms of this model

Estimation of the production function as a regression model with conditional mean zero errors is open to criticism. The main line of criticism concerns the strict exogeneity of the value of K and L. Firms clearly choose their capital stock and labor force. When they do so they must take into account particular features of their production environment not captured in the deterministic relation (5.1). Such factors, for example the fertility of the fields if the firm is a farm, enter into the error term of the model, ε, since they are part of the reason why there is variation in output for the same levels of capital and labor. Since firms take account of (components of) ε there is reason to doubt the independence of ε and K and L. This is the criticism that capital and labor will be endogenous, not exogenous. One econometric solution to the problem of endogeneity of capital and labor stocks in the model is to introduce additional restrictions (information). Profit maximization in the product, capital and labor markets and perfect competition provide one way forward and this restriction can be incorporated stochastically in the Bayesian approach. Since the present chapter concerns regression models we shall pick up this point again in later chapters. A more statistical answer is to obtain panel data and then allow for an unobserved, time-invariant, component of the error using the approaches to be described in chapter 7.

Another line of thought argues that while (5.1) provides an efficient production frontier in that Y measures the maximum output obtainable from the given quantities of capital and labor, not all firms achieve this output and many produce less. The distance of a firm's output from the frontier measures its inefficiency. This leads to the notion of **frontier production functions** and their estimation. In this literature the argument is that the realized output of any firm differs from Y by a non-positive amount. It essentially introduces an additional source of error into the model over and above ε. Panel data involving repeated observations on each firm can help to test this theory and measure the inefficiencies if we assume that the degree of inefficiency is constant over time while actual quantities of capital and labour applied vary.

A further criticism is that the analysis makes no allowance for measurement error in the output/labor and output/capital ratios.

We conclude this section with the remark that under strict exogeneity of capital and labor there is no particular numerical difficulty in Bayesian inference about a non-linear regression model like (5.5). The main issues are economic not statistical.

5.2 BINARY CHOICE

We have used binary choice as an example on several occasions already so we shall give a fairly short treatment here. Suppose that you are modeling the choice of economic agents between two alternatives. Each choice is supposed to provide each agent with a certain utility and your economic model is that each agent makes the choice that provides him with the largest utility. If we could observe these utilities (measured on some common agreed scale) then the theory may be trivially compared with the data. But we cannot observe utilities; we can only model them. So let the choices be labeled zero and one and consider a model in which, for each agent i, the utilities of these choices are modeled as functions of two types of covariate. The first, called z, are characteristics of the choices, for example the cost to agent i of that choice, and the second, called w, are characteristics of the agent, for example income or car ownership. So we can write for the utilities of each choice for agent i,

$$u_{i1} = g_1(z_{i1}, w_i); \quad u_{i0} = g_0(z_{i0}, w_i).$$

Of course the simplest version of the model would be that in which the functions $\{g_i\}$ are linear leading to

$$u_{i0} = \alpha_0 + z_{i0}\delta + w_i\gamma_0; \quad u_{i1} = \alpha_1 + z_{i1}\delta + w_i\gamma_1$$

but again we do not find that agents and choices with the same characteristics always lead to the same choices, so we try to allow for this fact by including error terms that recognize the inadequacy of our effort to model the determinants of utility. This leads to a model which is, in principle, refutable by study of the evidence. This is

$$u_{i0} = \alpha_0 + z_{i0}\delta + w_i\gamma_0 + \varepsilon_{i0},$$
$$u_{i1} = \alpha_1 + z_{i1}\delta + w_i\gamma_1 + \varepsilon_{i1}.$$

Choice 1 is made if u_{i1} exceeds u_{i0}, otherwise choice zero is made. Now if our data consists just in the identity of the choice(s) made (and the covariates, of course) then we will be, in effect, observing whether u_{i1} exceeds u_{i0} or falls below it. So the likelihood for this problem will simply involve the distribution of

$$u_{i1} - u_{i0} = \alpha_1 - \alpha_0 + (z_{i1} - z_{i0})\delta + w_i(\gamma_1 - \gamma_0) + \varepsilon_{i1} - \varepsilon_{i0}.$$

More compactly we can write the difference in utilities as

$$u_{i1} - u_{i0} = x_i\beta + \varepsilon_i$$

where a term in $x_i\beta$ (apart from the constant term) represents either the differential effect of agent characteristics or the common effect of (differential) choice characteristics; and ε_i is the difference of the errors in each choice utility. In the context of choice of mode of transport an element of $x_i\beta$ could be either the effect of different journey times or the differential effect of income.

5.2.1 *Probit likelihoods*

We get to observe the choice each agent makes, call it y_i, where $y_i = 1$ if agent i makes choice 1 and $y_i = 0$ if he makes choice 0, together with the covariates x_i. Now by the hypothesis that agents make utility maximizing choices we see that

$$y_i = 1 \quad \text{if} \quad x_i\beta + \varepsilon_i > 0$$

and otherwise $y_i = 0$. Thus the model becomes

$$y_i = 1 \quad \text{if} \quad \varepsilon_i > -x_i\beta \tag{5.6}$$

and zero otherwise. If, as one of many possible choices, we take the ε_i to be iid $n(0, \tau)$ we must have

$$P(y_i = 1 | x_i, \beta, \tau) = 1 - \Phi(-x_i\beta\tau^{1/2}) = \Phi(x_i\beta\tau^{1/2}),$$
$$P(y_i = 0 | x_i, \beta, \tau) = \Phi(-x_i\beta\tau^{1/2}) = 1 - \Phi(x_i\beta\tau^{1/2})$$

since $P(\varepsilon_i > -x_i\beta) = P(\tau^{1/2}\varepsilon_i > -x_i\beta\tau^{1/2}) = 1 - \Phi(-x_i\beta\tau^{1/2}) = \Phi(x_i\beta\tau^{1/2})$ since $\tau^{1/2}\varepsilon_i \sim n(0, 1)$ and using the symmetry of the normal density function.

Now note that β and τ appear in these probabilities, of which the likelihood will be composed, only in the form $\beta\tau^{1/2}$ so that, from the likelihood alone we could never separately calculate β and $\tau^{1/2}$ – we could only learn their product.[1] So we follow standard practice in (arbitrarily) setting τ equal to one and the model becomes

$$P(y_i = 1 | x_i, \beta) = \Phi(x_i\beta),$$
$$P(y_i = 0 | x_i, \beta) = 1 - \Phi(x_i\beta). \tag{5.7}$$

This is called the **probit model** for choice probabilities – it arises when you choose normality for the prior on the difference in utility error terms. The inverse function to $\Phi(u)$ – the quantile function – is in this context called the probit function. Thus if $p_i = P(y_i = 1 | x_i, \beta)$ then $p_i = \Phi(x_i\beta)$ and $x_i\beta = probit(p_i)$. Note that $E(Y_i | x_i, \beta) = P(Y_i = 1 | x_i, \beta) = \Phi(x_i\beta)$ so we have a non-linear regression model.

In view of the assumed independence of the $\{\varepsilon_i\}$ given the $\{x_i\}$ and β the likelihood is equal to the product

$$\ell(\beta; y, x) \propto \prod_{i=1}^{n} \Phi(x_i\beta)^{y_i}[1 - \Phi(x_i\beta)]^{1-y_i}. \tag{5.8}$$

This expression is a generalization of the Bernoulli trials model of chapter 1 in which $\Phi(x_i\beta)$ appears as p, constant across agents. It is also a generalization of the one covariate probit model also used there as an illustration.

The parameters β are not usually of economic interest in themselves, because they have been arbitrarily scaled by the choice $\tau = 1$, although of course you may well want to know if β_k is zero, i.e. whether x_k has *any* effect on choice. Most often, interest will center on the marginal effect of a variation in, say, x_k on the probability of choice 1. This is

$$\frac{\partial P(y_i = 1 | x_i, \beta)}{\partial x_{ik}} = \beta_k \phi(x_i\beta). \tag{5.9}$$

Note that this marginal effect is itself a function of x so to report it you have to select the covariate vector at which to calculate it. Common choices are typical x vectors in your data set e.g. gender, owns a car, average income, etc. Another possibility is to report the posterior distribution of $\partial P/\partial x_j(x)$ averaged over the x vectors in your sample – the average derivative.

In algorithm 4.4 we gave a short program to compute the probit posterior using data augmentation. If you would rather employ a package, here is how you might tell BUGS to do it.

```
model
{for(i in 1:n){
y[i]~dbin(p[i],1)  # or dbern(p[i])
```

---

1 From a deeper point of view, utilities are unique only up to an increasing linear transformation. So we could multiply u_1 and u_0 by any positive number and still have the same choice model. Setting $\tau = 1$ eliminates this ambiguity.

```
p[i]<-phi(b0+b1*x1[i]+b2*x2[i])
}
b0~dnorm(0,0.001)
b1~dnorm(0,0.001)
b2~dnorm(0,0.001)
}
list(b0=0,b1=1,b2=-1)  # initial values
```

in which phi is the function $\Phi(.)$. Lines 6–8 specify a fairly diffuse prior for the β coefficients in which they are taken to be independent. If you wish to study the derivative of the choice probability, (5.9), at some specific x vector, for example the mean, you can add an extra line before the prior for b0 of the form

```
der2 <- b2 * exp(-0.5 * (b0 + b1*mean(x1) + b2*mean(x2)))* 0.39894
```

and this will produce realizations of this new function of the parameters which can then be studied graphically or numerically.

We leave sampling of the probit model as an exercise.

5.2.2   *Criticisms of the probit model*

One line of criticism of the model says that it is sensitive to heteroscedasticity in the $\{\varepsilon_i\}$ though we must be careful to specify what "it" is in this sentence. It may be that the posterior densities of the β coefficients are sensitive to departures from the dogmatic prior that asserts the errors are homoscedastic but that the derivatives, (5.9), are, for most vectors x not very sensitive to this assumption. A reaction to this criticism is to allow for heteroscedasticity in the errors in the same way that we did in the linear model, namely by taking each agent to have his own precision with these precisions taken themselves to be, say, gamma distributed with unit mean and precision, say, v, as in section 5 of chapter 3. This would lead to errors with a Student's t distribution instead of a normal to which it would tend as $v \to \infty$.

Then there is the standard econometric criticism that the x's are probably correlated with errors in the model so that the regression formulation of the model is incorrect. A standard response is to look for panel data. An alternative is to look for instrumental variables. We shall consider both these possibilities in chapters 7 and 8.

5.2.3   *Other models for binary choice*

Alternative choice models can be produced by making different choices about the marginal distribution of the $\{\varepsilon_i\}$ since the likelihood depends only on (5.6) which requires us to specify $P(\varepsilon_i > -x_i\beta)$. If we write this probability as $F(x_i\beta)$ where F is chosen to be a probability, lying between zero and one, for all possible values of $x_i\beta$ then the general form of the likelihood is

$$\ell(\beta; y, z) \propto \prod_{i=1}^{n} F(x_i\beta)^{y_i}[1 - F(x_i\beta)]^{1-y_i}$$

which reduces to (5.8) when $F(.) = \Phi(.)$. The values of β are not comparable between different choices of $F(.)$.

The most common alternative model is to have

$$F(u) = \frac{e^u}{1 + e^u}; \quad -\infty < u < \infty$$

which is the standard logistic distribution function of mean zero and variance $\pi^2/3$. This has the nice property that the odds on choice 1 are given by

$$\frac{P(y_i = 1|x_i, \beta)}{P(y_i = 0|x_i, \beta)} = \frac{e^{x_i\beta}}{1 + e^{x_i\beta}} \frac{1 + e^{x_i\beta}}{1} = e^{x_i\beta}$$

so the logarithm of the odds – the lodds – is linear in x. This is called the **logit model** and the inverse function to $F(u)$, namely $u = \log(F/(1 - F))$, is called the logit function. Thus, in this model $x\beta = \text{logit}(p)$. It may be implemented in BUGS by changing the fourth line in the probit program above to

```
logit(p[i])  =  b0  +  b1  *  x1[i]  +  b2  *  x2[i].
```

A third choice of F is the distribution function of a uniform random variable on the interval from 0 to 1. This is $F(u) = u, 0 \leq u \leq 1$ and it leads to the choice model

$$F(x_i\beta) = P(Y_i = 1|x_i, \beta) = x_i\beta.$$

This is called the **linear probability model**. Compared to the probit and logit model it has the disadvantage that both the prior and the posterior distribution of β must have support confined to the set of β values such that, for every i, $x_i\beta$ must lie between zero and one (because $F(x_i\beta)$ is a probability). For this reason it is rarely used in serious work.

We showed in chapter 4 how a Gibbs Sampler algorithm can be easily implemented after augmenting the posterior with the utility differences $\{u_{i1} - u_{i0} = y_i^*\}$.

Generalizations

It is also possible, but rather difficult, to treat F as an additional parameter and to let the evidence lead to a posterior distribution for both β and F. This would involve placing a prior distribution on the space of distribution functions which can be done but this remains a relatively advanced technique. Treating F as a parameter relaxes the dogmatic prior implicit in probit, logit and similar models that F is normal, logistic, etc. Probably a better strategy in the present state of technology is to report posterior densities from a variety of choices of the prior $F(.)$, including normal, t, logistic etc. Note that it is not meaningful to report the posteriors for β under these models since β is a model-specific parameter. A more sensible choice might be to report alternative posteriors for the derivatives like (5.9). It is straightforward within BUGS to run several simultaneous MCMC runs using different priors.

In our chapter on linear models we showed how linearity of the dependence of the regression on any covariate x can be relaxed and that was computationally easy by treating the covariate as a factor. If you want to find the (approximate) maximum likelihood estimates, perhaps in order to derive initial values for an MCMC calculation, you can use the generalized linear model (glm) function in S. Its shortest form is

```
results <- glm(y~x,family=binomial("probit"))
```

Note the analogy to the `lm` function. The second argument is the choice of family and the choice of link. The family refers to the distribution of Y, binary data lie within the binomial family. The argument to family is the link. This is the function that relates $x\beta$ to the mean (μ) of Y so it specifies the form of the regression function. For the probit model, as we have seen, $x\beta = \text{probit}(\mu)$; for the logit it is $x\beta = \text{logit}(\mu)$, which is the default link for the binomial. Notice the slightly confusing point that the link function does not express the mean as a function of $x\beta$ – it is the other way round; it expresses $x\beta$ as a function of the mean. If you are using the default link there is no need to put anything after the family name. Some families with their default links are

```
binomial(link = "logit")
gaussian(link = "identity")  # this gives you the normal linear model
Gamma(link = "inverse")
inverse.gaussian(link = "1/mu^2")
poisson(link = "log")
```

A list of families and links can be obtained in R by `help(family)` and `help(link)`.

5.3   ORDERED MULTINOMIAL CHOICE

Consider now a situation in which an agent must make one of several choices or make one of several responses and these choices are **naturally ordered**. Let Y indicate one of $J + 1$ ordered categories, for example "small, medium, large" and we code these categories as $0, 1, 2, ..., J$. Each agent's choice is just one of these categories and we observe the choice and a vector of covariates x.

An econometrically natural way of handling such data is to suppose that there exists a utility function associated with an underlying continuous variable that generates the categories that we observe. Thus suppose that variable is size and that each agent chooses the size that maximizes utility. We do not, however, get to know the size that is chosen but only learn whether it is small, medium or large. Let the size chosen by agent i have the representation

$$s_i = x_i\beta + \varepsilon_i,$$

where x is a collection of factors that influence the optimal choice of s, and ε arises because of the empirical observation that agents with the same x do not invariably make the same choices.

The category that we observe is now determined by the magnitude of s. Specifically,

$$\text{if} \quad s < \gamma_1 \quad \text{we observe } y = 0,$$
$$\text{if} \quad \gamma_1 < s < \gamma_2 \quad \text{we observe } y = 1,$$
$$\dots \quad \dots$$
$$\text{if} \quad s > \gamma_J \quad \text{we observe } y = J.$$

To complete the model we need a likelihood and a prior. Perhaps the most common likelihood is got by assigning the $\{\varepsilon_i\}$ independent standard normal distributions. This is the ordered probit model and gives for the probability that $Y = 0$

$$P(Y = 0 \,|\, x, \beta) = P(S < \gamma_1 \,|\, x, \beta) = P(x\beta + \varepsilon < \gamma_1 \,|\, x, \beta)$$
$$= P(\varepsilon < \gamma_1 - x\beta \,|\, x, \beta) = \Phi(\gamma_1 - x\beta),$$

and for the probability that $Y = 1$ we have

$$P(Y = 1 \,|\, x, \beta) = P(\gamma_1 < s < \gamma_2 \,|\, x, \beta)$$
$$= P(\gamma_1 - x\beta < \varepsilon < \gamma_2 - x\beta \,|\, x, \beta)$$
$$= \Phi(\gamma_2 - x\beta) - \Phi(\gamma_1 - x\beta),$$

and so on.

Thus the likelihood for γ, β for an individual agent is

$$\ell(\beta, \gamma; y, x) \propto \sum_{j=0}^{J} 1(y_i = j)[\Phi(\gamma_{j+1} - x_i\beta) - \Phi(\gamma_j - x_i\beta)]$$

where $\gamma_0 = -\infty$ and $\gamma_{J+1} = \infty$. The parameters are $\gamma_1, \gamma_2, \dots, \gamma_J$ and the K elements of β. Thus the parameters number $K + J$. The regression function $x\beta$ *must not include an intercept* because such a parameter could never be distinguished from the γ's. Notice also that, as in the probit model, the variance of ε is taken to be one. As in that model, this is because the elements of β and γ are only determined up to scale. The γ parameters are subject to the order restriction that

$$\gamma_1 \leq \gamma_2 \leq \dots \leq \gamma_{J+1}. \tag{5.10}$$

A natural prior for the elements of β might be independent imprecise normals, but that for the γ's must take account of the order restriction. One way of doing this is to assign γ_1 a vague normal prior and then to assign the increments $\gamma_{j+1} - \gamma_j$ priors that are confined to the non-negative axis. This will ensure that the posterior density of the γ's satisfies the order restrictions (5.10). The BUGS program listed in appendix 3 is written for $J = 4$ categories and assigns independent vague gamma priors to $\gamma_2 - \gamma_1$ and $\gamma_3 - \gamma_2$.

5.3.1   Data augmentation

As is usual with models involving a latent variable, in this case, s, a Gibbs algorithm using data augmentation is easy to write down and could be used if you wish to write your own program (though BUGS does the job perfectly well). As in the probit model, the idea is to treat the unobserved values of S, namely $s = (s_1, s_2, ..., s_n)$, as additional parameters so the total parameter set is s, β, γ. The algorithm proceeds by considering the component conditionals, $p(s|\beta, \gamma, data)$, $p(\gamma|\beta, s, data)$, and $p(\beta|\gamma, s, data)$. It is as follows.

Suppose you knew β, γ and the data, then if $y_i = j$ then $S_i \sim n(x_i\beta, 1)$ truncated to the interval γ_{j-1} to γ_j so, just as in the probit model, sampling the $\{S_i\}$ is just a matter of sampling truncated normal variates. The conditional density of γ_j given all remaining elements of γ, β and S is a bit trickier to derive. But recall that $Y_i = j$ if $\gamma_{j-1} < S_i \leq \gamma_j$ so it follows that γ_j must exceed both γ_{j-1} and all the S_i such that $Y_i = j$. Moreover, from $Y_i = j + 1$ if $\gamma_j < S_i \leq \gamma_{j+1}$ it follows that γ_j must be less than both γ_{j+1} and all the S_i associated with $Y_i = j + 1$. Finally, since there is nothing in the data to indicate where in this interval γ_j lies, its distribution must be the prior for γ_j truncated to this interval. The last component conditional is that of β given s, γ and the data. But if you know the data the posterior density of β must be that in a normal linear model with dependent variable s, covariate matrix X, and unit error precision. Thus a Gibbs algorithm would be:

ALGORITHM 5.1   *ORDERED PROBIT*
   1. $p(S_i|\beta, \gamma, y_i = j) = n(x_i\beta, 1)$ *truncated to* $\gamma_{j-1} < S < \gamma_j$.
   2. $p(\gamma_j|\gamma_k(k \neq j), \beta, s, y) =$ *the prior density of* γ_j *truncated to the interval* $(\max\{\max\{s_i : y_i = j\}, \gamma_{j-1}\}), \min\{\min\{s_i : y_i = j + 1\}, \gamma_{j+1}\})$.
   3. $p(\beta|\gamma, s, y) = n(b, X'X)$, *for* $b = (X'X)^{-1}X's$.
   4. Repeat nrep times.

5.3.2   Parameters of interest

The parameters of interest would typically be the derivatives of the choice probabilities with respect to the covariates, for example,

$$\frac{\partial P(Y = j | x, \beta)}{\partial x_k} = \beta_k[\phi(\gamma_j - x\beta) - \phi(\gamma_{j+1} - x\beta)].$$

The posterior distributions of such derivatives are readily calculated, for any particular value of x, using samples from the posterior density of β, γ.

5.4 MULTINOMIAL CHOICE

The binary choice model can be extended to choice among many categories with no natural ordering. Examples might be choice among competing brands of a product or choice among ways of traveling to work – bus, train, car, for example. In the binary choice we have, naturally, two categories and this leads to a single equation,

$$y_i^* = x_i'\beta + \varepsilon_i, \quad i = 1, 2, ..., N \tag{5.11}$$

in which y_i^* can be represented as the difference in utilities, for person i, of the choice labeled zero and the choice labeled one, so that if y_i^* was positive, choice 1 was made and otherwise choice 0. The variable $Y_i \in \{0, 1\}$ indicated which choice was made.

This framework extends naturally to multinomial choice in which there are, say, p categories labeled 0, 1, 2, ..., $p - 1$. Analogously to (5.11) there is a collection of $p - 1$ utility differences with the representation

$$y_i^* = X_i\beta + \varepsilon_i \tag{5.12}$$

where y_i^* is a column vector of length $p - 1$. In the **multinomial probit** model the vector ε_i is assumed to be $p - 1$ variate normal with mean zero and precision matrix Σ^{-1}, given X_i, β, Σ. y_{ij}^* can be thought of as the utility, to agent i, of choice j minus the utility of choice 0 so that in general,

$$y_{ij}^* = u_{ij} - u_{i0}, \quad j = 1, 2, ..., p - 1.$$

It follows that if all the y_{ij}^* are negative then person i makes choice 0 and the indicator Y_i takes the value zero. Otherwise, if at least one y_{ij}^* is positive, then person i makes the choice corresponding to the largest of the y_{ij}^* and Y_i indicates that choice.

An important consideration is that, since we only observe the ranks of the y_i^* and not their numerical values, we can multiply the equation (5.12) by a positive number c to get $cy_i^* = X_i(c\beta) + c\varepsilon_i$ so we could never tell, from the ranks of the elements of y_i^* alone, whether the parameters of the model were β, Σ or $c\beta$, $c^2\Sigma$. In the binary choice case, $p = 2$, Σ was scalar and it was arbitrarily assigned the value one to remove this indeterminacy. In the Bayesian literature so far this indeterminacy is removed by assigning the $(1, 1)$ element of Σ to be equal to one and constructing priors on β and the remaining elements of Σ. The paper by McCulloch, Polson and Rossi (2000) referenced in the bibliographic notes to this chapter describes Gibbs Samplers to implement two approaches to this task and compares the results with examples. Their general conclusions are that Gibbs Sampler sequences can be highly auto-correlated, necessitating long runs, and that the behavior of the Sampler is rather strongly dependent upon the prior specification for Σ.

5.5   TOBIT MODELS

5.5.1   *Censored linear models*

The probit and similar models apply when our data consist of indicators of which of several choices have been made. Often the choice is naturally discrete and binary as in working or not working, traveling by bus or not, and so on. But often the choice has a continuous dimension. Consider, for example, consumer purchases of a particular class of goods during a given time interval. Here the choice has two aspects. The first is whether to spend at all and the second is how much to spend. We can think of this as one problem with the solution either zero or some positive number and this is the natural approach if we think of the agent as maximizing a utility function subject to a budget constraint. Depending on the position of the budget line and the indifference curves the optimal expenditure may be a positive number of dollars or, the corner solution, nothing at all.

One framework for analyzing such data is to postulate, as with the binary choice models, an underlying linear model

$$y^* = x\beta + \varepsilon$$

and to connect this with data by supposing that what we observe is

$$y = \begin{cases} y^* & \text{if } y^* > 0 \\ 1_{\{y^* \le 0\}} & \text{otherwise} \end{cases}.$$

So we observe y^* if it is positive and we observe an indicator of $y^* \le 0$ otherwise. If y^* is positive the consumer spends y^*; if it is negative he spends nothing. In both cases we observe the agent's choice. In this framework we have an example of a censored linear model.

5.5.2   *Censoring and truncation*

A random variable is **censored** if we may only observe its value when it lies in a proper subset of its support and otherwise observe only that it lies outside that subset. For example, y^* may naturally have support on the real line but we get to see it only if it lies on the positive axis, otherwise we learn only that its value was non-positive. The standard censored data likelihood when the underlying model has distribution function $F(.)$ and density function $f(.)$ has the form

$$g^c(y) = f(y)^{I_{\{y \in S\}}} P(Y \in S^c)^{I_{\{y \in S^c\}}} \tag{5.13}$$

where S is the set of possible Y values where we are permitted to observe the value of Y, S^c is its complement, and $I_{\{y \in S\}}$ is the indicator of the event that Y falls in S.

This likelihood tells us the probability of the data we shall observe. This is $f(y)$ if $y \in S$ and $P(Y \in S^c)$ if y is not in S.

A related, but quite distinct, idea is that of **truncation**. Under truncation we get to observe Y only if its value lies in a proper subset of its support. Censored data is more informative than truncated data because with the former we get to know how many observations fall outside the subset. With truncated data we do not have this information. The two types of data lead to different likelihoods and, in contrast to (5.13), the likelihood for truncated data has the form

$$g^t(y) = \frac{f(y)}{P(Y \in S)}. \tag{5.14}$$

The ratio in the truncated data likelihood is the density of Y given that it lies in S. We do not need to use indicators in the truncated data likelihood because *all* data values lie in S.

The censored data likelihood (5.13) may be written as

$$g^c(y) = \left[\frac{f(y)}{P(Y \in S)}\right]^{I_{\{Y \in S\}}} P(Y \in S)^{I_{\{Y \in S\}}} P(Y \in S^c)^{I_{\{Y \in S^c\}}}$$

because the terms in $P(Y \in S)^{I_{\{Y \in S\}}}$ cancel. The second and third terms form a like-lihood for the binary event that an observation lies in S. The first term is the density of Y given that it lies in S – the truncated data likelihood – for observations lying in S. This is also a likelihood function. Because of this we can analyze the data in terms of two models, one for the binary event that Y lies in S, e.g. that Y is positive, the second for the distribution of Y given that it lies in S. If these two models have distinct parameters then, as long as the parameters are independent in the prior, they will be so in the posterior and in effect two distinct analyses can be done. We shall return to this point shortly.

Tobit models

Suppose there is a latent linear model $y^* = x\beta + \varepsilon$ determining the value of y^* and if this value is positive we observe it, otherwise we only know that it is not positive. Thus Y^* is censored. If $\varepsilon|x, \beta \sim n(0, \tau)$ then we have the **tobit model**. The set S is the positive axis and its complement is the rest of the real line. The probabilities required for the censored data likelihood are

$$f(y|x, \beta, \tau) = n(x\beta, \tau), \quad P(Y \in S^c|x, \beta, \tau) = \Phi(-x\beta\tau^{1/2}).$$

Thus for n agents for whom the ε_i are independent given the x vectors, β, and τ, the likelihood is

$$\ell(\beta, \tau) \propto \tau^{n_1/2} \exp\{-(\tau/2)(y - X\beta)'(y - X\beta)\}\prod_{i=1}^{n_0}\Phi(-x_i\beta\tau^{1/2}), \tag{5.15}$$

where n_1 observations have $y^* > 0$ and $n_0 = n - n_1$ have $y^* \le 0$. The matrices y, X contain the values of y with the x vectors for the agents who supplied the numerical value of y^*. The natural flat prior on β and $\log \tau$ then leads to the posterior distribution

$$p(\beta, \tau | data) \propto \tau^{n_1/2-1} \exp\{-(\tau/2)(y - X\beta)'(y - X\beta)\} \prod_{i=1}^{N_0} \Phi(-x_i \beta \tau^{1/2}).$$

This likelihood is rather easy to handle. In terms of the parametrization τ, $\beta^* = \beta \tau^{1/2}$ it is log-concave. This implies that it is straightforward to find the joint posterior mode or ml estimate which provides useful approximations to modes of the marginal posterior densities of the $K + 1$ parameters. Notice that unlike the binary choice model τ and β appear separately in the likelihood and so we are not obliged to set τ to some arbitrary value, we can identify it from the likelihood. A BUGS program to sample the posterior distribution of β, τ is given in appendix 3.

Data augmentation

The tobit posterior density is easily derived using a Gibbs Sampler algorithm with the parameter set augmented by y^* for censored observations. The component conditionals are

$$p(y^* | y = 0, \beta, \tau) \quad \text{and} \quad p(\beta, \tau | y^*).$$

The latter is the normal linear model posterior centered at $b = (X'X)^{-1}X'y^*$ with precision equal to $X'X$. The former is a product of normal $x_i \beta$, τ densities truncated above at zero.

Parameters of interest

As with binary choice the economically interesting parameters are not necessarily the β's, which show the marginal effect of x on the latent y^*'s. Probably of more interest is the effect of some covariate on, say, the expected value of Y given that it is positive. This would be the expected purchase given that you spend anything at all. From the appendix to this chapter we find that

$$E(Y | Y > 0) = \mu + \tau^{-1/2} \frac{\phi(\tau^{1/2}\mu)}{\Phi(\tau^{1/2}\mu)} \quad \text{where} \quad \mu = x\beta.$$

So the derivative of this expression with respect to a variation in x_j is

$$\frac{\partial E(Y | Y > 0)}{\partial x_j} = \beta_j [1 - \phi(z)(\phi(z) + z\Phi(z))], \quad \text{for} \quad z = \tau^{1/2} x\beta.$$

This depends on the parameters β and τ and so is uncertain, but its probability distribution is readily calculated, for any choice of x, by using MCMC realizations of β, τ.

SEPARATE DECISIONS

The tobit structure unites the decision to choose a positive value of y with the decision as to what positive value to choose. It does this by having the same coefficients β appearing in both the probit component of the censored data likelihood and the truncated normal component. As we noted earlier, it is possible to split the decision into two separate steps by estimating distinct models for the decision to have positive y and the decision on the value of y given that it is positive. With separate models with distinct coefficient vectors we can, by looking at how similar the coefficient vectors are, see if this tobit restriction is valid.

To implement this, suppose that the positive value of Y is determined by a linear model

$$y^* = x\beta + \varepsilon, \quad \varepsilon|x, \beta \sim n(0, \tau).$$

Then the density of Y is the normal distribution truncated on the left at zero,

$$p(y^*|x, \beta, \tau, Y > 0) = \frac{\tau^{1/2}\phi([y^* - x\beta]\tau^{1/2})}{\Phi(x\beta\tau^{1/2})}.$$

Then suppose that the decision to have a positive Y, to spend anything at all, is determined by a probit model with latent linear structure given by another linear model

$$y^* = x\gamma + v, \quad v \sim n(0, 1)$$

so that the distribution of the indicator y of choosing a positive amount is

$$p(1_{y^*>0}|x, \gamma) = \Phi(x\gamma)^{1_{\{y^*>0\}}}[1 - \Phi(x\gamma)]^{1-1_{\{y^*>0\}}}.$$

The two separate models together reduce to the tobit if $\beta = \gamma\tau^{1/2}$. The joint posterior density for n independent observations under uniform priors for β, γ and the improper prior $1/\tau$ for τ is

$$p(\beta, \gamma, \tau|data) \propto \tau^{n_1/2-1}\prod_{i=1}^{n_1}\left[\frac{\phi([y_i - x_i\beta]\tau^{1/2})}{\Phi(x_i\beta)}\right]\prod_{i=1}^{n}\Phi(x_i\gamma)^{1_{y^*>0}}[1 - \Phi(x_i\gamma)]^{1-1_{\{y^*>0\}}}.$$

It will be observed that β, τ, and γ are independent a posteriori – if they are so in the prior – since the joint density factors into the product of terms involving either only β, τ, or only γ. Thus we can do quite separate calculations to sample these $2k + 1$ parameters. The calculations to sample the probit posterior have already been described and illustrated, so it only remains to sample the truncated normal posterior density. This is readily done using the BUGS program given in appendix 3.

5.5.3   Selection models

Selection is ubiquitous in economic data. It arises when the theory refers to any member of a population, for example all women of working age, but the data comes from a potentially non-randomly selected subset, for example working women. People who have been out of work for six months are a potentially non-randomly selected subset of all the people who become unemployed. The respondents to a longitudinal survey at any date are a potentially non-randomly selected subset of all those who originally participated in the survey. To be convincing, an econometric model should involve probabilities that are conditional on the fact that the data are selected. Ignore this fact and your analysis may well be unconvincing. So how do you condition your likelihood and prior on the fact of selection? To examine this we look briefly at about the simplest selection model.

We adopt the language of wages and labor force participation since this has been classic since the early work of Gronau (1973) and Heckman (1974).[2] Suppose that a woman of working age and with certain levels of education and other character-istics x could potentially earn a wage of y^* if she had a job. Suppose also that she chooses to work if and only if her potential wage exceeds a threshold or reservation level w^r which itself depends on a set of covariates reflecting her preferences for "leisure" and income and let $d^* = y^* - w^r$. Then she works iff $d^* > 0$. This suggests, as a starter model, the formulation

$$y^* = x\beta + \varepsilon_1$$
$$d^* = z\gamma + \varepsilon_2$$

in which $\varepsilon = (\varepsilon_1, \varepsilon_2)$ is bivariate normal with mean zero and covariance matrix $\Sigma = \{\sigma_{ij}\}$ given $x, z, \beta, \gamma, \Sigma$. In Amemiya's (1985)[3] useful classification this is called a type 2 tobit model.

Now suppose that what we observe is a collection of women who tell us their wage if they are working and otherwise tell us they are not working.[4] Consider a likelihood term for a woman who is not working. This event is equivalent to $d^* < 0$ and so, from our discussion of the probit model, its probability is

$$P(d^* < 0 | x, z) = P(z\gamma + \varepsilon_2 < 0 | z, x) = \Phi(-z\gamma\tau_2^{1/2}) = 1 - \Phi(z\gamma\tau_2^{1/2}) \quad (5.16)$$

---

2   R. Gronau, The effect of children on the housewife's value of time, *Journal of Political Economy*, 81: S 168–99 (1973), J. J. Heckman, Shadow prices, market wages and labor supply, *Econometrica*, 42, 679–94 (1974).

3   T. Amemiya, *Advanced Econometrics*, Harvard University Press (1985).

4   Working for money in the paid labor force.

where $\tau_2 = 1/\sigma_{22}$. But for a woman who works and reports a wage equal to y_i^* we know two things, firstly that $d_i^* > 0$, and secondly the value of y_i^*. What she tells us has probability

$$P(d_i^* > 0 \mid x, z) p(y_i^* \mid d_i^* > 0, x, z). \tag{5.17}$$

The first term has probability $\Phi(z\gamma\tau_1^{1/2})$ but the second term is more complicated and is

$$p(y_i^* \mid d_i^* > 0, x, z) = \frac{\int_0^\infty p(y_i^*, u \mid x, z)\, du}{P(d_i^* > 0 \mid x, z)}$$

and so the whole likelihood contribution from this woman is

$$\int_0^\infty p(y_i^*, u \mid x, z)\, du = p(y_i^* \mid x, z) \int_0^\infty p(u \mid y_i^*, x, z)\, du. \tag{5.18}$$

But under normality, from the appendix to chapter 3, the distribution of d^* given y^* is $n(z\gamma + (\sigma_{12}/\sigma_{11})(y^* - x\beta), \sigma_{22}(1 - \rho^2))$ so a woman who works contributes (5.18), the product of a normal density for the wage she earns and the integral of a normal density. The result for the likelihood as a whole, being the product of terms like (5.16) and (5.18), is an inelegant expression, to say the least. Fortunately, the Bayesian perspective affords relief.

To construct a Gibbs algorithm we consider the very simple underlying, latent, structure which is a pair of possibly correlated normal linear models, one for the potential wage, y^*, and one for the difference between the wage and the reservation wage. Then such an algorithm, with the parameter set β, γ, Σ, $\{y_i^*, d_i^*\}$, would sample in turn from the component conditionals

    1. $p(\beta, \gamma \mid \{y_i^*, d_i^*\}, \Sigma, \text{data})$
    2. $p(\{y_i^*, d_i^*\} \mid \beta, \gamma, \Sigma, \text{data})$
    3. $p(\Sigma \mid \{y_i^*, d_i^*\}, \beta, \gamma, \text{data})$,

where "data" refers to the wages of those who work and the participation status of all. The first of these is the posterior distribution of the two coefficient vectors in a pair of correlated normal linear models with known error covariance matrix, and a straightforward extension of the analyses of chapter 3 will give the form of this multi-variate normal distribution. The second is a product of terms for each woman. For a woman who works we know her wage and the only uncertainty is over d_i^* whose distribution given the wage is given above. For a woman who does not work in the paid labor market we are uncertain about both y_i^* and d_i^* and we must draw from their joint distribution given the condition that $d_i^* < 0$. This can be done by first drawing d^* subject to the condition that it is negative and then drawing from the conditional normal distribution of y^* given that value of d^*. The third part of the Gibbs step is simple because if we know $\{y_i^*, d_i^*\}$, β, γ then we know ε, a vector of bivariate normal variates, and the likelihood combines with a (natural conjugate) Wishart prior for the precision matrix Σ^{-1} to produce a Wishart posterior – see definition 3.5 of the appendix to chapter 3 (section 3.8.3).

Criticisms of the selection model

The model we have chosen to discuss is the earliest in a long line of increasingly rich models. Criticisms are the by now familiar ones of potential endogeneity of the covariates, and reliance on homoscedastic normality and linearity of covariate effects. The latter statistical problems may be resolved by enlarging the model space; that is, by more programming. But the endogeneity issue remains, of course.

5.6   COUNT DATA

Count data arise when, during the period of observation, an event may occur many times. The data are the number of times the event occurred which is called a count. The natural sample space for Y is zero plus the positive integers. Possible examples include the numbers of patents filed during a year by a particular firm; the number of visits to hospital during a year by a particular individual; and the number of strikes during a year at a particular firm.

The poisson model

The most natural probability model[5] for a count is the poisson distribution which is a single parameter family with mass function

$$p(y|\lambda) = \frac{e^{-\lambda}\lambda^y}{y!}, \quad y = 0, 1, 2, 3, \ldots \quad \lambda > 0.$$

The parameter λ is the mean of the Y and also the variance, so for poisson data the mean and variance are equal. It can be sampled in S by the commands

- `rpois(n,λ)`; This gives n pseudo-random realizations of the poisson variate with mean λ.
- `dpois(y,λ)`; This gives the value of the mass function at `y`.
- `ppois(y,λ)`; This gives the distribution function at `y`.
- `qpois(p,λ)`; The quantile function at `p`. This is the smallest y value such that $P(Y \le y) \ge p$.

The standard way to introduce covariates into the model is by specifying the mean λ as a function of the covariate vector x and since λ must be positive this is most easily done by choosing

$$\lambda_i = \exp\{x_i\beta\}. \tag{5.19}$$

---

5   Though it rarely, if ever, has a justification in economic theory.

For n observations that are stochastically independent given x and β the likelihood is therefore

$$\ell(\beta) \propto \prod_{i=1}^{n} \exp\{-e^{x_i\beta}\} e^{y_i x_i \beta}. \tag{5.20}$$

If you wish to generate observations satisfying a poisson regression model then the following S code will do the trick:

```
n <- 100; b0 <- 0; b1 <- 1;
x <- rnorm(n)
y <- rpois(n, exp(b0+b1*x))
```

A BUGS program to sample from the posterior density of β is very easy to write – one is given in appendix 3 – and convergence of the sampler is typically very fast. To locate the likelihood maximum you can use glm in S as

```
results <- glm(y ~ x, family = poisson)
```

since (5.19) is the default link. BIC values to compare two model specifications can be calculated by substituting the ml estimates under each model into (5.20).

5.6.1 Unmeasured heterogeneity in non-linear regression

In the linear model of chapter 3 we started from a deterministic model showing how Y depended on x but recognized that in practice such a model could not fit the data and we were obliged to extend the model by adding an error term ε. This term was an attempt to make allowance for variations among agents in their choice of Y due to factors either unrecognized in the theory or factors that were part of the theory but unmeasured by the econometrician. Similar considerations arise in models for limited dependent variables where econometricians are inclined to add an error term to represent the effect of unmeasured covariates. Such additional variation is usually called **unmeasured heterogeneity** to contrast it with the variability in Y that is accounted for by the covariates included in the model.[6] We shall discuss one example of a model with unmeasured heterogeneity in this section and note other examples in the course of subsequent discussions.

Heterogeneous poisson regression

As an example of how a model can be extended to allow for additional unmeasured heterogeneity consider extending the poisson regression by writing the mean for agent i as

$$E(Y_i | x_i, \beta, v_i) = v_i \exp\{x_i \beta\}.$$

---

6   Models with unmeasured heterogeneity are sometimes called **doubly stochastic** models.

In this model v_i represents the collective effect of unmeasured covariates on the mean count. Since the model now has more parameters than observations it is necessary to use a proper prior for the unknowns β and $v = (v_1, v_2, ..., v_n)$, and the usual way of doing this is to take β and v as independent with β having the usual flat prior and the $\{v_i\}$ independent given a hyperparameter α. A common choice for this prior distribution, given the covariates, is

$$v_i \sim iid\ gamma(\alpha, \alpha)$$

so the v_i have mean one and precision α. This gives the joint posterior distribution

$$p(\beta, v|data, \alpha) \propto \prod_{i=1}^{n} \exp\{-v_i e^{x_i\beta}\} e^{y_i x_i \beta} e^{-\alpha v_i} v_i^{y_i+\alpha-1}.$$

The scalar α can also be assigned a prior distribution which would then provide a joint posterior distribution for α, β, v or the posterior distribution of β can be studied for alternative choices of α. This is another example of a Bayesian hierarchical model.

The heterogeneous poisson model elaborates the poisson regression model by allowing for additional dispersion in the counts. If we write $\lambda = \exp(x\beta)$ then, conditional on λ and v, the mean and variance of the count are

$$E(Y|v, \lambda) = v\lambda = V(Y|v, \lambda)$$

since a property of the poisson distribution is that the mean and variance are equal.[7] But, unconditionally on v, the mean is $E_v(v\lambda) = \lambda$ assuming that v is distributed independently of x, β with mean one, and the variance of the count is

$$V(Y|\lambda) = E(v\lambda|\lambda) + V(v\lambda|\lambda)$$
$$= \lambda + \lambda^2 V(v)$$

which exceeds λ.[8] So unlike the homogeneous poisson the heterogeneous poisson has a variance that exceeds the mean and it is in that sense overdispersed. Of course if the variance of v is zero the heterogeneous model reduces to the homogeneous one, so the posterior distribution of the $\{v_i\}$ will be informative about whether the heterogeneous extension is necessary.

EXAMPLE 5.2   INFERENCE ABOUT HETERO-GENEOUS POISSON REGRESSION   *To illustrate inference with this model we generated some* homogeneous *poisson data using the commands given above with* $n = 100$, $\beta_0 = 0$, $\beta_1 = 1$ *and using standard normal*

---

7   The appendix to this chapter gives an account of the poisson family.

8   In this derivation we have used the fact that the variance of $v\lambda$ is equal to the mean of the conditional variances plus the variance of the conditional mean. This is one form of the law of iterated expectations.

covariate values. Thus the variance of the gamma density of v is zero which implies, since the variance of a gamma(α, α) density is $1/\alpha$, that the parameter α is infinite and its posterior distribution should show this fact. We choose to assign a gamma prior to $1/\alpha$ whose true value is zero. The BUGS program of appendix 3 was run using 2 chains to check convergence, each of length 10,000, discarding the first 5,000. The posteriors of the resulting $2 \times 5,000 = 10,000$ realizations are shown in figure 5.2. The first two plots in figure 5.2 show smoothed histograms of the regression parameters β_0 and β_1. These are bell shaped and centered about the true values of 0 and 1 respectively. The (unsmoothed) histogram of the realizations of $1/\alpha$ peaks at the origin, which is the value generating the data, and most values are less than 0.2 which corresponds to most α values exceeding 5. This picture seems consistent with the hypothesis that the data are probably not overdispersed.

For a second example we generated data with heterogeneity present following a gamma distribution with mean one, as before, but variance equal to one so that $\alpha = 1$. So these data really are heterogeneous. Plots of the three marginal posterior distributions are shown in figure 5.3. The distributions of β_0 and β_1 are similar to those of the earlier (homogeneous) figure, but more dispersed, but the unsmoothed histogram of the realizations of $1/\alpha$ is now quite different, having a mode not far from one. This graph has essentially no mass near zero and shows that the data are clearly overdispersed or heterogeneous.

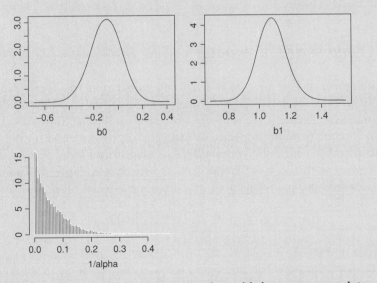

Figure 5.2 Heterogeneous poisson regression with homogeneous data

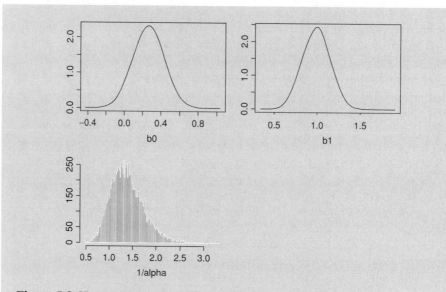

Figure 5.3 Heterogeneous poisson regression with heterogeneous data

The poisson model augmented with gamma multiplicative heterogeneity in the mean is usually called the negative binomial model since if we integrate v out of the poisson likelihood with respect to a gamma(α, α) distribution we find the resulting mass function is that of a negative binomial distribution. The derivation is in the appendix to this chapter.

5.6.2   Time series of counts

The count model that we have been describing is applicable to a set-up in which we observe one count for each of n individuals, which is a cross-sectional perspective. Perhaps more convincing is the situation where the data form a time series of counts in which, for either a single individual or many such agents, we observe the sequence of counts together with the corresponding sequence of covariate vectors. Thus, for any particular agent, the mean count may be written as $v \exp\{x_t\beta\}$ leading, if the counts are conditionally independent, to a likelihood of the form

$$\ell(\beta, v; y, x) \propto \exp\{-v \exp\{\textstyle\sum_{t=1}^T x_t\beta\}\}\textstyle\prod_{t=1}^T (v e^{x_t\beta})^{y_t}. \qquad (5.21)$$

The interest of this time series variant is that, unlike the cross-sectional case, we have repeated observations involving the same heterogeneity term, v. In this context we can be much more relaxed over the prior and even consider the possibility of an improper prior on v. Suppose for example we consider a uniform prior on log v,

$p(v) \propto 1/v$. Then on multiplying the likelihood (5.21) by $1/v$ and integrating out v using the gamma integral formula we have a posterior distribution for β of the form

$$p(\beta|y, x) \propto \frac{e^{\Sigma x_t y_t \beta}}{\left(\Sigma e^{x_t \beta}\right)^{\Sigma y_t}} \tag{5.22}$$

leaving aside the prior for β, assuming it is independent of v. This is a proper posterior density as long as there is some variation in the x sequence (and we observe at least one event!). We shall deal with time series of counts in a little more detail in the chapter on panel data.

We have just seen how to extend the poisson model to allow for additional unmeasured sources of variation – unmeasured heterogeneity. We might think of applying this idea to the probit and tobit set-ups. Both these models are driven by a latent linear structure, $y^* = x\beta + \varepsilon$. If we add, on the right hand side, an additional source of random variation analogous to log v in the poisson case then there will be, in general and without essentially arbitrary assumptions, no way of distinguishing this term from ε itself. It is the fact that the poisson model is not driven by an underlying linear model that makes it possible to distinguish extra, additive, omitted variation. On the other hand it is common to allow for additional variability via the slope coefficients of $x\beta$ by writing it for agent i as $\Sigma_{j=1}^{k} x_{ij}\beta_{ij}$. So each agent has his own parameter vector. The model is completed by assigning a hierarchical prior structure to the β parameters in which β_{ij} has mean β_j and variance $\sigma_{\beta_j}^2$. Posterior interest might then center on the $\{\beta_j\}$. Models like this are common in the biostatistical literature under the name of random effects or mixed models and BUGS is particularly suited to handling them.

5.7 DURATION DATA

Economists often find themselves thinking about the length of time that some event lasts. Examples include the duration of a period of unemployment or the length of time before a mortgage is paid off. Data that represent an interval of time are called duration data and in a regression model we are interested in understanding how covariates affect the distribution of duration. The most natural way for an economist to think about such covariate effects is to imagine an agent at a sequence of time points at each of which he must choose to terminate the event or not. The total duration of the event is then determined by the sequence of decisions to stop or to carry on and the duration, Y, is determined by the first occasion on which he decides to stop.

Consider then a given time instant, t, and an agent with covariates x who must decide whether or not to continue. He has a binary choice and we can construct a model by specifying the probability that he stops as a function both of the covariates and of the time, t, that has elapsed since the event began. More specifically consider a short interval of time from t to $t + \delta t$ and write the probability of stopping in t, $t + \delta t$ as

$$\theta(t)\,\delta t = P(t < Y \le t + \delta t | Y > t) \tag{5.23}$$

where θ depends also on x but we suppress this dependence to simplify notation. Notice the conditioning on $Y > t$ which implies that the duration is at least t. Obviously if the duration was less than t the agent would have already decided to stop and the question of whether to stop at t is meaningless! The function $\theta(t, x)$ is called the **hazard function** at t and it completely determines the probability model for Y. To see this note that if G is the distribution function of Y and g is the density function then

$$\theta(t)\,\delta t = P(t < Y \le t + \delta t | Y > t)$$

$$= \frac{P(t < Y \le t + \delta t)}{P(Y > t)}$$

$$= \frac{G(t + \delta t) - G(t)}{1 - G(t)}.$$

Dividing both sides by δt and letting $\delta t \to 0$ gives

$$\theta(t) = \frac{g(t)}{1 - G(t)} = \frac{g(t)}{\bar{G}(t)}. \tag{5.24}$$

The second line here is just a version of $P(A|B) = P(A \cup B)/P(B)$.

Here, $g(t)$ is the density function of the duration (survival, unemployment) time at t and $\bar{G}(t) = 1 - G(t)$ is called the **survivor function**. Since (5.24) is a differential equation we may solve it subject to the condition that G is a distribution function to find a representation of the distribution and density functions of survival time as

$$1 - G(t) = \exp\left\{-\int_0^t \theta(u)\,du\right\},$$

$$\Rightarrow g(t) = \theta(t)\exp\left\{-\int_0^t \theta(u)\,du\right\}. \tag{5.25}$$

Here the second line follows by differentiation of the first. Thus, remarkably, by specifying a sequence of binary choice probabilities for each instant of time we have deduced the entire distribution of the duration. Since we now have a model for the density function of Y we have a likelihood and can proceed to inference. All that remains is to specify a functional form for the hazard. Each such choice leads to a specific model and we shall study two such models both of which are examples of **proportional hazard models**. The hazard is proportional when it takes the form $\theta(t, x) = \theta_0(t)\psi(x)$. In this case the hazard at any time t is shifted proportionally up or down by the factor $\psi(x)$. The function $\theta_0(t)$ is called the **baseline hazard**.

5.7.1   Exponential durations

Suppose that θ does not depend on t. Then $g(t) = \theta e^{-\theta t}$ which is the exponential distribution – a subfamily of the gamma distributions with $\alpha = 1$ and $\beta = \theta$. A constant hazard implies that the decision whether or not to stop is independent of how much time has passed since the event began. If we allow for dependence on a covariate vector x as for example by setting $\theta = e^{x\beta}$ we have an exponential regression function. In particular, since the mean of an exponential(θ) variate is $1/\theta$ we see that the regression function for this constant (time-invariant) hazard model is

$$E(Y|x, \beta) = \exp\{-x\beta\}.$$

Thus we have a non-linear regression model.

It is common to find that duration data is censored in the sense that for some agent we know only that he had not stopped by t. Such a censored duration contributes the probability $1 - G(t) = \exp\{-\theta t\}$ to the likelihood. If we denote by δ an indicator of a duration being uncensored the likelihood for n agents whose durations are stochastically independent takes the form

$$\begin{aligned} \ell(\beta; y) &\propto \prod_{i=1}^{n} g(y_i)^{\delta_i}(1 - G(y_i))^{1-\delta_i}, \\ &= \prod_{i=1}^{n} e^{x_i\beta\delta_i} \exp\{-y_i e^{x_i\beta}\}. \end{aligned} \tag{5.26}$$

If no observation is right censored this expression reduces to the product of n conditionally independent exponential densities with means of the form $\exp\{-x_i\beta\}$. The symbol y in this expression represents a duration if $\delta = 1$ and a censoring time otherwise.

Computation

The joint posterior density of β is proportional to (5.26) times a prior for β. Sampling such a posterior is not difficult. For most users the easiest method is BUGS, and within BUGS there are several ways to proceed. The software provides a specific device to handle censored data. This is to write the model statement in the form

```
y ~ ddist(theta)I(lower, upper)
```

If upper is missing and the statement reads `I(lower,)` then `y` is censored at lower. If both lower and upper are missing and `I` takes the form `I(,)` then this is equivalent to no censoring. With censored duration data `lower` would be zero for uncensored data and the censoring time otherwise. `ddist` stands for any of the BUGS distributional forms e.g. `dnorm`, `dexp`, etc. Thus to model right censored exponential data the model statement might be

```
model{
for(i in 1:n){
y[i]  ~ dexp(mu[i])I(cen[i],)
mu[i] <- exp(b0 +b1*x[i])
}}
```

The data file would here contain three columns. The first would be the values of y, with right censored observations treated as missing (NA); the second would be the censoring times – cen – with zeros for the uncensored data and the censoring times for censored data; and the third would be the x data.

5.7.2   Weibull durations

Returning to the general model in which the hazard, $\theta(t, x)$, depends upon both time, t, and covariates, x, we see that the exponential model imposes the restriction that the hazard does not depend on the elapsed duration. This means roughly that however long the event has lasted the probability of it ending "next day" remains the same. This may well be unreasonable in many economic applications. For example if the event is holding a job then empirical studies seem to indicate that the chance of the job ending, by quit or termination, is initially low, rises to a peak and then falls. This pattern is consistent with some models of optimal employer/employee behavior.

A simple way of allowing for a non-constant hazard is to allow it to be monotone, though this doesn't fit the job tenure hazard we have just described. A monotone hazard is created by allowing the hazard to take the form

$$\theta(t, x) = \alpha t^{\alpha-1}\psi(x), \quad \alpha > 0.$$

The integrated hazard is clearly equal to $t^{\alpha}\psi(x)$ and so, from (5.26), the density function of the duration, given x, is

$$g(t) = \alpha t^{\alpha-1}\psi(x)\exp\{-t^{\alpha}\psi(x)\}. \tag{5.27}$$

This is the weibull model, named after a Swedish statistician. It is widely used in econometrics. If $\alpha = 1$ the model reduces to the exponential; if $\alpha > 1$ the hazard is decreasing from infinity at the origin to zero as $t \to \infty$; and if $0 < \alpha < 1$ the hazard increases from zero at the origin towards infinity. Fitting the weibull model with a likelihood proportional to the product of n terms like (5.27), possibly with right censoring, is straightforward in BUGS. In the program for exponential data just change dexp(mu[i]) to dweib(a,mu[i]) and then provide a prior for α using any distribution on the non-negative axis.

5.7.3 Piecewise constant hazards

The exponential and weibull models adopt simple parametric forms for the way in which the hazard function varies over time. Often we would like to avoid such strong priors and allow the hazard to vary in some arbitrary, but reasonably smooth manner. We can achieve this by defining a partition of the time axis and letting the hazard assume the values

$$\theta(t, x) = \alpha_j \psi(x) \quad \text{for} \quad t_{j-1} < t \le t_j, \quad j = 1, 2, ..., J$$

where the $\{\alpha_j\}$ are any positive numbers. Thus, given the alphas, the hazard behaves like a step function of time. Smoothness of the hazard can then be enforced by adopting a prior in which successive increments in the alphas are positively correlated.

5.7.4 Heterogeneous duration models

Just as with count data, we can extend duration modeling to deal with unmeasured sources of heterogeneity by introducing additional observation specific parameters. The usual way to do this is write the hazard function for agent i as $v_i \theta(t, x_i)$. For example, with an underlying exponential model we would have the hazard as $v_i e^{x_i \beta}$ and with weibull data it would be $v_i \alpha t^{\alpha-1} e^{x_i \beta}$. The latter leads to the heterogeneous weibull model with density function conditional on α, β, v_i

$$p(t|v_i, x_i, \alpha, \beta) = v_i \alpha t^{\alpha-1} e^{x_i \beta} \exp\{-v_i e^{x_i \beta} t^\alpha\}. \tag{5.28}$$

The $\{v_i\}$ are then assumed to be independent conditional on the $\{x_i\}, \alpha, \beta$ and some hyperparameters with α, β having standard, typically gamma/uniform, priors. The standard model would assign independent mean one, variance σ^2 priors to the $\{v_i\}$ with α, σ^{-2} having diffuse gamma densities and β being diffuse normal. This model, specified by (5.28) and the conditional prior

$$p(v|\delta) \propto v^{\delta-1} e^{-\delta v}, \quad \delta = 1/\sigma^2,$$

has a hazard function marginal with respect to v that may be non-monotone as a function of t and thus possibly able to describe job tenure data.

Parameters of interest would be σ, as a check on the presence of unmeasured heterogeneity; α as a measure of the curvature of the hazard; and the elements of β which show how the hazard shifts when covariates change.

Appendix 3 provides a BUGS program to sample the marginal posterior densities of α, δ, β in this model.

Criticism of duration models

The main objection to models such as the exponential or weibull that specify particular parametric forms for the hazard is that they lose track of the econometric foundations of the problem, namely, as we said at the beginning of the section, that agents are making a series of binary choices, to stop or not to stop. Mechanical forms lead away from serious consideration of such choices. There is now a small but potentially exciting literature that takes seriously the modeling of optimal stopping and, more generally, of agents making sequences of discrete choices. Some references are given in the bibliographic notes. Bayesian work in this area has scarcely begun.

5.8 CONCLUDING REMARKS

In this chapter we have described a number of non-linear regression models and described how they can be implemented, typically using MCMC methods. Many of the techniques described in the linear regression chapter can be used in a non-linear context. These include the use of dummy indicator variables; the construction of interaction terms to study possible departures from constant regression effects; and the use of semiparametric methods. The S function `gam`, whose use was illustrated in chapter 3, section 3.6.2, to fit smooth possibly non-linear effects applies here also. In the linear model we used it as

```
gam(y ~s(x))
```

which fits a smooth regression function. In a non-linear model which fits into the class of models that can be estimated using the generalized linear model function `glm` – these include count and binary data – the S call would be something like

```
gam(y ~ s(x), family = poisson)
```

for example.[9]

A notable omission from this chapter has been discussion of model choice and residual analysis. Partly this has been for reasons of space and the desire not to be repetitious. Bayes factors for model choice – between logit and probit models for example – can be constructed, although there have been few examples published to date. But partly it has been because model checking is less easy in many non-linear models. Residuals are well defined in the CES production function example and their study can be carried out in much the same way as for linear models; but residuals for discrete choice or partly discrete choice models or for duration models are less obvious. There has been a good deal of frequentist work on this subject but rather little Bayesian material so far.

---

9 You should enter `library(mgcv)` in an S session to make `gam` available. This is a frequentist program; Bayesian counterparts are less well developed.

5.9 EXERCISES

(1) Find or generate some binary data with associated covariates and run the BUGS program of section 5.2 or its logit variant. Study convergence of the sampler. To generate some data in R use, say,

```
n <- 100; x_rnorm(n); b0 <- 0; b1 <- 1;
y <- rbinom(n, 1, pnorm(b0 + b1*x))
```

Compare your answers with ml estimates computed in S using the `glm` function.

(2) To generate data satisfying an ordered probit model with, say, 4 categories generate some x's as in the previous exercise and choose parameter values; then choose cut-off points $\gamma_1, \gamma_2, \gamma_3$; generate s values following a normal linear model with mean linear in x and unit precision; finally calculate the category into which each s value falls by setting y_i equal to 0 if $s_i < \gamma_1$, equal to 1 if $\gamma_1 < s_i < \gamma_2$, etc. Generate some data and use the BUGS function from appendix 3 to simulate from the posterior densities of γ_j, β_j.

(3) Study Bayesian inference about count data by finding or generating a sequence of counts and their covariate values. To generate some time series data you might use

```
n <- 5; beta <- 1; x <- rnorm(n); y <- rpois(n, exp(beta*x)).
```

You can then draw the time series posterior (5.23) which allows for possible agent specific time invariant heterogeneity in the mean. To draw it you could use

```
bv <- seq(-4, 4, length=100);
plot(bv, exp(bv * sum(x*y))/(sum(exp(x*bv)))^(sum(y))).
```

(4) You can explore Bayesian modeling of duration data by generating some, say, weibull data by

```
n <- 100; x <- rnorm(n); alpha <- 1.2; beta <- 1; y
<- rweib(n, alpha, exp(x*beta))
```

and running the BUGS program from appendix 3.

(5) You can explore the S function `glm` as a device for locating approximate posterior modes by creating some data satisfying a generalized linear model, for example count data or binary data. Then you could compare the point estimates and standard errors produced by a call to `glm` with the output of BUGS runs.

(6) You can try out the frequentist regression smoother in `gam` by generating generalized linear model data with a non-linear regression function and asking the program to detect the shape of that function.

5.10 APPENDIX TO CHAPTER 5: SOME FURTHER DISTRIBUTIONS

5.10.1 *The lognormal family*

A lognormal variate is one whose logarithm is normally distributed. To put it the other way round, if X is normal with mean μ and precision τ, then $Y = e^X$ is lognormally distributed with the same two parameters. We write $Y \sim \Lambda(\mu, \tau)$.

Since $P(Y \le y | \mu, \tau) = P(e^X \le y | \mu, \tau) = P(X \le \log y | \mu, \tau)$ it follows that the distribution function and density function of a $\Lambda(\mu, \tau)$ variate are

$$F(y) = P(Y \le y) = \Phi(\tau^{1/2}(\log y - \mu));$$

$$f(y) = \frac{\tau^{1/2}}{y} \phi(\tau^{1/2}(\log y - \mu)); \quad y > 0.$$

Written out explicitly the density function is

$$f(y; \mu, \sigma^2) = \frac{1}{\sqrt{2\pi}} \frac{\tau^{1/2}}{y} \exp\{-(\tau/2)(\log y - \mu)^2\}, \quad y > 0.$$

The distribution is skewed, with a long tail to the right, so the mean exceeds the mode and median. Empirical frequency distributions of wealth and income often seem to be roughly lognormal. This is one reason why econometric regression models explaining income or output or wealth typically work with the logarithms of these variables which can be expected to be more nearly normal.

The moments of the distribution are easily deduced from the moment generating function of the normal distribution which, from the appendix to chapter 1, is $E(e^{tX}) = \exp\{t\mu + t^2/2\tau\}$. Since $e^{tX} = Y^t$ it follows that

$$E(Y^t | \mu, \tau) = \exp\left\{t\mu + \frac{t^2}{2\tau}\right\}, \tag{5.29}$$

which implies that the mean is $E(Y|\mu, \tau) = \exp\{\mu + \frac{1}{2\tau}\}$. The coefficient of variation is $\sqrt{(e^{1/\tau} - 1)}$ which is approximately equal to $\tau^{-1/2}$ when τ is large. It is interesting that although Y has moments of all positive order, given by (5.29), it does not itself have a moment generating function since $\int_0^\infty e^{ty} f(y)\, dy$ fails to converge in an interval about $t = 0$.

5.10.2 *Truncated normal distributions*

It is often the case in econometrics that we need to consider normal distributions that are truncated on the left or the right so that we only observe realizations which are all above or all below a given number. Specifically, consider a normal distribution of mean μ and precision τ truncated on the left at zero, so that we only observe positive realizations. The density of such a left truncated normal variate is

$$g(y \mid y > 0) = \frac{\tau^{1/2} \phi(\tau^{1/2}(y - \mu))}{\Phi(\tau^{1/2}\mu)}, \quad y > 0, \tag{5.30}$$

where, as usual, ϕ and Φ are the standard normal density and distribution functions. The role of the denominator in this expression is to ensure that the density integrates to one over the positive axis.

To find the moments of this truncated distribution it is best to work out the moment generating function. This is

$$M(t) = E(e^{tY} \mid Y > 0) = \frac{\int_0^\infty \tau^{1/2} \exp\{ty - (\tau/2)(y - \mu)^2\} \, dy / \sqrt{2\pi}}{\int_0^\infty \tau^{1/2} \exp\{-(\tau/2)(y - \mu)^2\} \, dy / \sqrt{2\pi}}.$$

If we complete the square in the exponent of the numerator of this expression we can put it in the form

$$M(t) = \frac{e^{t\mu + t^2/2\tau} \int_0^\infty \tau^{1/2} \exp\{-(\tau/2)(y - m)^2\} \, dy / \sqrt{2\pi}}{\int_0^\infty \tau^{1/2} \exp\{-(\tau/2)(y - \mu)^2\} \, dy / \sqrt{2\pi}}$$

$$= e^{t\mu + t^2/2\tau} \frac{\Phi(\tau^{1/2}m)}{\Phi(\tau^{1/2}\mu)} \quad \text{for} \quad m = \mu + t/\tau.$$

The first term is the mgf of an untruncated normal and the second term corrects this to allow for the truncation. The cumulant generating function is found from this expression to be

$$K(t) = t\mu + t^2/2\tau + \log \Phi(\tau^{1/2}(\mu + t/\tau)) + \text{constant}.$$

Differentiating this expression with respect to t at the point $t = 0$ gives the mean as

$$E(Y \mid Y > 0) = \mu + \tau^{-1/2} \frac{\phi(\tau^{1/2}\mu)}{\Phi(\tau^{1/2}\mu)}. \tag{5.31}$$

In the more general case of truncation on the left at, say, c, the cgf is

$$K(t) = t\mu + t^2/2\tau + \log \Phi(\tau^{1/2}(\mu - c + t/\tau)) + \text{constant}$$

with mean

$$E(Y|Y > c) = \mu + \tau^{-1/2} \frac{\phi(\tau^{1/2}(\mu - c))}{\Phi(\tau^{1/2}(\mu - c))}.$$

For truncation on the right at c replace t by $-t$ and μ by $-\mu$ in these expressions.

5.10.3   The poisson family

The family of poisson distributions is indexed by a scalar λ and the probability mass function is

$$p(y|\lambda) = \frac{e^{-\lambda}\lambda^y}{y!}, \quad y = 0, 1, 2, \ldots; \quad \lambda > 0.$$

That this expression sums to one follows from the expansion $e^{\lambda} = 1 + \lambda + \lambda^2/2! + \lambda^3/3! + \ldots$

The moment generating function is

$$M(t) = E(e^{tY}|\lambda) = \sum_{s=0}^{\infty} \frac{e^{ts}e^{-\lambda}\lambda^s}{s!}$$

$$= e^{-\lambda}\sum_{s=0}^{\infty} \frac{(\lambda e^t)^s}{s!} = \exp\{\lambda(e^t - 1)\}$$

with cgf $K(t) = \log M(t) = \lambda(e^t - 1)$. It follows by differentiation that

$$E(Y|\lambda) = \lambda; \quad V(Y|\lambda) = \lambda$$

and indeed all cumulants are equal to λ.

5.10.4   The heterogeneous poisson or negative binomial family

Consider a poisson distribution with mean $v\lambda$ given v and λ and then assign v a gamma distribution of mean one and variance $1/\alpha$. Thus

$$p(y|v, \lambda) = \frac{e^{-v\lambda}(v\lambda)^y}{y!} \quad \text{and} \quad p(v|\alpha) = \frac{v^{\alpha-1}e^{-\alpha v}}{\Gamma(\alpha)\alpha^{-\alpha}}, \quad \alpha, v > 0; y = 0, 1, 2, \ldots$$

The joint distribution v and y given λ, α is the product of these two terms and so the marginal distribution of y is

$$p(y|\lambda, \alpha) = \frac{\lambda^y}{y!\Gamma(\alpha)\alpha^{-\alpha}} \int_0^\infty \exp\{-v(\lambda + \alpha)\} v^{y+\alpha-1} \, dv$$

$$= \frac{\lambda^y}{y!\Gamma(\alpha)\alpha^{-\alpha}} \Gamma(y + \alpha)(\lambda + \alpha)^{-(y+\alpha)}.$$

This is a (slightly disguised) version of the negative binomial probability mass function. It may be put into standard form by defining

$$q = \frac{\alpha}{\lambda + \alpha}$$

so the mass function becomes

$$p(y|q, \alpha) = \frac{\Gamma(y + \alpha)}{\Gamma(y + 1)\Gamma(\alpha)} q^\alpha (1 - q)^y,$$

where we have used $x! = \Gamma(x + 1)$ when x is integer.

The moment generating function is best derived from that of the poisson with conditional mean $v\lambda$. Thus

$$M(t) = E(\exp\{v\lambda(e^t - 1)\})$$

$$= \left(\frac{1}{1 - \theta/\alpha}\right)^\alpha, \quad \text{for } \theta = \lambda(e^t - 1).$$

This gives the mean and variance as

$$E(Y|\alpha, \lambda) = \lambda, \quad V(Y|\alpha, \lambda) = \lambda\left[1 + \frac{\lambda}{\alpha}\right]$$

or, in terms of α, q,

$$M(t) = \left(\frac{q}{1 - e^t(1 - q)}\right)^\alpha, \quad E(Y|\alpha, q) = \frac{1 - q}{q}\alpha, \quad V(Y|\alpha, q) = \alpha\frac{(1 - q)}{q^2}.$$

5.10.5 *The weibull family*

This is a two parameter family with densities of the form

$$p(t) = \alpha t^{\alpha-1}\lambda \exp\{-\lambda t^\alpha\}, \quad \alpha, \lambda > 0. \tag{5.32}$$

The survivor function is

$$P(T > t) = e^{-\lambda t^\alpha} \tag{5.33}$$

giving the median duration as

$$\text{median } (T) = \left[\frac{\log(2)}{\lambda}\right]^{1/\alpha}.$$

The s'th moment of T is

$$E(T^s) = \lambda \alpha \int_0^\infty t^{s+\alpha-1} e^{-\lambda t^\alpha} dt$$

$$= \lambda \int_0^\infty z^{s/\alpha} e^{-\lambda z} dz$$

$$= \lambda^{-s/\alpha} \Gamma\left(1 + \frac{s}{\alpha}\right), \tag{5.34}$$

where the second line follows from the change of variable $z = t^\alpha$ with jacobian $dt = (1/\alpha)z^{(1/\alpha)-1} dz$ and the third from use of the gamma integral formula. The mean and variance of T are therefore

$$E(T) = \lambda^{-1/\alpha} \Gamma\left(1 + \frac{1}{\alpha}\right),$$

$$V(T) = \lambda^{-2/\alpha}\left(\Gamma\left(1 + \frac{2}{\alpha}\right) - \Gamma^2\left(1 + \frac{1}{\alpha}\right)\right).$$

These expressions reduce to the moments of an exponential(λ) variate when $\alpha = 1$, namely $E(T) = 1/\lambda$, $V(T) = 1/\lambda^2$, etc.

The regression version of the weibull is got by setting $\lambda = \psi(x)$, e.g. $\lambda = e^{x\beta}$.

The heterogeneous weibull

The heterogeneous weibull has conditional hazard equal to $v\alpha t^{\alpha-1}\lambda$. The standard heterogeneous model is that in which v has density

$$p(v) \propto v^{\delta-1} e^{-\delta v},$$

a unit mean gamma distribution with variance equal to $1/\delta$. Interest often centers on the distribution of T marginal with respect to v. Using (5.33), the survivor function is

$$P(T > t) = E(P(T > t|v))$$

$$= \int_0^\infty v^{\delta-1} e^{-\delta v} \exp\{-v\lambda t^\alpha\} \, dv / \Gamma(\delta)\delta^{-\delta}$$

$$= \int_0^\infty \exp\{-v(\delta + \lambda t^\alpha\} v^{\delta-1} \, dv / \Gamma(\delta)\delta^{-\delta}$$

$$= \left[\frac{(\delta + \lambda t^\alpha)}{\delta} \right]^{-\delta}$$

$$= (1 + \lambda t^\alpha \sigma^2)^{-1/\sigma^2}, \quad \text{for} \quad \sigma^2 = 1/\delta. \tag{5.35}$$

The parameter σ^2 is the variance of v. This expression reduces to (5.34) as $\sigma^2 \to 0$. This gamma mixture of weibulls is sometimes called the Burr family – it has three parameters as compared to the weibull's two.

The hazard function of the weibull is, of course, $\lambda \alpha t^{\alpha-1}$ which is monotone in t, but that of the mixed weibull or Burr is, by differentiation of the negative of the logarithm of (5.35), equal to

$$\theta(t) = \frac{\lambda \alpha t^{\alpha-1}}{(1 + \lambda t^\alpha \sigma^2)}$$

and this is not necessarily monotone. In particular, it can rise from zero to a single maximum and then fall again towards zero. Notice that in the regression version of this model with λ equal to $e^{x\beta}$, say, the hazard is no longer proportional. It does not factor into the product of a function of t and a function of x.

Moments of the heterogeneous weibull family are readily found by replacing λ in (5.34) by $v\lambda$ and taking expectations with respect to v. Thus for example,

$$E(T) = E(v^{-1/\alpha})\lambda^{-1/\alpha}\Gamma\left(1 + \frac{1}{\alpha}\right)$$

$$= (\delta/\lambda)^{1/\alpha} \frac{\Gamma(\delta - 1/\alpha)}{\Gamma(\delta)} \Gamma\left(1 + \frac{1}{\alpha}\right).$$

5.11 BIBLIOGRAPHIC NOTES

The literature on Bayesian analysis of non-linear regression models is now quite large. Much of it deals with proposals for particular MCMC algorithms, often exploiting latent linear models and using data augmentation and the Gibbs Sampler. In a sense this literature is being superseded by the advent of packages such as BUGS. Papers on logit models include Koop and Poirier (1997: 139–51) and Poirier (1996: 163–81). A nested discrete choice model arises in modeling sequential choice situations in which an initial choice opens up a new choice set and a choice from this then opens a new set etc. The logit arises because at each stage the discrete choice model is logit or multinomial logit. Albert and Chib (1993: 669–79) was an early Bayesian study of discrete choice modeling exploiting data augmentation. McCulloch, Polson, and Rossi (2000: 173–93) is perhaps the most recent discussion of inference in the multinomial probit model. They offer an answer to the question of how to construct priors on covariance matrices when one of the variances is constrained to be one.

Discrete choice models with flexible forms for the error distribution are explored in Geweke and Keane (1999).

Sequential discrete choice holds many possibilities for Bayesian methods. W. van der Klaauw (2002) is a recent study of this class of model.

There have been nice surveys of selection models, for example Amemiya (1985) and more recently in Vella (1998: 127–69), but all are written from a frequentist perspective and ignore Bayesian inference. A Bayesian survey would be useful.

Fernandez, Osiewalski, and Steel (1997: 169–93) provide an interesting discussion of (frontier) production function inference emphasizing how improper priors can, unlike in simpler models, sometimes lead to the non-existence of proper posterior distributions. Congdon (2001) and (2003) provide many examples of non-linear regression models and links to relevant BUGS code.

For a biostatistical take on generalized linear models with random coefficients and hierarchical priors look at Clayton (1996), in *Markov Chain Monte Carlo in Practice*, eds. Gilks, Richardson, and Spiegelhalter. This volume contains many papers on both the theory and application of MCMC and is well worth consulting. There is a growing literature on Bayesian analysis of duration or survival data with the baseline hazard specified non-parametrically. See, for example, Ibrahim, Chen, and Sinha (2001).

Yatchew and Griliches (1985: 134–9) provide an insightful discussion of what in Bayesian terms are sensitivities to prior beliefs in probit models, though their approach is entirely frequentist.

Chapter 6

RANDOMIZED, CONTROLLED, AND OBSERVATIONAL DATA

The numbers in an economists's data file are almost always **observational data**. This means that they arise out of his/her observations of the working of the economic system – of watching people or firms as they interact in the market place or of looking at the aggregate effects of such interactions. This fact is of fundamental importance. In this short chapter we shall describe what is meant by the phrase "observational data" and distinguish such data from that arising out of randomized or controlled experimentation. We shall then give an account of the consequences of the fact that our data are observational. Foremost among these consequences is that econometric models are, in general, *not* regression models, though such models may arise after further analysis. In the following two chapters we give an account of the use of panel and clustered data and then of the use of instrumental variables. These are two ways of trying to solve the problems raised by the non-randomized character of our data.

6.1 INTRODUCTION

Recall that the starting point[1] for an econometric analysis is an equation

$$g(y, x) = 0 \qquad (6.1)$$

that describes the solution of an economic model in the sense that for each x it may be uniquely solved for y. It may be linearized to give $y = x\beta$ as an approximate explicit form of the solution. To confront the model with data we add a term ε that varies from one agent or market to another to recognize that the theory represented by (6.1) will generally be descriptively inaccurate. This gives $y = x\beta + \varepsilon$ in the case where $g(y, x) = y - x\beta$. Alternatively, and more generally, one can write the enlarged model as

$$g(y, x, \varepsilon) = 0. \qquad (6.2)$$

---

1 This has been the standard approach for at least 50 years. See the paper by Koopmans cited in the bibliographical notes at the end of this chapter.

Equations (6.1) or (6.2) form the **structural** model in the sense that they represent your theory about the way in which y is determined by x (and ε). Note that $g(,)$ is generally a set of equations equal in number to the dimension of y. Objects that appear in these expressions and will be unknown after y, x have been observed are **structural parameters**. These might be β, ε in the linearized version, or ε and the function $g(., ., .)$ in the general version of the structure. The objective of econometric inference is to make probability statements about these parameters in the light of the data. To proceed with Bayesian inference we need a probability distribution for y. This would follow from a joint probability distribution for x, ε since y is determined if these numbers are known.

The issue that then arises is to formulate credible prior beliefs about x and ε. In chapters 3 and 5, dealing with regression models, we assumed that it was credible that the values of x and ε were independent, that is, x is *exogenous*, but gave no reason why any reader should find this belief credible. There are some circumstances, arguably uncommon in economics, in which it will be credible that x is exogenous. Foremost among these are when the data arise from a randomized or a controlled experiment.

6.2   DESIGNED EXPERIMENTS

In this section we shall describe some situations in which it might be credible to view x as exogenous. To make the discussion more concrete let us think in terms of the linear(ized) version of (6.2), namely

$$y = x\beta + \varepsilon. \tag{6.3}$$

6.2.1   *Randomization*

Suppose that you know that the y, x data were produced by first using a random number generator to choose a value for x and then observing the chosen y values that, by assumption, are determined by (6.3) for some β and ε. Now ε is intended to capture the factors that determine y other than x, factors that have been omitted in the theorizing that lead to (6.1). These factors are specific to the agent or market and the environment in which they operate. But since x was chosen in a way – from a random number generator – that is apparently physically independent of such agent or market specific factors it follows that for most people (stochastic) independence of x and ε will be plausible. This independence in turn implies that (6.3) is a regression model and the results of chapter 3 apply.

This **random allocation** of covariates does occur, particularly in agricultural and medical statistics. In an agricultural experiment the level of fertilizer allocated to a field, x, is typically randomly determined and ε represents the effect on yield of factors that were not measured, perhaps temperature, shade, rainfall and so on. The random choice of treatment, x, makes it seem plausible that x and ε are statistically independent and so differences in yield as we look across plots can reasonably be thought to be, on average, attributable to the differences in treatment of such plots.

In medical statistics random allocation of treatments x to patients is the basis of the **randomized clinical trial**, the idea being that it is vital to assign treatments independently of particular unmeasured characteristics of the patient and his environment. When treatment has been randomized to patients, differences in outcomes between patients can plausibly be attributed, on average, to differences in treatments. A randomized trial provides the basis for widely credible inference about treatment (covariate) effects.

Analyses in which treatments are not randomized have much less credibility in medical statistics. And indeed this field has its share of observational and non-randomized data, an early and not untypical example being the observed correlations of smoking rates and lung cancer occurrence. Because smoking practices were not randomly assigned, many people, including the statistician R. A. Fisher, argued that the observed correlation failed to show, convincingly, a casual effect. Their argument was, in effect, that people with different smoking rates, x, could have systematically different error terms, ε, where the error represents the effect of unmeasured factors, for example hereditary ones, that predispose individuals both to get cancer and to smoke. It was not until data of a different type, from controlled laboratory experimentation, became available that most people accepted the view that smoking caused cancer.

6.2.2 *Controlled experimentation*

A controlled experiment is one in which extraneous factors that might affect y other than x are held constant by the experimenter and only x is changed. The ideal is a laboratory setting in which, through control of the physical environment in which the experiment is conducted, the scientist can vary x, and watch its effect on y while all other possible causes of variation in y remain the same. Thus any variation in y can be confidently attributed to variation in x. In terms of the linear model, x is changed but ε remains the same. From a technical point of view control makes it possible to absorb ε into the intercept of a linear model. When the error term is a constant the question of endogeneity or exogeneity of x doesn't arise.

It is important to note that the word "control" is also used in several rather different senses in econometrics. One of these is when there is a binary covariate which can be interpreted as indicating receipt of treatment, for example participation in a job-training program – $x_i = 1$ – or not – $x_i = 0$. Then people assigned to the program are called the **treated** and those not assigned are called "the **controls**."

Another use of the word control by economists is when a covariate, for example years of education, is included in a regression model; then it is often said that education has been "controlled for." If another variable included in the model is, say, age then one says something like "the effect of age on y, controlling for education, is . . ." when reporting the estimated coefficient of age. The idea behind this usage is that in a (fully) controlled experiment ε is not allowed to vary as x does, but if you cannot control ε but know a component of it, such as years of education, you can include that variable as an additional covariate. And you can, at least in principle, do your calculations within subgroups all of whom have the same education, so that within such a group the education component of the error term *is* kept constant. It's not a lab technician keeping education constant, it is you – the econometrician. Then all you have to worry about are the *remaining* unmeasured variables whose effect goes to make up ε. Including a variable in the regression equation has (approximately) the same mathematical effect as physically holding it constant during an experiment.

Digression   *In epidemiology and biostatistics regression analyses of observational or imperfectly randomized data typically include many "controls" in the sense of the last paragraph. Examples are standard covariates such as age and gender as well as many pre-treatment measures of health status, blood pressure, weight and the like. It seems to be widely felt that such control covariates effectively eliminate the problem of correlation between the error term and their main covariate, typically some measure of "treatment." In cross-section and panel data econometrics economists also add controls but, in contrast, do not generally feel that by doing so they solve the problem of endogeneity. This distinction is sometimes called that between "selection on observables" – the common biostatistics belief – and "selection on unobservables" – a common belief of economists. So what may be a credible model in biostatistics may be an incredible one in economics.[2] The explanation for the difference of view – assuming I have characterized it correctly – is unclear.*

6.2.3   *Randomization and control in economics*

Randomized allocation of covariates is uncommon in economics, partly for ethical reasons – imagine randomly allocating tax rates or years of education to individuals – though it sometimes occurs.[3]

EXAMPLE 6.1   *RANDOMIZATION BY ACCIDENT*   *Randomization can occasionally appear as the accidental by-product of policies designed to achieve fairness. For example, the liability of young American men to serve in the Vietnam war was determined in part by lottery. But military service is not equivalent to civilian work so you have a situation in which an important economic variable, civilian labor market experience, was partly randomized.*

2   Some of the biostatisticians' optimism has recently crept into economics in the recent literature on propensity scores.

3   One well known example is a study in California of health care usage in which families were randomly allocated to insurance plans. See the references at the end of this chapter.

Controlled experimentation is rarely feasible either. Moreover economic agents are not inanimate laboratory material, they will be aware that they are subjects in an experiment and their behavior may change as x changes just because of that awareness. Economic data are, in almost all cases, produced by the working of the economy; they are not produced as the output of a designed (randomized or controlled) experiment. This is what makes econometrics difficult and its results, in the view of some observers, less than compelling.

Randomized choice of x makes independence of x and ε credible and controlled experimentation is designed to eliminate all variability in ε. Are there other circumstances that would make such exogeneity at least plausible? Most of the arguments that are available tend to argue against exogeneity, unfortunately. Indeed you often have, in economics, two arguments against exogeneity. The first is that the covariates are not randomly assigned. The second is that the economics of the model leads you to conclude that covariates and errors *must* be correlated. Here are some leading examples within the context of which exogeneity can be debated.

6.2.4 Exogeneity and endogeneity in economics

In a model of consumer demand in which x is price and y is quantity demanded it may be plausible to believe that price is not chosen by an agent but is rather given to him and determined by a market process that has no evident dependence on his characteristics. Price is not randomized to the agent but nonetheless it may be plausible that it is independent of ε, at least at the level of the individual agent. But at the level of the aggregate demand of the whole market in which price is determined at the intersection of an aggregate demand and supply curve, then price typically must be correlated with the aggregate effect of unmeasured factors – the aggregate error term. Indeed the econometric study of price and market demand was one of the first topics in which there arose econometric equations that are not interpretable as regressions.

EXAMPLE 6.2 *MARKET DEMAND AND SUPPLY*

To see this important case more clearly consider linear demand *and* supply *equations*

$$q_d = \alpha_d + \beta_d p + \varepsilon_d,$$
$$q_s = \alpha_s + \beta_s p + \varepsilon_s, \tag{6.4}$$

where q_d is the aggregate demand that would be forthcoming at price p and q_s is the corresponding aggregate supply function in this market. The equations (6.4) correspond to the general formulation $g(y, x, \varepsilon) = 0$ in which y is the pair, q_d, q_s, and x is p. Now, we must bring into the argument the process by which price, p, is determined. If price could be randomly assigned and the quantities demanded and supplied could be measured then a regression analysis using the model (6.4) *would be appropriate. But in fact, of course, economists normally find it appropriate to believe that observed prices clear the market by equating the quantities that would be demanded and supplied. So in the data that we observe it is assumed that p is such that $q_d = q_s = q$, say. Then the equations (6.4) become*

$$q = \alpha_d + \beta_d p + \varepsilon_d, \tag{6.5}$$

$$q = \alpha_s + \beta_s p + \varepsilon_s. \tag{6.6}$$

This is a pair of simultaneous equations in the two unknowns q and p and it may be solved for q and p, if $\beta_d \neq \beta_s$, as is plausible since surely $\beta_d < 0$ and $\beta_s > 0$. The solution for p, q is

$$p = \frac{\alpha_s - \alpha_d}{\beta_d - \beta_s} + \frac{\varepsilon_s - \varepsilon_d}{\beta_d - \beta_s},$$

$$q = \frac{\alpha_s \beta_d - \alpha_d \beta_s}{\beta_d - \beta_s} + \frac{\varepsilon_s \beta_d - \varepsilon_d \beta_s}{\beta_d - \beta_s}. \tag{6.7}$$

*It will be evident from these equations, called the **reduced form** corresponding to the **structural form** of (6.5) and (6.6), that p and q must, in general, be correlated with both ε_s and ε_d. It follows that neither $\alpha_d + \beta_d p$ nor $\alpha_s + \beta_s p$ is equal to $E(q \mid p)$ – they are not regressions – p is necessarily correlated with the errors because of our hypothesis that we see the market in equilibrium where demand and supply are equated. If you attempt to estimate α_d, β_d by assuming that p and ε_d are independent you will be adopting beliefs that are inconsistent with your own model and your results will have no credibility. This is a good example of the point that economics can often give you a very good reason why potential covariates and error terms should be correlated.*

Two other remarks about this model are worth making, though both are quite distinct from the main point of this example – that p (and q) must be endogenous. One is that the reduced form equations, (6.7), are both regressions in the sense that the first expressions on the right hand side of both equations are conditional means, assuming both ε_d and ε_s have marginal means of zero. The other is that, in this version of the supply and demand model, it will not be possible to determine all four parameters, α_d, α_s, β_d, β_s from the likelihood alone; only two functions of them, the reduced form means, are likelihood identified.[4]

We argued above that while price may be exogenous at the level of the individual household it could not be so at the level of the whole market – the economics of the problem forces you to rule out exogeneity of price. There are many contexts in which the economics of the problem dictates, or strongly suggests, that certain variables

---

4 We shall say a little more about market equilibrium models in chapter 8.

are likely to be correlated with the error term. The reasoning here is that it is often persuasive to believe that agents choose, at least in part, their own covariate values and they do so in the light of information not possessed by the observing economist.

EXAMPLE 6.3 *AGRICULTURAL PRODUCTION FUNCTIONS* *A classic example[5] is that of an agricultural production function in which the output of the farm, bushels of wheat for example, is taken to depend on the levels of factor inputs such as the amounts of labor and capital that are used, so that, for example*

$$q = \alpha + \beta_1 k + \beta_2 l + \varepsilon$$

where q is output, k, l are measures of capital and labor inputs (usually measured in logarithms) and ε summarizes all other sources of variations in output. (The Cobb–Douglas production considered in chapter 5 was of this form.) In a randomized experiment k and l would be allocated to a farm by a random number generator and so they can be plausibly assumed independent of the unmeasured determinants of output represented by ε. In a controlled experiment matters will be arranged so that when k and l are changed ε remains the same. But without these conditions we surely must believe that farmers choose their capital and labor inputs and that they do so in the light of some of the factors that enter into ε. These may include particular features of the land being farmed, of the weather, of the anticipated behavior of competitors, etc. This line of thought suggests that independence of ε and k, l is unpersuasive.

EXAMPLE 6.4 *EXPLAINING WAGES* *The standard model for the determination of the wage (rate) earned by different individuals has it depend on each person's education and experience or age. We might have*

$$w = \alpha + \beta_1 e + \beta_2 a + \beta_3 a^2 + \varepsilon$$

which is linear in years of education, e, and quadratic in age, a. But in most countries, children and their parents have latitude in choosing the amount (and perhaps also the quality) of education that the child receives. To the extent that this is true, that choice may well be influenced by factors, unmeasured by the economist but known to the family, that will also affect the wage that the child will subsequently earn. The obvious example is the child's ability or abilities. If ability measures are not included as covariates in the wage equation there is a strong a priori case for believing ε and e to be correlated. An analysis that assumes that education is exogenous will not be persuasive.

5 Cf. section 1 of chapter 5.

EXAMPLE 6.5 *INCOME AS A COVARIATE*

Often in a microeconometric analysis theory suggests that consumer or household income should be a determinant of whatever is under study, for example expenditure on some class of consumer good. But agents typically have some latitude in choosing their income by deciding on their hours of work through choice of overtime, if available, or full versus part time work, or choice of seasonal as opposed to year round work. To the extent that the income choice depends on factors that also affect the choice of the dependent variable and are not observed by the economist, income will plausibly be endogenous.

In these examples, and many others can be given, economists have not merely no good reason to believe x and ε to be independent, they have some reason to believe that ε and x *are* dependent. The implication of these arguments is that often the econometric model $y = x\beta + \varepsilon$ is *not* a regression equation in the sense that $x\beta$ is not the expected value of y given x. It follows that the regression modeling of chapters 3 and 5 may well not apply to inference about economic models.

6.3   SIMPSON'S PARADOX

We have emphasized the importance of taking a view about the relationship between covariates and errors and that economists may (a) have no good reason for supposing the terms independent but even (b) have reason to suppose that they must be dependent. But one may ask "is lack of independence important?", "does it matter if I treat the relation between y and x as a regression even though I am unconvinced that x is exogenous?" Here is the best-known example showing that radically different inferences can be made depending on whether you do or do not treat x as exogenous.

The data in the table below show the aggregate relation between the covariate x, which is binary, and the dependent variable y, which is also binary.

The regressor x takes the two values x and $\bar{x}$ and the outcome y takes the two values y and $\bar{y}$. The standard interpretation of the table is medical and x, $\bar{x}$ mean treated or not treated and y, $\bar{y}$ represent lived or died. So the table represents 80

Table 6.1

		Response		
		y	$\bar{y}$	recovery rate
Treatment	x	20	20	40	50%
	$\bar{x}$	16	24	40	40%
		36	44	80	

people of whom half were treated and of whom 44 died. And, of the 40 people treated half died, and of the 40 people not treated 24 died. The effect of treatment (x) on survival (y) is positive, treated people survive more often. But you can easily translate this example into economics. Let x indicate receipt of unemployment benefit and let y indicate finding a job in the next month. Or, in a cross-country study, let x indicate a tax regime and let y represent the presence or otherwise of economic growth. We shall continue with the medical story.

If it helps, you can fit this into the linear model framework. Let y^* be a latent variable triggering $y = 1$ if it is positive and $y = 0$ if it is negative. Then we can write

$$y_i^* = \alpha + \beta x_i + \varepsilon_i, \quad i = 1, 2, \ldots, n.$$

If you create some individual data satisfying the constraints implied by the table then assume x is exogenous with respect to ε and fit a probit model to the y, x data, you will find posterior modes for α and β of -0.25 and 0.25 respectively. These figures imply recovery rates among the treated of 50% and among the untreated of 40%. So the modal effect of treatment on survival is positive, which sounds like very important information.[6]

But now suppose you find a third variable, also binary, for example gender, z, then you can break down the data by z and have separate tables for men and women. Suppose these are, respectively:

Table 6.2

		Men Response			
		y	$\bar{y}$		recovery rate
Treatment	x	18	12	30	60%
	$\bar{x}$	7	3	10	70%
		25	15		

Table 6.3

		Women Response			
		y	$\bar{y}$		recovery rate
Treatment	x	2	8	10	20%
	$\bar{x}$	9	21	30	30%
		11	29		

6 Though the posterior standard deviation of β is 0.28 and so β is within a standard error of zero. This is immaterial though. You can multiply all numbers by 1,000 and the same paradox will arise.

So 60% of the treated men recover, but 70% of the untreated men recover. And 20% of the treated women recover but 30% of the untreated women recover. Thus treatment is worst for men; treatment is worst for women; but treatment is best for all! This is Simpson's paradox.

Again, if it helps, you can work with the latent linear model which is now extended to

$$y_i^* = \alpha + \beta x_i + \gamma z_i + \varepsilon_i'.$$

Putting individual level data corresponding to the information in the last two tables through a probit model gives posterior modes for α, β, γ of -0.53, -0.29 and 1.07. So the coefficient on treatment has changed signs, from 0.25 to -0.29, when we add the new covariate, gender, into the model. In the language discussed at the end of section 6.2.2 the effect of treatment on survival is positive, but the effect of treatment on survival *controlling for gender* is negative.

The crucial parameter, which would be called structural if this was economic data, is the effect of treatment on survival, holding everything else constant. But which posterior mode is the structural parameter? Is it the effect you can calculate from table 6.1, namely +10 percentage points, or is it the effect you can calculate from tables 6.2 and 6.3 of -10%, or neither? Our point of view is that to justify regression analyses, such as these, as a way of making inferences about a structural effect, you need to make it plausible that the covariates are, at worst, mean independent of the "errors" and, at best, independent. We are actually not told how these data were obtained, indeed they are probably fictional, but one thing is for sure, they do not look as though they were obtained from a designed experiment in which treatment was randomized to patients. The reason for this is that if treatment was randomized it should be (approximately) independent of other characteristics of the patient. But you can deduce from tables 6.2 and 6.3 that treatment is highly correlated with gender; 75 percent of men were treated but only 25 percent of women. Nor do they look as if they came from a controlled experiment in which "all other possibly relevant factors" were held constant, after all, gender wasn't held constant. So, in the absence of further information about how these data were obtained the answer must be *neither*. The answer to the question with which we began this section is that exogeneity is more than important, it is crucial.

Digression   *In the frequentist literature demonstration of the importance of exogeneity is usually shown by examining the bias[7] in the location of the sampling distribution of an estimator, typically least squares, when exogeneity fails.*

---

7   This is called "omitted variables bias."

6.4   CONCLUSIONS

Economists have become very adept at undermining claims of exogeneity. This is fine because it shows a high level of self-criticism, but it has the downside of making econometric work less and less persuasive. So how do economists react to these somewhat negative arguments? Many of them become theorists of course, but aside from this option there are two main responses.

The first is to look for panel or clustered data and the second is to look for an instrumental variable. As we shall see in the next chapter, panel or clustered data provide an opportunity to the economist to regard his data *as if* it had been produced by a controlled experiment in which the error, or rather an important part of it, had been held constant from one observation to another. By contrast, an instrumental variable is a randomizer with much the same properties as the output of a random number generator in determining treatment in a clinical trial. We shall deal with panel data next and show how it might help us construct credible models in the face of endogenous covariates. The following chapter, 8, deals with the search for an instrument.

6.5   APPENDIX TO CHAPTER 6: KOOPMANS' VIEWS ON EXOGENEITY

T. C. Koopmans (1950) made an early and influential statement about when it might be reasonable to believe that a variable is exogenous. He writes,

> [One principle] treats as exogenous those variables which are wholly or partly outside the scope of economics, like weather and climate, earthquakes, population, technical change, political events. . . . [Another principle] . . . regards as exogenous those variables which influence the remaining (endogenous) variables but are not influenced thereby.[8]

The first of these principles has, with the benefit of 50 years of hindsight, a somewhat ironical flavor. Though economists have yet, I think, to claim that earthquakes are explicable, in part, by economic activity, all the other categories are now viewed as part of a collection of jointly dependent variables that both influence and are influenced by the workings of the economy. In particular, legislation is now viewed as responding to market pressures, as is technical or scientific advance and innovation, as is the level and rate of change of population.

6.6   BIBLIOGRAPHIC NOTES

Readers who want to pursue the smoking and lung cancer controversy and examine Fisher's views might care to look at R. A. Fisher, Dangers of cigarette smoking,

---

8   The second principle appears to be tautological.

British Medical Journal, July 6, 1957, p. 43 and August 3, 1957, pp. 297–8. For a discussion of his views there are Cook (1980) and Stolley (1991: 416, 425).

Lindley and Novick (1981: 45–58) discuss Simpson's paradox and its connection with exchangeable beliefs. Our whole treatment of the relation between covariates and errors could be, and probably should be, recast as a requirement that certain beliefs be exchangeable. Lindley and Novick point the way to such a treatment. Rubin (1978: 34–58) discusses exchangeability and causal inference. Imbens and Rubin (1997: 305–27) look at endogeneity induced by non-compliance in an otherwise randomized trial and develop a data augmentation algorithm to do Bayesian inference.

For another recent methodological essay see Angrist and Krueger (1999).

The best known example of a deliberately randomized experiment in economics is the Health Insurance Experiment described in Manning *et al.* (1987).

Accidental randomization of civilian labor force experience is exploited in Angrist (1990: 313–36). Some applied economists lay stress on accidental randomization, often called natural experiments, and prefer to search for instances of such data rather than work with standard data sources.

For Koopmans' remarks about exogeneity see Koopmans (1950: 393–409).

Chapter 7
MODELS FOR PANEL DATA

7.1 PANEL DATA

Panel or **longitudinal data** are increasingly available to economists and provide an opportunity to relax some of the more dogmatic features of models applied to pure cross-section and pure time series data. In particular, and crucially, with panel data we can relax the assumption that the covariates are independent of the errors. They do this by providing what, on certain additional assumptions, amounts to a "controlled experiment."

DEFINITION 7.1 PANEL DATA *A panel is a collection of people (agents) who are interviewed repeatedly. Some people call the evidence that these agents provide* longitudinal data *to emphasize that the data refer to the same agents at successive dates. The i'th agent supplies data* $\{y_{it}, x_{it}\}$ *on* T_i *occasions that are equally spaced in time. Thus if the panel has N agents the total data collected is* $N\Sigma_i T_i$ *pairs of the form* $\{y_{it}, x_{it}\}$ *for* $i = 1, 2, ..., N$ *and* $t = 1, 2, ..., T_i$. *Data for which we observe each agent for the same length of time, say T, is called a* **balanced panel** *and, of course data in which agents are observed for differing time spans is called unbalanced. Balance is not necessary, it simply makes the exposition a little bit tidier and we shall assume it in what follows.*[1] *A time series arises as the special case of a panel in which* $N = 1$. *A cross-section is the special case of a panel in which* $T = 1$.

A closely related type of data is called clustered.

DEFINITION 7.2 CLUSTERED DATA *Closely related to panel data are* clustered data. *Clustering is where the data fall naturally into groups the members of which can be presumed to share relevant unmeasured characteristics. Examples of such groups might be members of the same family who may have similar tastes; households in*

---

[1] Of course with an unbalanced panel you might want to ask yourself precisely why you have, say, $T_a = 3$ observations for agent a but 10 for agent b. This sort of question leads one to think about "dropout" from a panel, censoring and the general question of missing observations. We shall avoid these issues and take the $\{T_i\}$ as data, providing in themselves no information about model parameters.

*the same village whose land might have similar characteristics; firms in the same indus-
try, and so on. With clustering we don't have repeated observations on the same agent
but we have sets of observations on similar agents. The purest case of clustered data occurs
when our observations consist of N {y, x} pairs for identical twins who, of course, share
the same genetic inheritance. Here we are observing, not the same person but the same
genetic entity on T = 2 occasions. In so far as unmeasured factors in the model are
attributable to genetic factors we may be able to argue that their effect on Y is constant
within the same twin pair.*

Panel and clustered data can provide a situation close to controlled experimentation.
Take the example of identical twins. If the error term is largely determined by genetic
factors that have not been measured then because the twins are genetically identical
the error term is at least approximately constant as x varies from one twin to the
other. Similar, though usually less persuasive, arguments can be made with panel data.

In this chapter we shall focus on panel data and explain and illustrate some useful models and their Bayesian analysis. But before doing so we shall try to give some
intuitive understanding of how panel data can help us to make inferences about
structural parameters even when covariates are not randomized and experiments not
tightly controlled.

7.2   HOW DO PANELS HELP?

The crucial characteristic of panel data for an econometrician is the fact that it contains repeated observations on the *same agent*. This sameness makes it plausible that
unmeasured factors that enter the error term in a model are similar over time for
the same agent. For example, if you observe the same firm in T years it is, perhaps,
plausible that unmeasured factors influencing y and possibly correlated with x, such as
the identity of the management or the physical location of the plant, are constant,
at least over a short horizon. The similarity of unmeasured factors in observations
on the same agent on different occasions can make it possible to reduce inference
about structural parameters to a regression calculation. To see this consider a linear
model with a single agent observed twice.

EXAMPLE 7.1   *A SINGLE AGENT OBSERVED
TWICE*   *Consider a single agent observed on occasions 1 and 2 so that we
have, for some particular agent,*

$$y_1 = x_1 \beta + \varepsilon_1,$$
$$y_2 = x_2 \beta + \varepsilon_2.$$

(7.1)

*Now if the values of x are not randomly assigned, the covariate values in each
period must be presumed correlated with the two error terms, so neither equation*

is a regression. But because we are dealing with the same agent it is plausible that many of the unmeasured factors that enter the error terms ε_1 and ε_2 are the same in period 2 as in period 1. In particular, to capture this idea, suppose that the error terms admit the representation

$$\varepsilon_1 = \alpha + v_1$$
$$\varepsilon_2 = \alpha + v_2 \tag{7.2}$$

*where α may be correlated with the x values but v_1, v_2 are not so that the dependence of x on ε is entirely attributable to its dependence on α. Thus $x = (x_1, x_2)$ is assumed to be independent of $v = (v_1, v_2)$ but dependent on α. The term α is often called a **fixed effect**[2] or an **individual effect** – we shall use the latter expression. It may vary from agent to agent but is constant over time for the same agent. In this case (7.1) and (7.2) imply*

$$y_1 = x_1\beta + (\alpha + v_1)$$
$$y_2 = x_2\beta + (\alpha + v_2). \tag{7.3}$$

Neither of these equations are regressions because of the dependence between x and α. Thus in the first equation $E(y_1|x_1, \beta) = x_1\beta + E(\alpha|x_1, \beta) \neq x_1\beta$. But these equations imply that

$$y_2 - y_1 = (x_2 - x_1)\beta + v_2 - v_1, \tag{7.4}$$

and this is a regression because of the independence of $x(= x_1, x_2)$ and $v(= v_1, v_2)$. (Note especially that independence between (x_1, x_2) and (v_1, v_2) implies, for example, that $E(v_1|x_2) = 0$: this condition rules out the case in which x_2 is equal to y_1, as it might be in an autoregressive model.) It follows from this independence that all the standard methods for inference in linear regression models apply with data that are N pairs $\{y_{i2} - y_{i1}, x_{i2} - x_{i1}\}$.

This example shows that, with panel data we can (sometimes) reduce inference about structural parameters to a regression analysis on a transformation of the data. It is applicable if the following conditions are satisfied. It will be plain that the argument leading to (7.4) cannot work if the errors are not additive and the decomposition of ε into α and v is not additive also. It will be equally clear that if x does not change between periods 1 and 2 then this method will fail because $\sum_{i=1}^{n}(x_{i2} - x_{i1} - (\bar{x}_2 - \bar{x}_1))^2$ will be zero. Thus it is not panel data per se that enables us to convert the problem of inference about β into a standard regression problem, it requires panel data plus linearity plus additivity of the error decomposition (7.2) plus time constancy of the individual effect.

---

2 Sometimes it is called a **random effect**. These two names reflect the frequentist distinction between parameters that do or do not have probability distributions. The distinction is irrelevant to Bayesians for whom all parameters have probability distributions.

A less algebraic, less formal and perhaps more intuitive way of understanding the potential of panel data can be provided as follows. In the cross-sectional case the model is $y_i = x_i\beta + \varepsilon_i$. We get our information about β, in effect, by taking pairs of agents, with distinct x's, and comparing their y values. But the difficulty with this calculation is that the agent with the larger x may also have the larger ε and so when we attribute the difference in y to the difference in x we may well be mistaken – it may also be due to the difference in ε. The effects on y of differences in x and differences in ε will be **confounded**.[3] But if we can rule out a priori any systematic association between x and ε we will be correct, at least on average over a lot of such pairwise comparisons, in attributing y differences to x differences. We can do this with a fully controlled experiment in which the ε's are not allowed to vary or, less powerfully, in a randomized experiment in which the ε's do vary but in a way that is independent of the x's. On the other hand, if we cannot rule out such a systematic association between differences in x and differences in ε then we will be unable to disentangle the effect of x on y from the effect of ε on y. Ruling out this systematic association between x and ε is precisely what the hypothesis of strict exogeneity does, though, as we have remarked, such an assumption often lacks credibility.

But when we have repeated observations on each agent we can write the error term as in (7.2) and then attribute any systematic association between the error and x as being *entirely* due to the possibility the $\{\alpha_i\}$ may be associated with the covariate value as we look across agents. Then if, as the notation indicates, the $\{\alpha_i\}$ are constant over time, we can get information about β not by comparing two distinct agents with different covariate values, but by comparing the same agent on two different occasions, between which his covariate has changed but, by assumption, his α has not. A change in y between two time points then must be due to the change in x if α didn't change (and v is independent of x). So the critical assumptions with panel data are that (a) we can separate out, additively, an individual effect from the error term and that (b) individual effect does not vary over time but the covariates do. If we can credibly assert this then all our information about the effect of x on y derives from the comparison of the same agents at different times and none from the comparison of different agents. As it is usually put, we use the *within* (*agent*) information to identify β.

Although we are emphasizing the special character of panel data here, from another point of view what we are doing when we introduce additive individual effects in a panel data model is exactly what economists traditionally do when they introduce additional "controls" in a linear model, as we explained in chapter 6. The function of these additional covariates is to try to reduce, even eliminate, the dependence between the error term and the already included covariates. Individual-specific effects correspond to the introduction of N new dummy covariates, as we shall see formally in the next section, and these act as additional "controls."

We should also emphasize that the point of the argument leading to (7.4) is not to recommend treating a linear model for balanced data by converting it into a regres-

---

3   The smoking and lung cancer controversy mentioned in chapter 6 is an example of this point. In effect, Fisher was arguing that the effect of smoking on cancer occurrence will be confounded with the effects of omitted variables correlated with both smoking habits and proneness to cancer.

sion model for the differenced data. The Bayesian approach requires us to place a prior distribution on all parameters, including the $\{\alpha_i\}$, and then, if interest centers on β, integrate out the $\{\alpha_i\}$ and any other so-called nuisance parameters. Bayesians integrate – they do not eliminate nuisance parameters by differencing the data. Nevertheless, differencing to eliminate the α_i is so evidently a sensible thing to do that one would hope that a formal Bayesian approach would lead to differencing for some not entirely unreasonable choice of prior, as indeed it does – see below. And anyway, differencing the data is not a method that works outside the linear model.

One might be interested in a non-linear model for panel data. This might arise when Y is binary so that we repeatedly observe a binary choice by each agent, for example Y_{it} might be an indicator whether or not household i purchased a particular good during period t. Or it might occur with count data when Y_{it} might be the number of times an event happened. A well-known example is the number of patent applications filed by firm i during year t. Or it might be that Y_{it} is the length of the t'th spell of unemployment for person i. In each case a factoring of error similar to (7.2) can be constructed and the panel character of the data exploited to produce a possibly persuasive posterior density for β. We shall first look at Bayesian inference about linear models and then at some non-linear models.

7.3 LINEAR MODELS ON PANEL DATA

Write the general balanced panel data linear equation as

$$y_{it} = x_{it}\beta + \varepsilon_{it}, \quad i = 1, 2, ..., N; \; t = 1, 2, ..., T,$$

where y_{it} is the observation of y for agent i at time t. The standard way of relaxing the independence of ε and x is to write ε as the sum of two terms. The first is a parameter, say α_i, that is constant over time but specific to an individual agent. This is an **individual effect**. The second component is a term which, like ε itself, varies over both time and agents. Then the hypothesis is that x_{it} is independent of ε_{it} given α_i. To save on notation we shall continue to denote this component by the symbol ε. Thus the linear panel model with individual effects for agent i at time t is

$$y_{it} = x_{it}\beta + \alpha_i + \varepsilon_{it}, \quad \varepsilon_{it}|x_{it}, \beta, \alpha_i, \tau \sim n(0, \tau). \tag{7.5}$$

The NT parameters that constitute the errors, $\{\varepsilon_{it}\}$, have here been assigned a prior distribution in which they are independently conditionally normal with means zero and precision τ given the covariate values and the remaining parameters. The individual effect α_i plays the role of an agent-specific intercept in this model and consequently the covariates in x_{it} cannot contain a column of ones. It is this separation of the error into two additive components that will be critical in allowing us to relax the independence of error and covariate. In effect, by allowing for agent-specific intercepts that are unchanging over time we have, if we adopt this model, convinced ourselves that the covariates are exogenous.

In this section we shall give some of the analytical results for this model under alternative priors. There is no real practical difficulty in applying this model, whatever your priors are, but some analysis is conventional and, up to a point, it is insightful.

7.3.1 Likelihood

Moving now to the model for all the data supplied by agent i we write the regressor matrix as X_i which is of order $T \times k$ and whose t'th row contains x_{it}, and introduce the column vector of T ones which will be called j_T. Then

$$y_i = X_i \beta + \alpha_i j_T + \varepsilon_i, \quad \varepsilon_i | X_i, \beta, \alpha_i \sim n(0, \tau I_T). \tag{7.6}$$

Here, y_i is a column vector of length T giving the consecutive y values for this agent, X_i is a $T \times k$ matrix of covariate values and β is a k vector of coefficients common to all agents and is the primary object of inference; and ε_i is the $T \times 1$ error vector that is normal, homoscedastic, and not autocorrelated and independent of X_i, α_i, and β. Thus X_i is strictly exogenous with respect to ε_i given α_i. Observations for different agents are stochastically independent given the covariate matrices, β, and the individual effects. All of these beliefs about ε except its independence of X given α are readily relaxed and independence of ε_i and X_i can be weakened. We can write (7.6) for all agents as

$$y = \begin{bmatrix} y_1 \\ y_2 \\ . \\ . \\ y_N \end{bmatrix} = \begin{bmatrix} X_1 & j_T & 0 & . & . & 0 \\ X_2 & 0 & j_T & . & . & 0 \\ . & & & & & . \\ . & & & & j_T & 0 \\ X_N & 0 & . & . & 0 & j_T \end{bmatrix} \begin{bmatrix} \beta \\ \alpha_1 \\ . \\ . \\ \alpha_N \end{bmatrix} + \begin{bmatrix} \varepsilon_1 \\ \varepsilon_2 \\ . \\ . \\ \varepsilon_N \end{bmatrix}, \tag{7.7}$$

where y is of length NT, the covariate matrix is of order $NT \times (k + N)$, and the coefficient vector is of length $k + N$. Note that we have enlarged the covariate matrix by adding N columns, in other words we have N additional dummy or indicator covariates. These are controls in the sense discussed in chapter 6.

To write panel expressions more compactly it is useful to recall the definition of the Kronecker product.

DEFINITION 7.3 KRONECKER PRODUCT OF TWO MATRICES, $A \otimes B$ *This product of A of order $m \times n$ and B of order $p \times q$ is a matrix of order $mp \times nq$ of the form*

$$A \otimes B = \begin{bmatrix} a_{11}B & . & . & . & a_{1n}B \\ a_{21}B & . & . & . & . \\ . & . & . & . & . \\ . & . & . & . & . \\ a_{m1}B & . & . & . & a_{mn}B \end{bmatrix}.$$

It can be shown that

$$(A \otimes B)' = A' \otimes B'; \quad (A \otimes B)^{-1} = A^{-1} \otimes B^{-1};$$
$$|A \otimes B| = |A|^p |B|^m \quad (\textit{if } A, B \textit{ are square});$$
$$(A \otimes B)(C \otimes D) = AC \otimes BD \quad (\textit{if } AC \textit{ and } BD \textit{ are defined});$$

and in particular,

$$I \otimes B = \begin{bmatrix} B & 0 & . & . & 0 \\ 0 & B & 0 & . & . \\ . & 0 & . & . & . \\ . & . & . & B & 0 \\ 0 & 0 & . & 0 & B \end{bmatrix}. \tag{7.8}$$

The S command has the form `kronecker(A,B)`.

We can then represent the right hand block of the regressor matrix as a Kronecker product of the form $I_N \otimes j_T$ and thus we can write the whole system more concisely as

$$y = [X \quad R]\begin{bmatrix} \beta \\ \alpha \end{bmatrix} + \varepsilon, \quad \text{for } R = [I_N \otimes j_T] \tag{7.9}$$

$$\text{or} \quad y = Z\delta + \varepsilon, \quad \varepsilon | Z, \delta \sim n(0, \tau I_{NT}) \tag{7.10}$$

where Z is of order $NT \times (k + N)$. The columns of R are the N additional control covariates mentioned in section 7.2. (Notice that as we moved from the single agent at one time point to the single agent at T time points to the all agent all time points versions of the model we are using progressively stronger exogeneity conditions. In (7.5) ε_{it} must be independent of x_{it}; in (7.6) it must be independent of X_i; and in (7.10) it must be independent of all covariate values for whatever time or agent, and for each case the independence is conditional on α_i or even on $\{\alpha_i\}$.)

The marginal distribution of the error vector in (7.10) is normal, homoscedastic and non-autocorrelated, while Z is strictly exogenous by assumption. It follows from this that we are dealing with the standard normal linear regression model of chapter 3. And it follows immediately from the discussion there that the likelihood corresponding to the model (7.10) is

$$\ell(\beta, \alpha, \tau; y, Z) \propto \tau^{NT/2} \exp\{-\tau(\delta - d)'Z'Z(\delta - d)/2\} \exp\{-\tau e'e/2\}, \tag{7.11}$$

where d is the least squares (ls) estimate, $d = (Z'Z)^{-1}Z'y$, and e contains the ls residuals, $e = y - Zd$.

The remaining issue is to formulate a prior distribution for $\delta = (\beta, \alpha)$ that is consistent with the beliefs about α and X that we sketched earlier. We first consider what appears to be the analytically simplest choice. This choice leads to the Bayesian analogue of a common frequentist procedure.

7.3.2 A uniform prior on the individual effects

Suppose we take the $\{\alpha_i\}$ to be independently uniformly distributed on the real line. If we also adopt default uniform priors for β and $\log \tau$ the prior is

$$p(\beta, \alpha, \tau) = p(\delta, \tau) \propto 1/\tau, \qquad (7.12)$$

and we are back to the Bayesian analysis of the simplest normal linear model with $k + N$ regression parameters and a scalar precision matrix, τI_{NT}, that was described in chapter 3, section 3.3. From previous results we know that δ is normal with mean equal to the least squares estimate $d = (Z'Z)^{-1}Z'y$ and precision equal to $\tau Z'Z$, all conditional on τ, and that marginally τ is gamma with parameters $(NT - k - N)/2$ and $e'e/2$ where $e = y - Zd$ – the residual vector – and $k + N$ is the number of regression parameters consisting of k elements of β and N individual effects. Even though we have arrived at what is essentially the normal linear model with default priors it is worth saying more about this model – usually called the **fixed effects model** – since it is so widely used in applied economics and is analytically tractable.

The structure of the least squares estimate

Consider the least squares estimate, d, which satisfies the normal equations $Z'Zd = Z'y$. If we write this system of equations in partitioned form we have

$$\begin{bmatrix} X'X & X'R \\ R'X & R'R \end{bmatrix} \begin{bmatrix} b \\ a \end{bmatrix} = \begin{bmatrix} X'y \\ R'y \end{bmatrix}. \qquad (7.13)$$

Because the matrix R has the form $[I_N \otimes j_T]$ an easy calculation, using the Kronecker product rules given above, shows that

$$R'R = TI_N \quad \text{and} \quad RR' = I_N \otimes J_T$$

where $J_T = j_T j_T'$ is a $T \times T$ matrix of ones. If we now treat the system (7.13) as a set of two simultaneous equations we can solve it for both b and a as

$$b = (X'HX)^{-1}X'Hy, \qquad (7.14)$$

$$a = \bar{y} - \bar{x}b. \qquad (7.15)$$

Here $\bar{y}$ is a column of N means of the y's for each agent and $\bar{x}$ is an $N \times k$ matrix whose j'th column contains the means of covariate j for each agent. These objects contain the agent-specific means of the y's and the x's. The matrix H, of order $NT \times NT$, is equal to

$$H = I_{NT} - (1/T)RR' = I_{NT} - (1/T)(I_N \otimes J_T)$$

and has the general form

$$\begin{bmatrix} H_T & 0 & . & . & . \\ 0 & H_T & 0 & . & . \\ . & . & . & . & . \\ . & . & . & H_T & 0 \\ 0 & . & . & 0 & H_T \end{bmatrix}$$

where $H_T = I_T - (1/T)J_T$. The matrix H_T operates on a vector of length T to measure its elements from their means. Thus, for example,

$$H_T y = \begin{bmatrix} y_1 - \bar{y} \\ y_2 - \bar{y} \\ . \\ . \\ y_T - \bar{y} \end{bmatrix}.$$

With these interpretations we see from (7.14) and (7.15) that the ls estimate of the slope coefficients is a least squares estimate based on the regression of the y's, measured from their agent-specific means, on the x's, measured from their agent-specific means. For this reason it is often called the **within (agent) estimate** of β. So b has two least squares interpretations, it is both the ls estimate in a regression of y on X and N additional dummy covariates[4] and the ls estimate in the regression of y on X when all data are measured from their agent-specific means.

The derivation of a, b that we have just given involves some slightly tedious matrix algebra. We could have avoided this by remembering the remark made as a digression in chapter 3, section 3.3, that if we measure the covariates from their means the likelihood, given τ, factorizes into a part involving only β and a part involving reparametrized intercepts of the form $\alpha^* = \alpha + \beta\bar{x}$. The matrix H transforms vectors so that they are measured from their means and we can rewrite (7.6) as

$$y_i = HX_i\beta + \alpha_i^* j_T + \varepsilon_i,$$
$$\text{where} \quad \alpha_i^* = \alpha_i + \bar{x}_i\beta$$

where $\bar{x}_i$ is the vector of means of the covariate values for agent i. Then if the X's in (7.7) are replaced by HX the new version of Z is such that $Z'Z$ is diagonal, $X'HR = 0$, and it is immediate that

$$b = (X'HX)^{-1}X'Hy,$$
$$\hat{a}^* = \bar{y},$$

---

4   Hence the name **least squares dummy variables** (lsdv) that is sometimes used for it.

and the second equation then implies $\hat{a} = \bar{y} - \bar{x}b$. Redefining the intercepts in this way is an example of the technique of parameter separation.

There is yet a third interpretation of b; it is a generalized least squares estimate for data in which the y's and x's are replaced by their first differences. To see this consider the $T - 1 \times T$ matrix D_T that operates to first difference a vector of length T. Thus

$$
D_T y = \begin{bmatrix} 1 & -1 & 0 & .. & 0 \\ 0 & 1 & -1 & .. & 0 \\ 0 & & & .. & .. \\ .. & & -1 & .. & \\ 0 & 0 & .. & 1 & -1 \end{bmatrix} \begin{bmatrix} y_T \\ y_{T-1} \\ . \\ . \\ y_1 \end{bmatrix} = \begin{bmatrix} y_T - y_{T-1} \\ y_{T-1} - y_{T-2} \\ . \\ . \\ y_2 - y_1 \end{bmatrix}.
$$

A little matrix algebra shows that D_T and H_T are related by $H_T = D_T'(D_T D_T')^{-1} D_T$ which means that we can also write b as

$$
b = (X'D'(DD')^{-1}DX)^{-1} X'D'(DD')^{-1}Dy, \tag{7.16}
$$

where $D'(DD')^{-1}D$ is a block diagonal matrix of order NT with each diagonal element equal to $D_T'(D_T D_T')^{-1} D_T$. This has the form of a generalized least squares estimate applied to the data $\{D_T y_i, D_T X_i\}$ with precision matrix proportional to $(D_T D_T')^{-1}$. So another way of thinking about our results concerning β is that they arise out of first differencing the data. Note that

$$
\begin{aligned} D_T y_i &= D_T X_i \beta + \alpha_i D_T j_T + D_T \varepsilon_i \\ &= D_T X_i \beta + D_T \varepsilon_i, \end{aligned}
$$

since the first differences of a column of ones are zero. So **differencing** is sometimes said to "eliminate" the individual effects from the model. Since the precision matrix of $D_T \varepsilon_i$ is indeed $\propto (D_T D_T')^{-1}$ we see that yet another interpretation of b is as GLS applied to first differenced data. This implies that the apparently reasonable operation of differencing the data, discussed in section 6.1.1, can in fact be justified, in Bayesian terms, by the adoption of independent uniform priors for the individual effects. Whether this is a persuasive prior is, of course, a matter of opinion and of the context of the investigation.

EXAMPLE 7.2   T = 2   *In the special but important case in which $T = 2$ the matrix D takes the form $(1\ -1)$ and $DD' = 2$ which is scalar and cancels from (7.16). So b reduces to ordinary, not generalized, least squares applied to the first differenced data.*

We can summarize our results on this uniform prior or **fixed effects model**, as it is called in the frequentist literature, in:

THEOREM 7.1 INFERENCE ABOUT β UNDER a UNIFORM PRIOR

1. The marginal posterior mean of β is the within estimator provided by least squares regression using the data which are the departures of each y and each column of X from their agent-specific means.

2. This mean is also equal to the generalized least squares estimator based on data which are the first differences of the y_i and the X_i.

3. It is also the least squares estimate in a model with covariates equal to X plus N agent-specific dummy variables as in the matrix R above.

4. The marginal posterior distribution of β is Student's t with $v = N(T-1) - K$ degrees of freedom, mean b and precision equal to

$$P(\beta) = \frac{v-2}{v} X'HX\frac{1}{s^2}, \quad \text{for } s^2 = e'e/v,$$

provided $v > 2$.

5. The $\{\alpha_i\}$ are distributed normally given τ with means $\bar{y}_i - \bar{x}_i b$ and precisions all equal to $T\tau$.

Remark *Unidentifiability* One important feature of b is that the matrix $H_T X_i$ will contain a column of zeros for every covariate that does not vary over the T periods of observation because the deviations of a constant from its mean are all zero. If this constancy is true for every agent then the β coefficients of such time-constant covariates will vanish from the model, being, in effect, absorbed into the individual effects. So we must interpret the β and b vectors as referring only to the coefficients of the covariates that are time varying for at least one agent. It follows that when we move to the β, τ marginal, the coefficients of the time-constant covariates do not appear and so their posterior distribution is uniform. Since their prior was also uniform the distribution of such coefficients is unmodified by the data and they are **unidentified** in this model. A good example of such a time-invariant covariate might be "gender." Suppose, for example, that your model for agent i is

$$y_{it} = \alpha_i + \beta_1 g_i + \beta_2 x_{it} + \varepsilon_{it}$$

where g_i is the gender of agent i, so the effect of being, say, male, is to shift your response up or down by the amount β_1. But this coefficient cannot be determined under flat priors because this model is observationally equivalent to

$$y_{it} = \alpha_i^* + \beta x_{it} + \varepsilon_{it}, \quad \text{for } \alpha_i^* = \alpha_i + \beta_1 g_i.$$

EXAMPLE 7.3   *NO REAL COVARIATES*   *An import-*
ant special case of the panel data model is where there are no covariates so the
model and (7.5) become

$$y_{it} = \alpha_i + \varepsilon_{it}, \quad \varepsilon_{it}|\alpha_i, \tau = n(0, \tau), \quad i = 1, ..., N, \; t = 1, ..., T. \quad (7.17)$$

It follows from (7.15) that the conditional posterior distribution of the $\{\alpha_i\}$ is
normal with means equal to $\{\bar{y}_i\}$ and common precision $T\tau$. As an application
suppose that α_i is permanent income for agent i and the $\{y_{it}\}$ are measured
values of income that differ from permanent or "lifetime average" income by
random error. Then this model, under a uniform prior, will estimate permanent
income by average income for each agent. This is not a particularly sensible model
to adopt – see the later discussion of shrinkage.

Time and other dummy variables

The dummy variables on which we have concentrated are identifiers of individual
agents, these are the agent-specific individual effects. Another common type of dummy
is a period identifier or time dummy. Consider for example a model with two agents
and two time periods written as

$$y_{11} = \alpha_1 + \gamma_1 + \varepsilon_{11},$$
$$y_{12} = \alpha_1 + \gamma_2 + \varepsilon_{12},$$
$$y_{21} = \alpha_2 + \gamma_1 + \varepsilon_{21},$$
$$y_{22} = \alpha_2 + \gamma_2 + \varepsilon_{22}.$$

The first subscript on y identifies the agent and the second identifies the time period,
so the model has an agent-specific, time-invariant effect α and a time-specific agent-
invariant effect γ. (We have ignored any real covariates in order to focus on the agent
and time dummies.) The covariate matrix for this system is

$$R = \begin{bmatrix} 1 & 0 & 1 & 0 \\ 1 & 0 & 0 & 1 \\ 0 & 1 & 1 & 0 \\ 0 & 1 & 0 & 1 \end{bmatrix}$$

and it will be noticed that this matrix is not of full column rank, $R'R$ is singular.
One restriction on the α's or γ's will remove this singularity and it is usual to remove
this lack of identification by setting the first time dummy equal to zero, giving the
identifiable system

$$y_{11} = \alpha_1 + \varepsilon_{11},$$
$$y_{12} = \alpha_1 + \gamma + \varepsilon_{12},$$
$$y_{21} = \alpha_2 + \varepsilon_{21},$$
$$y_{22} = \alpha_2 + \gamma + \varepsilon_{22},$$

$$(7.18)$$

with

$$R = \begin{bmatrix} 1 & 0 & 0 \\ 1 & 0 & 1 \\ 0 & 1 & 0 \\ 0 & 1 & 1 \end{bmatrix}$$

which is of full column rank.

The model could, equivalently, have been written explicitly as a linear regression model with three regressors; one a binary variable indicating agent 1, with coefficient α_1; the second a binary variable indicating agent 2, with coefficient α_2; and the third a binary variable indicating period 2, with coefficient γ.

EXAMPLE 7.4 *THE EMPLOYMENT EFFECT OF RAISING THE MINIMUM WAGE* *A well-known application of the linear panel data model with time and individual effects is a study of the effect of raising the minimum wage on employment in low wage jobs. Card and Krueger (1994) consider a panel of $N = 399$ restaurants (agents) on $T = 2$ occasions. The restaurants were located in one of two adjoining American states, New Jersey (NJ) and Pennsylvania (PA). Between the first and second periods the legal minimum wage was raised in New Jersey but not in Pennsylvania. Let $\{\Delta y_i\}$ be the change in employment at each restaurant – employment in the second period minus employment in the first period and let $\{x_i\}$ be an indicator of the restaurant being in NJ, 1 if it is, 0 if it isn't. The simplest version of the model they used is*

$$\Delta y_i = \gamma + \beta x_i + \varepsilon_i \qquad (7.19)$$

where the errors are homoscedastic, uncorrelated and of mean zero. The key coefficient is β which although it measures only the effect of the restaurant being located in NJ,[5] is interpreted as the effect of introduction of the raised minimum wage on the change in employment. Under normality and uniform priors the posterior mode of β is the least squares estimate $b = \sum(x_i - \bar{x})\Delta y_i / \sum(x_i - \bar{x})^2$ which simplifies, because x is binary, to

$$b = \overline{\Delta y}_{NJ} - \overline{\Delta y}_{PA}$$

---

5   The authors also use a different measure of the size of the minimum wage change as an alternative to the New Jersey dummy.

> *which is the average change in employment at New Jersey restaurants minus the average change in employment at Pennsylvania restaurants. Since the estimator is a difference of average differences (in employment) it is called a difference in differences, "diffs in diffs," procedure.*

Since the interest of the authors was in the effect of the change in minimum wages on the change in employment it is natural to write the model in the form (7.19), which is a pure cross-sectional model. But because they have panel data the model could have been written in terms of the levels of employment, as, say,

$$y_{it} = \alpha_i + \gamma t + \lambda x_i + \beta t x_i + v_i, \quad t = 1, 2; \quad i = 1, 2, ..., 399, \qquad (7.20)$$

where $\{\alpha_i\}$ are restaurant-specific effects, t is a period dummy variable taking the value one in the second period and zero in the first, just as in (7.18); and the final regression term, $t x_i$, is an *interaction* between the time effect and the effect of being in NJ. Then a uniform prior on the restaurant-specific effects would, as we have just seen, have led to inference about the remaining parameters being based on the first differenced data, namely

$$y_{i2} - y_{i1} = \Delta y_i = \gamma + \beta x_i + v_{i2} - v_{i2}$$

which is (7.19).

Notice that λ has vanished from the first differenced version of the model and is likelihood unidentified. This remark helps to explain why the model the authors actually fitted was not (7.19) but rather

$$\Delta y_i = \gamma + \beta x_i + \delta Z_i + \varepsilon_i \qquad (7.21)$$

where the vector Z_i contains time-invariant measured characteristics of restaurant i. Suppose that the levels model, (7.20), contained an additional term in which the effects of these time-invariant restaurant characteristics were allowed to depend on time as in

$$y_{it} = \alpha_i + \gamma t + \lambda x_i + \beta t x_i + \delta t Z_i + v_i, \quad t = 1, 2; \quad i = 1, 2, ..., 399.$$

Then first differencing this model leads to (7.21). Thus when they include time-invariant covariates in a model for the change in employment they are allowing for the presence in the levels model of time-invariant covariates with a time-dependent effect. (It turns out there is no evidence in their data that δ is non-zero.)

This example has illustrated some of the many uses of dummy covariates in a panel data model; they may be agent-, time-, or location-specific indicators and they may interact with real variables to create subtly time-varying regression effects.

7.3.3   *Exact sampling*

Exact sampling of the posterior for readers who wish to do it themselves[6] is entirely straightforward with this normal linear model and vague prior and just follows the method described in chapter 3. It is:

ALGORITHM 7.1

1. Compute $d = (b, a)$, the least squares estimate, $d = (Z'Z)^{-1}Z'y$, and $e'e$ for $e = y - Zd$;
2. Sample τ from its marginal gamma$(v/2, e'e/2)$ distribution;
3. Using the τ values, sample β from its multivariate normal$(b, \tau\sum_{i=1}^{N} X_i' H X_i)$ distribution;
4. Using the β, τ values sample the $\{\alpha_i\}$ from their normal$(a_i, T\tau)$ distributions.

This algorithm corresponds to the representation of the joint posterior distribution as

$$p(\beta, \alpha, \tau | data) = p(\alpha | \beta, \tau, data) p(\beta | \tau, data) p(\tau | data).$$

7.3.4   *A hierarchical prior*

A uniform prior on the individual effects is a strong assertion. In many applied economic contexts one would expect these effects to be at least broadly similar. This suggests that we consider a prior on the $\{\alpha_i\}$ that asserts that they are probably similar. One way of expressing this view is by a hierarchical prior.

EXAMPLE 7.5   *NO REAL COVARIATES AGAIN*

The simplest case of a linear panel data model is that in which there are no (real) covariates and interest centers on the intercepts. For example, as before, suppose that each agent supplies several years of income data and that each reported income can be thought of as an imperfect measure of that agent's permanent or lifetime average income. Then if the income data are thought of as the y_{it}, $t = 1, 2, ..., T$ and if we interpret α_i as permanent income for that agent then we have a set-up that fits the panel linear model without covariates, (7.17). In this application it might well be reasonable to think of the values of permanent income for different agents as broadly similar, or exchangeable. This suggests that we look at proper, hierarchical priors for these coefficients. By doing so we shall provide a generalization of the model of the last section.

---

6   A BUGS program to do the sampling under (nearly) uniform or normal or virtually any prior is given in section 7.3.5.

The uniform prior for the $\{\alpha_i\}$ that leads to the within-estimate of β can be thought of as a limiting case of a proper prior whose precision goes to zero. So a generalization of the previous model would be to assign these coefficients a prior in which you regard them as independent realizations of a normal variate with mean, say, α (without a subscript) and precision, say, ϕ. In turn, you could assign α a prior, $p(\alpha|\phi)$, and assign ϕ some prior, say, $p(\phi)$. Thus the new prior would be

$$p(\beta, \tau, \{\alpha_i\}, \bar{\alpha}, \phi) = p(\beta, \tau)p(\{\alpha_i\}\bar{\alpha}, \phi)p(\alpha)p(\phi) \tag{7.22}$$

$$\propto \frac{1}{\tau}\phi^{N/2}\exp\{-(\phi/2)\Sigma_{i=1}^{N}(\alpha_i - \bar{\alpha})^2\}p(\alpha)p(\phi).$$

To explore this model we could write down and then simplify the joint posterior density of β, $\{\alpha_i\}$, τ, α, and ϕ found by multiplying the likelihood for (7.17), which is

$$\ell(\beta, \tau, \{\alpha_i\}; \{X_i, y_i\}) \propto \tau^{NT/2}\exp\{-(\tau/2)(\Sigma_{i=1}^{N}(y_i - X_i\beta - \alpha_i j_T)'(y_i - X_i\beta - \alpha_i j_T)\}$$

by (7.22).

It is, however, simpler and perhaps more insightful first to look at the model in linear equation form by writing

$$y_i = X_i\beta + \alpha_i j + \varepsilon_i, \tag{7.23}$$
$$\alpha_i = \alpha + \eta_i$$

where $\{\varepsilon_i, \eta_i\}$ are independently normal with precisions τ and ϕ respectively given X_i, β, τ, α. Substituting the second of these equations into the first gives

$$y_i = X_i\beta + \alpha j + (\varepsilon_i + \eta_i j) \tag{7.24}$$

where the composite error term is mean zero normal, given X_i, β, τ, ϕ, α, with covariance matrix and precision given by

$$V(\varepsilon_i + \eta_i j_T) = E(\varepsilon\varepsilon') + E(\eta^2)j_T j_T' = (1/\tau)I_T + (1/\phi)J_T, \tag{7.25}$$

$$P(\varepsilon_i + \eta_i j_T) = \tau\left[I_T - \frac{1}{T + \phi/\tau}J_T\right] \tag{7.26}$$

where J_T is a $T \times T$ matrix of ones. (To verify that P inverts V just multiply them together to get I_T.)

We can assemble the equations (7.24) for all N agents as

$$y = \begin{bmatrix} y_1 \\ y_2 \\ . \\ . \\ . \\ y_N \end{bmatrix} = \begin{bmatrix} X_1 & j_T \\ X_2 & j_T \\ . & . \\ . & . \\ . & . \\ X_N & j_T \end{bmatrix}\begin{bmatrix} \beta \\ \alpha \end{bmatrix} + \begin{bmatrix} \varepsilon_1 + j_T\eta_1 \\ \varepsilon_2 + j_T\eta_2 \\ . \\ . \\ . \\ \varepsilon_N + j_T\eta_N \end{bmatrix} = Z\delta + v. \tag{7.27}$$

Inspection of the model defined by (7.27) shows that, for given τ, ϕ, it is a normal linear model but with a non-scalar covariance matrix. The errors are homoscedastic, with common variance equal to $1/\tau + 1/\phi$, but errors for the same agent are correlated. In fact they are equi-correlated in that the covariance of ε_{is} with ε_{it} is $1/\phi$ for all $s \neq t$. It follows from this that, conditional on τ, ϕ, we can use the results of chapter 3 on the linear model with non-scalar covariance matrix to deduce that $\delta(= \alpha, \beta)$ is normally distributed with mean d given by the generalized least squares estimate – $\delta | \tau, \phi,$ data $\sim n(d, Z'PZ)$

$$d = (Z'PZ)^{-1}Z'Py. \qquad (7.28)$$

The marginal distribution of δ in the **hierarchical normal linear model** depends on the prior distribution of τ, ϕ and is generally hard to calculate analytically and the whole model is best handled by simulation which is, with one caveat, straightforward enough.

7.3.5 BUGS program

The following BUGS program shows how straightforward it is to write down this model. This model is written for a scalar covariate, the extension to k covariates just involves adding a third subscript. You would normally provide two or more sets of priors and a corresponding number of sets of initial values and run several chains at once, the comparison of which provides a check on the convergence of the MCMC algorithm.

```
model{
for(i in 1:N){for(t in 1:T){
y[i,t]~dnorm(mu[i,t],tau)
mu[i,t]<-beta*x[i,t] + alpha[i]}
alpha[i]~dnorm(alphabar,phi)}
alphabar~dnorm(0,0.0001) # alphabar is α in the text
beta~dnorm(0,0.0001)
tau~dgamma(0.01,0.01)
phi~dgamma(0.01,0.01)
}
```

The fixed effects structure is a special case of this model in which the $\{\alpha_i\}$ are assigned uniform priors and to get this you would delete lines 6 and 9, and change the fifth line to something like

```
for(i in 1:N){alpha[i]~dnorm(0,0.0001)}.
```

The caveat mentioned above is that a uniform prior for the precision of the individual effects leads to an improper posterior distribution for all parameters. Such a prior is therefore unacceptable in Bayesian inference. Moreover, in practice, very diffuse priors on ϕ can lead to slow convergence of MCMC algorithms.

The frequentist analogue of this hierarchical model is known in the traditional literature as "*random effects*."[7]

7.3.6　Shrinkage

A comparison of the fixed and random effects procedures that is illuminating is to look at the case in which there no covariates. This might correspond to the example in which the α_i were the permanent incomes of the N agents. In this case the model is

$$y_{it} = \alpha_i + \varepsilon_{it}, \quad \varepsilon_{it}|\{\alpha_i\}, \tau \sim iid\ n(0, \tau) \tag{7.29}$$

$$\begin{aligned} \text{with} \quad & p(\alpha_i|\tau) \propto 1, \\ \text{or} \quad & p(\alpha_i|\alpha, \phi, \tau) \sim iid\ n(\alpha, \phi) \quad \text{for} \quad i = 1, 2, ..., N. \end{aligned} \tag{7.30}$$

The first prior corresponds to the fixed and the second to the random effects priors. Notice that with no covariates present there is no endogeneity problem here. Under the uniform prior it is not difficult to see that $\{\alpha_i\}$ will have posterior conditional (on τ) normal distributions with means[8]

$$E(\alpha_i|\text{data}) = \bar{y}_i. \tag{7.31}$$

So, roughly speaking, under the fixed effects or uniform prior model, you estimate each person's permanent income by his average income. Under the normal (random effects) prior a slightly more complicated calculation shows that the $\{\alpha_i\}$ will have posterior normal distributions (conditional on τ, ϕ) that are of the form[9]

$$E(\alpha_i|\tau, \phi, \text{data}) = \frac{\phi\dfrac{N-1}{N}\bar{y} + \tau T \bar{y}_i}{\phi\dfrac{N-1}{N} + \tau T}. \tag{7.32}$$

This shows that the estimates (conditional posterior means) of each person's permanent income are a weighted average of his mean recorded income and the average recorded income of the entire sample.[10] The estimate is "shrunk" towards the average. In many circumstances this is a highly plausible thing to do, for surely the set of agent mean incomes will be more variable than the set of permanent incomes and it will seem wise to pull in some of the more extreme averages. Note the agreeable

---

7　There are many "random effects" non-linear models in the econometrics literature and we shall mention some of them later in this chapter.

8　As a special case of (7.15).

9　This is a special case of (7.28) in which there are no covariates and no β coefficients.

10　This will also be approximately true unconditionally on τ, ϕ.

feature that as more data becomes available for each agent, $T \to \infty$, then (7.32) tends towards the $\bar{y}_i$ (7.31) and shrinkage diminishes. If ϕ is dogmatically set equal to zero in the prior then we revert to the fixed effects model and get

$$E(\alpha_i | \tau, \phi = 0, \text{data}) = \bar{y}_i. \tag{7.33}$$

Thus there is no shrinkage with the fixed effects formulation.[11]

7.3.7 A richer prior for the individual effects

The iid normal prior of the last model, though favored by statisticians, appears to economists to neglect the presumed correlation of the individual effects and the covariate sequence. Economists have responded by choosing a prior for α_i in which it is normal with precision ϕ and mean that is a linear combination of all the covariates for agent i. In the case where $k = 1$ and there is a single scalar covariate we would have

$$\alpha_i = \lambda' x_i + \eta_i, \quad \eta_i | x_i, \lambda, \phi, \tau \sim n(0, \phi),$$

where $\lambda' = (\lambda_1, ..., \lambda_T)$. If we substitute this equation into (7.23) we have

$$\begin{aligned} y_i &= \beta x_i + j_T \lambda' x_i + (\varepsilon_i + j_T \eta_i), \\ &= [\beta I_T + j_T \lambda'] x_i + (\varepsilon_i + j_T \eta_i), \\ &= \Pi x_i + (\varepsilon_i + j_T \eta_i). \end{aligned}$$

In this model the value of y for agent i at time t depends not only on x at t but on x at all values, past, current and future. This is because of our presumption that the individual effect is correlated with the entire x sequence. Notice that the coefficients on the covariates, which we have denoted by the $T \times T$ matrix Π, take a special form which, in the case $T = 2$, is

$$\Pi = \begin{bmatrix} \beta & 0 \\ 0 & \beta \end{bmatrix} + \begin{bmatrix} \lambda_1 & \lambda_2 \\ \lambda_1 & \lambda_2 \end{bmatrix}.$$

This model for the prior dependence of the $\{\alpha_i\}$ on the x sequence is usually called the pi matrix model. It was developed by Chamberlain in a frequentist context following earlier work by Mundlak.

To implement this model under a (possibly unreasonable) uniform prior for the $\{\lambda_i\}$ and with a balanced panel takes only a minor change in the BUGS program given earlier.

---

11 Shrinking estimates of a collection of similar parameters is generally desirable even from a frequentist point of view. Estimates that do not shrink typically have inadmissible sampling distributions.

```
model{
for(i in 1:N){for(t in 1:T){
Y[i,t]~dnorm(mu[i,t],tau)
mu[i,t]<-beta*X[i,t] + alpha[i]}
alpha[i]~dnorm(v[i],phi)
v[i] <- lambda[1]*X[i,1]+lambda[2]*X[i,2] + ...+lambda[T]*X[i,T]}
for(t in 1:T){lambda[t]~dnorm(0,0.0001)}
beta~dnorm(0,0.0001)
tau~dgamma(0.01,0.01)
phi~dgamma(0.01,0.01)
}
```

This program specifies that α has prior mean equal to a linear combination of the covariate values with coefficients that are effectively uniform. As with the earlier version of this program it is probably wise to consider more accurate (reasonable) priors for the precision parameters τ and ϕ than these default gamma densities. Note that if the panel is unbalanced – varying values of T from agent to agent – complications arise. These can be handled by treating unobserved covariate values as missing data but the calculations will not be as simple as in the balanced case. An alternative is to write the prior as

$$\alpha_i = \lambda'_{T_i} x_i + \eta_i, \quad \eta_i | x_i, \lambda_{T_i}, \phi_{T_i}, \tau_{T_i} \sim n(0, \phi_{T_i})$$

with separate priors for ϕ, τ corresponding to different values of T.

We now turn to look at some non-linear panel data models. Some of the material in the following sections dealing with reparametrization in non-linear models is rather more difficult than the rest of the book.

7.4   PANEL COUNTS

Data in which we observe the number of events that occur in several (usually successive) time intervals for each of a number of agents is panel count data. Standard examples are the number of patents filed each year by a collection of firms, or the number of strikes occurring in each year in each of several industries. In this chapter we shall extend the count data model of chapter 5 to its panel counterpart. An analysis parallel to that of the linear model is relatively simple.

Suppose our theory indicates that the count for agent i at time t should have the form $y_{it} = e^{x_{it}\beta}$ where we have chosen a functional form that recognizes the non-negativity of counts. This would be the analogue of (6.1). We now introduce the inevitable error, ε_{it}, also multiplicatively, to get

$$y_{it} = \exp\{x_{it}\beta + \varepsilon_{it}\}$$

and, just as in the linear case, we attempt to exploit the panel nature of our data by writing the error as a sum of an individual effect and a second term which we shall assume to be distributed mean independently of the covariate values.[12] Thus,

$$y_{it} = \exp\{x_{it}\beta + \alpha_i + \varepsilon_{it}\}.$$

Choice of an appropriate (prior) distribution for the $\{\varepsilon_{it}\}$ must recognize that y will take on only non-negative integer values. In the light of this restriction the most natural model would be to have $y_{it}|x_{it}, \beta, \alpha_i$ distributed as a poisson variate with mean equal to

$$E(Y_{it}|x_{it}, \beta, \alpha_i) = \exp\{x_{it}\beta + \alpha_i\}. \qquad (7.34)$$

This defines the distribution of $\varepsilon_{it}|x_{it}, \beta, \alpha_i$ implicitly. In particular, the expected value of $e^{\varepsilon_{it}}$ given x_{it}, β, α_i is equal to

$$E(e^{\varepsilon_{it}}|x_{it}, \beta, \alpha_i) = E\left(\frac{Y_{it}}{\exp\{x_{it}\beta + \alpha_i\}}\bigg| x_{it}, \beta, \alpha_i\right) = 1$$

so the "error term" defined to be $e^{\varepsilon_{it}}$ is mean independent of x_{it} given α_i which is analogous to the linear model where we only require the error to be mean independent of the covariates.[13] Note that (7.34) is a non-linear regression model.

If we write λ_{it} for $\exp\{x_{it}\beta + \alpha_i\}$, for simplicity of notation, then the likelihood for an individual agent and period is

$$\ell_{it}(\alpha_i, \beta; y_{it}) \propto \lambda_{it}^{y_{it}} e^{-\lambda_{it}}$$

which is the poisson(λ_{it}) probability mass function after neglecting the irrelevant constant y_{it}! With N agents each observed on T occasions (so the panel is balanced) and observations independent conditional on the $\{x_{it}, \alpha_i\}$ and β the whole likelihood is the product of such terms over all i and t.

Inference requires prior distributions for β and $\{\alpha_i\}$ and there is no restriction on your choice except, of course, that your readers must find them not unconvincing. We consider two choices that are analogous to the fixed and random effects versions of the panel linear model. The first is a uniform prior on the $\{\alpha_i\}$ (and β).

7.4.1 A uniform prior on the individual effects

A natural starting point for inference in this model is to consider the $\{\alpha_i\}$ as independently uniformly distributed independent of β which is also uniform. (This implies

---

12   In chapter 5 we used the notation $v_i = e^{\alpha_i}$.
13   The error here is not, however, independent of the covariate given the individual effect, it is only mean independent.

improper priors for $v_i = e^{\alpha_i}$ that are proportional to $1/v_i$.) For this choice the contribution of agent i to the posterior density of β is

$$p_i(\beta|y_i, x_i) \propto \int_{-\infty}^{\infty} \prod_{t=1}^{T} e^{\alpha_i y_{it} + \beta x_{it} y_{it}} \exp\{-e^{\alpha_i + \beta x_{it}}\} \, d\alpha_i$$

$$= e^{\beta \Sigma_t x_{it} y_{it}} \int_{-\infty}^{\infty} e^{\alpha_i s_i} \exp\{-e^{\alpha_i} \Sigma_t e^{\beta x_{it}}\} \, d\alpha_i, \quad \text{for } s = \Sigma_t y_{it}.$$

$$= e^{\beta \Sigma_t x_{it} y_{it}} \int_0^{\infty} v_i^{s_i-1} \exp\{-v_i \Sigma_t e^{\beta x_{it}}\} \, dv_i$$

$$\propto \frac{e^{\beta \Sigma_t x_{it} y_{it}}}{(\Sigma_t e^{\beta x_{it}})^{s_i}}. \tag{7.35}$$

In the third line we changed the variable from α_i to $v_i = e^{\alpha_i}$ with jacobian $1/v_i$. The symbol $s_i = \Sigma_t y_{it}$ is the total number of events experienced by agent i. The move from the third to the fourth line uses the gamma integral formula from the appendix to chapter 1. The expression (7.35) generalizes the result for $N = 1$ (5.23), given in chapter 5.

The kernel (7.35) is that of a multinomial likelihood, as in chapter 1, whose interpretation is as follows. Imagine T cells and $s_i = \Sigma_t y_{it}$ balls to be placed in them. Each ball is placed in cell t with probability equal to

$$p_t = \frac{e^{\beta x_{it}}}{\Sigma_t e^{\beta x_{it}}}, \quad t = 1, 2, \ldots, T,$$

and the placing of the balls is done independently. Then (7.35) represents the probability distribution of the placement of the balls. It is as if for any firm there is a given number of patents, and inferences about β are made by inspecting how many of these patents are filed in periods in which the x's are large or small. Essentially, inferences about β are being made solely from the "within" agent data, just as in the fixed effects version of the linear model.[14] Repeating the integration for each agent we find the posterior density of β to have the form

$$p(\beta|\text{data}) \propto \prod_{i=1}^{N} \frac{e^{\beta \Sigma_t x_{it} y_{it}}}{(\Sigma_t e^{\beta x_{it}})^{s_i}}. \tag{7.36}$$

This is the uniform prior (or fixed effects) posterior density for poisson counts. If a non-uniform prior for β is required then (7.36) would just be multiplied by $p(\beta)$.

---

14   The expression (7.35) can also be reached by using as your likelihood not the joint distribution of the data but only its distribution conditional on the total numbers of events occurring for each agent. The parameters $\{\alpha_i\}$ do not appear in this conditional likelihood which is essentially (7.35). This conditional likelihood argument is the standard way to reach (7.35) in the frequentist literature, which then recommends maximizing (7.36) with respect to β.

Notice that if $T = 1$ for each agent, so you don't have panel data, then $s_i = y_{it}$ and $\sum_t e^{\beta x_{it}} = e^{\beta x_{it}}$ and each term in (7.36) is equal to 1. This means that without panel data the marginal posterior density of β will be equal to the prior density and this parameter is not likelihood identified so that panel data are essential for this approach. If β is scalar this density can be plotted, but the best and most general procedure for studying your results is to sample from the joint posterior density of β, $\{\alpha_i\}$. We shall give a little BUGS program to do this after giving a "random effects" version of the model.

7.4.2 A gamma prior for the individual effects

A proper, hierarchical, prior for the individual effects is most naturally constructed by considering the factors $v_i = e^{\alpha_i}$ as independent gamma variates. This is because the gamma is a natural conjugate prior for this model. So let us suppose that

$$p(v_i | \delta, \gamma) = \frac{v_i^{\delta-1} e^{-\gamma v_i}}{\Gamma(\delta)\gamma^{-\delta}} \tag{7.37}$$

where δ, γ are (positive) hyperparameters. If we also assume that the v_i are distributed independently, given δ, γ, and independent of β, then a little analytical progress can be made. In particular the contribution of agent i to the marginal posterior density of β, δ, γ is

$$p_i(\beta, \delta, \gamma | \text{data}) \propto \int_0^\infty (\prod_t v_i^{y_{it}}) e^{\beta \sum_t x_{it} \, y_{it}} \exp\{-v_i \sum_t e^{\beta x_{it}}\} v_i^{\delta-1} e^{-\gamma v_i} dv_i / [\Gamma(\delta)\gamma^{-\delta}],$$

$$= e^{\beta \sum_t x_{it} y_{it}} \int_0^\infty v_i^{s_i+\delta-1} \exp\{-v_i[\sum_t e^{\beta x_{it}} + \gamma]\} dv_i / [\Gamma(\delta)\gamma^{-\delta}],$$

$$= e^{\beta \sum_t x_{it} y_{it}} \frac{\Gamma(s_i + \delta)}{\Gamma(\delta)} \left(\frac{\gamma}{\gamma + \sum_t e^{\beta x_{it}}}\right)^\delta \frac{1}{(\gamma + \sum_t e^{\beta x_{it}})^{s_i}}$$

where $s_i = \sum_t y_{it}$. The product of N such terms multiplied by $p(\beta, \delta, \gamma)$, the prior density of β, δ, γ, will be the marginal posterior density of β, δ, γ. In the second line we have used the gamma integral formula from chapter 1.

From the results given in the appendix to chapter 1 the expected value of v_i in (7.37) is δ/γ. If $x\beta$ contains an intercept parameter then it is sensible to constrain v_i to have mean one and this leads to the restriction $\delta = \gamma$.

Little further insight is gained by additional mathematics so we shall next give a BUGS program to implement both the fixed and random effects versions of this model.

7.4.3 Calculation in the panel count model

```
model{
for(i in 1:n){
for (j in 1:1){
y[i,j] ~ dpois(lam[i,j])
lam[i,j] <- v[i]*exp(a + b*x[i,j])
}
v[i] ~ dgamma(d,d)
}
d ~ dgamma(.01,.01)
a ~ dnorm(0,0.001)
b ~ dnorm(0,0.001)
}
```

The panel length is here denoted by 1 and its width by n. The fourth line states that each value of Y is poisson with its own parameter λ; the fifth line states that λ is equal to an individual effect multiplying an exponential regression function. The remaining lines specify independent nearly uniform priors for the intercept and slope and a hierarchical prior for the $\{v_i\}$ whose mean is constrained to be one. So this is the random effects prior. It asserts that the v_i are independent conditional on δ but dependent unconditionally. So the $\{v_i\}$ are held to be "similar" in this formulation. For the fixed effects version delete the line beginning d ~ and then replace the prior for v_i by something like

```
v[i] ~ dgamma(0.001,0.001).
```

As with every BUGS calculation, multiple runs from diverse starting points should be used and convergence statistics checked. In non-linear models such as this it is particularly important to consider, and even report, the results of varying the model and, in particular, choosing different priors.

It would be possible to use the pi matrix approach of section 7.3.7 in this non-linear context.

7.5   PANEL DURATION DATA

In chapter 5 we examined exponential and weibull models for the duration of an event. Here we shall draw on that material and extend the analysis to the panel context in which we have repeated durations for several agents. The weibull extension is interesting because in order to carry out a fixed effect default prior analysis we have to draw upon the idea of parameter separation that we described in chapter 1. The hazard function, representing the conditional probability of exit shortly after time t given survival to that date, is $\alpha t^{\alpha-1} e^{x\beta} dt$. In this chapter, because we have been using α to denote the fixed or random effect we shall write the hazard for the weibull model as $\theta t^{\theta-1} e^{\alpha+x\beta} \, dt$ so now the so-called shape parameter is denoted by θ and the symbol α denotes an intercept that enters additively into the log hazard. As in the rest of this chapter we let α be an agent-specific intercept or individual effect.[15] Thus the hazard and density function for agent i in his j'th spell at time t are

$$h_{ij}(t) = \theta t^{\theta-1} e^{\alpha_i + x_{ij}\beta} \tag{7.38}$$

$$p_{ij}(t \mid \alpha_i, \beta, \theta, x_{it}) = \theta t^{\theta-1} e^{\alpha_i + x_{ij}\beta} \exp\{-t^\theta e^{\alpha_i + x_{ij}\beta}\}, \tag{7.39}$$

where $t > 0$, $\alpha > 0$. In this formulation the agents are allowed to have hazard functions that are shifted up and down relative to each other by the factor e^{α_i}. It is important to notice that the covariates x are allowed to differ from spell to spell (duration to duration) and between agents but within any spell they are time invariant. Thus if the data refer to spells of unemployment then agent, say, 3, begins his second spell with $x = x_{32}$ and ends it with x at that level – it is unchanging within a spell. This may, of course, be restrictive. Another debatable feature of the model is that the effect of a covariate on the hazard is restricted to be the same at all time points within a spell. Under independence of durations across spells and agents the likelihood function will be the product of terms like (7.39).[16]

It remains to formulate prior beliefs and to sample the resulting posterior distribution. For a "fixed effect" analysis we would consider uniform priors, but on what? If you take the logarithm of (7.39), differentiate twice with respect to α, β and θ, and then take expectations with respect to T, you find that the information matrix that results is not block diagonal as between α and β, θ. This suggests that we might try to find a reparametrization such that the new individual effect is information orthogonal to the remaining parameters, for each agent. This can be done and, if we work in terms of $v_i = \exp\{\alpha_i\}$ we find that the new individual effect v_i^* defined by

$$v_i = \exp\{\psi(2) + \theta v_i^*\} \tag{7.40}$$

is information orthogonal to θ, β.[17] (Here $\psi(2) = 0.4228$.)

This suggests that we write the likelihood for the T spells provided by agent i in terms of the parametrization β, θ, v^* and assign these parameters *independent* priors. This is straightforward in BUGS. It would be plausible to assign θ a prior that reflects the salience of the exponential case, $\theta = 1$.

---

15 There is no reason why one cannot have agent-specific slopes too, of course, but we shall stay with the simpler set-up here.

16 Independence across time is often unappealing in duration data because of the way in which data are collected. Suppose, for example, you can observe an agent for only two years. Then since the second spell cannot start before the first is ended the lengths of two successive spells will be necessarily connected. Subtle issues need confronting to find a convincing likelihood for such data.

17 Unfortunately this orthogonality no longer holds if some durations are subject to censoring, as is common with duration data.

> **Digression**   *There is a formal connection to frequentist methods here in that if you assign a uniform prior to v^*, form the posterior and then integrate out v^* to find the marginal posterior density of β, θ the result (apart from the β, θ prior) is the likelihood that you would have formed if you only had access to the first differences of the log durations. So differencing once again eliminates the individual effect just as in the linear model, and once again it is equivalent to integration with respect to a uniform prior. The difference from the linear model is that here the uniform prior is placed on the transformed individual effect.*

We have focused here on the use of independent vague priors on orthogonal parameters. Alternatives include, of course, proper, possibly hierarchical priors and there is no practical reason why such priors can't let means of individual effects depend on covariate sequences, as in the pi matrix approach. Sensitivity of important inferences to alternative priors should be studied.

7.6   PANEL BINARY DATA

A common situation is that in which we observe for each agent a sequence of indicators of the occurrence of some event. This is count data except that at most one event can occur in each time interval. From another perspective this would be the panel extension of the binary choice models considered in chapter 5.

Let the data for agent i at time t be $y_{it} \in (0, 1)$ and x_{it} and let the probability that $y_{it} = 1$ be given by the probit form

$$P(Y_{it} = 1 \mid x_{it}, \alpha_i, \beta) = \Phi(\alpha_i + x_{it}\beta).$$

Other forms, such as the logit, that constrain this probability to lie between zero and one could be used without any computational problem. As in the discussion of the probit model in chapter 5 we could derive this expression from an underlying latent normal linear model of the form

$$y_{it}^* = \alpha_i + x_{it}\beta + \varepsilon_i$$

where the $\{\varepsilon_{it}\}$ are independent standard normal variates and we, in fact, only observe the sign of y^*. Assuming that observations are independent conditional on the $\{x_{it}, \alpha_i, \beta\}$ the likelihood contribution of agent i is

$$\ell_i(\alpha_i, \beta) \propto \prod_t \Phi(\alpha_i + x_{it}\beta)^{y_{it}}[1 - \Phi(\alpha_i + x_{it}\beta)]^{1-y_{it}} \tag{7.41}$$

and with the further assumption of independence across agents the whole sample likelihood would be the product of N such terms.

7.6.1   *Parameters of interest*

In our earlier discussion of probit and similar models we pointed out that the parameters of interest to an economist are not usually the slope coefficients $\{\beta_j\}$ but rather the marginal effects of changes in the covariates on the choice probability. So that in a non-panel context, without individual effects, and with $P(Y = 1|x, \alpha, \beta) = \Phi(\alpha + x\beta)$ one might want to know about

$$\frac{\partial P}{\partial x_j} = \beta_j \phi(\alpha + x\beta)$$

for example. The posterior distribution of this quantity at any given x vector is readily found from simulation output by averaging it over the nrep realizations from the joint posterior density of α, β. Similarly, if you wish to predict whether an agent with a specific covariate, say x^*, will experience an event then the relevant prediction is

$$E(\Phi(\alpha + x^*\beta)|\text{data})$$

and this again can be computed by averaging over your simulation output. Matters are a good deal more subtle when the model includes an agent-specific, individual effect. The reason for this is that if you wish to predict P for some other agent at some other time you need to take a view on what his α is likely to be.

7.6.2   *Choices of prior*

The remaining tasks are to choose the prior and compute marginal posterior densities of quantities of interest. This is a more important and more subtle issue than in linear models because posterior distributions here, and in other non-linear models, can be quite sensitive to the choices you make. This means that you have a more complex reporting task since you will need to display a range of inferences corresponding to alternative defensible choices of prior.

In previous sections we considered primarily (a) diffuse priors for individual effects and (b) proper priors dependent on hyperparameters. If we try to apply this program we can run into difficulties with the uniform prior. To see why this happens recall that a diffuse prior means that the likelihood and the posterior density coincide and, in particular, the posterior mode will coincide with the maximum likelihood estimate. But there is a well-known difficulty with maximum likelihood (ml) estimates in models such as the one we are considering that have many agent-specific parameters – in fact at least as many parameters as agents. This is called the incidental parameter problem.[18] By theoretical or numerical examination of the behavior of ml estimates it can be shown that these estimates tend to be displaced from the

---

18   This discussion applies to most non-linear panel data regression models, including the duration modeling of the last section.

values that they are trying to estimate when T is small. So under a flat prior you can obtain posterior densities that are extremely misleading. This occurs especially when T, the length of the panel, is small relative to N, the number both of agents and of individual effects. The reason for this is that in this context you have both many parameters and data, consisting only of the signs of the latent variables, that in some sense are not very informative. The uniformity of the prior seems to have a strong impact on the location of the posterior.

The reader can observe this phenomenon for himself by running the first of the two BUGS programs given below.

Diffuse prior program

```
model{
for(i in 1:n){
for(j in 1:1){
y[i,j]~dbin(p[i,j],1)
p[i,j] <- phi(a[i]+ b*x[i,j])}
a[i] ~dnorm(0, 0.001)}
b ~dnorm(0,0.001)}
```

Hierarchical prior program

```
model{
for(i in 1:n){
for(j in 1:1){
y[i,j]~dbin(p[i,j],1)
p[i,j] <- phi(a[i]+ b*x[i,j])}
a[i] ~dnorm(0,tau)}
tau ~dgamma(0.25,0.25)
b ~dnorm(0,0.001)}
```

The models[19] are identical except for the choice of prior for the $\{\alpha_i\}$. In each, the fourth line states that y is binary with choice probability p, and the fifth line states that p is equal to $\Phi(\alpha_i + x_{it}\beta)$. In both models the (scalar) slope coefficient is assigned a low precision (variance = 1,000) or rather diffuse normal distribution. The first model has the $\{\alpha_i\}$ independently normal with a large variance, and this corresponds roughly to a diffuse prior and to what seems somewhat analogous to the frequentists' fixed effect model. The second has a hierarchical, or random effects, prior for the $\{\alpha_i\}$ with the second level precision parameter, τ, having a gamma prior with unit mean and variance equal to 4. So this is a fairly informative prior. We can then use these two programs with real or simulated data to see what they produce, and in partic-ular to study the sensitivity of inference, particularly about β, to changes in the prior.

An easy extension of the model is to specify that the prior mean of α_i depends on the sequence of x values for agent i; this is the pi matrix approach. But this exten-sion is left to the reader.

---

19 We have to use $j = 1 : l$ instead of $t = 1 : T$ because the symbol t is protected in S.

EXAMPLE 7.6   *For a small example consider panel data with N = 10 agents observed on T = 20 occasions and one covariate whose coefficient is unity. The data were generated from an underlying normal linear model with errors having mean zero and precision one. The $\{\alpha_i\}$ were themselves normal with mean zero and precision equal to one. The y data obtained by just recording the sign of the dependent variable in the latent model had 88 zeros and 112 ones.*

The results of running the first program are interesting. We find that the marginal posterior densities of the $\{\alpha_i\}$ are centered close to the values of these 10 parameters used in simulating the model. But the marginal posterior density of β is typically located some distance away from the value of one that we used to provide the data. The same is true if we use the logit version of the model in which the fifth line of the program is replaced by

```
logit(p[i,j]) <- a[i] + b*x[i,j]
```

This poor behavior of the posterior distribution of β under a diffuse prior is a manifestation of the incidental parameter problem. Even though we have $10 \times 20 = 200$ observations these are not enough to dominate the prior.

Again, it seems as though default priors on the original parametrization of the model may be misleading and a possible solution is to try to orthogonalize the parametrization.

7.6.3   *Orthogonal reparametrizations*

Clearly the choice of prior for these models needs deeper thought. One line of attack is to attempt to separate the individual effects from the (β) parameters of interest in the way briefly described in chapter 1 and which we proposed applying to panel duration data. This is an attempt to reduce the dependence of inference about β on the choice of prior for the individual effects. The idea is to find a new parametrization from $\{\alpha_i\}, \beta$ to, say, $\{g_i\}, \beta$ in such a way that the likelihood factors into a component that involves only the $\{g_i\}$ and a component that involves only β. Exact factoring cannot be done in general but in a large class of models such factoring can be achieved approximately in the sense that we can make the information matrix for $\{g_i\}, \beta$ block diagonal. This is an (information matrix) orthogonalization.

Such a reparametrization exists for all panel data models of the form $P(Y_{it} = 1 | x_{it}, \alpha_i, \beta) = H(\alpha_i + \beta x_{it})$ where H is a distribution function. This class includes the panel probit, in which $H(z) = \Phi(z)$ and the panel logit in which $H(z) = \Lambda(z)$, the logistic distribution function. Such a reparametrization has[20]

---

20   To verify this take the log likelihood of the data provided by agent i regarded as a function of g_i and β and differentiate it twice with respect to these two parameters. After taking expectations with respect to the sampling distribution of $y_{i1}, ..., y_{iT}$ given these two parameters the matrix of second derivatives will be found to be diagonal.

$$\alpha_i^* = \sum_{t=1}^{T} H(\alpha_i + \beta x_{it}). \tag{7.42}$$

The second part of the orthogonal program is to use a prior in which the $\{\alpha_i^*\}$ and β are independent and in which the $\{\alpha_i^*\}$ are assigned independent and flat distributions. Supposing that α_i^* is uniform on its range, which is from 0 to T, the conditional density of α_i is the (proper) distribution

$$p(\alpha_i|\beta) \propto \sum_{t=1}^{T} h(\alpha_i + \beta x_{it}) \tag{7.43}$$

where $h(.)$ is the density function corresponding to $H(.)$.

Recall that a finite mixture distribution has the form $p(x) = \sum_{t=1}^{T} p_t h_t(x)$ where each h_t is a density function and the $\{p_t\}$ are probabilities that sum to one. This is called a T component mixture and we can recognize the conditional (on β) distributions in (7.43) as such finite mixtures with each p_t equal to $1/T$. A finite mixture distribution can be, and typically is, multimodal. One useful way of thinking about such a mixture is to imagine how you would sample from it – for a given β. One way to do this is to define a new finite discrete random variable, say Z, with support on the points $1, 2, ..., T$ and such that $P(Z = t) = p_t$, $t = 1, 2, ..., T$ where in (7.43) $p_t = 1/T$ for all such t. We could then draw a realization of Z; and, if the realization is t, take a realization from h_t and report that as your result. Realizations generated in this way have exactly the mixture distribution required. To prove this in general note that

$$p(x) = \int p(x|z)p(z)\,dz$$

$$= \sum_{t=1}^{T} p_t h_t(x)$$

which in our case is

$$p(\alpha_i|\beta) = \sum_{t=1}^{T}(1/T)h(\alpha_i + \beta x_{it})$$

which is (7.43). This observation suggests an implementation of the panel discrete choice model with a uniform prior on the orthogonal individual effects.

7.6.4   *Implementation of the model*

Introduce an extra set of indicator variables $\{z_t\} = z$ into the model and note that the joint distribution of all the T observations supplied by all the N agents is

$$p(y|\alpha, \beta, z) = \prod_{i=1}^{N}\prod_{t=1}^{T} H(\alpha_i + \beta x_{it})^{y_{it}}(1 - H(\alpha_i + \beta x_{it}))^{1-y_{it}}.$$

It follows from Bayes' theorem that

$$p(\alpha, \beta, z|y) \propto \prod_{i=1}^{N}\prod_{t=1}^{T}H(\alpha_i + \beta x_{it})^{y_{it}}(1 - H(\alpha_i + \beta x_{it}))^{1-y_{it}}p(\alpha_i|\beta, z)p(\beta)p(z)$$

in which $p(\alpha_i|\beta, z = t) = h(\alpha_i + \beta x_{it})$ and $p(z)$ allocates probability $1/T$ to each integer $1, 2, ..., T$. This procedure is an example of data augmentation in which we introduce additional variables (actually parameters!) in order to bring simplicity and clarity into an otherwise rather complicated model. Though the posterior density now involves a total of $2N + K$ arguments its MCMC implementation is now seen to be rather simple. A BUGS program for panel logit might look like:

```
model{
for(i in 1:n){
for(j in 1:l){
y[i,j] ~dbern(mu[i,j])
logit(mu[i,j]) <- a[i] + b*x[i,j]}
a[i] ~dlogis(nu[i],1)
nu[i] <- lam[i,z[i]]
z[i] ~dcat(P[])
lam[i,1] <- -b*x[i,1]
lam[i,2] <- -b*x[i,2] #etc to lam[i,l]=-b*x[i,l]
}
b ~dnorm(0,.001)
}
```

The interpretation of this program line by line is as follows:

(1) Lines 2, 3. n is N and l is T.
(2) Line 4. y for agent i in period t is a binary (Bernoulli) variate with parameter (probability) equal to mu[i, j].
(3) Line 5. The probability is of logit form, $\Lambda(\alpha_i + \beta x_{it})$ – any other form, e.g. probit, could be used. This line completes the likelihood for agent i.
(4) Lines 6, 7. The prior for α_i given z is logistic (normal, etc.) with a location depending on z and equal to $-bx_{it}$ if $z = t$. This is because $h(\alpha_i + \beta x_{it})$ is a logistic (normal, etc.) density for α_i with mean equal to $-\beta x_{it}$ and scale one.
(5) Line 8. This uses the BUGS supplied distribution dcat(p) which generates an integer from 1 to T with probabilities given by the vector p. The line says that the augmentation variable z has such a distribution.
(6) Line 12. Completes the prior which in this case states that β (here univariate) has a fairly flat normal distribution centered at the origin. Any other prior can be used, of course.

For a probit model line 5 would become `probit(mu[i,j]) <- a[i] + b*x[i,j]` or, equivalently, `mu[i,j] <- phi(a[i] +b*x[i,j])`. And line 6 would become `a[i] ~dnorm(nu[i],1)`.

The data to be supplied to the program would be $N \times T$ matrices Y and X if the covariate is scalar, otherwise X would be $N \times T \times K$ if x has K elements and there would be more elaborate expressions for mu and lam in the BUGS program, together with the values n and l and a vector P of length l containing $1/l$ repeated l times.

7.7   CONCLUDING REMARKS

We have discussed in the chapter some of the simpler linear and non-linear regression models that apply when the data permit repeated observations on the same agent. Uniform priors on (possibly redefined) individual effects typically (though not always) correspond to standard frequentist procedures such as differencing and conditioning. Hierarchical priors on such effects, possibly allowing for mean dependence on the covariate sequences, are not difficult to implement. Starting points for MCMC calculations are conveniently found by exploiting the fact that most such models fall into the category of **generalized linear models** and point estimates, with rough guides to marginal posterior standard errors able to be found using the glm command in R. Generalized linear models in which all coefficients are allowed to be agent-specific and have hierarchical priors are becoming common in the biostatistics literature under the name **mixed models** and many of the examples in the BUGS on-line manual are of this type. Often, the aim of these calculations seems to be the statistical one of fitting the data well rather than the econometric one of making inferences about structural parameters with a clear economic theoretical interpretation.

Among the challenging extensions to the class of panel data models is the development of approriate priors for autoregressive non-linear models in which, for example, with binary data, the occurrence of an event at time t depends upon whether it had occurred previously.

One final remark is that one can encounter convergence issues in the MCMC implementation of non-linear models and so careful checking of sampler output is required.

7.8   EXERCISES

(1) **Solving the normal equations**   Take the normal equations for $(b\ a)$, (7.13), and solve them for a in terms of b to verify (7.15). Next take the solution for a and insert it into the first of the two equations to verify (7.14).

(2) **Properties of R (7.9)**   Verify that $R'R = TI_N$ and $RR' = I_N \otimes J_T$ when $R = [I_N \otimes j_T]$.

(3) The BUGS code for weibull data given in appendix 3 can be modified to allow for repeat durations for each agent. Do this modification and try out the modification for alternative choices of parametrization, as discussed in section 7.5, and choice of prior.

(4) By forming the likelihood for an individual agent, differentiating its logarithm and then taking expectations with respect to the conditional distribution from which the likelihood was derived, show that α_i given in (7.42) is information orthogonal to the remaining parameters.

(5) Repeat problem (4) for the parameter v_i^* of (7.40). This is slightly more complicated than the previous problem and you will need to use the moments given in the distribution appendix to chapter 5.

(6) Generate some count data by, for example, `n <- 100; beta <- 1; x <- rnorm(n); y <- rpois(n,exp(x))`, and get point estimates and approximate posterior standard errors using the `glm` command in S, as `glm(y ~ x, family = poisson)`.

(7) Repeat exercise (6) with binary data, (`y <- rbinom(n, 1, pnorm(beta * x))`) using the command `glm(y~x, family=binomial(link= probit))`.

(8) Try the same but now with (exponential) duration data, (`y <- rexp(n, exp(beta * x))`) using the command `glm(y~x, family = Gamma(link= log))`. (Note that you get minus beta since the program uses exp(-beta*x) as the parameter.)

(9) With reference to (7.19), if x is a dummy variable indicating membership in one of two groups show that the least squares estimate of the slope of the linear regression of y on x is the difference of the means of y in the two groups.

(10) You can redo exercises (6) through (8) to fit a smoothed regression response using the S function `gam` as in `gam(y~s(x), family = poisson)`.

7.9 BIBLIOGRAPHIC NOTES

Hobert and Casella (1996: 1461–73) give a valuable discussion of MCMC methods for the linear panel data model with individual effects. They show that a conventional improper prior on the variance of the individual effects leads to an improper posterior and, more importantly, that this impropriety may be hard to detect in sampler output! Chib, Greenberg, and Winkelmann (1998: 33–54) deal with a more general version of the panel count model; see also Gelfand, Sahu, and Carlin (1996: 165–80).

One of several good econometric examples of the use of simple linear panel data models, discussed in section 7.3.2, is Card and Krueger (1994: 772–93). The study is notable for its active search for new data to test a theory and for its attention to model checking.

The question of unbalanced panels referred to in the first footnote in this chapter leads into the general question of missing data in panel surveys. A clear exposition of the issue is contained in Hirano *et al.* (2001: 1645–60). Hogan, Lin, and Herman (2003) is an example of the treatment of non-response in the biostatistical literature.

Gelfand, Sahu, and Carlin (1995: 479–88) discuss computationally effective ways of parametrizing random effects panel data models. Fernandez, Osiewalski, and Steel (1997) has a general discussion of the non-existence of posterior distributions in panel data models with individual effects and how this non-existence can fail to be revealed during MCMC calculations.

The survey chapter by Chamberlain in volume 2 of the *Handbook of Econometrics* (1984) is important for the way the author connects panel model specification to theory. (See also Heckman and MacCurdy, 1980: 47–74.) Chamberlain's survey also develops and applies, in a frequentist way, the pi matrix approach discussed briefly in section 7.4. This survey is related to an earlier paper by Mundlak (1961: 44–56), which is also an important source.

For an early example of a non-linear random effects model in econometrics see Lancaster (1979: 939–56). Bayesian count data models are studied in Chib, Greenberg, and Winkelmann (1998: 33–54).

Parameter separation in models with individual effects is discussed in Lancaster (2000: 391–413) and Lancaster (2002: 647–66). Orthogonal parametrizations are discussed and applied also in papers by Woutersen and Voia (2002), and Woutersen (2001).

Chapter 8
INSTRUMENTAL VARIABLES

8.1 INTRODUCTION

As we argued in chapter 6 and earlier a model that exhibits the dependence of y on x with the deterministic relationship disturbed by error, ε, requires some assumption or belief regarding the connection, if any, between x and ε. In the linear model, $y = x\beta + \varepsilon$, we need a joint probability distribution for x, ε to enable inference about β to proceed. The belief that the values of x have been randomly assigned would justify an assumption of independence of these two quantities but in the absence of randomization we seem to need further information. As we showed in the last chapter this could be in the form of panel data together with a further assumption about the structure of the error term. But a more common way of resolving this difficulty in econometrics is the introduction into the model of **instrumental variables**.

   In this chapter we shall state what an instrumental variable is and relate the idea to that of a randomizer such as would be used in a randomized experiment. We then analyze a particular linear structure in which an instrumental variable can be used to solve the problem caused by endogenous covariates, that is, variables whose effects are confounded with those of unmeasured variables. We show how to use Bayes' theorem to make inferences about important structural parameters and provide a BUGS program to do the computations. We then illustrate the approach by two sorts of calculations. The first uses simulated data to explore the properties of posterior distributions when instruments are highly correlated with the endogenous covariate and when they are not. This latter is the well-known **weak instrument** problem. We then apply the approach to real data using a weak instrument with a very large sample. A final section describes generalizations of the instrumental variable approach.

8.2 RANDOMIZERS AND INSTRUMENTS

Consider again the process of randomization. If it was possible we would take some objective device capable of generating numbers by a chance mechanism – tossing a coin, for example – and use the output of this device, call it z, to select values for x. Because z originates in a physical mechanism apparently unrelated to the agents under study it will typically seem plausible to assume that z, and hence x, will be independent of ε. This variable z is an example of an instrumental variable.[1] It has the key properties that (a) it is plausibly independent of ε and (b) it will be dependent on x (because you use z to determine x). You can think of this mechanism as a system of two relations,

$$x \leftarrow z \tag{8.1}$$

$$y \leftarrow x, \varepsilon \tag{8.2}$$

representing z determining x and then x and the error determining y. For example, one can imagine tossing a coin and letting z represent either heads or tails. The first relationship might then say, "if z is heads assign this individual to health insurance plan A, if it is tails assign her to plan B." Then the outcome y, which might be, say, the number of visits to the doctor, is determined by both the insurance plan, which is the covariate x, and by the error term which represents the combined effect of all other factors that affect doctor visits – age, gender, income, wealth, etc. By construction, z (and therefore x) is plausibly independent of all these factors – the coin is not aware that the next person is a rich woman, or a poor man. To make matters more concrete we could write down a linear version of these two equations which would be

$$x = \gamma + \delta z, \tag{8.3}$$

$$y = \alpha + \beta x + \varepsilon. \tag{8.4}$$

If z, and hence x, is indeed thought to be independent of ε then the second of these equations is a (linear) regression model with $\alpha + \beta x$ representing the conditional mean of y given x.[2]

The process we have just described is randomized choice of covariate. But what is the relevance of this to economics where randomized experiments are rarely feasible? The answer lies in a generalization of the system (8.3) and (8.4) and this generalization is the key to all instrumental variable work in econometrics.

8.3 MODELS AND INSTRUMENTAL VARIABLES

Let us suppose that the randomizing equation (8.3) is imperfect in that x is determined not only by z but by additional unknown factors whose combined effect

---

1 Though it is not called this in the (primarily medical) literature where randomization is most frequently undertaken. "Instrumental variable" is an exclusively econometric phrase.

2 Recall that we always take error terms to have zero (marginal) means because this can always be achieved by redefining the intercept.

varies from agent to agent, just like ε. In the linear version of the model we might then write

$$x_i = \gamma + \delta z_i + \varepsilon_{1i} \qquad (8.5)$$

$$y_i = \alpha + \beta x_i + \varepsilon_{2i}. \qquad (8.6)$$

In this system x is determined partly by the randomizer and partly by an "error term," ε_{1i}. The randomizer, or instrument, z is now assumed (believed) to be distributed independently of *both* error terms, ε_{1i} and ε_{2i}. When econometricians introduce an instrumental variable in this way it is, of course, rare that z represents the outcome of a physical randomizing machine. It is instead typically an economic variable for which a more or less convincing case can be made that it behaves *as if* it was a randomizer.

The system of equations (8.5) and (8.6) is called recursive.

DEFINITION 8.1 RECURSIVE EQUATIONS *A system of equations of the form*

$$x = \gamma + \delta z$$
$$y = \alpha + \beta x$$

*is called recursive in that it can be solved for x and y in terms of z and the parameters by solving the first equation for x and then using this solution in the second equation to solve for y. When we add error terms as in (8.5) and those error terms are stochastically independent the system is called **fully recursive**.*

DEFINITION 8.2 ENDOGENOUS VARIABLES *A variable (like x) that appears on the right hand side of an econometric equation system (so it is a causal variable in the theorist's underlying deterministic model), and that is presumed to be correlated with the errors in the model is called endogenous.*

The new error term, ε_1, might be interpreted as due to measurement error in x in that there exists a correct value of x, say x^*, which is determined exactly by the randomizer but in fact "clerical error" records x^* as x and the agent actually receives "treatment" x. A variant on this story is to suppose that the agent is assigned a "treatment" x^* but some agents choose not to comply with the assigned treatment and instead choose as their covariate (treatment) the value x, so in some cases x is the assigned treatment and in others it is not. In this case the relation between x and z will depend on an additional parameter or error term ε, measuring non-compliance, which is independent of z but not necessarily independent of the error in the relation between y and x. There are many other stories one can invent to explain the existence of an error term in the randomizing equation. Which story is plausible will depend very much on context. In systems such as (8.5) with the variable z having the properties that it is correlated with x but independent of the error terms, z is no longer called a randomizer but is instead called an instrumental variable.

DEFINITION 8.3   INSTRUMENTAL VARIABLES   *A variable that is uncorrelated with the errors in the model but correlated with the endogenous covariate is called a (valid) instrument.*

Examples of variables that have been used as instruments in economics include time, location, and lottery draws.

This generalization, (8.5), has the following important consequence. Suppose that we ask whether the second equation, (8.6), is still a regression. It will be so if $\alpha + \beta x_i$ is the conditional mean of y_i. So let's take expectations, initially conditional on both x and z.

$$
\begin{aligned}
E(y|x, z) &= \alpha + \beta x + E(\varepsilon_2|x, z) \\
&= \alpha + \beta x + E(\varepsilon_2|\varepsilon_1, z) \\
&= \alpha + \beta x + E(\varepsilon_2|\varepsilon_1)
\end{aligned}
$$

where the second line follows because x is a function of ε_1 and z, and the last line follows since z is independent of $\varepsilon = (\varepsilon_1, \varepsilon_2)$. It follows from this that recursive systems are not, in general, sets of regression equations. The second equation *is* a regression if and only if ε_2 and ε_1 are mean independent, and so the error in the randomization equation[3] is uncorrelated with that in the equation of interest.[4] It follows that if you are willing to believe that the two error terms are stochastically (or at least, mean) independent then standard Bayesian regression methods apply. It is when you cannot believe this independence and the system is recursive, but not fully recursive, that interesting complications arise. (Notice that if we return to the deterministic randomizing model in which ε_1 is absent it will automatically be true – because $E(\varepsilon_2|\varepsilon_1, z) = E(\varepsilon_2|z) = 0$ – that $\alpha + \beta x$ is the regression of y on x.)

Since it is the recursive form that is most frequently used in applied work we shall focus on this model in this chapter.

---

3   The first equation is more usually called the "selection equation" because it shows how the covariate value, x, to be applied to agent i is chosen or selected.

4   Actually, we have shown that $\alpha + \beta x$ is equal to $E(y|x, z)$ if the errors are mean independent. But if $E(y|x, z) = \alpha + \beta x$ then $E(y|x) = \alpha + \beta x$.

8.4 THE STRUCTURE OF A RECURSIVE EQUATIONS MODEL

Consider the recursive model with a stochastic selection equation,

$$x_i = \gamma + \delta z_i + \varepsilon_{1i} \tag{8.7}$$

$$y_i = \alpha + \beta x_i + \varepsilon_{2i}. \tag{8.8}$$

This is a pair of equations designed to show (a) how the covariate x is selected and (b) how that covariate value helps to determine y. The variable z, the randomizer or instrument, is assumed (believed) to be independent of the error terms ε_1, ε_2 or at least mean independent. We shall allow for z, and hence δ, to be vector valued so there may be many instruments. Interest focuses on the response of y to variation in x represented by the coefficient β, assumed the same for all agents. This is the structural coefficient.

An equation system written as (8.7) and (8.8) is called a **structural form** because its equations show how each variable is connected to others according to the theory and its equations generally have a clear theoretical interpretation, for example β is the response of y to a unit variation in x holding constant, α, β, ε_2. In the context of a recursive equations system the variables whose values the equations are designed to determine, $\{y, x\}$, are called **jointly dependent variables**.

DEFINITION 8.4 THE STRUCTURAL FORM *The structural form of a model shows the theoretical, and causal, relationships between the jointly dependent variables. The parameters are intended to have a direct behavioral or technical interpretation.*

It is helpful in thinking about inference in this model to solve the system to show explicitly the way in which x and y are determined. Such a solved system is called the **reduced form**.

DEFINITION 8.5 THE REDUCED FORM *The reduced form of a linear recursive system expresses the jointly dependent variables as explicit functions of the instruments.*

In a single equation model such as we discussed in chapter 1 the structural and reduced forms coincide.

This solution of the linear recursive system is easily found to be

$$x = \gamma + \delta z + v_1 \qquad (8.9)$$
$$y = \alpha^* + \beta \delta z + v_2$$
where $\alpha^* = \alpha + \beta\gamma$, $v_1 = \varepsilon_1$ and $v_2 = \varepsilon_2 + \beta\varepsilon_1$.

These equations show the dependence of both y and x on the instrumental variable(s). Unlike the structural form, both equations of the reduced form are regressions, because of the (mean) independence of z and the errors – if z is independent of $(\varepsilon_1, \varepsilon_2)$ it is necessarily independent of (v_1, v_2). So a recursive system may be transformed into a collection of regression equations.

8.4.1 Identification

In (8.9) the parameter of interest, β, appears in the reduced form only as part of the coefficient of z in the equation for y. So the question that arises is whether β is (likelihood) identified. Recall that the definition of identification given in chapter 1 states that a parameter θ is identified if it can be deduced uniquely from a knowledge of the joint distribution of the data. In the present case this means that if we knew the joint distribution of (y, x, z) given $\theta = (\gamma, \alpha, \delta, \beta)$ we could deduce β. But is this true? It is clear that if we knew this joint distribution we would know the regressions of (y, x) on z. This in turn implies that we could know γ, δ, α^* and $\beta\delta$, but could we deduce β from this knowledge? The answer is clearly yes if $\delta \neq 0$ for then we can calculate β as the ratio of the coefficient of z in the equation for y to the coefficient of z in the equation for x. And if there were several instruments any one of these ratios would supply β and the answer would be unique.

On the other hand if $\delta = 0$ then β could not be determined because the reduced form reduces to

$$x = \gamma + v_1,$$
$$y = \alpha^* + v_2,$$

and β has disappeared from the model.[5] So β is identified from the likelihood if, and only if, $\delta \neq 0$. The practical interpretation of the statement that $\delta = 0$ is that x is not randomized, not even partially, so our conclusion is that β is identified only if there is at least some randomization of x. This conclusion is often described as **local non-identification** in that there is a portion of the β, δ parameter space that does not permit the deduction of β.

Next we consider inference about β.

---

5 It is, of course, formally present in the definitions of α^* and in the covariance matrix of v. But it cannot be deduced from a knowledge of α^* or from knowledge of that covariance matrix.

8.5   INFERENCE IN A RECURSIVE SYSTEM

Let us examine the structure of the likelihood for the recursive equation system under the hypothesis that the reduced form errors $v = (v_1, v_2)$ have a bivariate normal distribution with means zero and precision matrix Q. This is equivalent to asserting that the structural form errors, $\varepsilon = (\varepsilon_1, \varepsilon_2)$, are jointly normal since the two sets of errors are linearly related. The joint density of v for a single agent is then

$$\ell(\alpha^*, \beta, \delta, \gamma; y, x, z) \propto |Q|^{1/2} \exp\{-0.5 * v'Qv\}, \qquad (8.10)$$

$$\text{where} \quad v = \begin{bmatrix} x - \gamma - \delta z \\ y - \alpha^* - \beta\delta z \end{bmatrix}$$

and this is also the likelihood based on the conditional distribution of y, x given z, since the jacobian from v to y, x is one.

This is the likelihood for a pair of linear regression models in which the parameter of interest is the ratio of one slope coefficient to the other. But it has the interesting feature that when there is more than one covariate (instrument) there are fewer parameters in the model than regression coefficients. The parameters of the reduced form are $(\alpha^*, \gamma, \beta, \delta, Q)$ which number $1 + 1 + 1 + k + 3 = k + 6$ if there are k instruments (elements of z). However the regression coefficients are $k + 1$ in number in the first equation and $k + 1$ in the second, for a total of $2k + 2$ plus the three distinct elements of Q, totaling $2k + 5$. Thus there are more coefficients than free parameters in the system if $k > 1$. The excess, equal to $k - 1$, is called the **degree of over-identification** of the system. When k is equal to one so that both x and δ are scalar the system is called **just identified**. With an over-identified system the reduced form is called **restricted**.

DEFINITION 8.6   JUST AND OVER-IDENTIFICATION   *A recursive equation system is over-identified if there are more (linearly independent) valid instruments than endogenous covariates. If there are as many instruments as right hand endogenous variables it is just identified.*

Digression   *Two stage least squares*   From a statistical point of view the one instrument or just identified case is rather trivial. This is because β is uniquely defined as the ratio of one regression slope to another as can be seen from (8.9). The "obvious" way to estimate β is by estimating each coefficient by least squares and forming an estimate of β by calculating their ratio. Since the least squares regression coefficient of x on z is equal to $cov(x, z)/var(z)$

and the least squares regression coefficient of y on z is cov(y, z)/var(z), their ratio is

$$b_{iv} = \frac{cov(y, z)}{cov(x, z)}$$

and this is the traditional instrumental variables estimator referred to above. This also is the β component of the joint posterior mode under a Bayesian analysis with a flat prior. This common sense procedure doesn't work when the equation of interest is over-identified because then β is equal to the ratio of the coefficients of z_1 in the two reduced form equations, but it is also equal to the ratio of the coefficients of z_2! So how do you proceed in this case? A method widely used in the frequentist literature is to make a least squares estimate of the δ coefficients in the selection equation, say $\hat{\delta}$, and then to calculate the least squares regression of y on z$\hat{\delta}$, taking the coefficient on this scalar covariate as an estimate of β. This method is called two stage least squares. It has no Bayesian interpretation. In the Bayesian procedure there is no real difficulty in handling any degree of identification.

8.5.1 Likelihood surfaces with weak instruments

We showed above that β is identified from this likelihood except locally when δ = 0. We can see how this non-identification affects the likelihood by looking at a graph of the likelihood for δ, β taking the remaining parameters as known. Along the line corresponding to δ = 0 in this δ, β space the likelihood surface does not depend on the value of β. This means there is a ridge in the surface along this line. It is instructive to study this ridge graphically and in figures 8.1, 8.2, and 8.3 we have taken Q

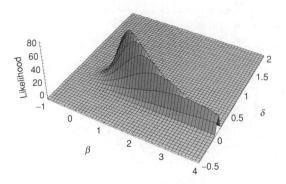

Figure 8.1 Instrumental variable likelihood surface: $\rho = 0.1$

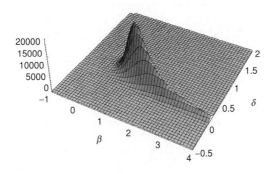

Figure 8.2 Instrumental variable likelihood surface: $\rho = 0.2$

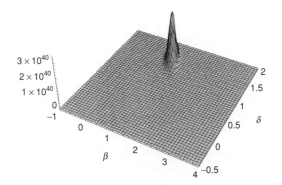

Figure 8.3 Instrumental variable likelihood surface: $\rho = 0.7$

as known and set γ, α^* equal to zero so the likelihood is just a function of the scalars β and δ. We then chose the data to have sums of squares and products of the size that would be produced by a model in which the squared correlation between the instrument and the endogenous covariate ranges from small to large – from a weak(ish) instrument to a strong one. The three figures show the likelihood surface in each case.

It can be seen that when the instrument is weakly correlated with the endogenous variable the ridge of non-identifiability plays a major role in determining the likelihood surface's shape and in particular this ridge at $\delta = 0$ is responsible for the long tail to the right in the β marginal corresponding to figure 8.1 and, to a lesser extent, figure 8.2. As this correlation increases – the instrument becomes stronger – the surface pulls away from the ridge, which finally becomes invisible, and the likelihood begins to take on the standard bivariate normal form corresponding to figure 8.3. It seems clear from these figures that weak correlation or very incomplete randomization will produce very non-normal posterior distributions when the priors are diffuse and the likelihood and the posterior are close.

Digression   *Jeffreys' prior* *It is interesting to see what Jeffreys'
method produces for the prior when Q is known and α* and γ are set equal to
zero.[6] Taking the log of the likelihood, (8.10), differentiating twice with respect
to β and δ, changing the sign, taking expectations and evaluating the matrix at
the "true" parameter values produces the (β, δ) information matrix*

$$
I_{\beta,\delta} \propto \begin{bmatrix} q_{11}\delta^2 & (q_{22}\beta + q_{12})\delta \\ (q_{11}\beta + q_{12})\delta & (q_{22}\beta^2 + 2q_{12}\beta + q_{11}) \end{bmatrix}
$$

*and the determinant of this matrix is $\delta^2 |Q|$. Jeffreys' principle then gives a prior
for β, δ that is proportional to $|\delta|$. This is a prior that assigns zero probability
density to the troublesome ridge δ = 0. A possible objection to the use of this prior
is that in many econometric applications an instrumental variable that has no
regression on the included endogenous variable is all too probable, and to rule it
out, dogmatically, a priori, may be unwise.[7]*

8.6   A NUMERICAL STUDY OF INFERENCE WITH INSTRUMENTAL VARIABLES

In this section we shall show, using simulated data, how to study numerically the
marginal posterior density of β in a simple recursive system with one or more instrumental variables and with δ being close to or far from zero. These exercises will demonstrate the variety of result that can be obtained when using instrumental variables.
They should also enable the reader to do Bayesian inference him or herself when
the model is a two equation linear recursive system.

   The model is (8.9) and to generate some data for illustrative purposes we select
some specific parameter values. Specifically, with one instrument,

$$
\gamma = \alpha^* = 0; \quad \delta = \text{either 1 or 0.2}, \quad \beta = 2.
$$

Through the calculations of this section we shall produce data generated by reduced
form errors, (v_1, v_2), which are independent normal variates with means zero and
unit precisions. The sample size will be $n = 1{,}000$ throughout this subsection. The
values of the instruments are iid $n(0, 1)$.

   In the first calculation we generate data with $\delta = 1$. This implies a squared
correlation of 0.5 between the instrument and the endogenous variable so about
half the variation in x is attributable to variation in the randomizer. This would
normally be thought of in econometrics as quite a strong instrument. In the second

---

6   The more general case gives essentially the same result.
7   Chao and Phillips (2002), who explore, theoretically, the application of Jeffreys' prior, take a different view.

calculation we generate data with $\delta = 0.2$ and this implies a squared correlation between the instrument and the endogenous variable equal to about 0.04. This instrument is weak.

8.6.1 Generating data for a simulation study

First we explain how you might generate some data, having already set the parameter values. Suitable S commands would be

```
z <- rnorm(n)...........values for the instrumental variables;
x <- γ+δ*z + rnorm(n)........values for the endogenous covariate;
y <- α*+β*δ*x + rnorm(n).......values for remaining dependent variable.
```

These three statements generate data according to the reduced form of the model. In this numerical study the structural form errors ε_1, ε_2 are iid standard normal variates but you can of course choose whatever joint distribution you like.

8.6.2 A BUGS model statement

A possible BUGS model statement based on the reduced form might be:

```
model{
for(i in 1:n){
y[i,1:2] ~dmnorm(mu[i,],q[,])
mu[i,1] <- g + d*z[i]
mu[i,2] <- as + b*d*z[i]
}
q[1:2,1:2] ~dwish(r[,],2)
as ~dnorm(0,0.001)
b ~dnorm(0,0.001)
d ~dnorm(0,0.001)
g ~dnorm(0,0.001)
}
```

The do loop specifies that for each i, y_1 and y_2 are bivariate normal with means mu and precision matrix q and that the two regression functions are as specified in (8.9). The likelihood is written for the case of one instrument. If you wish to use more than one then the fourth and fifth lines would be changed to, say

```
mu[i,1] <- g + d₁*z[i,1] + d₂*z[i,2]+ ... + dₖz[i,k]
mu[i,2] <- as + b*(d₁*z[i,1] + d₂*z[i,2]+ ... + dₖz[i,k])
```

for the case of k instruments. A prior for d_2, ..., d_k would also be required. Note that when we present the model to BUGS we are presenting it as a restricted reduced form when there is more than one instrument.

The prior specification begins by putting a Wishart prior on q with a location specified by the matrix $\mathbf{r}$ and scale parameter equal to 2 which gives the two-dimensional analogue to a gamma prior with small values of α and β. The last four statements of the prior specify standard low precision normal densities for the four parameters of the structural form.

8.6.3   Simulation results

In these calculations the sampler was run for three parallel chains from diverse starting points and convergence checks carried out. The length of the chains was 1,000 and the first 500 steps were discarded. This gives a total of 1,500 realizations from the joint posterior density of α^*, γ, β, δ and the three parameters of the reduced form error covariance matrix. The data were generated with $n = 1,000$, so this is, in traditional terms, a large sample study.

Figures 8.4, 8.5, and 8.6, show some of the results when data are generated with a strong instrument in which $\delta = 1$ and the r^2 between x and z was 0.5.

Figure 8.4 suggests a roughly bivariate normal joint posterior density of β and δ and figure 8.5 shows an apparently nearly normal marginal posterior density of β centered around the value, $\beta = 2$, used to generate the data. A 95% hpd interval for β calculated from the realizations underlying these figures runs from 1.89 to 2.01. The QQ plot, figure 8.6, confirms the marginal posterior normality of β. So for these data we seem to be in the situation depicted in figure 8.3 above in which a multivariate normal approximation to the joint posterior density works fine.

The second set of figures, 8.7, 8.8, and 8.9, use the data generated with $\delta = 0.2$ implying an r^2 of about 0.04 between x and z. This corresponds to a weak instrument.

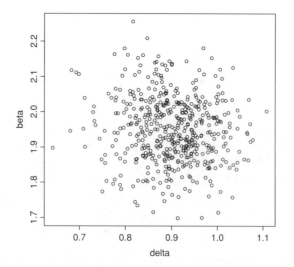

Figure 8.4 Joint posterior density of β and δ with a strong instrument

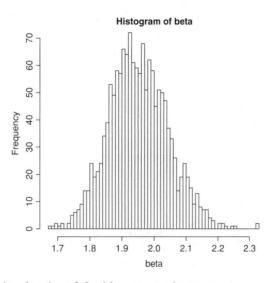

Figure 8.5 Posterior density of β with a strong instrument

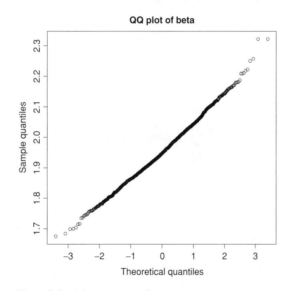

Figure 8.6 Normality of β with a strong instrument

The histogram of the marginal posterior density of β, figure 8.7, shows a distribution with remarkably thick tails – note the numbers on the x axis. While it is roughly centered near $\beta = 2$, values as large as ±30 or 40 have some probability and in fact a 95% hpd interval based on the 1,500 realizations of β runs from -28 to 27. More remarkable than this is the joint posterior density of β, δ shown in figure 8.8. The star shape shows very clearly the ridge in the likelihood that we showed in the earlier plots (figures 8.1 and 8.2). The QQ plot in figure 8.9 demonstrates

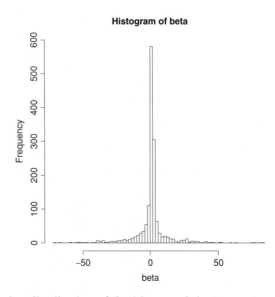

Figure 8.7 Posterior distribution of β with a weak instrument

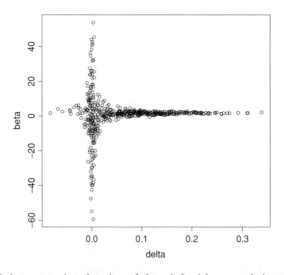

Figure 8.8 The joint posterior density of β and δ with a weak instrument

the strong non-normality of the posterior density for β in the weak instrument case. The speed of convergence of the MCMC sampler is also affected by weakness of the instrument although this is only marked in the case of the (weakly identified) structural parameter β. Longer chains than would be usually needed are necessary in order to have reasonable confidence that realizations are coming from the desired joint posterior distribution.

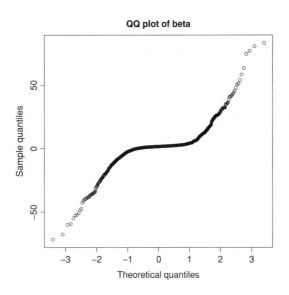

Figure 8.9 Non-normality of β with a weak instrument

Conclusions

- It seems clear from these calculations that asymptotic multivariate normal approximations can be poor. Exact calculations for the data and sample size that you have are essential to making appropriate inferences.
- Posterior distributions of weakly identified structural parameters can be very thick tailed.
- Convergence of markov chain samplers can be slow in models with parameters that are weakly identified.

In the next section we show how these theoretical calculations are relevant to a real application.

8.7   AN APPLICATION OF IV METHODS TO WAGES AND EDUCATION

Economists calculate the marginal rate of return to education by relating wages to years of education, and the rate of return is the slope coefficient in such a model which would, at its simplest, be of the form

$$\text{wages} = \alpha + \beta \text{ education.} \tag{8.11}$$

Typically, education is measured in years and "wages" is the logarithm of the weekly wage rate, so that β measures the proportionate return to an additional year of education and 100β is the percentage marginal return. On general grounds one would expect this number to be comparable to rates of return on other risky assets, say, somewhere between 5% and 30% implying values for β of the order of 0.05 to 0.30. The difficulty is that when we add an error term to (8.11) to represent the effect of all those unobserved factors that affect wages of individuals, then there is a presumption that many such factors also affect the amount of education that he or she acquires. Think of such unobserved factors as strength of character, energy, health, stamina, intelligence, and so on, and it must be clear that these variables can, and probably do, affect both education and wages. In other words, there is a presumption that *education is endogenous.*

In this section we shall make inferences about β using data on wages, education, and an instrumental variable suggested in an ingenious paper by Angrist and Krueger[8] (AK) (1991). AK suggested that the quarter of the year in which a person was born could be used as an instrument for education. They argued that years of education should show a systematic variation with quarter of birth due to the existence of laws regulating the age at which children are permitted to leave school.

> The experiment[9] stems from the fact that children born in different months of the year start school at different ages, while compulsory schooling laws generally require students to remain in school until their sixteenth or seventeenth birthday. In effect, the interaction of school entry requirements and compulsory schooling laws compel(s) students born in certain months to attend school longer than students born in other months.

They also argued that quarter of birth should be independent of factors such as those mentioned above that affect wages in addition to education. Thus, if *you* share the authors' beliefs, quarter of birth is a valid instrument for education and we can proceed to infer the marginal rate of return to education using the methods we have just described and used with simulated data.

The model is in the general framework of equations (8.1) and (8.2), reproduced below,

$$x \leftarrow z$$
$$y \leftarrow x, \varepsilon$$

in which z is quarter of birth, x is years of education and y is log weekly wage. It seems inappropriate to specialize the first of these relations to the linear form of (8.3) and (8.4) because there is no reason to expect the relation between quarter of birth and education to be monotone. A better way of proceeding with this categorical

---

8   See the bibliographic notes at the end of this chapter.

9   There is no experiment behind these data. The authors use the word "experiment" to refer to so-called natural experiments in which, for example, an unintended consequence of legislation is to create a situation *analogous* to a randomized experiment. Another example is where an unintended consequence of, for example, biology produces a situation analogous to a controlled experiment, for example the birth of identical twins allows the researcher to "control for" heredity.

covariate is to allow individuals born in different quarters to have different mean years of education and we can do this by defining three dummy or indicator variables, q_1, q_2, and q_3, such that $q_j = 1$ if the agent was born in quarter j and is zero otherwise, $q_j = I$ (birth in quarter j), $j = 1, 2, 3$, and writing the selection equation, $x \leftarrow z$, as

$$\text{educ} = \gamma + \delta_1 q_1 + \delta_2 q_2 + \delta_3 q_3 + \varepsilon_1 \tag{8.12}$$

where ε_1 will be assumed normal[10] with mean zero. This model implies that the expected education of someone born in quarter j is $\gamma + \delta_j$, $j = 1, 2, 3$ and the expected earnings of someone born in the fourth quarter of the year is γ. So the δ_j are the differences in average education between someone born in quarter j and someone born in the fourth quarter. The second structural equation relates wages to education and we write it as

$$\text{wage} = \alpha + \beta \, \text{educ} + \varepsilon_2 \tag{8.13}$$

since we would expect the relation between education and wages to be monotone and, at least roughly, linear, perhaps. The model, in structural form, composed of (8.12) and (8.13) will be recognized as an over-identified recursive model. It is over-identified because there are, in fact, three instrumental variables, q_1, q_2 and q_3, but only one right hand endogenous variable, education. Under an assumption of bivariate normality for ε_1, ε_2 it can be simulated using the BUGS program given earlier in section 8.6.2 extended to allow three instruments in the way indicated.

The data refer to $n = 35,805$ men born in 1939 and are a subset of the AK data which used men born in many different years and allowed for year of birth as an additional covariate. The average number of years of education was 13 and the median number was 12, with 59 men having zero years and 1,322 having the maximum education of 20 years; 38% of the men had 12 years, corresponding to completion of high school. For the relation between quarter of birth and education we find the following results:

Table 8.1 Quarter of birth and education

Quarter of birth	Years of education
first	13.003
second	13.013
third	12.989
fourth	13.116

---

10   This is not entirely reasonable since "years of education" is a discrete variable. However in our data it takes on 21 distinct values and in fact normality, though false, is not a terrible approximation as a QQ plot shows.

The differences are, as one might have expected, small; the difference between 13.116 and 12.989 is about six and half weeks of education and this is about one percent of the median years of education in the whole sample. It is these tiny differences, which are in fact statistically significant by a (frequentist) F test, that are the basis of the attempt to eliminate the endogeneity of education. These instruments certainly qualify as "weak," so it is interesting to see what the posterior distribution of the rate of return will look like.

To form this posterior we need to choose a prior and, quite unlike the use of artificial simulated data, when we have a real data application we have a context within which we can think meaningfully about priors. Take the return to education, which we argued above should not be outrageously different from the return on any other risky investment and be of the order of, say 0.05 to 0.30, possibly larger, possibly smaller. A prior that may command general assent among economists and perhaps encompasses a range of professional opinion, might be something like normal with a mean near 0.10, or 10% return, and a standard deviation of, say, 0.10. This states that while the rate could be any real number – it is not dogmatic – it is highly likely to lie between −20% and +30% although of course most of us, if we had to bet real money, would choose a much tighter distribution.

Next consider priors on the coefficients on the instruments, δ_1, δ_2 and δ_3, trying to imagine that we had not seen table 8.1. If we think about the proposed mechanism by which quarter of birth should influence length of schooling it should be apparent that the effect, if there at all, is likely to be small – a matter of weeks, not months. Moreover if we think of all three effects together it seems highly plausible that the coefficients should be of similar magnitude. If someone told you that δ_1 was, say, −0.11, which corresponds to a five-week difference from those born in the fourth quarter, it is likely that we would feel that the other coefficients were also of the same order of magnitude, though maybe of different signs. In this situation in which a collection of coefficients have the same dimension and have similar interpretations the standard Bayesian response is to regard them as exchangeable and, in consequence, to construct a hierarchical prior in which these coefficients are viewed as themselves conditionally independent draws from some distribution that itself involves (hyper)parameters. This is one way of expressing the idea that these coefficients are likely to be similar. A possible hierarchical prior is

$$\delta_1, \delta_2, \delta_3 | \mu, \tau \sim_{iid} n(\mu, \tau)$$

with μ assigned a diffuse prior, and with the standard deviation taken to be, say, 0.10 implying $\tau = 100$. This expresses the view that most differential effects of quarter of birth on education are likely to be within 0.20 of a year – or 10 weeks – of the mean.

Alternatively one can choose a default prior in which β and the δ_j, together with the intercepts, are assigned highly dispersed independent normal distributions. In the calculations that follow we shall try both priors.

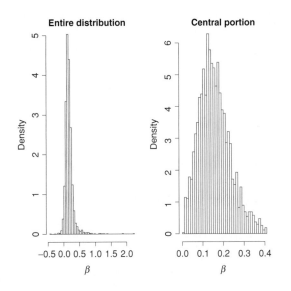

Figure 8.10 Posterior distribution of the rate of return – diffuse prior

Diffuse prior

The sampler was run through 2,000 steps with the first 1,000 discarded and three parallel chains were run to check convergence – this gives a total of 3,000 realizations from the joint posterior. Figure 8.10 shows the marginal posterior for β under the diffuse prior set-up. The left frame gives the entire histogram for all 3,000 realizations and the right frame provides a close-up of the middle 90% of the distribution.

It can be seen that the distribution is very dispersed; the smallest realization (of 3,000) corresponds to a return (a loss) of minus 40% and the largest to a gain of 220%. An (approximate) 95% hpd interval runs from a rate of return of essentially zero to one of about 45%.

The distribution is very far from normal (see the QQ plot in figure 8.11) and it is also very far from the prior which, if superimposed on the left hand frame of figure 8.10, would look almost flat. Clearly, we have learned something but not, perhaps, very much. As can be seen on the right frame of figure 8.10, the posterior points towards rates of return of the order of 10 to 20% a year, but very considerable uncertainty remains. The ideal might be to be able to pin down the rate of return to within one or two percentage points, but we are very far from this accuracy. The posterior mean of β under this prior is 17% and the median is 15%; 75% of all realizations lie within the range from 10% to 21%.

Informative prior

For contrast let us see what happens when we use the relatively informative prior described above in which β is $n(0.10, 100)$ and the three δ coefficients are con-

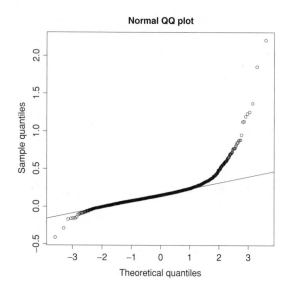

Figure 8.11 Posterior of β under a diffuse prior

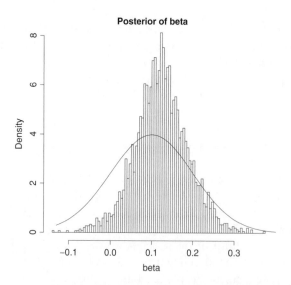

Figure 8.12 The posterior distribution of β with an informative prior

strained to be similar. We again ran the sampler for 2,000 steps three times and retained the final 1,000 of each chain giving 3,000 realizations from the joint posterior distribution. The marginal posterior histogram for β is shown in figure 8.12, with the prior density superimposed as the solid line.

Comparison of posteriors under diffuse and informative priors

One interesting comparison is between the marginal densities under the diffuse and informative priors shown here and in the left frame of figure 8.10. It seems that the principal effect of the informative prior is to more or less eliminate the extreme tails of the distribution. This is an example of shrinkage that we discussed in section 7.3.6. In figure 8.12 we no longer see the realizations of −40% or +200% that were present in figure 8.10, and indeed a QQ plot shows that the new posterior is almost normal and in this respect quite unlike the bizarrely thick-tailed earlier distribution.

For a numerical comparison we can look at the 95% hpd intervals which are as shown in table 8.2.

Table 8.2 HPD intervals under two priors

	lower	upper
diffuse	0	46%
informative	−1%	25%

The length of the confidence interval has been sharply reduced, but it is still very wide. Another comparison is to look at the quantiles and these, expressed in percentages, are as shown in table 8.3.

Table 8.3 Quantiles of the rate of return

	min	q_{25}	q_{50}	mean	q_{75}	max
diffuse	−40	10	15	17	21	220
informative	−15	8	12	12	16	37

Comparison of priors and posteriors

When we compare the relatively informative prior with the posterior histogram in figure 8.12 we see some change, but not a lot. The locations are roughly the same but the posterior is somewhat more concentrated than the prior. Relative to these prior beliefs the instruments seem to have provided a rather small amount of information.

What do we conclude?

- It appears that even with about 36,000 observations and a simple model with very few parameters there is not enough information to make precise estimates of the marginal rate of return. This is true even under relatively informative prior beliefs. The data transform such beliefs into less dispersed and more peaked posteriors but these are still not adequate to provide an accurate assessment of the rate of return.

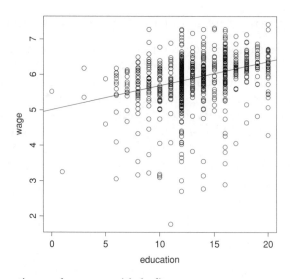

Figure 8.13 Education and wages, with ls fit

- Another valuable conclusion is that, even with this sample size, it is vital to compute exact posterior distributions that reveal the true nature of our uncertainty.
- A third implication of this section is that by using MCMC methods such exact inferences can be made very easily.

8.7.1   Is education endogenous?

These rather imprecise inferences about a parameter that is of major importance, the rate of return to investment in education, are disappointing. It would have been so much simpler to regress (log) wages on education by least squares. Here is what happens if you do. Figure 8.13 plots a randomly selected subsample of size 1,000 of the education and wage data with the least squares fit (using the whole sample) superimposed upon it.

The least squares line is

$$\text{wage} = 5.010(0.014) + 0.0680(0.001) \text{ education}$$

The coefficients are very sharply determined and the posterior mean, median and mode of the rate of return is 6.8% with a standard error of one tenth of one percent. Why can't we accept this estimate? The answer is, of course, that we have been presuming that education is endogenous, that its effect on wages is confounded with that of the numerous other potential determinants of wages. And under this belief the least squares estimates are (very precisely) wrong. But there is still hope for the least squares estimate since we have not, yet, shown that this presumption is true!

Consider how we might check to see whether education really is endogenous. We reproduce the structural form of the model for convenience here. It is

$$educ_i = \gamma + \delta z_i + \varepsilon_{1i}$$
$$wage_i = \alpha + \beta \, educ_i + \varepsilon_{2i},$$

where z stands for the quarter of birth instruments. We showed earlier that if ε_2 and ε_1 are uncorrelated then the second equation is a regression, the system is fully recursive, and standard regression methods, like least squares, can be used to make inferences about β. But if ε_2 and ε_1 are correlated then these methods are inappropriate and we must proceed as above with the consequent disappointing precision. So why don't we see if these errors are correlated? One way of doing this is to look at the posterior distribution of the correlation coefficient of ε_2 and ε_1. We can do this as follows. For the purposes of our calculation we represented the model as the restricted reduced form

$$educ_i = \gamma + \delta z_i + v_{1i}$$
$$wage_i = \alpha^* + \beta\delta z_i + v_{2i}.$$

The relation between the structural and reduced form errors is

$$\begin{pmatrix} \varepsilon_1 \\ \varepsilon_2 \end{pmatrix} = \begin{pmatrix} 1 & 0 \\ -\beta & 1 \end{pmatrix} \begin{pmatrix} v_1 \\ v_2 \end{pmatrix} \tag{8.14}$$

or $\varepsilon = Bv$. Thus $V(\varepsilon) = BV(v)B' = BP^{-1}(v)B'$, where $P(v)$ is the precision of the reduced form errors which, in our BUGS program, we denoted by q, thus $V(\varepsilon) = Bq^{-1}B'$. We can now use this equation to express the correlation between the structural form errors in terms of β and the reduced form precision matrix q, and we find

$$\rho_{\varepsilon_2, \varepsilon_1} = \frac{-\beta q_{22} - q_{12}}{\sqrt{q_{22}(q_{11} + 2\beta q_{12} + \beta^2 q_{22})}}.$$

Finally, to inspect the posterior distribution of ρ we substitute the 3,000 realizations of the four parameters on the right into this formula and the result is the same number of realizations from the posterior distribution of ρ whose histogram is shown in figure 8.14.

The mean and median correlation are both about -0.25 but the standard deviation is 0.26, and 517 out of 3,000 realizations are positive. The posterior suggests that the structural form errors are negatively correlated and this is a bit surprising on the hypothesis that a major element of both ε_1 and ε_2 is "ability" and this variable tends to affect positively both education and wages. But the evidence is very far from conclusive.

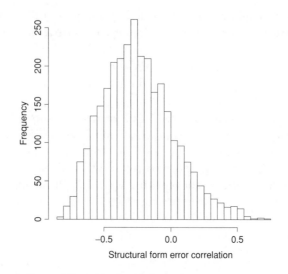

Figure 8.14 Correlation of the structural form errors

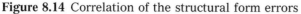

Digression ***Poorly measured education*** *Years of schooling is surely a poor measure of the "amount" of education. Suppose that there is a correct measure of education, call it x*, and it is this that determines the wage. On the other hand, quarter of birth determines years of schooling. So an alternative system is*

$$x = \gamma + \delta z + \varepsilon_1$$
$$y = \alpha + \beta x^* + \varepsilon_2.$$

Let the error in x be denoted by x** so that x = x* + x**. Then these equations imply

$$x = \gamma + \delta z + \varepsilon_1$$
$$y = \alpha + \beta x + (\varepsilon_2 - \beta x^{**}).$$

Now if β, the marginal return to a year of education, is positive we might expect ε_1 and $\varepsilon_2 - \beta x^{**}$ to be negatively correlated, though of course the actual correlation depends also on the association of ε_1 and ε_2. This is because when x, and so x**, is unexpectedly large there is a presumption that $\varepsilon_2 - \beta x^{**}$ will be unexpectedly small. This is a possible explanation for the negative correlation of the structural form errors suggested by figure 8.14.[11]

---

[11] This argument was suggested by Griliches (1977). It and several other possibilities are discussed by Card (2001). See the bibliographic notes.

- So is education endogenous? The evidence leaves us unsure. A weak instrument makes it difficult to come to a precise conclusion about the rate of return and, ironically, it also makes it difficult to be sure that an instrumental variable was needed in the first place!

This concludes our study of the application of instrumental variable methods to a real economic problem. We now turn briefly to a look at a classic econometric problem that arises when we observe a market in equilibrium. The connection between this problem and the recursive equations that we have just been studying is that a market equilibrium model leads to a system of equations that, in a formal sense, generalizes the recursive structure.

8.8 SIMULTANEOUS EQUATIONS

The two equation linear recursive structure we have been studying is probably the simplest likelihood structure when the model is described by a system of equations, but the idea of an instrumental variable or randomizer is far more general.

A mathematical generalization of the linear recursive model that has had great importance in econometrics and which was in fact the first instance of endogeneity in linear systems to be studied, as long ago as 1930, is the simultaneous equations model. This derives from thinking about markets that are in equilibrium. Revisiting example 6.2 of chapter 6, let $d = d(p, z_d)$ represent the market demand curve for a good or service, for example potatoes, and let $s = s(p, z_s)$ be the corresponding supply curve. Thus d represents the amount that would (collectively) be demanded if the price were to be p and a set of other variables that affect demand has the value z_d, and there is a similar interpretation for the supply curve. Equilibrium comes in when we can only observe d and s when the price p is such as to *clear the market*, that is, to equate d and s. There is some mechanism that is *left unspecified in the theory* that ensures that all trades are made at the market clearing price. Thus p solves $d(p, z_d) = s(p, z_s) = q$, say, where q is the quantity of the good or service traded at that equilibrium price. Again, to make matters concrete, consider linear demand and supply equations

$$d = \alpha_0 + \alpha_1 p + \alpha_2 z_d$$
$$s = \beta_0 + \beta_1 p + \beta_2 z_s. \tag{8.15}$$

But since we only observe the market when the price p clears it, the observed data are q, p satisfying

$$q = \alpha_0 + \alpha_1 p + \alpha_2 z_d$$
$$q = \beta_0 + \beta_1 p + \beta_2 z_s.$$

This is a pair of simultaneous (not recursive) equations in q and p and it admits of a unique solution provided $\alpha_1 \neq \beta_1$. To see this subtract the first equation from the second and, if $\alpha_1 \neq \beta_1$, solve for p;[12] then substitute the solution for p in either equation to solve for q. The result is

$$p = \frac{\beta_0 - \alpha_0}{\alpha_1 - \beta_1} - \frac{\alpha_2}{\alpha_1 - \beta_1} z_d + \frac{\beta_2}{\alpha_1 - \beta_1} z_s$$

$$q = \frac{\alpha_1 \beta_0 - \alpha_0 \beta_1}{\alpha_1 - \beta_1} - \frac{\beta_1 \alpha_2}{\alpha_1 - \beta_1} z_d + \frac{\alpha_1 \beta_2}{\alpha_1 - \beta_1} z_s.$$

(8.16)

The system (8.15) is of the form $g(y, z) = 0$, with y identified as (q, p) and z identified as (z_d, z_s), and thus is of the general form that we have been arguing is the starting point for a specifically *econometric* analysis. The system (8.16) shows explicitly the solution for the variables that the economic model is designed to explain.

If we now modify our deterministic specification of the demand and supply curves to allow for "error" terms we get

$$q = \alpha_0 + \alpha_1 p + \alpha_2 z_d + \varepsilon_d \tag{8.17}$$

$$q = \beta_0 + \beta_1 p + \beta_2 z_s + \varepsilon_s. \tag{8.18}$$

This is the structural form of the model in the sense that each of the two relations between q and p, (8.17) and (8.18), correspond to objects appearing in our theory, namely, the demand curve and the supply curve. If we now compare this system to that derived by the randomization argument given earlier, (8.5) and (8.6), and we can see that the present system, with the interpretations, say, $p = x$, $q = y$, $\{z_d, z_s\} = z$, is, at least mathematically, a generalization of the earlier one to which it reduces when $\alpha_1 = \beta_2 = 0$, for the structural form then becomes

$$q = \alpha_0 + \alpha_2 z_d + \varepsilon_d$$
$$q = \beta_0 + \beta_1 p + \varepsilon_s.$$

This is just (8.7) and (8.8) with the roles of q and p interchanged in the second equation. It should be emphasized, however, that this resemblance is only mathematical. There was no hypothesis of equilibrium in our formulation of the recursive system.

---

12 If $\alpha_1 = \beta_1 = \gamma$, say, then subtract the second equation of (8.15) from the first to find that $\alpha_0 + \alpha_2 z_d = \beta_0 + \beta_2 z_s = c$, say, so the structural form reduces to

$$q = c + \gamma p,$$
$$q = c + \gamma p.$$

In other words there is only one equation available to solve for the two unknowns and there will be, not a unique solution for (q, p), but an infinity of such solutions! Note that α_1 is the marginal response of demand to price, and presumably negative, and β_1 is the marginal response of supply to price, and presumably positive, so the condition that $\alpha_1 \neq \beta_1$ is plausible.

The coefficients in these equations are objects of economic interest and we need to see whether we can recover them from observations on q, p and the z's made when the market is in equilibrium. The answer to this question is "yes, if . . ." And, as with recursive systems, the answer hinges on what we can learn from the reduced form.

Digression *Random prices* *Before answering this question let us briefly return to the point made in chapter 1 that there is usually more than one type of data that could be used to estimate and test an economic model. Here, for example, one could imagine a designed experiment in which the investigator randomly announces prices to potential consumers who respond with a statement of how much they, collectively, are willing to buy at that price, and similarly potential suppliers announce how much they are willing to supply. This means that you are observing values for d and s at randomly selected values of p. The first set of responses must trace out the demand curve and the second the supply curve. The parameters of these curves can then be estimated by regressions of d on p and of s on p, in view of the fact that the covariate p has been randomized. This remark implies that the difficulties of identification and inference that we are now discussing are, in a sense, entirely due to the assumption that the markets we observe are in equilibrium.*[13]

Solving the structural system for q and p gives

$$p = \frac{\beta_0 - \alpha_0}{\alpha_1 - \beta_1} - \frac{\alpha_2}{\alpha_1 - \beta_1} z_d + \frac{\beta_2}{\alpha_1 - \beta_1} z_s + \frac{\varepsilon_s - \varepsilon_d}{\alpha_1 - \beta_1} \tag{8.19}$$

$$q = \frac{\alpha_1 \beta_0 - \alpha_0 \beta_1}{\alpha_1 - \beta_1} - \frac{\beta_1 \alpha_2}{\alpha_1 - \beta_1} z_d + \frac{\alpha_1 \beta_2}{\alpha_1 - \beta_1} z_s + \frac{\alpha_1 \varepsilon_s - \beta_1 \varepsilon_d}{\alpha_1 - \beta_1}. \tag{8.20}$$

The variables in z_d and z_s in this approach are typically assumed to have the properties of instrumental variables in that they are taken to be distributed independently of the error terms and, by hypothesis, they are correlated with the variables q, p which are jointly dependent variables in this model. There is no general argument as to why the covariates in z_d and z_s should be independent of the error terms. The credibility of this belief needs to be established on a case by case basis.[14] So this set-up is quite different from the earlier situation in which z is selected by a chance mechanism.

---

13 It is possible to write down and estimate a model in which the market is not in equilibrium. But in this case you have to state how price is determined if it is neither market clearing nor randomized.

14 For an early discussion see the paper by Koopmans cited in the bibliographical material for chapter 6.

We now show that neither structural form equation is, in general, a regression model.

THEOREM 8.1　*Neither equation of the structural form is a regression equation.*

　Proof　*To see this let us rewrite the rather complex equations (8.19) and (8.20) as*

$$p = \mu_p + v_p$$
$$q = \mu_q + v_q$$

where μ_p, μ_q stand for the linear functions of the covariates z_d, z_s in these equations and v_p, v_q stand for the two linear combinations of the structural form errors. Then since, given z_d, z_s, q and p are bivariate normal the regression of q on p[15] is of the form

$$E(q|p, z_d, z_d) = \mu_q + \frac{\sigma_{qp}}{\sigma_{pp}}(p - \mu_p)$$

where the σ's are the covariance of v_p, v_s and the variance of v_p. If we write these expressions in terms of the variances and covariances of ε_s, ε_p we find that the coefficient of p in the regression of q on p, z_d, z_s is

$$\frac{\sigma_{qp}}{\sigma_{pp}} = \frac{\alpha_1 var \, \varepsilon_s + \beta_1 var \, \varepsilon_d - (\beta_1 + \alpha_1) cov \, \varepsilon_s \varepsilon_d}{var \, \varepsilon_s + var \, \varepsilon_d - 2 \, cov \, \varepsilon_s \varepsilon_d}. \tag{8.21}$$

This expression is not equal to α_1 nor is it equal to β_1 so neither (8.17) nor (8.18) represents the regression of q on p.

This agument generalizes that at the end of section 8.3 where we showed that $E(y|x, z)$ was not a regression either. Generally speaking, linear relations between jointly dependent variables in an equation system are not regressions and must not be analyzed, using linear model techniques, as though they are.

8.8.1　*Likelihood identification*

The major issue with simultaneous equations systems is whether the parameters of the structural form can be identified from the joint distribution of the (potential) data. We have already seen an example of likelihood non-identification in our discussion of the recursive model in which, if the coefficient on the instrument is zero, the joint distribution of the data carries no information about β. With the supply

---

15　See section 3.8.3 of the appendix to chapter 3.

and demand model the likelihood is given by the joint distribution of q, p as given by the reduced form, (8.19) and (8.20). Inspection of this expression shows that q, p are jointly normally distributed with mean μ_p, μ_q and covariance matrix that of v_p, v_s. The question of likelihood identification is whether, from a knowledge of the coefficients appearing in these means and covariance matrix, we could deduce the parameters of the structural form (8.17) and (8.18). That this is a serious issue can be seen from the observation that we made in chapter 6 that if neither z_d nor z_s appear in the model, i.e. both α_2 and β_2 are zero, then neither the demand elasticity, α_1, nor the supply elasticity, β_1, could be deduced from the likelihood. Without the presence of exogenous covariates, i.e. instruments, the fundamental relations of our theory cannot be determined from data on markets in equilibrium.

The answer to this question as given in the traditional literature is to show that if the structural coefficients satisfy certain exact linear restrictions then some or all of the remaining structural coefficients could be deduced from a knowledge of the reduced form. (Examples of such beliefs are that certain elements of α_2 or β_2 are zero; these are called **exclusion** restrictions.) This amounts to asserting that a given set of dogmatic prior beliefs suffices to identify other structural coefficients. The Bayesian point of view on these questions is rather different. In this the question is whether certain prior beliefs, dogmatic or otherwise, combine with the likelihood to produce a proper posterior distribution. If they do, then what, if anything, do we learn from the data about the key structural coefficients? Such prior beliefs can be, of course, not only dogmatic but also stochastic. For example one widely acceptable belief that is readily incorporated in a Bayesian belief is that demand curves probably slope down, $\alpha_1 < 0$, and that market supply curves slope up, $\beta_1 > 0$!

We now turn briefly to inference and explain the basis for the BUGS program for simultaneous equations models given in appendix 3.

8.8.2 Inference in simultaneous equations models

Given a simultaneous equations model in structural form, such as (8.17) and (8.18), we can solve it for the reduced form, as in (8.19) and (8.20). Under bivariate normality for the reduced form errors, given z_d, z_s, the joint distribution of q, p is itself normal with means given by μ_p, μ_q. With independence across observations the likelihood is the product of such terms and so the heart of BUGS code for a simultaneous equations model would look something like the following, which slightly generalizes the code given in section 8.6.2.

```
model{
for(i in 1:n){y[i,1:2] ~dmnorm(mu[i,],R[,])
mu[i,1] <- ap + bp[1]*zd[i] + bp[2] * zs[i]
mu[i,2] <- aq + bq[1]*zd[i] + bq[2] * zs[i]
}
#the columns of y are p and q.
```

```
ap ~dnorm(0,.001)
aq ~dnorm(0,.001)
for(i in 1:2){bp[i] ~dnorm(0,.001)
bq[i] ~dnorm(0,.001)}
R[1:2,1:2] ~dwish(Omega[,],2)}
}
```

This models the reduced form with all coefficients being given conventional priors. Since econometric interest centers on the structural form coefficients these could be calculated from the sampler realizations of bp and bq, the relations between them being provided by (8.19) and (8.20). This is all right if there is a one-to-one relation between structural and reduced form coefficients, but when the structure is over-identified and the reduced form is restricted the model will have to be written in terms of the restricted reduced form by writing, say, -alpha2/(alpha1 - beta1) for bp[1], etc. This is also more appropriate since the econometrician's prior beliefs will typically refer to the structural and not to the reduced form coefficients. We leave this as an exercise for the reader. There is a moderately extensive Bayesian literature on simultaneous equations: for example, the work of Drèze and co-authors mentioned in the bibliographic notes. This work tends to be heavily algebraic and largely pre-dates the development of MCMC methods. There have been remarkably few empirical Bayesian simultaneous equations models published and none, I think, using BUGS.

8.9 CONCLUDING REMARKS ABOUT INSTRUMENTAL VARIABLES

An argument that some variable is a valid instrument is, in effect, a claim that some set of explanatory variables has been, at least in part, randomly allocated to agents. If this argument is accepted then inference about structural parameters can proceed as if the observational data that is available to economists has the character of the results of a randomized trial. In this chapter we have shown how Bayesian inference can proceed, under this belief, in a situation where the relations of interest are linear. The argument can be extended to non-linear models. Consider, for example, binary data where in the latent data model the explanatory variables must be presumed correlated with the error term, but there is available an instrumental variable correlated with the included explanatory variables but independent of the errors. Very much the same argument as that given above will apply here and plausible posterior distributions can be computed. We shall not pursue the non-linear extensions, but note that the same issues that arise with weak instruments in the linear case will be relevant in the non-linear case as well. In particular, it will be critical to compute exact posterior distibutions and not to rely on asymptotic normal approximations to the posterior.

8.10 BIBLIOGRAPHIC NOTES

Posterior densities in linear models with instrumental variables have been studied mathematically by many writers. Notable references include Chao and Phillips (2002: 251–83); Kleibergen and van Dijk (1998: 701–43); Kleibergen and Zivot (*forthcoming* 2003). A frequent conclusion of these researchers is that when instruments are weak and priors diffuse, marginal posterior densities tend to look like (thick-tailed) Cauchy distributions. The marginal posterior densities shown in this chapter in the weak instrument/diffuse prior cases look like Cauchy densities. For a graphical approach similar to the one taken in this chapter see the unpublished note from Princeton University, *Thinking about Instrumental Variables*, by C. Sims. Kleibergen and van Dijk drew graphs similar to figures 8.7 and 8.8 in their study of another case of non-identifiability which arises in time series econometrics.

Earlier work on simultaneous equations is summarized in Drèze and Richard (1983). The Angrist and Krueger paper using the data studied in section 8.6 is J. D. Angrist and A. B. Krueger, Does compulsory school attendance affect schooling and earnings, *Quarterly Journal of Economics*, 106, 979–1014, 1991. Their analysis was frequentist and relied heavily on asymptotic normal approximations to sampling distributions. A number of subsequent papers, e.g. Staiger (1997: 557–86); Bound, Jaeger, and Baker (1995: 443–50), have shown that such approximations can be very poor when instruments are weak and have proposed alternative approximations to sampling distributions in such contexts. See also Jaeger and Bound (1994). Chamberlain and Imbens (circa 1996) seem to have been the first to use hierarchical priors in the context of recursive simultaneous systems in econometrics.

Griliches (1977: 1–22) is a major source on the relation between wages and education. Card (2001: 1127–60), particularly pages 1155–7, in effect discusses potential correlations of structural form errors, although he does so in an indirect, frequentist, way by focusing on differences between least squares and "instrumental variable" estimates. Such differences reflect the correlation in the structural form errors – for example if they are uncorrelated the differences should not exist.

There are many expositions of simultaneous equations models in the literature but it is still worth looking at one of the very first, namely J. Tinbergen, Determination and interpretation of supply curves, originally published, in German, in *Zeitschrift fur Nationalokonomie*, 1930, I, pp. 669–79 and translated in *The Foundations of Econometric Analysis*, eds. D. F. Hendry and M. S. Morgan, Cambridge University Press (1995). This foundational paper is recommended reading.

Chapter 9
SOME TIMES SERIES MODELS

Time series data typically exhibit dependence between successive observations. A characteristic example of a model for time series data is the autoregression in which the model specifies that successive values of a series are correlated and the object of interest is the type and numerical value of this dependence – how strongly, and in what way y_t depends on y_{t-1} and preceding values in the series. The output of an MCMC calculation is a time series. Time series models are sometimes analyzed as though they were a slight variant of the linear regression models of chapter 3, but this is not so and, in particular, they can create special problems for a default or objective Bayesian analysis.

The goal of this chapter is to explain the essentials of the Bayesian approach to inference about time series models.[1] We shall try to do this by studying two specific time series models. For each of these we shall explain the model and demonstrate how the relevant posterior and predictive distributions can be calculated. We shall begin with a simple autoregression in which the dependence lies between the means of successive observations and go on to another model in which the dependence arises in the second moments. There are many time series models that have been of interest to economists and the reader, after reviewing this chapter, should be able to make Bayesian inferences about them.

9.1 FIRST ORDER AUTOREGRESSION

A model we have considered several times already, both in chapter 1 and in our discussion of markov processes in chapter 4, is the first order autoregression that can be described, in part, by the equations

$$y_t = \alpha + \rho y_{t-1} + \varepsilon_t, \quad t = 1, 2, ..., T. \tag{9.1}$$

---

1   There is a very large number of models for time series that are used in econometrics. I shall make no attempt to survey these. The text by Hamilton (1994) gives a clear account of such models, although his approach to inference about them is almost entirely frequentist.

This model asserts that for $t = 1, 2, \ldots, T$ each value of Y is a linear function of the previous value in the series plus an error, just as in a regression model. And just as in the regression model this model is over-parametrized and we can proceed only by adopting a proper prior, for example for the vector $\varepsilon = (\varepsilon_1, \varepsilon_2, \ldots, \varepsilon_T)$. As with the normal linear model a natural and simple starting point is to view these T unknowns hierarchically as independently normally distributed with means zero and common precision τ. This specification must however be conditional on the remaining model parameters which in this case are α, ρ and y_0, the initial condition. Thus the specification is

$$p(\varepsilon \,|\, \alpha, \rho, \tau, y_0) = \text{iid } n(0, \tau I_T). \tag{9.2}$$

The belief (9.2) is sufficient to define the joint distribution of the data $y = (y_1, y_2, \ldots, y_T)$ given α, ρ, τ and y_0. To see this, consider the change of variable from ε to y and work out the jacobian of the transformation. For example, consider the case $T = 2$ and write out the equations of (9.1) as

$$\begin{aligned} y_2 &= \alpha + \rho y_1 + \varepsilon_2 \\ y_1 &= \alpha + \rho y_0 + \varepsilon_1. \end{aligned} \tag{9.3}$$

Then the jacobian matrix is

$$\frac{\partial \varepsilon}{\partial y} = \begin{bmatrix} \dfrac{\partial \varepsilon_2}{\partial y_2} & \dfrac{\partial \varepsilon_2}{\partial y_1} \\[2ex] \dfrac{\partial \varepsilon_1}{\partial y_2} & \dfrac{\partial \varepsilon_1}{\partial y_1} \end{bmatrix} = \begin{bmatrix} 1 & -\rho \\ 0 & 1 \end{bmatrix}$$

whose determinant is one.[2] This is true, in fact, for every T and so the joint distribution of y can be found simply by substituting $y_t - \alpha - \rho y_{t-1}$ in place of ε_t in the joint normal distribution of ε. This gives a likelihood conditional on α, ρ, τ and y_0 as

$$p(y \,|\, y_0, \alpha, \rho, \tau) = \ell(\alpha, \rho \,|\, y, y_0) \propto \tau^{T/2} \exp\{-(\tau/2)\Sigma_{t=1}^{T}(y_t - \alpha - \rho y_{t-1})^2\};$$
$$\text{for} \quad -\infty < \alpha, \rho < \infty; \quad \tau > 0. \tag{9.4}$$

The data here are $y_0, y_1, \ldots, y_T$ but the likelihood is written for the distribution of the last T of these variables, conditional on the first, y_0.

It is possible that you are also willing to assign a distribution to Y_0. One way of doing this is to suppose that the random variables that you are about to observe form a section of a markov process which is in stationary equilibrium in the sense

---

2 The determinant of a triangular matrix, such as this one, is the product of the diagonal elements.

defined in chapter 4. In this case, it will be recalled, each realization of Y comes from the stationary distribution of the process which, for the present model, is[3]

$$p(y|\alpha, \rho, \tau) = n\left(\frac{\alpha}{1 - \rho}, \tau(1 - \rho^2)\right).$$

Then you could assign this distribution to Y_0 and and multiply it into (9.4) to form a likelihood for the whole series of length $T + 1$ rather than for the last T given the first. This only makes sense if the process could be in stationary equilibrium, which requires that $|\rho| < 1$. Whether it is plausible to assign Y_0 this distribution and to adopt $|\rho| < 1$ as a dogmatic restriction on the parameter space is context specific. For example, if Y is the wages of a person in successive years beginning with the year after he leaves school, talk of stationary equilibrium seems far fetched. In another context it may be more persuasive. But, either way, it is not *necessary* to model Y_0 – you can argue conditionally on its observed value.

The model composed of (9.1) and (9.2) is called an autoregression but in what sense is there a regression function involved? Consider the expectation of Y_t given y_{t-1}, α and ρ. This is $E(Y_t|y_{t-1}, \alpha, \rho)$ and from (9.1) this is equal to $\alpha + \rho y_{t-1} + E(\varepsilon_t|\alpha, \rho, y_{t-1})$. But as can be seen from (9.1) y_{t-1} is a function only of α, ρ and values of ε dated before period t. And since (9.2) specifies that the $\{\varepsilon_t\}$ are independent it follows that $E(\varepsilon_t|\alpha, \rho, y_{t-1})$ is equal to its marginal expectation of zero. Hence

$$E(Y_t|y_{t-1}...y_1, \alpha, \rho) = \alpha + \rho y_{t-1}.$$

The mean of Y_t given previous realizations is a linear function of, and only of, y_{t-1} (together with parameters). This is why the model composed of (9.1) and (9.2) is called an *auto*regressive model.

STRICTLY EXOGENOUS AND PREDETERMINED VARIABLES

We can formally write the autoregressive model for all $T + 1$ observations as

$$y = \alpha j_T + \rho y_- + \varepsilon \tag{9.5}$$

where y_- is the vector containing $(y_0, y_1, ..., y_{T-1})$ and $y = (y_1, y_2, ..., y_T)$. This looks like a linear regression model with intercept α and regressor vector given by y_-. But in the present model, with prior (9.2), the error vector and "regressor" vector y_- are necessarily dependent! To see this consider the case $T = 2$ represented by the equations (9.3). The covariance of ε_1 with y_2 is

---

3   To verify that this is so you may substitute this density as $p(x)$ into equation (4.13), using $n(\alpha + \rho x, \tau)$ as the transition kernel, and see that such a $p(.)$ solves the equation.

$$E(\varepsilon_1 y_2) = E(\varepsilon_1[\alpha + \rho y_1 + \varepsilon_2])$$
$$= \rho E(\varepsilon_1 y_1) \quad \text{since } E(\varepsilon_1) = E(\varepsilon_1 \varepsilon_2) = 0$$
$$= \rho E(\varepsilon_1[\alpha + \rho y_0 + \varepsilon_1])$$
$$= \rho \, var(\varepsilon_1) \quad \text{since } E(\varepsilon_1 | \alpha, \rho, y_0) = 0$$

and this is not zero unless ρ is zero. It follows that although (9.5) looks like a linear regression model of the type considered in chapter 3 for which we took the errors and the covariates to be independent, in this model the errors and "covariate" y_- cannot be independent. The vector y_- is not exogenous. Instead we call it **predetermined**. The reason for this is that calculations of the type just given show that each element of y_- is correlated with all elements of ε that refer to earlier dates but not with contemporaneous or future elements of ε. In the case $T = 3$, if we put ε and y_- side by side we have

$$\begin{bmatrix} \varepsilon_3 \\ \varepsilon_2 \\ \varepsilon_1 \end{bmatrix}, \quad \begin{bmatrix} y_2 \\ y_1 \\ y_0 \end{bmatrix}$$

and we see that, from the model, y_2 is necessarily correlated with ε_2 and ε_1 but not with ε_3; similarly y_1 is necessarily correlated with ε_1 but not with ε_2 or ε_3. In these circumstances we say that a vector like y_- is a vector of **predetermined variables** which are dependent on previous elements of the error vector but not on their contemporaneous values.

Interpretation of parameters

The interpretation of the parameters is critical to a satisfactory Bayesian analysis because if you don't understand what job a parameter does then how can you form a view about its likely value? Interpretation of parameters in models such as the present one needs some thought and can be quite complicated. For example, the interpretation of one parameter can depend on the value taken by another. Consider the interpretation of the intercept parameter α. To understand this let us represent each y_t in the model as a function of the initial value, y_0, and the sequence of error terms. We can do this by replacing y_{t-1} in (9.1) by $\alpha + \rho y_{t-2} + \varepsilon_{t-1}$ to get

$$y_t = \alpha + \alpha\rho + \rho^2 y_{t-2} + \varepsilon_t + \rho\varepsilon_{t-1},$$

and continuing in this way we eventually find that

$$y_t = \alpha(1 + \rho + \rho^2 + \ldots + \rho^{t-1}) + \rho^t y_0 + (\varepsilon_t + \rho\varepsilon_{t-1} + \ldots + \rho^{t-1}\varepsilon_1), \quad (9.6)$$

for $t = 1, 2, \ldots, T$. From this representation we can immediately see that, because the ε_t have zero means, the mean value of Y_t changes from period to period[4] and is,

---

4 Unless $y_0 = \alpha/1 - \rho$.

in each period, a complicated function of both α and ρ and the initial condition. This is in sharp contrast to a linear model of the form $y_t = \alpha + \beta(x_t - \bar{x}) + \varepsilon_t$ in which α is the expectation of the average of the Y values appearing in the sample.

If the process is stationary and $|\rho| < 1$ the first sum on the right hand side of (9.6) will be close to $\alpha/(1 - \rho)$, the stationary mean of Y, when t is large, and the term $\rho^t y_0$ will be negligible. So in this case α is proportional to the (equilibrium) mean of each Y_t. On the other hand if $\rho = 1$ then

$$y_t = t\alpha + y_0 + (\varepsilon_t + \varepsilon_{t-1} + \ldots + \varepsilon_1) \tag{9.7}$$

whose expectation is $t\alpha + y_0$. In this case α is the coefficient on a time trend in the mean. This is what we meant by saying that the interpretation of a parameter can depend on the value taken by another parameter, in this case ρ.

The case in which $\rho = 1$ is an instance of a process with a **unit root**. When $\rho = 1$, equation (9.1) becomes

$$y_t = \alpha + y_{t-1} + \varepsilon_t, \quad \text{or} \quad y_t - y_{t-1} = \alpha + \varepsilon_t \tag{9.8}$$

which is called a **random walk** with **drift** α. Such a process is not stationary and, as can be seen from (9.7), the realization at any date t always depends on the initial value, y_0, and is equally dependent on all error terms no matter how far in the past they occurred. Some people argue that such "persistence of shocks" is of economic significance and this controversy has given rise to many attempts to determine whether macroeconomic time series show evidence of a unit root.

9.1.1 Likelihoods and priors

Let us recapitulate the likelihood under the hypothesis that $\varepsilon_1, \varepsilon_3, \ldots, \varepsilon_T$ are iid $n(0, \tau)$ given y_0, α and ρ.

$$p(y|y_0, \alpha, \rho, \tau) \propto \ell(\alpha, \rho, \tau; y_1, y)$$
$$\propto \tau^{T/2} \exp\{-(\tau/2)\Sigma_{t=1}^{T}(y_t - \alpha - \rho y_{t-1})^2\}; \tag{9.9}$$
$$\text{for} \quad -\infty < \alpha, \rho < \infty; \quad \tau > 0.$$

An alternative likelihood is available under the stationarity condition $|\rho| < 1$ and the additional assumption that the process when observed is remote from its origin because in this case we know the marginal distribution of Y_0 which is $n(\mu, \tau(1 - \rho^2))$ where $\mu = \alpha/(1 - \rho)$. In this case we can use the joint distribution of $Y_0, \ldots, Y_T$ and not its conditional distribution given Y_0. This gives the likelihood

$$p(y, y_0|\alpha, \rho, \tau) = p(y|y_0, \alpha, \rho, \tau)p(y_0|\alpha, \rho, \tau)$$
$$= \tau^{T/2} \exp\{-(\tau/2)\Sigma_{t=1}^{T}(y_t - \alpha - \rho y_{t-1})^2\}$$
$$\times \tau^{1/2}(1 - \rho^2)^{1/2} \exp\{-(\tau/2)(1 - \rho^2)(y_0 - \mu)^2\} \tag{9.10}$$
$$-\infty < \alpha < \infty; \quad |\rho| < 1; \tau > 0,$$

where $\mu = \alpha/(1 - \rho)$. Alternatively we can write the likelihood as a function of μ, ρ and τ:

$$\ell(\mu, \rho, \tau) \propto \tau^{T/2} \exp\{-(\tau/2)\Sigma_{t=1}^{T}(y_t - \mu(1 - \rho) - \rho y_{t-1})^2\}\tau^{1/2}(1 - \rho^2)^{1/2}$$
$$\times \exp\{-(\tau/2)(1 - \rho^2)(y_0 - \mu)^2\}. \tag{9.11}$$

These likelihoods are simple enough under normality (and many other choices can easily be made for the marginal distributions of the $\{\varepsilon_t\}$) and the remaining problem is to formulate a prior.

Many choices of "objective" prior have been proposed in the literature, particularly in connection with the possibility that $\rho = 1$, the unit root hypothesis. In the case where it is asserted a priori that $|\rho| < 1$, so that you dogmatically rule out a unit root, it night be natural to take the prior for ρ as allowing for ρ to be anywhere between plus and minus one. One possibility is a uniform distribution $p(\rho) \propto 1$, $-1 < \rho < 1$. Another is $p(\rho) \propto (1 - \rho^2)^{-1/2}$ which is a proper, U-shaped, prior on $(-1, 1)$.[5] This particular prior, while it may have some objective rationale, would not seem to agree with most people's views about ρ in most contexts that this writer can think of.

In the case in which $\rho \geq 1$ is not dogmatically ruled out someone who prefers to use "objective" rules to formulate their prior beliefs might look to Jeffreys' rule. Phillips (1991) studied this possibility. Jeffreys' prior in this model is algebraically rather complex and, perhaps unfortunately, depends upon the sample size[6] T. This means that your prior views about α and ρ depend upon how long you propose to observe the series. This seems very odd. So Jeffreys' prior in this case appears hard to justify.

In the simpler model in which $y_t = \rho y_{t-1} + \varepsilon_t$, the reference prior approach, mentioned in chapter 1, has been applied by Berger and Yang (1994). A reference prior turns out to have different algebraic forms within and outside the stationary interval $|\rho| < 1$. No further work on this approach in autoregressive problems seems to be available. Berger and Yang remark that even the simple model $y_t = \rho y_{t-1} + \varepsilon_t$ is "surprisingly challenging to 'objective' Bayesians."

Turning to the joint prior for α and ρ we are led to ask whether it is reasonable to take these parameters as independent a priori. Since, under stationarity, the long-run mean is $\mu = \alpha/(1 - \rho)$ some writers argue that it is more appropriate to work in terms of μ and ρ and to take these as independent.

Exact analytical results

In this subsection we give some exact results on posterior distributions for two of the more obvious models.

---

5   To see this, transform according to $z = 1 - \rho^2$ with $d\rho = (1 - z)^{-1/2}dz$ which transforms the integral of ρ from -1 to 1 into that of a beta density on $(0, 1)$ with parameters $\alpha = \beta = 1/2$, which is proper.
6   This is because T appears in the information matrix in a way that is not multiplicative.

Examination of the likelihood (9.9) shows that it has exactly the form of the likelihood for a normal linear regression[7] of the type studied in chapter 3 which, it will be recalled, had kernel given by $\tau^{N/2} \exp\{-(\tau/2)\sum_{i=1}^{N}(y_i - \alpha - \beta x_i)^2\}$, if we interpret N as T and x as y_-. The implication of this remark is that exact analytical results are available *under uniform priors*[8] for α, ρ and $\log \tau$. In particular, given τ, the parameters α, ρ are bivariate normal with precision matrix

$$P(\alpha, \rho) = \tau \begin{bmatrix} N & \sum_{t=1}^{T} y_{t-1} \\ \sum_{t=1}^{T} y_{t-1} & \sum_{t=1}^{T} y_{t-1}^2 \end{bmatrix}.$$

If we reparametrize the model to

$$y_t - \bar{y} = \alpha^* + \rho(y_{t-1} - \bar{y}_-) + \varepsilon_t$$
$$\text{where} \quad \alpha^* = \alpha + \rho \bar{y}_-$$

and $\bar{y}$ is the mean of observations 1 to T and $\bar{y}_-$ is the mean of observations 0 to $T - 1$, then the posterior precision matrix for α^* and ρ becomes diagonal and is

$$P(\alpha^*, \rho) = \tau \begin{bmatrix} N & 0 \\ 0 & \sum_{t=1}^{T}(y_{t-1} - \bar{y}_-)^2 \end{bmatrix}.$$

Furthermore, the posterior mean and median of the α^* and ρ are the least squares estimates, namely

$$E(\alpha^* | \tau, \text{data}) = \widehat{\alpha^*} = \bar{y}$$

$$E(\rho | \tau, \text{data}) = \hat{\rho} = \frac{\sum_{t=1}^{T} y_t(y_{t-1} - \bar{y}_-)}{\sum_{t=1}^{T}(y_{t-1} - \bar{y}_-)^2}.$$

Since these do not depend on τ they are also the unconditional posterior means.

As in chapter 3 the marginal distributions of α and ρ are Student's t densities centered at $\bar{y}$ and the least squares estimate $\hat{\rho}$. So, if your views are well represented by a uniform prior on α, ρ, $\log \tau$, you can proceed exactly as in the linear model and inference is straightforward.

On the other hand, if your views are well represented by a uniform prior on μ, ρ and $\log \tau$ then it is also straightforward to deduce analytically the marginal posterior distribution of ρ. We leave this as an exercise.

---

7   This is another example of the Janus-like character of the autoregressive model – from several points of view it looks like a linear regression model, but fundamentally it is quite different.
8   Similarly, exact analytical results are available for natural conjugate priors.

> **Digression**   *The **sampling distribution** of $\hat{\rho}$ which, of course, depends on ρ, is skewed and takes different forms asymptotically according as $|\rho| < 1$ or $\rho = 1$. So this model provides an instance in which there is a radical practical divergence between Bayesian and frequentist analysts. The paper by Sims and Uhlig (1991) and the responses and discussion in the Journal of Applied Econometrics (1991) trace this controversy.*

9.1.2 BUGS implementation

Implementation of time series models in BUGS is mostly straightforward. Let us examine the general form of the code by considering a model with ρ constrained to be less than one in modulus and in which μ is assigned a diffuse prior and ρ is taken to be uniform between plus and minus one.

```
model{
for(i in 2:n){
y[i] ~ dnorm(m[i],tau)
m[i] <- mu*(1-rho) + rho*y[i-1]
}
rho ~ dunif(-.999,.999)
mu ~ dnorm(0,.001)
tau ~ dgamma(.001,.001)
}
```

This code uses the likelihood conditioned on the (observed) initial value, y_0, so the data input would be $y_0, y_1, y_2, ..., y_n$ but no model is given for y_0. The autoregressive parameter ρ is assigned a uniform prior over the stationary interval from -1 to 1, while the long-run mean of the process, μ (under stationarity), is given a diffuse normal distribution and the precision is given the conventional diffuse gamma. As in all the illustrations in this book there is absolutely no presumption that these priors are sensible. In a practical application you would replace lines 6–8 with your own (defensible) beliefs.

If you wish to model in terms of α, ρ, τ then the fourth line would be replaced by

```
m[i] <- alpha + rho * y[i-1]
```

and the sixth by, say,

```
rho ~ dnorm(0,0.001).
```

If you wish to model the initial observation, y_0, then you could add a statement after line five of the form `y[1]~ . . . .` For example the statement[9]

---

9   Rather irritatingly, you have to use $y[1]$ for the initial observation because S does not accept $y[0]$ as an element of a vector.

```
y[1] ~ dnorm(mu, tau1)
tau1 <- tau*(1-rho^2)
```

would assign to Y_0 its stationary distribution. This only makes sense if stationarity, $|\rho| < 1$, is imposed by the prior.

9.1.3 Some calculations

In this section we shall show some illustrative BUGS calculations using simulated data.[10] The calculations are designed to show two things. The first is how simple it is to calculate posterior distributions in time series models using MCMC. The second is to show the dangers involved in naive use of "objective" priors.

> **EXAMPLE 9.1 POSTERIOR CALCULATIONS WHEN THE LIKELIHOOD IS CONDITIONED ON THE INITIAL OBSERVATION** *We generated a time series of length $n = 51$ following an autoregressive process with $\alpha = 0.3$, $\rho = 0.9$ and $\tau = 1$. The initial value was set as the long-run mean, $\mu = \alpha/(1 - \rho) = 3$. We analyzed the data using two different vague priors. The first uses relatively diffuse priors on α, ρ and $\log \tau$. The second uses correspondingly diffuse priors on μ, ρ and $\log \tau$.[11]*
>
> *Figure 9.1 below plots the data. Figure 9.2 shows the results of two analyses of these data in the form of smoothed histograms of 3,000 realizations of α, μ and ρ derived from parallel BUGS runs of length 2,000 after retaining the second half of each series. Vertical lines have been drawn at the values used to generate the data.*
>
> *The first row of figure 2 shows the posterior densities of α and ρ that follow from a uniform prior on α, ρ. The density of ρ is centered at the least squares estimate which is $\hat{\rho} = 0.816$ in accordance with our analytical results. It shows a characteristic feature of least squares in this model, namely that it is too low, although the true value of ρ, namely 0.9, does not receive low probability density. It has been known since Hurwicz (1950)[12] that the sampling distribution of the least squares estimator of the slope in this model is centered below the true value and this in turn implies that the posterior mean of ρ under this prior will usually be "too low."*
>
> *The second row shows the posterior densities of μ and ρ derived using a diffuse prior on μ, ρ. A glance at the horizontal axis for the first of these figures shows an extraordinarily dispersed and thick-tailed distribution of μ, the stationary mean*

---

10   Readers are strongly advised to carry out analogous calculations for themselves.

11   The calculations using three runs of length 2,000 are virtually instantaneous on a modern laptop computer.

12   L. Hurwicz, Least squares bias in time series, in Koopmans, T. C. (ed.) *Statistical Inference in Dynamic Economic Models*, Cowles Commission Monograph 10, 365–83, New York, Wiley, 1950.

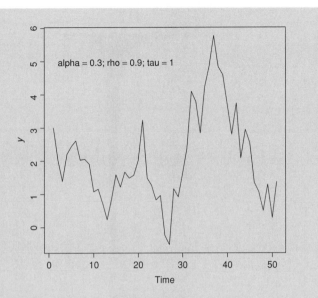

Figure 9.1 An autoregressive time series

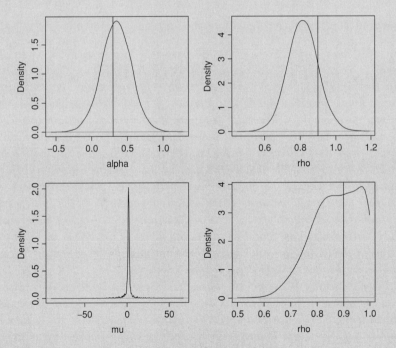

Figure 9.2 Posterior densities using different priors

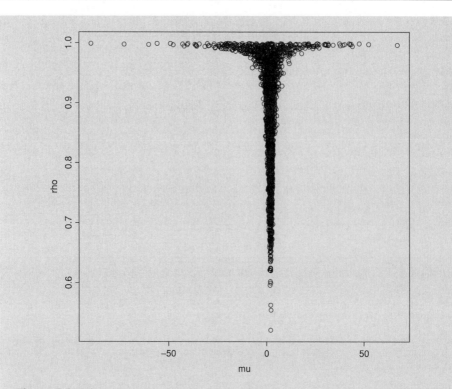

Figure 9.3 Joint posterior density of rho and mu

*of the process. This figure is reminiscent of the density shown in the weak instru-
ments example of section 8.6.3. This is because a similar phenomenon is at work,
local non-identifiability. You will recall from chapter 8 that when the instrument
is uncorrelated with the right hand endogenous variable the coefficient of interest
vanishes from the likelihood. This means that there is a ridge in the likelihood
surface. When that correlation is weak such a ridge remains a dominant feature
of the likelihood surface. The present model of (9.9) with α replaced by μ(1 − ρ)
shows that when ρ = 1 the parameter μ vanishes from the likelihood function and
a similar ridge occurs. When ρ is "nearly" one that ridge remains prominent, μ
will be poorly determined and, from the second figure on the second row, that ridge
emerges in the form of a second mode of the marginal posterior density of ρ near
ρ = 1, even though ρ = 1 has zero posterior density.*

*Instead of looking at the marginal densities of μ and ρ it is even more instruct-
ive to consider their joint density in the form of a scatter diagram of the 3,000
μ, ρ realizations. This scatter diagram is displayed in figure 9.3. The resemblance
to figure 8.8 is striking. It shows clearly the ridge in the likelihood surface near
ρ = 1.*

What should one make of these calculations? Firstly, comparing the two posterior densities for ρ it is clear that inferences about this object are very sensitive to the choice of prior. The likelihood is not dominant for these data. Secondly, neither prior can be thought of as non-informative relative to the data set that we have examined. So neither of these analyses seems to be satisfactory. Choice of prior in this and similar models[13] continues to be a subject of research. In practical terms, sensitivity to the prior indicates that a serious analysis of time series data should consider the consequences of alternative choices of prior. This is straightforward to do, in BUGS for example where you can calculate posterior distributions under many alternative priors within the same MCMC run, but it will make the presentation of your results more complex, though more honest. The second recommendation is that these alternative priors should be chosen to represent a range of defensible views in the light of the economics of the phenomenon under study. A third comment is that since the interpretation of one parameter depends on the values taken by another it might be wise, in thinking about your prior, to think conditionally by, for example, assessing your views conditional on ρ and then forming your views about ρ.

Prediction

Suppose that you wish to predict some future value of the time series, say the values of Y_{T+1} and Y_{T+2}. Since neither of these are in your data set they are uncertain both before and after you have seen the data. Therefore they are parameters. Consider first Y_{T+1} which, from the model, has the representation

$$Y_{T+1} = \alpha + \rho y_T + \varepsilon_{T+1}. \tag{9.12}$$

This formula expresses Y_{T+1} as a function of other model parameters and the realized value of y_T. We wish to study the predictions of Y_{T+1} that are implied by the model and data and the best way to do this is to simulate from its posterior predictive distribution. We see that we can do this by simulating from the posterior distribution of the parameters α, ρ and ε_{T+1}. We already know how to simulate from the joint posterior distribution of α, ρ – such realizations will be generated from the BUGS output. It remains to simulate from the posterior distribution of ε_{T+1}. But, from the model, ε_{T+1} is $n(0, \tau)$ given τ and unconditionally on τ it can be simulated by simulating from the posterior distribution of τ and drawing an $n(0, \tau)$ realization for each such draw. To implement these simulations in BUGS only involves defining the new parameter Y_{T+1} and asking for simulations of its posterior distribution to be included in the output file. To do this involves adding the additional statements, say:

---

13   C. A. Sims (1991) Comment by Christopher A. Sims on "To criticize the critics", by Peter C. B. Phillips, *Journal of Applied Econometrics*, 6, 423–34 contains a more extensive discussion of choice of prior in the autoregressive and related models. This article is strongly recommended.

```
yp1~dnorm(mu1,tau)
mu1 <- mu*(1-rho)+rho*y[n]¹⁴
```

These lines effectively define a new parameter for the model and if you add `yp1` to the parameter list you will find in your output file realizations from the posterior (predictive) distribution of Y_{T+1}.

Similarly, Y_{T+2} has the representation

$$Y_{T+2} = \alpha + \rho Y_{T+1} + \varepsilon_{T+2} \tag{9.13}$$

in which Y_{T+2} is represented as a function now of four parameters, α, ρ, Y_{T+1} and ε_{T+2}. Notice that since there are four unknowns now instead of the three involved in Y_{T+1}, predictions of Y_{T+2} will be more uncertain than those of Y_{T+1}. To produce samples from the posterior distribution of Y_{T+2} you must define this object as an extra parameter of the model with statements such as

```
yp2~dnorm(mu2,tau)
mu2 <- mu*(1-rho)+rho*yp1
```

Adding `yp2` to the list of parameters whose posterior distribution is to be output produces realizations from the posterior predictive distribution of Y_{T+2}. The samples from the posterior densities of Y_{T+1} and Y_{T+2} can then be plotted and studied and, for example, highest posterior density regions can be found so that you can make statements such as "with probability 0.95 the next two realizations will lie in such and such a region."

9.2 STOCHASTIC VOLATILITY

The second example is a model for time series that extends the earlier analysis of heteroscedastic errors by allowing the variances of the errors to be autocorrelated. Here the error variances not only vary from observation to observation but do so in a correlated way. This is a model with a weak economic theoretical foundation but it is rather one which responds to empirical observations that some financial time series appear to show periods of continued high variability and continued low variability. In other words the variances seem (positively) autocorrelated.

Consider the model for time series data $\{y_t\}$ described, for $t = 1, 2, ..., T$, by

$$y_t = e^{h_t/2} u_t, \tag{9.14}$$

$$h_t = \mu + \rho h_{t-1} + v_t \tag{9.15}$$

---

14   We are assuming you are working in the parametrization $\alpha = \mu(1 - \rho)$.

where $\{u_t\}$ and $\{v_t\}$ are independent sequences of $n(0, 1)$ and $n(0, \sigma^2)$[15] variates respectively and $-1 < \rho < 1$. Thus the $\{h_t\}$ follow a stationary first order autoregressive process with normal errors. For a given value of h_t the variance of y_t is e^{h_t} and this varies over time and, through (9.15), is autocorrelated. So the model has y both heteroscedastic and with variances that evolve in a correlated way.

Because of stationarity the marginal distribution of any h_t is normal with mean $\mu_h = \mu/(1 - \rho)$ and variance $\sigma_h^2 = \sigma^2/(1 - \rho^2)$. It follows that e^{h_t} is lognormal with these parameters. From these results we can readily deduce the moments of any y_t. In particular,

$$
\begin{aligned}
E(y_t) &= E(e^{h_t/2})E(u_t) = 0, \\
V(y_t) &= E(y_t^2) = E(e^{h_t})E(u_t^2) = \exp\{\mu_h + \sigma_h^2/2\}, \\
E(y_t^3) &= E(e^{3h_t/2})E(u_t^3) = 0 \\
E(y_t^4) &= E(e^{2h_t})E(u_t^4) = 3\exp\{2\mu_h + 2\sigma_h^2\}.
\end{aligned}
$$

These results follow from the moments of lognormal variates described in the appendix to chapter 5. They show that y_t has a mean and third moment of zero so it is symmetrically distributed about zero. And from the relationship between the second and fourth moments we can deduce that the density is more peaked than a normal distribution[16] – it has excess kurtosis.

From the independence of u_t and v_t the marginal distribution of any y_t is equal to

$$
p(y_t) \propto \int_0^\infty e^{-h_t/2} \exp\{-e^{-h_t}y_t^2/2\} \exp\{-(h_t - \mu_h)/2\sigma_h^2\}\, dh_t.
$$

This is a scale mixture of normals but the density, i.e. the integral, does not have a closed form representation. This means that we cannot obtain a representation of the likelihood other than as a high dimensional integral. But Bayesian inference with this model is no more difficult than with any other non-linear model.

To see this note first that the model is easy to simulate if you wish to generate your own data rather than use some real economic series. You first generate a realization of a stationary autoregressive sequence of h's and then you produce a sequence of independent normal y's with means zero and variances equal to e^{h_t}. The following S statements are one way of doing this.

```
n <- 500; alpha <- 0; rho <- 0.5; pv <- 1;
h <- rep(0,n)
h[1] <- rnorm(1, alpha/(1-rho), 1/sqrt(pv*(1-rho^2)))
for(j in 2:n){h[j] <- rnorm(1, alpha + rho*h[j-1], 1/sqrt(pv))}
y <- exp(h/2)*rnorm(n)
```

15 The second argument of the normal density will, in this section, be the variance and not the precision to conform to the usage in the literature.

16 A normal variate of variance σ^2 has fourth moment equal to $3\sigma^4$ so the ratio of the fourth moment to the square of the second is always 3. But from the moments given above, this ratio is equal to $3^{\sigma_h^2} > 3$ for the distribution of y_t.

Then the BUGS program to analyze these data proceeds analogously by first writing the likelihood conditionally on h_1, ..., h_n; then specifying the (prior) model for h's conditional on the precision pv, the autocorrelation coefficient rho and the intercept alpha; and finally specifying the priors for these three parameters. Note the hierarchical prior structure. The stochastic volatility program in appendix 3 does this job.

This stochastic volatility model is an alternative way of developing what are often called autoregressive conditional heteroscedasticity or ARCH models. Such models also allow for autocorrelated heteroscedasticity.

9.3   EXTENSIONS

There is a vast literature on time series econometrics. Very often in this literature models are not closely linked to economic structure. For example a common agenda is that of finding the best way of forecasting future values of the series from those that have been observed. This is more a statistical exercise than an econometric one.

Among the generalizations that are often used:

(1) Addition of a vector of strictly exogenous covariates to the model as $y_t = \alpha + \rho y_{t-1} + x_t \beta + \varepsilon_t$.
(2) Addition of extra lags of Y as, for example, second order autoregression $y_t = \alpha + \rho_1 y_{t-1} + \rho_2 y_{t-2} + \varepsilon_t$. This extension allows us to show an additional use of simulation. The second order autoregressive process is stationary, when $\varepsilon = (\varepsilon_1, \varepsilon_2, ..., \varepsilon_T)$ are iid $n(0, \tau)$, if and only if the coefficients satisfy the conditions

$$\rho_1 + \rho_2 < 1$$
$$\rho_1 - \rho_2 < 1$$
$$|\rho_2| < 1.$$

These inequalities define a region in ρ_1, ρ_2 space that is a regular triangle on a base running from $\rho_1 = -2$ to $\rho_1 = 2$ at $\rho_2 = -1$ and of height 2. One can check stationarity by simulating from the posterior distribution of ρ_1, ρ_2 and counting how many points lie outside the triangle. Alternatively one can impose stationarity on the model by taking the prior for these parameters to be some joint distribution over R^2 subject to the condition that they must lie in the stationary region.
(3) Allowing the error term in an autoregression to be a moving average as, say, $\varepsilon_t = u_t + \omega u_{t-1}$ where the $\{u_t\}$ are iid mean zero and homoscedastic.
(4) Vector autoregressive models in which each y_t is vector valued.

9.4   EXERCISES

You can easily explore the characteristics of time series models by simulating data and examining them graphically. Here's how you might do it in R.

```
n <- 200; mu <- 1; rho <- 1; y <- rep(0,n); eps <- rnorm(n);
for(i in 2:n){y[i] <- mu*(1-rho)+rho*y[i-1]+eps[i]}; plot(y)
```

The first line sets the time series length; the parameters of a first order auto-regressive model; a vector of zeros to hold the output; and a vector of $n(0, 1)$ errors. The second line generates and plots the series. In this case it is random walk without drift starting at zero. Many variants are possible. Try some and then explore second order models with the same method. If you download and attach the package "tseries" you can use the function acf, as in `acf(y)`, to plot the autocorrelation function of a time series. This plots the correlations between y_t and y_{t-l} as a function of the lag l, that is, the first, second, . . . , l'th order autocorrelation coefficients of the series.

(1) Try simulating some time series data and running the BUGS autoregression program from section 9.2.1.
(2) Hold back an observation at the end of your simulated series and try to predict it by generating its predictive distribution based on the first $T - 1$ observations, using the method outlined in section 9.1.3.
(3) Deduce the joint posterior density of μ, ρ, τ in the first order autoregressive model with a flat prior, a uniform prior for ρ over the stationary region and the standard diffuse prior for τ. Find the marginal density of ρ and show that it has a factor equal to $1/|1 - \rho|$ and that this accounts for the bimodality in the last plot of figure 9.2.
(4) Generate some time series data and fit a stochastic volatility model using the BUGS program of appendix 3. Examine the posterior distribution of ρ to see if the variances are autocorrelated; examine the posterior distribution of σ^2 to check for heteroscedasticity.

9.5 BIBLIOGRAPHIC NOTES

Bauwens, Lubrano and Richard (1999) is, perhaps, the only book-length Bayesian treatment of time series in the econometrics literature. Its material largely dates from the period before the mid-nineties when Bayesian computation was difficult. It contains many further references. One that is particularly worth mentioning is the symposium on Bayesian inference about unit roots published in the *Journal of Applied Econometrics* (1991: vol. 6). This includes a paper by Phillips (1991), giving a study of Jeffreys' prior for simple autoregressive models such as the one discussed in this chapter. Schotman and van Dijk (1991), and Schotman (1994) are worth reading on the issues of parametrization and local non-identifiability. Geweke (1994) explores alternative prior specification for real economic time series in an early econometric application of the Gibbs Sampler.

The paper on reference priors mentioned in this chapter is J. O. Berger and R.-Y. Yang's Noninformative priors for Bayesian testing for the AR(1) model in *Econometric Theory*, 10, 461–82, 1994.

Useful further references on time series models include Chib and Greenberg (1994); Jacquier, Polson, and Rossi (1994); and Chib, Nardari, and Shephard (2002). The latter two papers deal with Bayesian inference about stochastic volatility models. Berg, Meyer, and Yu (2004) is a very clear treatment of model choice in sv models. In particular, it describes the DIC criterion for model choice. DIC values are output by BUGS.

Sims and Uhlig (1991) contrast Bayesian inference about a simple autoregressive model with its frequentist counterpart. Sims (2000) contains some interesting arguments about time series methods in the near unit root case and argues for reporting posterior inferences under a range of economically plausible priors.

A CONVERSION MANUAL

Almost all current students of econometrics and an even higher proportion of existing applied economics researchers were trained to use a mode of statistical inference that is radically different from the one described in this book. So overwhelming is this approach that it is often *identified* with econometrics. We shall call it frequentist econometrics in order to distinguish it from the Bayesian method. In this section we shall give a brief comparative guide to the two approaches. We don't intend to argue here for the Bayesian approach. The purpose of this appendix is to contrast, perhaps rather starkly, the differences (and some similarities) between Bayesian and frequentist econometrics.

A1.1 THE FREQUENTIST APPROACH

Consider an investigator with a set of data, a question in mind, and the elements of a model within the framework of which that question can be answered. The frequentist approach is to envisage a population of economic agents such that the agents represented in the data can be regarded as a sample from that population. An example might be the set of all residents of the San Francisco Bay area who might travel to work by a rapid transit system. Or it might be all members of the US labor force who might be eligible for a training program. In macroeconomics the notion of the population is harder to define. Agents here may be countries or they may be distinct market days or trades. The population here is quite imaginary, involving a collection of potential periods of economic history – reruns of history. It is, perhaps, possible to imagine taking another sample – rerunning history – but impossible to actually do it.

   If the feature of the population that you are to observe is denoted by Y then the view is that Y will vary over the population. If you take a sample from the population then you will get a particular set of values for Y; if you take another sample you will get a different set of values. This is called sampling variation. If you choose a model for the variation in Y over the members of the population that is characterized by a parameter θ then there will be a particular value of θ, say θ_0, that is true in the sense that if your sample comprised the whole population, and your model is true, then you would, in effect, know θ_0.[1] For example your model might state that $E(Y) = \theta_0$ or, more generally, $E(g(Y, \theta_0)) = 0$ where $g(.)$ is some given function. The expectation, E, is interpreted as representing the average of Y or $g(Y, \theta_0)$ over the whole population. The parameter θ_0 is then thought of as a characteristic of the population, such as the proportion of all Americans who voted Republican in the 2000 presidential election. The object of econometrics is then to find out θ_0 from the evidence provided by the sample and assuming that the model is true, namely that in the distribution of Y over the population it really is the case that $E(g(Y, \theta_0)) = 0$ for some θ_0.

Frequentist econometrics is tied to the notion of a sample and population. The object of inference is θ_0 and the inference problem is posed as that of using the sample to provide an estimate of θ_0 or a test of a hypothesis about it.

The essence of the procedure is to select an estimator or a test statistic. These are formulae such as "take the average of the values of Y that appear in your sample." Any proposed estimator or statistic is then evaluated by computing its frequency distribution over repeated, similar, samples from the population. In the case of an estimator of θ_0 a "good" estimator is one which, on average over repeated samples, will be close to θ_0 so that an investigator will have the comfort of knowing that, even if the estimate of θ_0 provided by his own sample is badly in error, other investigators with other samples who use the same estimator will, on average, be close. In the case of a test statistic it is evaluated by its power which is the ability of the test to detect the falseness of the hypothesis in question when that hypothesis about θ_0 is in fact false. Typical ways of measuring "closeness" of an estimator $\hat{\theta}$ to θ_0 include bias, $E(\hat{\theta} - \theta_0)$; variance, $E(\hat{\theta} - E(\hat{\theta}))^2$; mean squared error, $E(\hat{\theta} - \theta_0)^2$; mean absolute deviation, $E|\hat{\theta} - \theta_0|$; etc., where all these expectations refer to averages over repeated, similar, samples from the population. They are features of the "sampling distribution" of the estimator.[2]

Often the sampling distribution is hard to calculate so that frequentist econometricians resort either to using limit theorems of probability theory to approximate the repeated sampling behavior of an estimator or test statistic when "the sample size is large," or they use a computer to simulate the sampling distribution similarly to the Bayesian use of it to sample from a complicated posterior distribution.

So dominant is the frequentist paradigm in econometrics that the word "distribution" is automatically taken to mean "sampling distribution" and the phrase "standard error" automatically means "standard deviation of the sampling distribution."

---

1   It is possible for an economist to write down a model for the population such that, even if the sample comprised the whole population, it would not be possible to deduce the value of θ_0. This is the problem of identification. It is an issue in the construction of models, not of inference about them.

2   The word frequentist in the phrase "frequentist econometrics" refers to this emphasis on the behavior of statistics in repeated samples.

A1.2 THE BAYESIAN CONTRAST

So how does Bayesian work depart from this familiar agenda? It does so principally in the following ways.

(1) The Bayesian must formulate a model and attach probabilities to the values of the data that he is about to observe. That is, he must formulate $p(y)$ and this is usually done in two stages by calculating the likelihood, $p(y|\theta)$, and the prior, $p(\theta)$, from which an integration over θ will provide the required full model. In thinking about the probabilities of prospective data it is reasonable and usually helpful to imagine a hypothetical population from which the data are to be drawn. But the Bayesian is not tied to this way of thinking. A Bayesian macroeconomist could ask himself "what would the economy (Y) look like – what values are plausible, what values are not – if the parameters (θ) of my model were to take this value or that value" – and this would give him a likelihood. And then he could ask about plausible value for his parameters, and this would give him his prior. This way of thinking does not require a population or a sample and the parameters are not necessarily to be identified with characteristics of a population. So a Bayesian could go along with thinking of data as arising out of a population of agents but he is not tied to this point of view.[3]

(2) A marked difference between the two approaches is that the Bayesian approach requires a likelihood, $p(y|\theta)$, a complete statement of what values of Y are probable and what values are improbable, for each potential value of θ. A frequentist can get away with less than a likelihood, for example, a statement that realizations Y are independently and identically distributed and such that, say, $E(g(Y, \theta_0)) = 0$, a moment condition. In this sense, a Bayesian analysis is more demanding. But of course you get what you pay for. A likelihood and a prior imply a posterior distribution and thus permit inferences that are "exact." A moment condition without a likelihood produces an estimator whose sampling distribution cannot be deduced since the model is not rich enough to specify it. Inference in this case has to rely on, possibly very good, approximations to or estimates of the unknown sampling distribution.

(3) In a Bayesian procedure there is, in a sense, only one "estimator," this is the (marginal) posterior distribution of the quantity (parameter) of interest, given the model and the data. The model and data imply the estimator. This contrasts sharply with frequentist econometrics in which, for any model and data, anyone with sufficient ingenuity can come up with a new estimator or test. Of course if a Bayesian is obliged to report a single numerical value for θ or, more generally,

---

3 Often Bayesians will refer to their data as "the sample" even though it does not originate in the sampling of any well-defined physical population. This is just historical usage.

to make a single decision on the basis of model and data he can certainly do so by, for example, reporting the marginal posterior mode. But this point aside, there is no such thing as "the" or even "a" Bayesian estimator. To speak of such is to confuse Bayesian inference with frequentist where there is a proliferation of estimators of various classes and types.

(4) The distributions that arise in Bayesian econometrics are prior or posterior distributions of quantities as yet unknown, "parameters," "future" observations – all generically called parameters, a word that refers to any unknown. The distributions that arise in frequentist econometrics are usually probability distributions of functions of the data – statistics – in hypothetical repeated samples. These are called sampling distributions and they are strictly irrelevant to a Bayesian. It follows that properties associated with sampling distributions are also irrelevant. These include bias, mean squared error, variance, and efficiency. For example, the Gauss–Markov theorem, the foundation stone of traditional econometrics texts, is irrelevant to Bayesian econometrics. This is because it refers to the bias and variance of the sampling distribution of a class of estimators.

We note in passing that the notion of a sampling distribution is fraught with ambiguity. The difficulty arises in defining what is to be meant by the phrase "repeated sampling." We referred above to repeated similar samples but what is meant by "similar"?

Here is an econometric example of how this ambiguity can arise. There is a well-defined population of people in the San Francisco Bay area who travel to work. They may travel to work by car or bus and the issue is how their choice depends on a set of covariates such as income, travel time, and location. One way of sampling this population is to randomly select, say, a hundred people who travel by bus and a hundred who travel by car and in each case measure their covariate values. A variant on this is to throw a fair coin and if it shows heads select a bus traveler and if tails a car traveler. Doing this 200 times will produce a sample in which there are close to, but not exactly, a hundred people of each type. The frequentist then chooses an estimator (of the parameters measuring the effect of the covariates on the choice) and proceeds to work out its distribution over repeated samples of size 200 gathered by repetitions of his sampling method. Suppose his method has produced 97 bus travelers and 103 car travelers. Is the econometrician to imagine repeated samples of sizes 97 and 103? Or is he to imagine repeated samples in which, for each sample, a coin is thrown 200 times and the numbers of the two types vary from sample to sample? The distinction matters and the inferences to be produced will depend on which repeated sampling choice is made.

Perhaps a more familiar example is a regression model in which one samples agents and measures an outcome, Y, and some regressors X. Is the sampling distribution of some estimator or test statistic one in which both Y and X vary from sample to sample, or one in which only Y is allowed to vary in this thought experiment? This choice matters to a frequentist and her inferences will depend on which repeated sampling definition is chosen.[4] It doesn't matter at all to a Bayesian; his inferences are conditional on the data he has, not on what might have happened had he had a different sample.

(5) Nonetheless, some Bayesians will occasionally refer to the repeated sampling properties of a Bayes decision or of some feature of a posterior such as its mode or mean. These are referred to as "operating characteristics" of a Bayesian inference and they are typically described in an effort to persuade a frequentist that Bayesian inferences are worth considering. We note that when these calculations are done the conclusion is almost always that Bayesian procedures have good repeated sampling properties.[5]

(6) Consistency of an estimator or test statistic is a dominant interest in traditional econometrics. Prizes are won by finding a new consistent estimator and its asymptotic sampling distribution. By contrast, consistency plays only a limited role in Bayesian inference. This is because consistency refers to the behavior of the sampling distribution when you have more data than you actually have! Bayesian inference works from the information that is in your data file.[6]

(7) It is also true that, for a number of textbook models, there is a common frequentist procedure and a common Bayesian procedure such that the same conclusions would be drawn by using either method. Here is a very simple example. Suppose n independent realizations are taken of a normal variate with mean μ and variance one. A frequentist investigator chooses the sample mean, $\bar{y}$, as his estimator of μ and will observe that, over repeated samples of size n, $\bar{y}$ will be distributed normally with expectation μ and standard deviation $1/\sqrt{n}$. He will then construct as the shortest 95% confidence interval for μ the interval from $l = \bar{y} - 1.96/\sqrt{n}$ to $u = \bar{y} + 1.96/\sqrt{n}$ and his conclusion will be the rather subtle statement that "in repeated samples of size n the interval constructed by adding and subtracting $1.96/\sqrt{n}$ to the sample mean will contain between its end-points the number μ on 95% of such occasions." The Bayesian with an (improper) uniform prior on μ will observe that the posterior distribution of μ is normal with mean $\bar{y}$ and standard deviation $1/\sqrt{n}$. He will then notice that

---

4   This issue has been discussed by statistical theorists for 75 years but never, so far as I am aware, by econometrics texts. Cox and Hinkley (1974) give a useful summary of the argument. Incidentally, the conclusion of the (frequentist) theorists is that in the first example one should think of repeated samples of size 97 and 103 and, in the second example, repeated samples in which the regressors are held at their values in the sample to hand.

5   For example, as long as the prior on θ is proper, Bayes procedures are admissible with respect to quadratic loss which means, roughly, that no other estimator has a smaller sampling mean squared error for all values of θ_0.

6   Actually, there is one place in Bayesian econometrics where limit theorems of probability theory, such as consistency, play a major role. This is MCMC work as described in chapter 4. But in this case the "sample" size is entirely under the control of the investigator and can be increased, without limit, in an unambiguous way.

There is also a small recent interest in consistency of posterior distributions in models with genuinely infinite dimensional parameter spaces.

the shortest interval containing 95% of the highest values of the posterior density is from l to u. Hence he will conclude that "the probability that μ lies between l and u is 0.95." The conclusions of Bayesians and frequentists are quite different in a formal sense, yet readers of either will take away from their reading the inference that μ is almost certainly between l and u. In this practical sense, in this model, the conclusions of Bayesians and frequentists are the same.

(8) Much of the literature of econometrics is concerned with the development of new estimators or test statistics or about getting a better understanding of the repeated sampling properties of existing procedures. The Bayesian agenda frees this journal space for the econometrician to focus on the first four letters of the last noun. He can focus on fundamental questions like what is the relation between my data and my model?; how do I handle the inevitable discrepancies between what I have measured and what theory suggests that I should have measured?; how can I find data that are more relevant to my theory than those that have been collected, often by people with different aims in mind?; how do I handle models for which there is more than one solution of $g(y, x) = 0$? – such models arise for example in game theory – etc.

Appendix 2
PROGRAMMING

This appendix provides a summary of the S language and of the use of WinBUGS with the emphasis on material useful for simulation. To use the S language you can either go with S-PLUS, a commercial implementation of S, or with R, an open-source implementation. The online help system in R is useful but not really for beginners for whom the best source is the text by Krause and Olson listed at the end of this chapter. The commands discussed below are common to both R and S-PLUS.

A2.1   S

The prompt is >

Assignment is _ or <-, e.g. y <- rnorm(100) or x _ y/2.

S objects are column **vectors** by default; the j'th element of vector y is y[j], so, for example, in dnorm(x) x is a vector (or matrix) so that, for example, if x <- c(-1,0,1) then dnorm(x) produces a three vector containing the standard normal density function values at these three points. The standard operators +, -, /, *, together with ** or ^ for raising to a power, operate element by element. Thus, if y1 and y2 are vectors of the same length (length is determined by the command length(y1)) then y1/y2 will produce a vector whose first element is the first element of y1 divided by the first of y2, whose second element is the second element of y1 divided by the second of y2 etc.

The function c (standing for **concatenation** – don't use c for anything else) is the way to enter data into a vector. **Matrices** can be created by, for example, X <- matrix(c(1,2,3,4,5,6),byrow=T, nrow=3) which returns a 3 × 2 matrix

$$
\begin{array}{cc}
1 & 2 \\
3 & 4 \\
5 & 6
\end{array}
$$

or X <- diag(20) which creates the 20-dimensional identity matrix. The i, j'th element is X[i,j]. They can also be created by **binding** together column or row vectors. Thus the commands x1 <- c(1,3,5) and x2 <- c(2,4,6) followed by cbind(x1,x2) will reproduce X above. The dimensions of a matrix can be found by dim(X).

Plot commands are an important part of S. Some simple commands that produce graphics are plot(x,y) producing a scatter diagram with x on the horizontal axis; hist(x) produces a histogram of the data in x – you might want to add the extra arguments nclasses=..; plot(density(x)) produces a kernel density plot of the data in x; plot(x) produces a plot of the elements of x against their position in the vector. All these commands have additional arguments enabling you to control the appearance of the plot – see the relevant **help** file found by ?plot for example.

Probability density or **mass functions** are of the form dnorm, dt, dbinom etc.; the arguments are, first, the value x at which the density function is to be calculated and, second, the values of the parameters of the distribution, e.g. y <- dnorm(1, -2,1.5) – the normal density with mean –2 and standard deviation 1.5 evaluated at the point 1. There are usually default parameter values; in the case of the normal these are mean zero and standard deviation 1, so if you want the density of this standard normal at x you can just do dnorm(x). If x has more than one element, say n, then the output will be an n vector of function values.

Probability distribution functions have a similar structure except the first letter is p, e.g. pnorm(1,-2,1.5), which returns 0.97725.

Quantile functions have a similar structure except that the first letter is q and the first argument is a probability, e.g. qnorm(0.97725,-2,1.5), which returns 1.000.

Random number generators have the same structure except that the first letter is r and the first argument is the number of independent realizations required, e.g. rnorm(100,-2,1.5) returns 100 independent realizations from n(–2, 1.5). The command mvrnorm(100, mean, var)[1] with mean a vector of length k and var a $k \times k$ positive definite matrix will return a matrix of dimension $100 \times k$ whose rows are independent realizations of the k-dimensional multivariate normal density with mean vector equal to mean and covariance matrix equal to var.

Useful matrix operations are **transposition**, e.g. Xprime <- t(X); **multiplication** A <- X%*%b; **inversion**, Xinverse <- solve(X); **eigenvectors and values** are produced by eigen(X). The output of this command is a list with two components of which the first is a vector of the eigenvalues and the second a matrix of eigenvectors. Particular **components of a list** can be referred to by using the $ symbol. Thus eigen(X)$val produces the eigenvalues.

Do loops are sometimes required in order to produce **simulated data**. They work as in:

---

1   If you are working in R you will have to load the mass library by typing library(MASS) before you can access mvrnorm. Other versions of R use rmvnorm.

```
n  <-  100                              # length of series
rho  <-  0.95                           # autoregression coefficient
tau  <-  2                              # normal precision
y  <-  rep(0,100)                       # create a vector of zeros to contain
                                          the generated data

for(i  in  2:n){
y[i]  <-  rho*y[i-1]
+rnorm(1,0,1/sqrt(tau))}²               #generate series with n(0, tau) errors.
```

(rep(x,n) produces a vector with n copies of x. The series here starts with y[1]=0.)

Multiplication using * produces different results from multiplication using %*%. Thus if x, y are vectors of the same length then x*y produces a vector containing products of corresponding elements in x and y; and x**2 produces a vector contaging the squares of the elements of x; x/y produces a vector containing the ratios of corresponding elements of x and y. The same applies if x and y are matrices of the same dimension.

A2.2 WINBUGS

BUGS stands for Bayesian statistical analysis Using the Gibbs[3] Sampler; WinBUGS is its Windows version. It's a package designed to facilitate the use of models for data that lead to likelihoods/priors that are best studied using markov chain monte carlo. It is somewhat analogous to the many (frequentist) econometric software products on the market. You supply the model, i.e. the likelihood and the prior; and you supply the data. But unlike frequentist programs its output produces not only point estimates and estimated standard errors, it also produces realizations from the complete posterior distributions of all model parameters. The language of WinBUGS is similar to but not identical with that of S. The program is still developing and imposes a short but sharp learning curve. This appendix is designed to minimize the pain. It takes you through analysis of a simple problem step by step.

There are two ways of using BUGS. One is to open the BUGS program and follow the instructions. It is a good idea to start by replicating the simple example given at the beginning of the online help manual. The other way is to use an interface to BUGS from some other software. With this approach you construct your model and organize your data outside BUGS and then issue a command to run BUGS from your external program. Most of the calculations reported in this book were done using an interface from R downloaded from the web site given in the bibliography for this chapter.

---

2 Note that we think of the normal distribution in terms of the precision τ but S requires us to specify it in terms of the standard deviation, $1/\sqrt{\tau}$.

3 Actually, the program will do several types of sampling, including Gibbs, Metropolis–Hastings and non-iterative sampling. The program decides what method to use.

We shall first describe the routine for running BUGS directly, then describe the method for using BUGS from within R, a method I prefer. It is also possible to run BUGS from Matlab – see the WinBUGS home page.

A2.2.1   *Formulating the model and inputting data from within BUGS*

(1)   Open the WinBUGS program.
(2)   Open a new document.
(3)   Type `model{`
(4)   Now input the model – likelihood and prior – which for a simple linear model might be

```
model{
for(i in 1:n){y[i] ˜ dnorm(mu[i],tau)
mu[i] <- alpha + beta1*x[i,1] + beta2*x[i,2]
}
alpha ˜ dnorm(0,0.0001)
beta1 ˜ dnorm(0,0.0001)
beta2 ˜ dnorm(0,0.0001)
tau ˜ dgamma(0.001,0.001)
}
```

The do (for) loop says that for each i, y is normally distributed with mean μ and precision τ and that μ varies across observations as a linear function of x_1 and x_2. The do loop provides the likelihood. Outside the do loop but within the model statement is the prior which in this case says that the four parameters are distributed (˜) either normally or as a gamma variate with parameters chosen to give very dispersed, low precision members of these families. (Try drawing these densities using the R plot function if you are not convinced of this.)

It is important to emphasize that you can place any prior distribution you like on the model parameters, including priors that show dependence between them. You can also, within the same calculation, compute posterior distributions for alternative sets of prior beliefs.

(5)   At this stage you must check that the syntax of your model statement is correct. Click on the **model** button; click on **specification**; then click on **check model**. If you have it right then "model is syntactically correct" will appear on the lower left of your screen; if you have made a mistake – a very high probability event for novice users – then an error message will appear there and a broken vertical bar (hard to see) will appear in your model statement at the point at which the error occurs. Apart from bracketing and punctuation errors there may well be less obvious ones and here is an example. Originally the model above was written as

```
for(i in 1:n){
y[i]~dnorm(alpha+beta1*x[i,1]+beta2*x[i,2],tau)}
alpha~dnorm(0,0.0001) etc.
```

This was a mistake and the first form is required (don't ask why), and an error symbol appeared after `alpha` in the second line.

(6) The next step is to load the data which, in this case, are the number of observations and n values each for y, x_1, x_2. Data may be supplied in several formats. For small data sets that can be easily typed a format is

```
list(n=5,y=c(1,3,3,3,5),x=structure(.Data=c(
1,2,
2,3,
3,1,
4,5,
5,2),
.Dim=c(5,2)))
```

But for larger data sets the best approach is to place them in a text file in the following form:

```
list(n=100)
y[,1]    x[,1]    x[,2]
-1.67    1.84     0.30
-1.37   -1.46     0.28
 0.75   -0.47     1.33
-2.40    1.01    -0.07
-0.26   -0.84     0.44
-0.54    1.54    -0.41
-3.54    1.89    -1.25
-0.70    0.14    -0.11
 2.40   -0.61     0.36
```

etc., where the columns of the data matrix are tab separated. (The array of numbers here has $n = 100$ rows.) To load these data open the file containing them alongside your model file; double click on **list** to highlight it; then click on **load data** in the specification tool; then double click on the first data symbol, in this case **y**, and click on **load data** again. You should get "data loaded" in the lower left of the screen. (Inputting data directly through the R interface is simpler than this – see below.)

(7) The next step is to decide whether you want to run multiple chains. If you want only a single chain then move to (8); otherwise go to the number of chains box in the specification tool and select the number you want.

(8) Now the model is ready to be compiled. Click on the **compile** button and you should get "model compiled" in the left hand corner.

(9)   The final step in setting up the model is to provide the Gibbs Sampler with initial values for each parameter for each chain. This may be done in two ways. One, which always works, is to type

```
list(alpha=0, beta1=0, beta2=0, tau=1)
```

for example, then double click **list** and click **load inits** in the specification tool. If you are running more than one chain then enter another list, highlight **list** and click **load inits**. Repeat for the chosen number of chains. Sometimes you can get the program to provide initial values for you by sampling from your prior. This is done using **gen inits**. Finally, you should see the message "initial values loaded; model initialized."

(10)   After this ordeal the model is set to run.

SUMMARY OF STEPS

Let us summarize these steps for easier reference:

- After inputting the model: Model/Specification/Check Model.
- After typing in the data or opening the data file: Model/Specification/Load Data.
- Choose number of chains: Model/Specification/Choose number of chains.
- Compile the program: Model/Specification/Compile.
- Input initial values for each chain: Model/Specification/Load Inits.
- Choose number of updates: Model/Update/Choose number of updates.
- Choose sequence of updates for analysis: Inference/Samples/ Choose begin and end.
- Choose parameters for study: Inference/Samples/Type node then click set for each.
- Follow evolution of the sampler: Inference/Samples/trace.
- With multiple chains check convergence: Inference/Samples/GR diag.
- If converged, study posterior using: Inference/Samples/quantiles, density etc.

A2.2.2   *Running the sampler*

When your model has compiled and the data are loaded you must choose your sampler options. Since the online user manual is pretty clear on most of the options we shall here just describe the minimal steps.

(1)   On the Model/Update screen choose update, the total length of the sampler runs – this will apply to each chain separately. A typical figure might be a run of length 10,000 updates.

(2)   On the Inference/Samples screen choose

- Begin and End. These refer to the subset of the run that will provide the sample from the posterior distribution. With a run of length 10,000 Begin might be set to 5,001 and End to 10,000.

- Node. In this window type the name of each parameter you wish to study, each time followed by clicking on **Set**.
- Node. Then type * in the node window to dynamically monitor the evolution of each parameter sequence or node.
- Trace. This will open windows for each node and these will display the progress of the sampler as the calculation proceeds.

(3) To start the sampler click on **Update** in the Update Tool window.

(4) After the sampler ends, convergence checks are provided by the Gelman–Rubin diagnostic, obtained by clicking on the **GR Diag** button. The window that emerges should show a red line that is close to one and all lines close to constancy to indicate that the sampler has reached convergence. (This will only work if you have run more than one chain simultaneously.) The time series plot for each parameter is provided by the **History** button. **Density** provides (sort of) smoothed estimates of the marginal posterior densities of each parameter using the pooled samples from all chains. The **Quantile** button gives point estimates and standard errors for each parameter. Recalling that MCMC samples are generally autocorrelated – after all, they are realizations of markov processes! – the numerical character of the autocorrelation in your output can be studied using **auto cor**. If these autocorrelations are slow to die out as the interval between observations, the lag length, increases, larger than usual lengths of sampler output will be needed to evaluate the posterior distribution with an acceptable precision.

(5) If the sampler stops with an error message (often hard to interpret), you have several options. Start again from different initial values; check the mathematics of your model; check the translation of that model given in your BUGS model file; check your data; run a simpler version of the model for which you can work out the posteriors analytically; consult the manual and FAQ and mailing list for other occurrences of your error; etc.

To send the sampler output to R for further analysis and construction of graphs you can take the following steps. (Again this is not necessary if you are running BUGS from within R or some other external program.)

(1) Click on **Coda** in the Sample Monitor Tool window and there will appear as many data files as there are chains plus one. The extra one indicates which of the sequences of numbers in the other output windows corresponds to which parameter.

(2) To transfer the output from any one chain select the appropriate output window and choose Save/Save in and then go to the working directory for, say, R, e.g. C:\Program Files\R\rw1062 and save the output file as, say, `mreg.txt` in "Plain Text" format.

(3) From within R open your sampler output file using

```
mreg_matrix(scan("mreg.txt"),byrow=T,ncol=2).
```

This will set up a matrix whose first column is the update number and whose second column contains the update sequence for each parameter. For example, if you have elected to study the samples for beta1 and beta2 from chain 1 the Coda Index file in WinBUGS will tell you that, say, beta1 realizations occupy the first 2,000 rows and beta2 realizations the second (and final) 2,000 and mreg will be a matrix of dimension 4,000 × 2. To pick out the beta1 values you can do, say, `beta1val_mreg[1:2000,2]` which picks up the first 2,000 elements in the second column of mreg. You can pool the output of all chains by repeating step 2 after selecting the Coda output files for the other chains and then, in R, use the concatenate function as, for example,

```
totalbeta1_c(beta1chain1, beta2chain2).
```

(4) Useful S tools for studying a vector – beta1 – of sampler realizations are:

- `summary(beta1)`   #mean, median, quartiles, extremes
- `tsplot(beta1)`   #time series plot
- `plot(density(beta1))`   #kernel density plot
- `acf(beta1)`   #autocorrelations plotted against lags
- `hist(beta1)`   #histogram.

(5) To study two vectors, say beta1 and beta2, you might choose:

- `plot(beta1,beta2)`   #scatter diagram
- `cor(beta1,beta2)`   #correlation coefficient
- `summary(lm(beta1~beta2))` #linear regression of beta1 on beta2.

A2.2.3   *Running BUGS from R*

There is a useful interface from R to WinBUGS which enables you to work entirely in R. This greatly simplifies the operation of inputting data and extracting sampler output for further analysis. The steps are:

(1) Create a *.txt file in your R working directory, e.g. reg.txt, and in it type the model – likelihood and prior – in the format given above. Save the file.
(2) You must then identify the parameters whose posterior distribution you wish to sample. This must have the format `parameters = c("beta1", "beta2", ...)`. Note the inverted commas.
(3) Create a list in R containing the initial values of all parameters, e.g. `inits <- list(alpha=0, beta1=0, beta2=0, tau=1)`. If, as you must with this interface, you are running several chains, you should create one initial values list for each chain. If they are called in1, in2, etc. then you create a list whose components are in1, in2, e.g. `inits <- list(in1, in2, ...)`.
(4) Finally you must create a data file. For example if the data consist of the sample size n, an n vector y, and an $n \times k$ matrix X you would write something like `data <- list(n=100, y=y, X=X)` where the left hand side y or X refers

to objects appearing in your model and right hand sides refer to your vector or matrix data stored in R. (If your dependent variable is an R vector called, say, "gascon" or "earnings" you would write y = gascon, etc.)

(5) To run BUGS from R you use the bugs function. For example, regsim <- bugs(data,inits,parameters,"reg.txt",n.chains=3,n.iter=1000, debug=T). This stores the output of your simulation as a list in regsim and orders up 3 chains of length 1,000 each. The command debug = T will give you some information about what went wrong if the simulation fails.

A2.2.4 Special likelihoods and the ones trick

The BUGS program supplies a collection of density/mass functions that you can call using a single command like dnorm or dgamma. But it often happens that in describing the likelihood or the prior you wish to use a probability distribution that is not supplied in BUGS. How do you proceed? One way is to use what amounts to a trick. Suppose that the density function that you wish to use in the model has the form $f(y, t)$ where y is the variable whose distribution is being described and t are the parameters of that distribution. We assume that you can write down f as an analytical expression. Now note that the mass function of a Bernoulli variate with parameter p is $p^z(1 - p)^{1-z}$ and that at $z = 1$ this expression is just p. Thus, if we write z ~ dbern(p) with $p = f(y, t)$ and input z data that are all equal to one we shall have written down code expressing the belief that y given t has density/mass function equal to $f(y, t)$. This may be implemented by the following code.

```
for (i in 1:n){
z[i] <- 1
z[i] ~ dbern(p[i])
p[i] <- f(y[i],t) / K
}
```

where K is a constant that is large enough to ensure that all sampled values of p[i] are less than one.

Finally, take heed of the health warning on BUGS.

A2.2.5 Computing references

On S

(1) *The Basics of S and S-PLUS*, A. Krause and M. Olson, Springer (1997). A good introductory text.

(2) *Modern Applied Statistics with S and S-PLUS*, W. Venables and B. Ripley, Springer, 2nd ed. (1999). A comprehensive but tightly written survey.

(3) *A Handbook of Statistical Analyses using S-PLUS*, B. Everitt, Chapman and Hall, first edition (1994). A book of example analyses that I have found very useful.
(4) http://lib.stat.cmu.edu/ is the best start point for finding useful S web sites.
(5) http://www.r-project.org/ will get you to the home page for the R implementation of S.

On BUGS

(1) http://www.statslab.cam.ac.uk/~mcmc/
(2) http://www.mrc-bsu.cam.ac.uk/bugs/ is the BUGS web site.
(3) www.stat.columbia.edu/~gelman/bugsR/ is the site for Andrew Gelman's interface from R to WinBUGS.
(4) Ross Ihaka and Robert Gentleman, R: A language for data analysis and graphics, *Journal of Computational and Graphical Statistics*, 5, 3, 299–314 (1996) is the source article for the R language.

Appendix 3
BUGS CODE

Here is a selection of BUGS programs covering some common models. The web site associated with recent books by P. Congdon, *Bayesian Statistical Modelling*, Wiley (2001) and *Applied Bayesian Modelling*, Wiley (2003), contains many more examples. In the examples below the priors are typically conventionally diffuse. You may, of course, choose whatever priors you wish. The code given here is not necessarily the most elegant or even efficient that could be written, but it does work.

A3.1   NORMAL LINEAR MODEL

This is code for the normal linear model with homoscedastic and non-autocorrelated errors.

```
model{
for(i in 1:n){y[i] ~dnorm(mu[i], tau)
mu[i] <- b0 + b1*x[i] + b2*z[i]
}
b0 ~ dnorm(0, 1.0E-6)
b1 ~ dnorm(0, 1.0E-6)
b2 ~ dnorm(0, 1.0E-6)
tau ~ dgamma(1.0E-3, 1.0E-3)}
```

A3.2   HETEROSCEDASTIC REGRESSION

This does linear regression with *t* distributed errors corresponding to gamma heterogeneity in the precisions of a normal linear model.

```
model{
for(i in 1:n){y[i] ~ dt(mu[i], tau, d)
mu[i] <- b0 + b1*x[i] + b2*z[i]
}
d <- 4   # degrees of freedom for the t distribution.
b0 ~ dnorm(0, 1.0E-6)
```

```
b1  ~ dnorm(0,  1.0E-6)
b2  ~ dnorm(0,  1.0E-6)
tau  ~ dgamma(1.0E-3,  1.0E-3)}
```

The first few lines of the data file are

```
list(n=100)
y[]        x[]       z[]
 1.40      0.25     -1.50
-0.80      0.09      1.62
```

A3.3   REGRESSION WITH AUTOCORRELATED ERRORS

This does linear regression allowing for first order autoregression in the errors.

```
model{
for(i in 2:n){
y[i]  ~ dnorm(mu[i],tau)
mu[i]  <- rho*y[i-1]+b0*(1-rho)+b1*x[i]-rho*b1*x[i-1]
}
y[1]  ~ dnorm(mu1,tau1)
mu1  <- b0+b1*x[1]
tau1  <- tau*(1-rho*rho)
b0  ~ dnorm(0,0.0001)
b1  ~ dnorm(0,0.0001)
tau  ~ dgamma(1.0E-3,1.0E-3)
rho  ~ dunif(-.999,.999)
}
```

A3.4   CES PRODUCTION FUNCTION

A non-linear regression model. yl and kl are output and capital per man, measured logarithmically. Careful choice of prior for sig, the elasticity of substitution, is important for convergence.

```
model{
for(i in 1:n)
{yl[i]  ~ dnorm(mu[i],tau)
mu[i]  <- a-(1/b)*log(d+(1-d)*exp(-b*kl[i]))
}
b <- (1/sig)-1
```

```
sig ~ dgamma(2,2)
a ~ dnorm(0,0.001)
d ~ dbeta(2,2)
tau ~ dgamma(0.001,0.001)
}
```

A3.5 PROBIT MODEL

The standard binary choice model – for logit change line 4 to `logit(p[i]) <- b0+b1*x1[i]+b2*x2[i]`.

```
model
{for(i in 1:n){
y[i] ~ dbin(p[i],1)
p[i] <- phi(b0+b1*x1[i]+b2*x2[i])
}
b0 ~ dnorm(0,0.001)
b1 ~ dnorm(0,0.001)
b2 ~ dnorm(0,0.001)
}
```

A3.6 TOBIT MODEL

An example of censored linear regression using the ones trick. Censoring on the left at zero.

```
model{
for(i in 1:n){
ones[i] <-1
ones[i] ~ dbern(p[i])
term1[i] <- 0.39894*pow(tau,1/2)*exp(-0.5*tau*pow(y[i] -mu[i],2))
term2[i] <- phi(-mu[i]*pow(tau,1/2))
p[i] <- pow(term1[i],ind[i])*pow(term2[i],1-ind[i])/10000
#pow(x,a) gives x^a.
mu[i] <- b0+b1*x[i]
}
b0 ~ dnorm(0,.001)
b1 ~ dnorm(0,.001)
tau ~ dgamma(.001,.001)
}
```

A3.7 TRUNCATED NORMAL

Truncated, not censored, linear regression also using the ones trick.

```
model{
for(i in 1:n)
{ones[i] <-1
ones[i] ~ dbern(p[i])
term1[i] <- 0.39894*pow(tau,1/2)*exp(-0.5*tau*pow(y[i] -mu[i],2))
term2[i] <- phi(mu[i]*pow(tau,1/2))
r[i] <- term1[i]/term2[i]
p[i] <- pow(r[i],ind[i])/10000
mu[i] <- b0+b1*x[i]
}
b0 ~ dnorm(0,.001)
b1 ~ dnorm(0,.001)
tau ~ dgamma(.001,.001)
}
```

First six lines of the data file for tobit and truncated normal

```
list(n=1000)
y[]      ind[]    x[]
0.00     0.00     -1.10
0.00     0.00     -1.71
0.00     0.00     -0.94
0.06     1.00     -0.06
0.56     1.00     -0.77
```

A3.8 ORDERED PROBIT

A linear model with the outcomes sorted in four ordered categories defined by the values of r, r+d, and r+d+e.

```
model{
for(i in 1:n){
y[i] ~ dcat(p[i,])
p[i,1] <- phi(r-mu[i])
p[i,4] <- 1-phi(r+d+e-mu[i])
p[i,2] <- phi(r+d-mu[i])-phi(r-mu[i])
p[i,3] <- phi(r+d+e-mu[i])-phi(r+d-mu[i])
mu[i] <- b*x[i]
}
r ~ dnorm(0,.001)
```

```
d ~ dgamma(.1,.1)
e ~ dgamma(.1,.1)
b ~ dnorm(0,.001)
}
```

A3.9   POISSON REGRESSION

Count data regression with $\exp\{x\beta\}$ for the mean.

```
model{
for(i in 1:n){
y[i] ~ dpois(mu[i])
mu[i] <- exp(b0+b1*x[i])
}
b0 ~ dnorm(0,.0001)
b1 ~ dnorm(0,.0001)
}
```

A3.10   HETEROGENEOUS POISSON REGRESSION

Multiplicative heterogeneity in the poisson mean.

```
model{
for(i in 1:n){
y[i] ~ dpois(mu[i])
mu[i] <- exp(b0+b1*x[i])*v[i]
v[i] ~ dgamma(a,a)
}
a <- 1/ra
ra ~ dgamma(1,1)
b0 ~ dnorm(0,.0001)
b1 ~ dnorm(0,.0001)
}
```

A3.11   RIGHT CENSORED WEIBULL DATA

This program uses the BUGS censoring function I(a, b) for data that must lie above a but below b. Guessed y values must be recorded as NA (not available). The extra variable cenind takes the value zero for uncensored observations and it gives the censoring time for censored observations.

```
model{
for(i in 1:n){
```

```
y[i] ~ dweib(alpha,r[i])I(cenind[i],)
r[i] <- exp(b0+b1*x[i])
}
b0 ~ dnorm(0,.0001)
b1 ~ dnorm(0,.0001)
alpha ~ dgamma(.001,.001)
}
```

The first few lines of the data file were

```
list(n=100)
y[]       cenind[]      x[]
0.31      0.00         -0.52
0.23      0.00         -1.61
0.30      0.00         -0.84
0.25      0.00          0.54
NA        1.40          0.68
0.49      0.00         -0.32
```

Note that the data were right censored at $t = 1.40$.
A slight modification of the preceding program gives the heterogeneous version.

A3.12   A CENSORED HETEROGENEOUS WEIBULL MODEL

```
model{
for(i in 1:n){
y[i] ~ dweib(alpha,r[i])I(cenind[i],)
r[i] <- v[i]*exp(b0+b1*x[i])
v[i] ~ dgamma(del,del)
}
```

the v's are neglected heterogeneity terms – random effects – given a gamma prior.

```
del ~ dgamma(.001,.001)
alpha ~ dgamma(.001,.001)
b0 ~ dnorm(0,.001)
b1 ~ dnorm(0,.001)
vari <- 1/del # the variance of the random effect
}
```

A3.13   AN OVER-IDENTIFIED RECURSIVE EQUATIONS MODEL

The likelihood is given as a restricted reduced form.

```
model{
for(i in 1:n){
y[i,1:2] ~ dmnorm(mu[i,], R[,])
mu[i,1] <- b0+b1*c0+b1*c1*z[i,1]+b1*c2*z[i,2]
mu[i,2] <- c0+c1*z[i,1]+c2*z[i,2]
}
R[1:2,1:2] ~ dwish(Omega[,],2)
b0 ~ dnorm(0,.0001)
b1 ~ dnorm(0,.0001)
c0 ~ dnorm(0,.0001)
c1 ~ dnorm(0,.0001)
c2 ~ dnorm(0,.0001)}
```

A3.14 A JUST IDENTIFIED SIMULTANEOUS EQUATIONS MODEL

The likelihood is given as an unrestricted reduced form.

```
model{
for(i in 1:n){y[i,1:2] ~ dmnorm(mu[i,],R[,])
mu[i,1] <- ap + bp[1]*zd[i] + bp[2] * zs[i]
mu[i,2] <- aq + bq[1]*zd[i] + bq[2] * zs[i]
}
ap ~ dnorm(0,.001)
aq ~ dnorm(0,.001)
for(i in 1:2){bp[i] ~ dnorm(0,.001)
bq[i] ~ dnorm(0,.001)}
R[1:2,1:2] ~ dwish(Omega[,],2)}
}
```

A3.15 A PANEL DATA LINEAR MODEL

A "random effects" panel linear model.

```
model{
for(i in 1:N){for(t in 1:T){
y[i,t] ~ dnorm(mu[i,t],tau)
mu[i,t] <- beta*x[i,t] + alpha[i]}}
for(i in 1:N){alpha[i] ~ dnorm(alphabar,phi)}
alphabar ~ dnorm(0,0.0001)
beta ~ dnorm(0,0.0001)
tau ~ dgamma(0.01,0.01)
phi ~ dgamma(0.01,0.01)
}
```

A3.16   A SECOND ORDER AUTOREGRESSION

```
model{
for(i in 3:n){
```

note 3 to *n* for a second order model, *k* + 1 to *n* for *k*'th order

```
y[i]  ˜ dnorm(mu[i],tau)
mu[i]  <- b0 + b1*y[i-1] + b2*y[i-2]
}
y[1] ˜ dnorm(0,0.0001)    # note priors for initial two observations
y[2] ˜ dnorm(0,0.0001)    # even though these are data
b0 ˜ dnorm(0,0.0001)
b1 ˜ dnorm(0,0.0001)
b2 ˜ dnorm(0,0.0001)
tau ˜ dgamma(0.001,0.001)
}
list(n=15,y=c(1,2,3,1,2,3,1,2,3,1,2,3,1,2,3))
```

made-up data to illustrate the format

A3.17   STOCHASTIC VOLATILITY

This is a model allowing first order autocorrelation in the precisions of a linear model.

```
model{
for(i in 1:n)
{y[i]  ˜ dnorm(0,p[i])
p[i]  <- exp(-h[i])
}
h[1]  ˜ dnorm(muh,qh)
muh  <- alpha/(1-rho)
qh  <- pv*(1-rho*rho)
for(j in 2:n){h[j]  ˜ dnorm(mu2[j],pv)
mu2[j]  <- alpha+rho*h[j-1]}
alpha ˜ dnorm(0,0.0001)
pv ˜ dgamma(1.0E-3,1.0E-3)
rho ˜ dunif(-0.999,0.999)
}
```

References

Aitchison, J. and Dunsmore, I. R. (1975). *Statistical Prediction Analysis.* Cambridge University Press.

Albert, J. H. and Chib, S. (1993). Bayesian analysis of binary and polychotomous response data, *Journal of the American Statistical Association*, 88.

Amemiya, T. (1985). *Advanced Econometrics.* Harvard University Press.

Angrist, J. D. (1990). Lifetime earnings and the Vietnam era draft lottery: evidence from Social Security Administration draft records, *American Economic Review*, 80, 3, 313–36.

Angrist, J. D. and Krueger, A. B. (1991). Does compulsory school attendance affect schooling and earnings, *Quarterly Journal of Economics*, 106, 979–1014.

Angrist, J. D. and Krueger, A. B. (1999). Empirical strategies in labor economics. In Ashenfelter, O. and Card, D. (eds) *The Handbook of Labor Economics*, volume 3. Elsevier.

Bauwens, L., Lubrano, M. and Richard, J.-F. (1999). *Bayesian Inference in Dynamic Econometric Models.* Oxford University Press.

Berg, A., Meyer, N. and Yu, J. (2004). Deviance information criterion for comparing stochastic volatility models, *Journal of Business and Economic Statistics*, 22, 1.

Berger, J. O. (1993). *Statistical Decision Theory and Bayesian Analysis.* Springer-Verlag.

Berger, J. O. and Pericchi, L. R. (2001). Objective Bayesian methods for model selection: Introduction and comparison in model selection. In P. Lahiri (ed.) *Institute of Mathematical Statistics Lecture Notes.*

Berger, J. O. and Wolpert, R. L. (1988). *The Likelihood Principle.* Institute of Mathematical Statistics Lecture Notes – Monograph Series, volume 6.

Berger, J. O. and Yang, R.-Y. (1994). Noninformative priors for Bayesian testing for the AR(1) model, *Econometric Theory*, 10, 461–82.

Bernardo, J. M. and Smith, A. F. M. (1994). *Bayesian Theory.* Wiley.

Bound, J., Jaeger, D. A., and Baker, R. M. (1995). Problems with instrumental variables estimation when the correlation between the instruments and the endogenous explanatory variable is weak, *Journal of the American Statistical Association*, 90, 443–50.

Box, G. E. P. and Tiao, G. C. (1973). *Bayesian Inference in Statistical Analysis.* Addison-Wesley.

Bremaud, P. (1998a). *An Introduction to Probabilistic Modeling.* Springer-Verlag.

Bremaud, P. (1998b). *Markov Chains.* Springer-Verlag.

Brooks, S. P. and Gelman, A. (1998). General methods for monitoring convergence of iterative simulations, *J.C.G.S.*, 7, 4.

Brooks, S. P. and Roberts, G. O. (1998). Assessing convergence of Markov Chain Monte Carlo algorithms, *Statistics and Computing*, 8.

Canova, F. (1994). Statistical inference in calibrated models, *Journal of Applied Econometrics*, 9.

Card, D. (2001). Estimating the return to schooling: Progress on some persistent econometric problems, *Econometrica*, 69, 5, 1127–60.

Card, D. and Krueger, A. B. (1994). Minimum wages and employment: A case study of the fast-food industry in New Jersey and Pennsylvania, *American Economic Review*, 84, 4, 772–93.

Casella, G. and George, E. I. (1992). Explaining the Gibbs Sampler, *The American Statistician*, 46, 3, August.

Chamberlain, G. (1984). Panel data. In Griliches, Z. and Intriligator, M. D. (eds) *The Handbook of Econometrics*, volume 2. Elsevier.

Chamberlain, G. (2000). Econometrics and decision theory, *Journal of Econometrics*, 95, 2, 255–84.

Chamberlain, G. and Imbens, G. (*c.* 1996). *Random Effects Estimators With Many Instrumental Variables*. Mimeo, Department of Economics, Harvard University. (2004) *Econometrica*, 72, 1, 295–306.

Chamberlain, G. and Imbens, G. W. (2003). Nonparametric Applications of Bayesian Inference, *Journal of Business and Economic Statistics*, 21, 1.

Chao, J. C. and Phillips, P. C. B. (2002). Jeffreys' prior analysis of the simultaneous equations model in the case of n + 1 endogenous variables, *Journal of Econometrics*, 111: 251–83.

Chib, S. (1993). Bayesian inference with autoregressive errors: A Gibbs Sampling approach, *Journal of Econometrics*, 58, 3, 275–94.

Chib, S. (1994). Bayesian inference in regression models with ARMA (p, q) errors, *Journal of Econometrics*, 64, 1–2, 183–206.

Chib, S. (1995). Marginal likelihood from the Gibbs sampler, *Journal of the American Statistical Association*, 90, 432, 1313–21.

Chib, S. (2001). Markov Chain Monte Carlo Methods: Computation and inference. In Heckman, J. J. and Leamer, E. E. (eds) *The Handbook of Econometrics*, volume 5. Elsevier.

Chib, S. and Greenberg, E. (1994). Bayesian inference for regression models with ARMA (p, q) errors, *Journal of Econometrics*, 64, 183–206.

Chib, S. and Greenberg, E. (1995). Understanding the Metropolis-Hastings algorithm, *The American Statistician*, 49, 327–35.

Chib, S., Greenberg, E. and Winkelmann, R. (1998). Posterior simulators and Bayes factors in panel count data models, *Journal of Econometrics*, 86, 33–54.

Chib, S., Nardari, F. and Shephard, N. (2002). Markov Chain Monte Carlo for stochastic volatility models, *Journal of Econometrics*, 108, 281–316.

Clayton, D. G. (1996). Generalized linear mixed models. In Gilks, W. R., Richardson, S., and Spiegelhalter, D. J. (eds) *Markov Chain Monte Carlo in Practice*. Chapman and Hall.

Congdon, P. (2001). *Bayesian Statistical Modelling*. Wiley.

Congdon, P. (2003). *Applied Bayesian Modelling*. Wiley.

Cook, R. Dennis (1980). Smoking and lung cancer. In "R. A. Fisher: An Appreciation," in Fienberg, S. E. and Hinkley, D. V. (eds) *Lecture Notes in Statistics*, 1. Springer-Verlag.

Cowles, M. K. and Carlin, B. P. (1995). Markov Chain Monte Carlo diagnostics: A comparative review, *Journal of the American Statistical Association*, 91, 883–904.

Cox, D. R. and Hinkley, V. (1974). *Theoretical Statistics*. Chapman and Hall.

Cox, R. T. (1961). *The Algebra of Probable Inference*. Baltimore: The Johns Hopkins Press.

Debreu, G. and Hernstein, I. N. (1953). Nonnegative square matrices, *Econometrica*, 21, 4.

de Finetti, B. (1974 and 1975). *Theory of Probability*. Wiley.

DeGroot, M. H. (1970). *Optimal Statistical Decisions*. McGraw-Hill.

Devroye, L. (1986). *Non-Uniform Random Variate Generation*. Springer-Verlag.

Drèze, J. H. and Richard, J.-F. (1983). Bayesian analysis of simultaneous equations systems. In Griliches, Z. and Intriligator, M. D. (eds) *Handbook of Econometrics*, vol. 1, ch. 9, North-Holland.

Edwards, W., Lindman, H. and Savage, L. J. (1963). Bayesian statistical inference for psychological research, *Psychological Review*, 70, 3, 193–242.

Edwards, W., Lindman, H. and Savage, L. J. (1981). Bayesian statistical inference for psychological research. In *The writings of Leonard Jimmie Savage – A memorial selection*. The American Statistical Association and the Institute of Mathematical Statistics.

Efron, B. and Gous, A. (2001). Scales of evidence for model selection: Fisher versus Jeffreys. In P. Lahiri (ed.) *Model Selection, Institute of Mathematical Statistics Lecture Notes*.

Efron, B. and Tibshirani, R. J. (1993). *An Introduction to the Bootstrap*. Chapman and Hall.

Everitt, B. (1994). *A Handbook of Statistical Analyses using S-PLUS*. Chapman and Hall.

Fernandez, C. and Steel, M. F. J. (2000). Bayesian regression analysis of scale mixtures of normals, *Econometric Theory*, 16, 80–101.

Fernandez, C., Ley, E. and Steel, M. F. J. (2001). Benchmark priors for Bayesian model averaging, *Journal of Econometrics*, 100.

Fernandez, C., Osiewalski, J. and Steel, M. J. F. (1997). On the use of panel data in stochastic frontier models with improper priors, *Journal of Econometrics*, 79, 169–93.

Fisher, R. A. (1922). On the mathematical foundations of theoretical statistics, *Phil. Trans. Royal Soc.*, A222, 309.

Fisher, R. A. (1957). Dangers of cigarette smoking, *British Medical Journal*, July 6, p. 43 and August 3, pp. 297–8.

Galton, Francis (1886). Regression towards mediocrity in hereditary stature, *Journal of the Anthropological Institute*, 15, 246–63. (http://www.mugu.com/galton/index.html. or www.elsevier.com/hes/books/02/menu02.htm.)

Gammerman, D. (1997). *Markov Chain Monte Carlo*. Chapman and Hall.

Geisser, S. (1993). *Predictive Inference: An Introduction*. Chapman and Hall.

Gelfand, A. E. and Dey, D. P. (1994). Bayesian model choice: Asymptotics and exact calculations, *Journal of the Royal Statistical Society*, (B), 56, 3, 501–14.

Gelfand, A. E. and Smith, A. F. M. (1990). Sampling-based approaches to calculating marginal densities, *Journal of the American Statistical Association*, 85, 398–409.

Gelfand, A. E., Sahu, S. K. and Carlin, B. P. (1995). Efficient parametrizations for normal linear mixed models, *Biometrika*, 82, 3, 479–88.

Gelfand, A. E., Sahu, S. K. and Carlin, B. P. (1996). Efficient parametrizations for generalized linear mixed models (with discussion). In Bernardo, J. M., Berger, J. O., Dawid, A. P. and Smith, A. F. M. (eds) *Bayesian Statistics 5*. Oxford University Press: 165–80.

Gelman, A. and Rubin, D. B. (1992). Inferences from iterative simulations using multiple sequences, *Statistical Science*, 7, 457–511.

Gelman, A., Carlin, J. B., Stern, H. S. and Rubin, D. B. (2003). *Bayesian Data Analysis*, 2nd edn. Chapman and Hall.

Geweke, J. (1994). Priors for macroeconomic time series and their application, *Economic Theory*, 10, 609–32.

Geweke, J. (1998). Simulation methods for model criticism and robustness analysis. In Bernardo, J. M., Berger, J. O., Dawid, A. P. and Smith, A. F. M. (eds) *Bayesian Statistics 6*. Oxford University Press.

Geweke, J. and Keane, M. (1999). Mixture of normal probit models. In Hsiao, C., Lahiri, P., Lee, L. F., and Pesaran, H. (eds) *Analysis of Panels and Limited Dependent Variable Models*. Cambridge University Press.

Geweke, J. and Keane, M. (2000). An empirical analysis of earnings dynamics among men in the PSID, *Journal of Econometrics*, 96, 2, 293–356.

Griliches, Z. (1977). Estimating the returns to schooling: Some econometric problems, *Econometrica*, 45: 1–22.

Gronau, R. (1973). The effect of children on the housewife's value of time, *Journal of Political Economy*, 81: S 168–99.

Hamilton, J. D. (1994). *Time Series Analysis*. Princeton University Press.

Hastie, T. J. and Tibshirani, R. J. (1990). *Generalized Additive Models*. Chapman and Hall.

Heckman, J. J. (1974). Shadow prices, market wages and labor supply, *Econometrica*, 42, 679–94.

Heckman, J. J. (2001). Micro data, heterogeneity and the evaluation of public policy: Nobel lecture, *Journal of Political Economy*, 109, 1, 673–748.

Heckman, J. J. and MacCurdy, T. (1980). A life-cycle model of female labor supply, *Review of Economic Studies*, 47, 47–74.

Heyde, C. C. and Johnstone, I. M. (1979). On asymptotic posterior normality for stochastic processes, *Journal of the Royal Statistical Society*, (B), 41, 184–9.

Hirano, K. (1998). A semiparametric model for labor earnings dynamics. In Dey, D. (ed.) *Practical Nonparametric and Semiparametric Bayesian Statistics*. MIT Press, Cambridge: 355–69.

Hirano, K. (2000). A semiparametric Bayesian inference in autoregressive panel data models, *Econometrica*, 70, 781–99.

Hirano, K., Imbens, G. W., Ridder, G. and Rubin, D. B. (2001). Combining panel data sets with attrition and refreshment samples, *Econometrica*, 69, 6, 1645–60.

Hobert, J. P. and Casella, G. (1996). The effects of improper priors on Gibbs sampling in hierarchical linear mixed models, *Journal of the American Statistical Association*, 91, 436, 1461–73.

Hogan, J. H., Lin, X. and Herman, B. (2003). *Mixtures of Varying Coefficient Models for Longitudinal Data with Discrete or Continuous Non-ignorable Dropout*. Brown University, Center for Statistical Sciences, working paper 03-002.

Hurwicz, L. (1950). Least squares bias in time series. In Koopmans, T. C. (ed.) *Statistical Inference in Dynamic Economic Models*, Cowles Commission Monograph 10. New York: Wiley, 365–83.

Ibrahim, J. G., Chen, M. H. and Sinha, D. (2001). *Bayesian Survival Analysis*. Springer-Verlag.

Ihaka, Ross and Gentleman, Robert (1996). R: A language for data analysis and graphics, *Journal of Computational and Graphical Statistics*, 5, 3, 299–314.

Imbens, G. W. and Rubin, D. B. (1997). Bayesian inference for causal effects in randomized experiments with noncompliance, *Annals of Statistics*, 25, 1, 305–27.

Jacquier, E., Polson, N. G. and Rossi, P. E. (1994). Bayesian analysis of stochastic volatility models, *Journal of Business and Economic Statistics*, 12, 4, 69–87.

Jaeger, D. and Bound, J. (1994). Evidence on the validity of cross-sectional and longitudinal labor market data, *Journal of Labor Economics*, 12, 3.

Jeffreys, Harold (1966). *Theory of Probability*, 3rd edn. Oxford: Clarendon Press.

Kadane, J. B. (1974). The role of identification in Bayesian theory. In S. E. Fienberg and A. Zellner (eds) *Studies in Bayesian Econometrics and Statistics: In Honor of Leonard J. Savage*. North-Holland: 175–91.

Kadane, J. B. and Lazar, N. A. (2001). *Methods and Criteria for Model Selection*. Mimeo, Carnegie Mellon University.

Kass, R. E. and Raftery, A. E. (1995). Bayes factors, *Journal of the American Statistical Association*, 90, 430.

Kass, R. E. and Wasserman, L. (1995). A reference Bayesian test for nested hypotheses and its relationship to the Schwarz criterion, *Journal of the American Statistical Association*, 90, 431, 928–34.

Keynes, J. M. (1920). Treatise on probability, volume VIII in *The Collected Writings of John Maynard Keynes*. Published for the Royal Economic Society, MacMillan.

Kleibergen, F. R. and van Dijk, H. K. (1994). On the shape of the likelihood/posterior in cointegration models, *Econometric Theory*, 10, 514–51.

Kleibergen, F. R. and van Dijk, H. K. (1998). Bayesian simultaneous equations analysis using reduced rank structures, *Econometric Theory*, 14, 701–43.

Kleibergen, F. R. and Zivot, E. (2003). Bayesian and classical approaches to instrumental variables regression, *Journal of Econometrics*, 114, 29–72.

Koop, G. and Poirier, D. J. (1997). Bayesian analysis of logit models using natural conjugate priors, *Journal of Econometrics*, 78, 139–51.

Koopmans, T. C. (1950). When is an equation system complete for statistical purposes? In *Statistical Inference in Dynamic Economic Models*, Cowles Commission Monographs 10. Wiley: 393–409.

Krause, A. and Olson, M. (1997). *The Basics of S and S-PLUS*. Springer.

Kyburg, H. E. and Smokler, H. E. (1964). *Studies in Subjective Probability*. Wiley.

Lahiri, P. (ed.) Institute of Mathematical Statistics Lecture Notes Volume 38, Model Selection.

Lancaster, T. (1979). Econometric methods for the duration of unemployment, *Econometrica*, 47, 4, 939–56.

Lancaster, T. (1997a). Bayes WESML: Posterior inference from choice-based samples, *Journal of Econometrics*, 79, 291–303.

Lancaster, T. (1997b). Exact structural inference in optimal job search models, *Journal of Business Economics and Statistics*, 15, 2, 165–79.

Lancaster, T. (2000). The incidental parameter problem since 1948. *Journal of Econometrics*, 95, 391–413.

Lancaster, T. (2002). Orthogonal parameters and panel data. *Review of Economic Studies*, 69, 3, 647–66.

Leamer, E. E. (1978). *Specification Searches: Ad Hoc Inference with Non Experimental Data*. Wiley.

Leamer, E. E. (1983). Model choice and specification analysis. In Griliches, Z. and Intriligator, M. D. (eds) *Handbook of Econometrics*, volume 1. North-Holland.

Leonard, T. and Hsu, J. S. J. (1999). *Bayesian Methods*. Cambridge Series in Statistical and Probabilistic Mathematics. CUP.

Lindley, D. V. and Novick, M. R. (1981). The role of exchangeability in inference, *Annals of Statistics*, 9, 1, 45–58.

Lindley, D. V. and Smith, A. F. M. (1972). Bayes estimates in the linear model, *Journal of the Royal Statistical Society*, (B), 34, 1–41.

Manning, W., Newhouse, J., Duan, N., Keeler, E., Leibowitz, A. and Marquis, M. (1987). Health insurance and the demand for medical care: Evidence from a randomized experiment, *American Economic Review*, 77, 3, 251–77.

McCulloch, R. E., Polson, N. G. and Rossi, P. E. (2000). A Bayesian analysis of the multinomial probit model with fully identified parameters, *Journal of Econometrics*, 99, 1, 173–93.

Meyn, S. P. and Tweedie, R. L. (1993). *Markov Chains and Stochastic Stability*. Springer-Verlag.

Mundlak, Y. (1961). Empirical production function free of management bias, *Journal of Farm Economics*, 43, 44–56.

Newton, W. K. and Raftery, A. E. (1994). Approximate Bayesian inference by the weighted likelihood bootstrap, *Journal of the Royal Statistical Society*, (B), 56, 3–48.

Norris, J. R. (1997). *Markov Chains*. Cambridge University Press.

Nummelin, E. (1984). *General Irreducible Markov Chains and Non-negative Operators*. Cambridge University Press.

Phillips, P. C. B. (1991). To criticize the critics: an objective Bayesian analysis of stochastic trends, *Journal of Applied Econometrics*, 6, 333–64.

Poirier, D. J. (1995). *Intermediate Statistics and Econometrics: A Comparative Approach*. MIT Press.

Poirier, D. J. (1996). A Bayesian analysis of nested logit models, *Journal of Econometrics*, 75, 163–81.

Press, S. J. (2003). *Subjective and Objective Bayesian Statistics*, 2nd edn. Wiley.

Ramsey, F. P. (1931). Truth and probability. In R. B. Braithwaite (ed.) *The Foundations of Mathematics and other Logical Essays*. London: Kegan, Paul, Trench, Trubner and Co.

Ripley, B. D. (1987). *Stochastic Simulation*. Wiley.

Robert, C. P. and Casella, G. (1999). *Monte Carlo Statistical Methods*. Springer-Verlag.

Rubin, D. B. (1978). Bayesian inference for causal effects, *Annals of Statistics*, 6, 34–58.

Rubin, D. B. (1981). The Bayesian bootstrap, *Annals of Statistics*, 9, 1, 130–40.

Schotman, P. C. (1994). Priors for the AR(1) model: Parametrization issues and time series considerations, *Econometric Theory*, 10, 3/4, 579–95.

Schotman, P. C. and van Dijk, H. K. (1991). A Bayesian analysis of the unit root in real exchange rates, *Journal of Econometrics*, 49, 1–2, 195–238.

Sims, C. A. (2000). Using a likelihood perspective to sharpen econometric discourse: Three examples, *Econometrica*, 95, 2, April, 443–62.

Sims, C. A. (2002). *Thinking about Instrumental Variables*, unpublished note from Princeton University.

Sims, C. A. and Uhlig, H. (1991). Understanding unit rooters: A helicopter tour, *Econometrica*, 59, 6, 1591–9.

Smith, A. F. M. and Gelfand, A. E. (1992). Bayesian statistics without tears; a sampling resampling perspective, *The American Statistician*, 46, 84–8.

Smith, A. F. M. and Roberts, G. O. (1993). Bayesian computation via the Gibbs sampler and related Markov chain Monte Carlo methods, *Journal of the Royal Statistical Society*, (B), 55, 3–23.

Spiegelhalter, D. J., Best, N. G., Carlin, B. P. and van der Linde, A. (2002). Bayesian measures of model complexity and fit, *Journal of the Royal Statistical Society*, (B), 64, 583–640.

Staiger, D. J. H. (1997). Stock instrumental variables regression with weak instruments, *Econometrica*, 65, 3, 557–86.

Stolley, Paul D. (1991). When genius errs: R. A. Fisher and the lung cancer controversy, *American Journal of Epidemiology*, 133, 416, 425.

Stone, M. (1974). Cross-validatory choice and assessment of statistical predictions, *Journal of the Royal Statistical Society*, (B), 36, 111–47.

Tinbergen, J. (1995). Determination and interpretation of supply curves. Originally published, in German, in *Zeitschrift fur Nationalokonomie*, 1930, I, 669–79; translated in Hendry, D. F. and Morgan, M. S. (eds) *The Foundations of Econometric Analysis*, 1995, Cambridge University Press.

van der Klaauw, W. (2002). *On the Use of Expectations Data in Estimating Structural Dynamic Models: An Analysis of Career Choice*. Department of Economics, University of North Carolina.

Vella, F. (1998). Estimating models with sample selection bias: A survey, *Journal of Human Resources*, 33, 1, 127–69.

Venables, W. and Ripley, B. (1999). *Modern Applied Statistics with S and S-PLUS*, 2nd edn. Springer.

Woutersen, T. (2001). *Robustness against Incidental Parameters and Mixing Distributions*. University of Western Ontario Economics Working Paper 2001–10.

Woutersen, T. and Voia, M. (2002). *Adaptive Estimation of the Dynamic Linear Model with Fixed Effects*. University of Western Ontario Economics Working Paper, 2002–10.

Yatchew, A. and Griliches, Z. (1985). Specification error in probit models, *Review of Economic Statistics*, 67, 1, 134–9.

Yatchew, A. and No, J. A. (2001). Household gasoline demand in Canada, *Econometrica*, 69, 6, 1697–709.

Zellner, A. (1971). *An Introduction to Bayesian Inference in Econometrics*. Wiley.

Zellner, A. (1975). Bayesian analysis of regression error terms, *Journal of the American Statistical Association*, 70, 349, 138–44.

Zellner, A. (1986). On assessing prior distributions and Bayesian regression analysis. In Goel, P. and Zellner, A. (eds) *Bayesian Inference and Decision Techniques*. Elsevier Science, B.V.: chapter 15.

Zellner, A. (ed.) (1997). *The Zellner View and Papers*. Edward Elgar.

Index